10-10
marks noted
on back page

P9-DHM-960

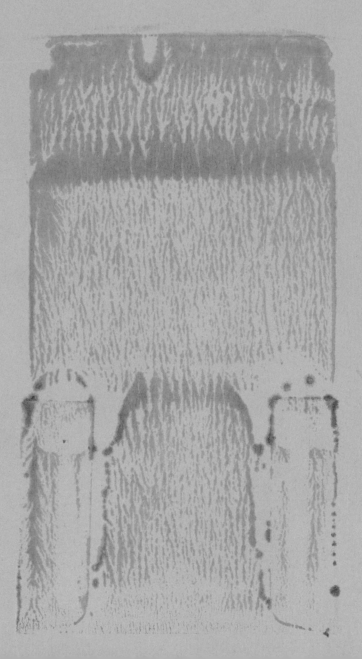

THE
TOWER
OF
LONDON

By the same author:

BIOGRAPHY

No. 10 Downing Street (Cassell)
The Edwardian Age (Cassell)
The Two Pillars of Charing Cross (Cassell)
Fanny and the Regent of Siam (Collins)
Carve Her Name with Pride (Collins)
The Private Papers of Hore-Belisha (Collins)
Clive of India (Hutchinson)
Chaplin, the Immortal Tramp (Newnes)
Viscount Southwood (Odhams)
Viscount Addison, Leader of the Lords (Odhams)
I Shall Fear No Evil: the Story of Dr. Alina Brewda (Kimber)
The Bogus Image of Bernard Shaw (Frewin)

NOVELS

The Road to Delhi (Bodley Head)
A Woman of France (Macdonald)
The Governor's Lady (Hutchinson)
Distant Drums (Chapman & Hall)
How Vainly Men . . . (Methuen)
Nothing to Lose (Macdonald)
Maki (Bodley Head)

TRAVEL

Hollywood by Starlight (Chapman & Hall)
Next Stop—Peking (Newnes)
India Marches Past (Hutchinson)
'Midst Himalayan Mists (Butterworth)

PLAYS

Gentle Caesar (with Osbert Sitwell) (Macmillan)
Clive of India (with W. P. Lipscomb) (Gollancz)
A Farthing Damages (with John McCormick)
The Voice of the People
They had His Number (with Juliet Rhys-Williams)

THE
TOWER
OF
LONDON

R. J. MINNEY

PRENTICE-HALL, INC.
Englewood Cliffs, New Jersey

The Tower Of London
by R. J. Minney

© 1970 by R. J. Minney

All rights reserved. No part of this book may be
reproduced in any form or by any means, except for
the inclusion of brief quotations in a review, without
permission in writing from the publisher.

Library of Congress Catalog Card Number: 72-123084
ISBN 0-13-925768-3

Published in the United States of America by Prentice-Hall, Inc.
Published in Great Britain by Cassell & Company Ltd.

Printed in the United States of America

For
Thomas, Hugo, Jamie & Richard
to read when they are older

Acknowledgements

The annals of the Tower, spread over many centuries, are not always explicit or detailed: at times they lack what one seeks most. Nor are the records of the early chroniclers always reliable. Shakespeare dipped into these for many of the dramatic scenes in his great historical plays ranging from *King John* to *Henry VIII*, which provided him with unforgettable moments of ferocity and violence, gentleness, compassion, piety, romance and laughter. From these and other contemporary sources much has been drawn for this book.

An irredeemable debt is owed by me to those who have written earlier of the Tower and have by diligent research and vivid narrative presented the lively and often inspiring story of the people who for nine hundred years have known the Tower and lived in awe of it.

Many have advised and helped me, chief of them being the Inspectors of Ancient Monuments, Messrs John Charlton, P. E. Curnow and Brian Davison; the Resident Governor of the Tower of London, Colonel Sir Thomas Butler, Bt; the Keeper of the Jewel House, Major-General H. D. W. Sitwell; Mr William Reid, Assistant Keeper in the Armouries of the Tower; Miss Sarah Barter, the Armoury Librarian; Chief Yeoman Warder G. A. Arnold; and Yeoman Clerk T. Randall.

For assistance with illustration research my thanks are due to Mrs M. E. Harper, Photographic Librarian at the Ministry of Public Buildings and Works, London. All Ministry of Works photographs reproduced in this book are British Crown Copyright.

Contents

Colour Plates

Prelude

The Ravens Never Tell

There have always been ravens in the Tower of London. They made their homes amid the rising turrets and battlements and for centuries did their scavenging there; and even after that service was no longer required, their presence has been encouraged, for the legend runs that if the ravens leave, the Tower will fall and the greatness and glory of Britain will vanish.

Six of these black creatures, described by Edgar Allan Poe as 'things of evil—prophet still, if bird or devil', are kept 'on the establishment' with their wings clipped so that they cannot fly away and a Yeoman Warder provides each of them with 2s 4d worth of meat a week—thus ensuring both their stay and Britain's survival.

Tower ravens on the Green (British Travel Association)

CHAPTER ONE

Twenty Towers

The Tower of London is the oldest fortified building still in occupation—older than the Doge's Palace in Venice, the Kremlin in Moscow, the Vatican in Rome and the Louvre in Paris. Its defensive strength, constantly augmented, was for many centuries able to withstand even attack by cannon. It can still be used as a prison, but the torture chambers, with their thumbscrew and rack, have been unused since the reign of James I, when it was ruled that torture was alien to the laws of England, as it was indeed unlawful even in the Middle Ages.

Other functions of the Tower have also fallen into disuse. Bows and arrows, and later firearms, were once made there. The National Observatory, installed in one of the turrets of the White Tower by Charles II, was moved to the Royal Observatory at Greenwich and more recently to Herstmonceux Castle in Sussex. The Royal Mint, the Zoo and the Public Record Office have been established elsewhere.

For many centuries there was a large resident population in the Tower. In addition to archers and men-at-arms, grooms in the stables, masons and carpenters, warders and gaolers, the executive and administrative staff, the prisoners who at times numbered more than a thousand, there were roadmenders, domestic servants male and female, cooks, barmaids and a constant flow of tradesmen and messengers. Now only fifty-six families live there.

The construction of the Tower as it now stands was begun by William the Conqueror and watched by Londoners with the utmost apprehension. As its terrifying walls and turrets rose above the riverside town it seemed like a huge, brooding monster, ready always to pounce. And pounce it did from time to time, devouring houses and whole streets to swell its great girth and augment its

sinister strength.

But those who have lived and worked in the Tower, apart from its numerous prisoners of course, have had for it an affection amounting almost to veneration. This is admirably conveyed by Dame Carruthers in the Gilbert and Sullivan opera *The Yeomen of the Guard*, which has so often been performed on the green of the old sunken moat under the great bulge of the Beauchamp Tower. 'Silence, you silly girl,' she chides a restless malcontent, 'you know not what you say. I was born in the old keep, and I've grown grey in it, and please God I shall die and be buried in it; and there's not a stone in the walls that is not as dear to me as my own right hand.'

Although it is always spoken of as 'the' Tower, in fact there are twenty towers and two bastions. The massive high-walled ancient fortress has always had a water entrance from the River Thames and a main land entrance from what is now known as Tower Hill.

The road slopes down to a wide modern gate with iron railings, beyond which can be seen the shimmer of the Thames and its shipping. Here once stood Bulwark Gate. Beyond this we see a causeway with its drawbridge pit—the remains of one of the three drawbridges which had to be crossed before the fortress could be entered.

On our right, where the refreshment room stands, is the site of the Lion Tower, beside which in the thirteenth century the King established his zoo with an assortment of wild animals which the public were allowed to come and see; it served as London's zoo until the animals were moved to Regent's Park in 1834. The Lion Tower, which was pulled down in the seventeenth century, was a semicircular barbican almost completely surrounded by the water of the moat: there is no water now and of the moat hardly anything is visible.

The causeway now turns left and brings us to the third of the Tower's entrances, known as the Middle Tower. Built in 1280, it consists of two large round towers, one on each side of the causeway; in the early days there was a portcullis under the entrance arch; a Yeoman Warder and his family now live in the rooms above. The Middle Tower looks relatively modern because it was largely rebuilt in 1717, when the finely carved coat of arms of King George I was placed above the arch.

Beyond the Middle Tower the causeway crosses what used to be the main moat, which once joined the Thames to encircle the Tower of London. It was very wide at this point, but was drained in 1843 and is now just a vast sunken stretch of green grass, most beautifully trimmed. The causeway ends at the next gate, known as the Byward Tower, which was built in 1280 on the Outer Wall about forty feet above the old moat. The Byward Tower (from 'by the Ward' as it admits you to the Outer Ward of the Tower) also has a portcullis and twin round towers, each of which has a fine vaulted chamber; the one on the right is an octagonal room with loopholed windows and an original stone fireplace known as the Warders' Lodge, by which you may just catch a glimpse of some of the Warders. Just

The Byward Gate and the moat before draining, from an early nineteenth-century print. (Ministry of Public Building and Works)

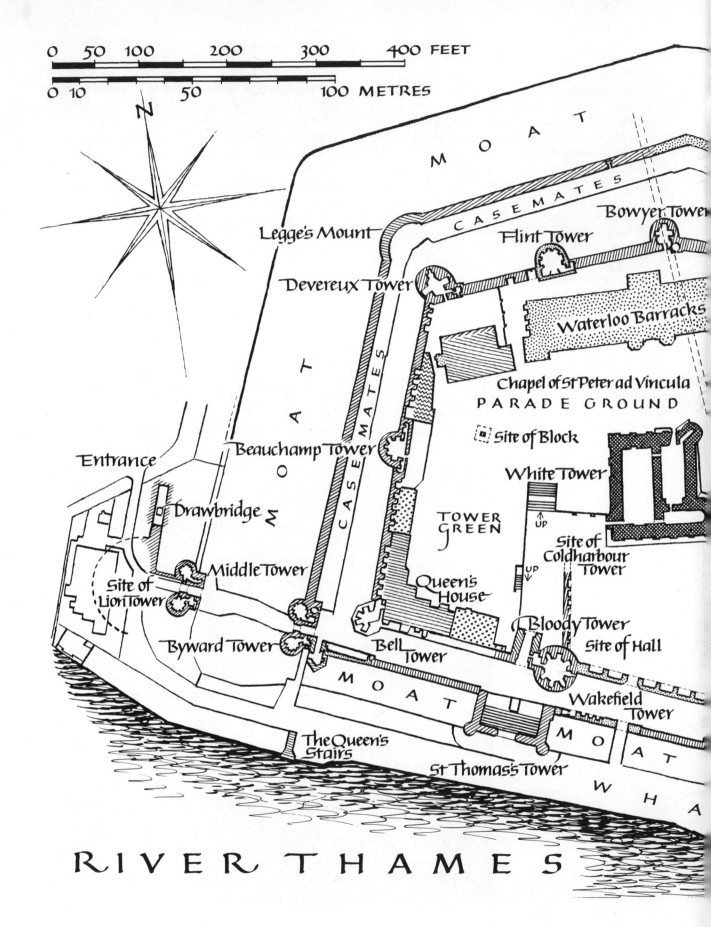

0   50   100   200   300   400 FEET

0   10   50   100 METRES

N

MOAT

CASEMATES

Legge's Mount

Flint Tower

Bowyer Tower

Devereux Tower

Waterloo Barracks

Chapel of St Peter ad Vincula

PARADE GROUND

Site of Block

Entrance

Beauchamp Tower

MOAT

CASEMATES

White Tower

Drawbridge

TOWER GREEN

UP

Site of Coldharbour Tower

Middle Tower

UP

Site of Lion Tower

Queen's House

Byward Tower

Bell Tower

Bloody Tower

Site of Hall

MOAT

Wakefield Tower

The Queen's Stairs

MOAT

St Thomas's Tower

WHA

RIVER THAMES

4

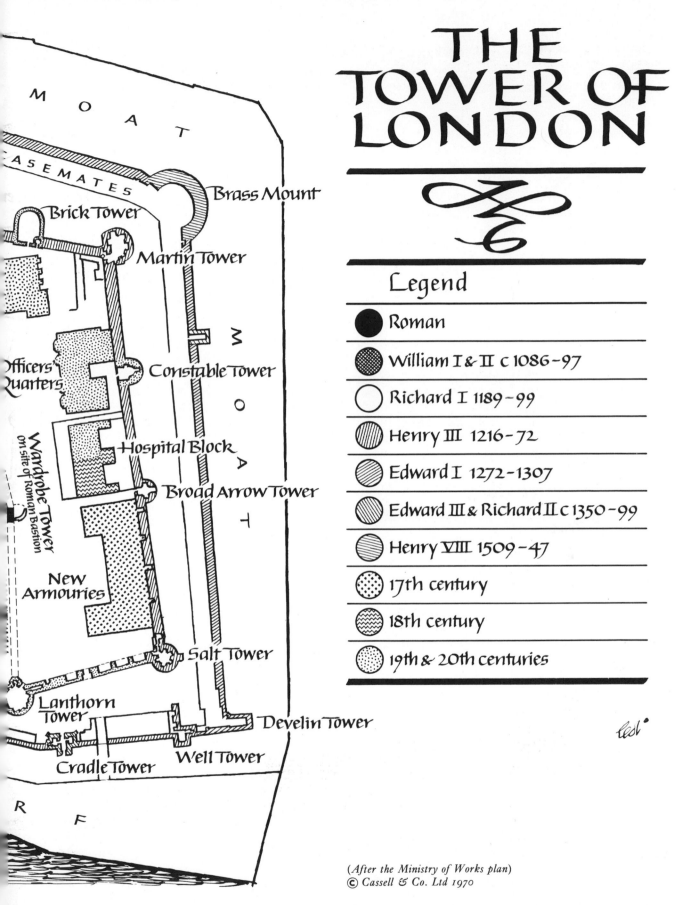

THE TOWER OF LONDON

Legend

- ● Roman
- ◉ William I & II c 1086–97
- ○ Richard I 1189–99
- ◍ Henry III 1216–72
- ◍ Edward I 1272–1307
- ◍ Edward III & Richard II c 1350–99
- ◍ Henry VIII 1509–47
- ◌ 17th century
- ◌ 18th century
- ◌ 19th & 20th centuries

(*After the Ministry of Works plan*)
© *Cassell & Co. Ltd 1970*

beyond it on the right is a passage (guarded by two heavy doors now normally shut) which led by a drawbridge across the moat to what are now known as the Queen's Steps (or the King's Steps, when the sovereign is a man).

Once through the Byward Gate we are actually in the Tower. Ahead lies a road with a high wall on each side—the Inner Wall on the left, the Outer Wall on the right. Centuries ago the River Thames used to flow where the road now runs and washed the base of the left-hand wall, at the time the only wall; the road is still called Water Lane and is just wide enough to take two cars abreast, though only one at a time can pass through the gates. All this land was reclaimed from the Thames, which now flows at some distance from the Outer Wall, beyond the dry bed of the old moat and the Wharf.

Water Lane runs right round the Tower, but only this stretch of it bears that name. On both sides of it there are towers. Let us look first at the one on the left, the Bell Tower, which stands at the point where Water Lane returns after its circuit.

The Bell Tower was built when the Inner Wall was erected in 1190. Immensely strong, its base is of solid masonry; it rises to a height of more than sixty feet—the original windows of the upper chamber, whose walls are eight feet thick, can still be seen and there is a little wooden turret above the parapet. In this turret is the bell that has been rung every morning and evening for centuries—it is the oldest curfew bell in London. Like the towers of the three main gates it was constantly manned by look-out men and archers. Among the more notable prisoners in its two chambers, one on each floor with no direct communication between them, were Sir Thomas More, Bishop John Fisher and Princess Elizabeth (later Queen Elizabeth I). The section of Water Lane running northward has a continuous line of small drab houses, some one-storied, others two-storied, built during the nineteenth century against the Outer Wall—these are known as the case-mates. Here in the old days were the workshops of the stone-masons, carpenters and armourers as well as the Royal Mint, which was at the far end, and this section of the street is known even now as Mint Street. Sir Isaac Newton lived in the Tower when he was Master of the Mint in the latter part of the seventeenth century. The Mint was moved outside the Tower into a special building beyond the northern wall in 1810. The Yeoman Warders live in the casemates, which now run only along the west and north sides but once extended on the east as well. The public are not allowed into this section. But visitors will see a metal stanchion on the west wall of the Bell Tower and another on the wall across the street, to which a golden chain was attached, carrying the sign of a tavern that was at No. 1 casemates.

Along Water Lane in the old days carts, wagons and hay wains, laden with straw and fodder for the cavalry horses and the King's hunters and with vast quantities of stores, used to clatter and creak by. In all, eight towers look down on Water Lane. The one immediately after the Bell Tower is the Bloody Tower; it was originally an archway set in the river wall in 1225 and was later made into a gate-tower. Like all the towers of the Inner Wall, it is perched high so that the archers could shoot over the wall at foes or rebels approaching by land or water. The Bloody Tower, originally called the Garden Tower because of a garden on its other side, is a square building, dark and menacing, with a heavy portcullis (there were two once) and a massive two-leaved and abundantly studded oak door which leads into the Inner Ward. It is worthwhile looking up at the attractive vaulting of the low, narrow arch. On the right flank of this gateway is the Wakefield Tower, a squat, circular structure with walls thirteen feet thick. It has just two rooms, the lower one octagonal and lit only by narrow slits; the upper, also octagonal, very lofty with large windows; the parapet is crenellated. Until recently the Crown Jewels were displayed here, and State documents, important treaties and other records were also housed in the Wakefield Tower for more than five hundred years, until they were moved to the Public Record Office in Chancery Lane in 1854.

Facing these two towers, on the river side of Water Lane, is St Thomas's Tower, a lofty, immensely wide structure built above the water-gate known as Traitors' Gate. St Thomas's has the largest arch in the Tower of London; it has no keystone, and has a span of sixty feet, wide enough to take three modern double-decker London buses abreast. A great many prisoners—queens, princes, prelates, statesmen, judges and courtiers—were brought to Traitors' Gate by boat under armed escort. St Thomas's Tower is built over the old moat, now dry. The Keeper of the Crown Jewels lives on the first floor, which is linked by an overhead passage with the Wakefield Tower on the other side of Water Lane.

Beyond St Thomas's Tower, projecting from

the Outer Wall on the same side, are three more towers—the Cradle Tower, the Well Tower and the Develin Tower, all of which overlooked the moat. Almost opposite the Cradle Tower is the Lanthorn Tower, built by Henry III into the Inner wall just beyond the Wakefield Tower; the river used to wash its base and there was a light at the top to guide river shipping. Eastward beyond it is the Salt Tower, at the corner of the Inner Wall where it turns northward. From the Salt Tower Edward I built two enclosing walls, one running south to the Well Tower, the other east to the Outer Wall behind the casemates, thus forming an enclosed square where invaders could be isolated and attacked by archers in both the Salt and Well Towers, as well as from the Develin Tower at the southeastern corner of the Outer Wall. This guarded the entrance from the easternmost Iron Gate. Only the ruins of these enclosing walls now remain.

If we turn north here and walk between the Inner and Outer Walls we will find on our left three more towers defending the Inner Wall— the Broad Arrow, the Constable and the Martin Towers; in the last of these the Crown Jewels were kept for a time and a daring attempt was made to steal them from there. There are no towers along the Outer Wall on the eastern side, only the dry channel of the old moat beyond it.

The Martin Tower is at the northeast corner of the Inner Wall and from this point both Inner and Outer Walls turn west. The corresponding corner of the Outer Wall is marked by what is known as the Brass Mount, a massive bastion erected in the reign of Henry VIII to bear the weight of cannon. There are no towers along the northern Outer Wall, but along the parallel Inner Wall there are five—after the Martin Tower they are the Brick, the Bowyer (where the bowmakers may have worked), the Flint and the Devereux Towers—the last-named at the northwestern corner, where the Inner Wall begins its southern course to join the Bell Tower. The Outer Wall turns similarly at another huge mount, Legge's Mount, also put up by Henry VIII for cannon. Midway between the two mounts a third was erected in the nineteenth century to cope with the Chartist rioters who were active from 1837 to 1848; it was twice hit by bombs in World War II and was completely destroyed. There are no towers along the western Outer Wall; the Inner Wall has just one, the Beauchamp Tower, standing exactly midway between the Devereux and the Bell Towers. In the very early years after the Norman Conquest the only landward gate

Tower Green, looking west. The Queen's House, the home of the Governor of the Tower, may be seen between the trees, at the corner of the L-shaped group of Tudor houses; it is entered by the door beneath the balcony. (Ministry of Public Building and Works)

into the Tower of London was here; it led right into the Inner Ward. Both the Beauchamp and the Devereux Towers, like the Bell, were used as prisons.

Now let us go through the gateway of the Bloody Tower into the Inner Ward. As we pass through the narrow sombre archway the scene begins to change. The sombreness fades and we shortly find ourselves in what might be an English country village. There is a long pleasant stretch of green on the left divided in two by a cobblestoned path with benches to sit on, an old church to the right with an L-shaped row of attractive Tudor houses opposite. At our backs, rising to a great height, stands the proudest of all the towers, not only in England but in all Europe —the White Tower, William the Conqueror's magnificent architectural legacy to posterity.

The road from the Bloody Tower gateway slopes upwards to a wide flight of stone steps at the far end. As we walk along it we will see on our right the remains of a long embrasured wall which falls short of the foundations of the double circular-towered gateway known as the Cold-harbour Tower (built in 1240), which once spanned the space from this wall to the White Tower and thus guarded the innermost enclosure of the great fortress. In this area Henry III built the Palace in which successive sovereigns lived until the reign of James I. A few traces of the Palace foundations remain, but not enough to indicate its size or plan: after the execution of Charles I, Oliver Cromwell obliterated it.

As we climb the wide sweep of steps, Tower Green comes into view on the left. It is haunted by harrowing memories, for on the scaffold here, the site of which was enclosed by Queen Victoria, three queens and four other famous people met their end. Beyond it is the Chapel of St Peter ad Vincula (St Peter in Chains) where many of the axe's victims were buried; it is thought to have been built by Henry I, and is mentioned in 1210 in the reign of King John; it was rebuilt by Henry III, and rebuilt yet again, after a devasta-ting fire, by Henry VIII. The curious name of the Chapel derives from the fact that it was con-secrated on 1 April, the date on which the chains of St Peter are exhibited each year in the Church of San Pietro in Vincoli in Rome, commemorating the apostle's imprisonment and eventual escape. Mr Doyne Bell, in an interesting monograph on this chapel in the Tower, states, 'With the ex-ception of the Abbey church of St Peter's at Westminster' (that is, Westminster Abbey) 'there is no ecclesiastic edifice in the United Kingdom in which (so far as it has been used as a place of sepulchre) is contained so much historical interest as this chapel.' Its peculiar dedication suggests that the Chapel was built for the prisoners in the Tower and possibly also for the use of the garrison and the officials. The sovereign and the court used St John's Chapel in the White Tower as their private place of worship until 'the King's houses' were built, after which the King and Queen often attended the services in St Peter's.

St Peter's was not the only religious building in the Tower. Some of the other towers, such as the Wakefield Tower, as well as the Palace, had their own small chapels; there is also the uniquely im-pressive Chapel of St John in the White Tower. At the side of St Peter's, against the Inner Wall, there are two eighteenth-century houses built for the chaplain and the doctor.

We now see the towers of the Inner Wall from a different angle. Here are their entrances. The Bell Tower can only be reached from the Queen's House, which was formerly called the Lieutenant's House, or 'Lodgings'; that is where the Governor now lives. It is the largest and most charming of the small gabled Tudor houses, standing almost in the centre of the group, and its staircase gives the only access to the upper chamber of the Bell Tower. It also provides access to the ramparts where Princess Elizabeth used to walk when she was a prisoner. The Lieutenant's House was built in the reign of Henry VIII, about the year 1530. Anne Boleyn spent part of her imprison-ment there, and Elizabeth had to use the Lieu-tenant's staircase to reach her cell in the Bell Tower. Though used as prisons from time to time, all these houses were really unfortified dwellings.

Next we see the flat front of the D-shaped Beauchamp Tower, with its two square turrets and battlemented roof. The entrance is now below ground level. Under the Tudors it was the Tower's principal prison, and was at times so crowded that not only all the floors, but even the basement had to be used. On the walls one can see ninety-one inscriptions carved by prisoners; some of these inscriptions have been moved here from other towers. Most of them are still decipher-able. The most elaborate is the memorial to the five brothers Dudley, sons of the Duke of Northumberland, carved by the eldest, John, styled Earl of Warwick. They and their father were confined in the Tower in 1553. North-umberland was executed for treason in the same

Aerial view of the Tower enclosure, the dry moat and the River Thames. (Aerofilms Ltd)

year and his fourth son, Lord Guildford Dudley, the husband of Lady Jane Grey, in 1554. To him is attributed the inscription of the single word 'Iane', said to refer to his wife. Another brother, Robert Dudley, Earl of Leicester, was the favourite of Queen Elizabeth I.

To the right of the Chapel of St Peter ad Vincula you will see the massive Waterloo Barracks built in 1845 by the great Duke of Wellington and named after his famous victory over Napoleon. The parapet and turrets were crenellated to be in harmony with the earlier buildings. In front of the barracks is the Parade Ground, beneath which, in a vast well-guarded underground chamber, the Crown Jewels are now displayed.

To the east is a smaller nineteenth-century building built close to the Inner Wall: it is the headquarters of the Royal Fusiliers (City of London Regiment) and houses the Royal Fusiliers Museum. Next to it are two houses built in the late seventeenth century and partially rebuilt after

9

being bombed in World War II—they are now the officers' married quarters. Adjoining is another attractive late seventeenth-century building in which the New Armouries are housed. The royal Palace and its gardens occupied the entire open space between the New Armouries and the ruined strip of embrasured wall running north from the Bloody Tower gateway; all that can be seen there now is a big cage which stands against the Inner Wall between the Lanthorn Tower and the Wakefield, where the ravens live.

There now remains but one building for us to look at—the White Tower, the focal point of the Tower of London and a superb example of Norman architecture. Before Henry III built the Palace, the two upper floors of the White Tower were used as the royal residence. The Council of State met there, as did also the courts of justice when the King was in residence. In the Chapel of St John on the second floor the sovereign and his family used to worship and it was here that the new Knights of the Bath held their vigil on the night before the King's coronation. In later times the crypt was used as a dungeon, with the torture chamber alongside. The White Tower now houses a magnificent display of old armour and weapons.

The visitor will see some ancient bricks and stonework to the east of this tower; they are the remains of the wall built by the Romans round London, which was still standing when the White Tower was erected. The section of it which ran through the Tower grounds was left undisturbed until the early years of the thirteenth century, when the three Roman towers along this wall were pulled down and rebuilt. The one at the southern end was replaced by the Lanthorn Tower; the one in the middle by the Wardrobe Tower (built in the twelfth century) of which only the stump, incorporating the base of the earlier Roman tower, can now be seen; the one to the north by the Bowyer Tower. The Roman wall, which ran parallel to the embrasured wall on the western side, was linked with the White Tower by a wall; this completed the innermost royal enclosure.

An adjunct to the Tower is the Wharf, which stretches from the site of the old Lion Tower to Tower Bridge and is reached by three bridges. Today it bristles with old cannon, and people use it as a place of relaxation, sitting on the many benches to talk or eat sandwiches and gaze at the shipping as it passes up and down the river.

CHAPTER TWO

How it Began

William the Conqueror, a man of swift decision and action, lost no time in building the Tower of London. After his victory at Hastings on 14 October 1066, he set out for the capital, but found the citizens of London prepared to resist him. They were encouraged by Stigand, the Archbishop of Canterbury, and by the powerful Earls Edwin and Morcar; they, with the full support of the Witan, the English Council of Wise Men, had sworn their allegiance to Edgar, the nephew of King Edward the Confessor, who had ruled the country until his death in January of that year. Realizing that he had insufficient forces to take London by storm, William swept through the southern counties, spreading havoc, devastation and terror; then turning north, he crossed the river at Wallingford. Stigand and the Earls submitted and the Conqueror entered the city from the northwest. He had already started building the Tower of London when he was crowned King of England at Westminster Abbey on Christmas Day, a bare ten weeks after landing in the country.

Some chroniclers dispute this, maintaining that twelve years elapsed before the construction of the Tower was begun. This is wholly out of keeping with the character of the Conqueror, who would certainly not have ignored the vital need for a fortress to guard the estuary of the Thames against invaders and to overawe the potentially rebellious citizens of London. Potential invaders there certainly were. Shortly before his defeat at Hastings, King Harold had beaten Hardrada, King of Norway, at the Battle of Stamford Bridge, but there were others of Danish stock linked by birth or marriage with King Canute who had ruled both England and Denmark until his death in 1035. Nor were the people of England prepared to submit willingly to the Norman conqueror; there were a series of revolts in various parts of the country. First the southwest, then York rebelled. Wales, Scotland and Ireland provided bases of operations for the disaffected, who received help not only from Edgar but also from the Danish King, Sweyn, who brought a large fleet to aid the rebellion in which even William's erstwhile ally the Count of Boulogne joined. After some years of swift marches and extensive terrorization, William was able to enforce the subjection of the country. 'A whole generation was wiped out in what amounted to genocide,' states Timothy Baker, drawing on contemporary chronicles for his book *The Normans*, 'so that Yorkshire was still a desert when the *Domesday* survey was carried out in 1086 and the scars were to outlive William's sons. Simeon, a monk of Durham, writing some fifty years later, tells of cannibalism and of the highways strewn with putrefying corpses, for starvation and pestilence followed in the wake of butchery.'

A thousand years earlier, on the very site chosen by William, the Romans had built not a tower but a large villa (possibly for a military governor) which was discovered during recent excavations. It extended right up to the Roman wall and large sections of its pavement were found; there was doubtless a fortress nearby. But after the Roman withdrawal from Britain in AD 407 the fortress must have suffered from neglect and decay, as well as damage from the successive attacks of hostile Angles, Saxons and later Danes, until King Alfred, deservedly called the Great, brought these devastating incursions to a halt less than a couple of hundred years before the coming of the Conqueror. The records show that Alfred kept all existing fortifications in repair, built a large number of others, and maintained all the garrisons at full strength.

William's Tower was built inside the walls of

London, which was a small but important city stretching for a mile along the north bank of the Thames and about a half mile inland. There were already settlements around it, including one on the south bank, which was linked with the city by a wooden bridge. Indeed, by this time London had been an important town for a thousand years. The Roman historian Tacitus (AD *c.* 55–120) described it as being filled with merchants and heavy traffic. To the north of the city stretched a vast forest where wild boar roamed (in the region of what is now St John's Wood and Hampstead); the marshes to the west and south had been drained by now and monks had been granted land for a monastery; Edward the Confessor erected his Abbey of Westminster there and was buried in it a few days after its consecration.

Far from being a primitive and savage country, civilized only after the Norman Conquest, England had been renowned for her learning, literature and art for five centuries before the Conqueror's ancestor, Rollo, a pagan Viking raider, was made duke of the coastal province of Normandy by Charles the Simple, King of the West Franks. Though England was sparsely populated in the north and west, which were cut off by forests and swamps from the rest of the country, the people had begun to coalesce into one nation; save for the earlier Celtic invaders, the settlers were essentially of kindred stock, and had established a unity under King Alfred and his successors. Almost all the people were Christians by the end of the seventh century. The church built at Canterbury in the days of the Romans had been rebuilt and there were a great many abbeys and monasteries which were rich in learning. The black-gowned Benedictine monks built churches, farmed, and cultivated vineyards, constructed granaries and developed the arts of architecture and sculpture, painting and music. In the eighth century the Venerable Bede, a monk in Jarrow, was recognized as the foremost scholar in Europe. 'Men from abroad came hither to this land in search of knowledge and instruction,' King Alfred noted. English embroidery and fine metal-work were among the exports to the Continent, and the considerable number of coins of that time which can now be seen in museums indicate that trade must have been brisk.

It is generally agreed that the administration of

England was far superior to that of Normandy. The early English kings were great law-givers and a large collection of their law-codes or *dooms*, going back to about the year 600, still survives. For the most part these were definitions of accepted custom; they show that justice was a royal right, although many great lords, bishops and some of the monasteries had been given leave by the King to hold their own courts. True feudalism, in which land was held only in return for military service, was unknown in England. It was introduced by William the Conqueror. In pre-Conquest times, the tie between lord and man was one of personal loyalty and honour.

William made the invasion of England a holy war, much in fashion at the time. The Pope gave the enterprise his blessing and it was under the consecrated papal banner that William prepared for the conquest of England.

Not only did he succeed in persuading the Norman barons to support him with men and ships in his effort to become king of another country, but he called for volunteers, who flocked to his standard. At stake was a rich prize, for England was five times the size of Normandy,

larger indeed than all the northwestern maritime states of the Continent put together. Nor were any of these states wholly independent; they owed allegiance to king or emperor. The King of England owed allegiance to none.

There were already quite a number of Normans in England, many of them occupying high positions. Some had been there for two generations. The court of Edward the Confessor, himself half-Norman, had been full of William's countrymen; many were barons, others bishops—one had even occupied the exalted position of Archbishop of Canterbury; but William could not have expected to receive any quisling help from them. As one of the greatest soldiers of the day, it was his purpose to decide the issue by battle. When William landed at Pevensey on 28 September, luck was also with him. King Harold was in York repelling the forces of his half-brother Tostig and Hardrada of Norway. Sixteen days later Harold lay dead on the battlefield at Hastings and William was master of England.

Duke William of Normandy, riding a black horse, arrives at the French coast with his followers to join his fleet and sail for England. From the Bayeux Tapestry, traditionally thought to have been designed by William's wife, Matilda of Flanders. (Giraudon)

CHAPTER THREE

Building the Tower

By the southeastern corner of London's Roman wall William began the construction of the Tower. He used the angle of the wall for two sides of his defensive enclosure and dug a dry ditch running northwards from the river and then eastwards to join the wall to complete its boundaries. The earth from the ditch was heaped up to form a high embankment, on the top of which he erected a timber palisade. From the bottom of the ditch to the top of the palisade would have been about thirty feet. The palisade was pierced by embrasures and loopholes for the archers and men with catapults. Inside this enclosure a large number of wooden huts were erected for storing weapons and provisions for the garrison. The Conqueror, William of Poitiers tells us, withdrew from London 'while certain strongholds were made in the town against the fickleness of the vast and fierce populace.'

This purely temporary structure was the first version of the present Tower of London. It was started before William's coronation and was completed in about three days. That a more solid structure would have to replace it was obvious and plans for erecting one were soon drawn up. The actual construction is thought to have been begun a few years later. Materials had first to be assembled, masons and other craftsmen had to be engaged and quarries selected for the supply of stone.

For at least two centuries before the Conquest, the craft of the mason and the architect had flourished in Britain. In England as on the Continent, the houses of the people were usually of wattle, straw and mud, a single room with one end partitioned off for the cattle. But the many magnificent churches and monasteries and the royal palaces, built on a large and impressive scale, exercised the skills of these master-craftsmen.

Under roofs decorated with glistening ornaments, in rooms hung with tapestries, the monarch dined, held meetings of his council, and received foreign ambassadors in audience. Alas, hardly any of these imposing edifices survived the energetic rebuilding activities of the Normans.

Edward the Confessor not only modelled Westminster Abbey on the abbeys he saw being erected in Normandy but also brought over from that country a number of master-masons to superintend the work. We know, however, and William must soon have learned, that Edward also used some brilliant English master-masons, to one of whom, 'Teinfrith, my church-wright', he gave an estate at Shepperton as a mark of his appreciation. Another of the master-masons whose name has survived was Leofsi Duddesunu.

English masons, artisans and highly skilled craftsmen were thus available in England and there were also abundant supplies of stone, marble, timber and rubble. But the Conqueror was not content to rely solely on local talent and materials. He preferred to employ the men he knew and who were familiar with the sort of work he wanted. The planning and supervision of the building of the Tower was entrusted to a Norman named Gundulf. He is not described as an architect or master-mason, but was one of the monks in the famous Abbey of Bec in Normandy. All learning at that time was the province of the Church. Gundulf had presumably devoted himself to the study of architecture, for he had been busy for some years designing and building cathedrals and castles in Normandy. By now in his fifties he lodged, we are told by Stow, in the house of Edmere, a burgess of London. A few years later he was appointed Bishop of Rochester and began building the cathedral there. Thus two projects were under his supervision.

The Conqueror gave instructions that the white limestone of Caen, which resembles marble, should be brought across the Channel, and that the hard and rough Kentish stone known as ragstone should be used with it. In addition, a local mudstone from the Thames known as septaria was used. All these can be seen in the White Tower to this day.

Boats brought Caen limestone up the Thames; the Kentish rag came from Maidstone along the Medway in barges. Gangs of labourers would unload them and trundle the stones in small carts to the site, where other workers were engaged in mixing sand and lime in immense vats to make mortar. Elsewhere men were busy in the forests outside London, felling trees which were then split by an axe and a wedge to form beams, or smoothed into planks with an adze, and fashioned by carpenters in the workshops on the site into massive doors, cupboards and shelves, or into benches and tables and even armchairs. Lead had to be brought for the roofs, and iron for clamps, though iron was costly and even the spades and shovels were of wood save for their small iron shoe. All around there were scaffolds and ladders, pulleys to raise and lower the cradles, baskets for hoisting stones, grindstones, trowels, axes, squares, plumb-lines to correct the levels, and string for measuring.

The man in charge on the building site was the master-mason. He was responsible for the design and the ground-plan and for organizing the various groups of craftsmen. Skilled men were not easily available during the latter part of the eleventh century, and at times, when persuasion failed, a royal command forced them to take on the work. Unskilled labour was more plentiful and transport had to be provided for the men as well as for the building materials. The master-masons were paid about twelve shillings a week. The carpenters, plasterers and others got from two-pence to threepence a day; in the winter, when they worked shorter hours, their pay was proportionately cut. Clad in long shirts that reached down to their knees, they had interpreters standing by each group to translate the orders of the Norman overseers (though used by many of the upper classes, French was unfamiliar to the English labourer). Often the work on the Tower must have gone on far into the night, with naked torches to light the scene; and doubtless large crowds of Londoners—the men ill-kempt in their workaday clothes, the women with tattered shawls over their heads—gathered round to gape at the

active teams straining at their loads to a rhythmic chant while the clatter went on amid swirling clouds of dust. And as the great White Tower rose to its immense height, with its lancet windows for the archers and its battlemented turrets, many among those spectators might justifiably have shuddered.

The White Tower was indeed a formidable stronghold. Its walls rose to a height of ninety-two feet and for much of the way up they were fifteen feet thick, tapering to eleven feet at the top. Strength was essential; light and ventilation

Medieval builders at work, from a late fifteenth-century Flemish Book of Hours. In the background on the left can be seen the mason's 'lodge', which served as a shelter for the stone-cutters. The crane is wound up by hand, and the thongs holding the scaffolding together are clearly visible. (By permission of the Trustees of the British Museum MS Add. 35313, fol. 34r)

The White Tower—fortress, palace and prison—the Conqueror's massive bequest to London. In the centre foreground, shaded by trees, is the stump of the twelfth-century Wardrobe Tower, itself incorporating the remains of an earlier Roman tower which once stood on the line of the Roman city wall. (Ministry of Public Building and Works)

mattered little, and the narrow slit windows served a defensive purpose.

To the eye the structure looks square. In fact it is an irregular shape. Of the four turrets at the corners, the one at the northeast is round, the other three are square; and there is a semi-circular bastion at the southeast corner to accommodate the apse of St John's Chapel and the crypt and the sub-crypt below it.

The only entrance was then on the south side, the door being about fifteen or twenty feet above the ground; it was at the west end of the wall and led directly to the first floor—a normal feature in Norman castles; the steps leading up to it from

the outside were removed whenever danger threatened.

For many centuries anyone entering would encounter heavily armed officers and men-at-arms wearing chain mail; sentries were also posted along the battlements and in the turrets, which commanded London and the river approaches.

The White Tower has four floors, each divided into three rooms; of these, one very large room occupies half the entire floor space. The ground floor, the north end of which is below ground level, has no outer windows at all. The three rooms on this floor were used as dungeons, though their original purpose was to store provisions, and there is a deep circular well, lined with ashlar.

Numerous prisoners were herded together in the biggest of these three rooms and the smaller one alongside contained a torture chamber: although torture was not permissible under the laws of England, it was used during the later Middle Ages and under the Tudors and Stuarts. The room was equipped with several racks, thumbscrews, iron collars, brakes for extracting or breaking the prisoners' teeth, iron stocks and bracelets, a horrible rack known as 'the Duke of Exeter's daughter' and other implements of torture. At one end of the room, inside the thickness of the wall, was the 'Little Ease', measuring four feet by four, with heavy oaken doors and without light or ventilation, in which the prisoner could neither stand nor lie down; Guy Fawkes was among those confined in it. There are very few instances of women having been tortured; the most famous was Anne Askew, a troublesome and violent religious reformer who was brought to the Tower in 1546 in the reign of Henry VIII. For a whole hour she was kept on the rack but still refused to incriminate others. She was eventually burnt at the stake. The third room, the sub-crypt of St John's Chapel, was also used as a prison. All the floors were of rough earth.

On the first floor, alongside the large entrance hall where the men-at-arms stood on guard, was another large room used by soldiers and the King's retainers. To the south was the crypt of the Chapel, which was also used as a prison; the prisoners' inscriptions can still be seen on the jamb of the doors.

On the second and third floors were the royal apartments. The largest room on the lower of these floors was used as the Banqueting Hall—it is ninety-five feet long; the smaller room alongside was used as sleeping quarters by the nobles of the King's court. St John's Chapel was on the south side—the finest room in the entire Tower, fifty-five feet long and built of white stone brought by the Conqueror from Caen. In the Chapel there are twelve massive round columns with carved capitals, some of which have a T-shaped cross—this, the only decoration, is peculiar in a building of this early date. The arches are quite plain. Above them is a clerestory lighted by a second tier of windows. The roof is lofty and rises through the floor above to the top of the Tower. The gallery is on a level with the upper floor and was used by the ladies-in-waiting and other women of the royal household. A barrel-shaped vault constructed like a tunnel spans the nave and apse and must be the earliest barrel vault to be seen in England today.

The back room on the top floor provided sleeping accommodation for the King and Queen. The long room above the Banqueting Hall was used as the Council Chamber; inside the thick outer wall on this floor runs a passage four feet wide, built into the thickness of the wall and used by archers, men with catapults, and others for passing from one defence position to the next without being exposed to the enemy. The roof is flat and covered with lead.

The only staircase in the White Tower is in the circular turret in the northeastern corner and leads right down to the dungeons. It mounts in a clockwise direction so that only the defenders would have enough space to use their right hands against attackers rushing up the stairs. There are three large fireplaces: two on the first floor and one on the second, in the Banqueting Hall. They were built into the outer walls and have no chimneys, only vents to let out the smoke; some Roman bricks were incorporated in their walling.

Each of the three main floors has two lavatories, with seats and chutes. One should try to imagine these rooms as they were when the King lived in them, the walls hung with lovely tapestries, enormous carpets stretched across the floors, and massive tables, chairs and beds in the rooms.

This was the only tower completed during or shortly after the reign of the Conqueror. Around it was an encampment for the garrison as well as for the King's mounted bodyguard and storehouses for food. The White Tower is the noblest of all the towers and even today it dominates the site, dwarfing the other nineteen towers into insignificance.

For many centuries the White Tower and later some of the other towers were referred to as 'Julius Caesar's Tower'. The name persisted right up to the time of Shakespeare, who in his play *Richard III* makes one of the two unfortunate Princes in the Tower ask his uncle, the Duke of Gloucester (later King Richard III), 'Did Julius Caesar build that place, my lord?' to which Gloucester replies, 'He did, my gracious lord, begin that place.' Then the Prince enquires, 'Is it upon record, or else reported successively from age to age, he built it?' The Duke of Buckingham cuts in with the confirmation, 'Upon record, my gracious lord.' Buckingham was wrong.

This was not the only tower William the Conqueror built in London. At the southwest corner of the city, within the old Roman wall and commanding both the river and the capital, he put up a fortress called Baynard's Castle, after one of his Norman barons; it stood at the western end of the city near where Blackfriars Bridge now stands. It was, however, completely destroyed in the Great Fire of London in 1666.

CHAPTER FOUR

The First Prisoner

The first known prisoner in the Tower was Rannulf Flambard, who was chief minister to the Conqueror's son William II, nicknamed Rufus; he had been appointed in 1087 to take over control of the building operations in the Tower from Gundulf. Like his predecessor he was a Norman and a churchman, and Rufus later appointed him Bishop of Durham.

It is not clear from the records when the White Tower was completed. According to Stow, whose *Survey of London* was written some centuries later, the date given is as early as 1078, nine years before the Conqueror's death. Others dispute this, stating that the work went on throughout the reign of Rufus and was unfinished when his brother Henry I came to the throne. Gundulf, already an old man, had been sent to Rochester, where he supervised the building of the cathedral and castle, dying while engaged in these operations in 1108 at the age of eighty-four.

Flambard was of extremely humble origin, and, unlike Gundulf, who was revered as a God-fearing and saintly man, he had worked his way up to a high position by flattery and treachery. As the King's chief minister he was dishonest, unscrupulous and arrogant. Loud were the outcries against him for his ceaseless and unjust extortions from the citizens of London; to swell the royal exchequer an endless succession of taxes were arbitrarily imposed and if they were not met, heavy fines followed. 'All justice slept—money was the Lord,' the chronicles record. When the clergy found that Flambard was selling church appointments to the highest bidder, their angry voices joined the roar of protests. But Rufus, with his exchequer filled to overflowing, refused to listen, and it was not until after his death that his successor Henry I arrested Flambard to allay the anger of the people. He was charged with simony (the buying and selling of ecclesiastical preferments) and imprisoned in the White Tower; there was great rejoicing all over England 'as if over the captivity of a raging lion'. Surprisingly, Flambard was allowed a number of privileges; he

The coronation of William Rufus, a manuscript miniature from the Flores Historiarum *of Matthew Paris. (By permission of the Feoffees of Chetham's Hospital and Library, Manchester)*

Henry I's awareness of public discontent leads him to dream that the three estates of the realm have risen up to destroy him. In the upper picture, peasants armed with farm implements crowd menacingly round his bed; below, he is threatened by armed knights. From the Chronicle of John of Worcester, *written in the mid-twelfth century. (By permission of the President and Fellows, Corpus Christi College, Oxford. MS CCC.157, fol. 382)*

had his own chaplains and servants to wait on him. The Saxon chronicler Vitalis tells us that in addition to the plentiful supply of food brought to him by the warders, he had vast quantities of provisions sent in from outside and a great many casks of wine. The records show that the Constable of the Tower was paid only 2s a day for Flambard's keep.

Appropriately, in view of his passion for food, Flambard was imprisoned in the Banqueting Hall. One night, as a gesture of magnanimity, he invited his guards to dine with him. In one of the casks of wine a length of rope had been concealed by his friends, and that evening Flambard made sure that his warders drank themselves into a stupor. He then brought out the rope and tied it to a pillar by one of the windows, only to find that

the window was hardly wide enough for his enormous girth. He managed nevertheless to squeeze through it, although greatly handicapped by his bishop's crozier, which he was determined to take with him. Clutching it firmly, he began to slide gently down the rope. But it proved to be too short for the drop of sixty-five feet and Flambard fell heavily to the ground. Badly bruised but otherwise uninjured, he picked himself up and was relieved to find that his crozier was undamaged.

He now encountered obstacles for which he had himself been responsible. The *Anglo-Saxon Chronicle* records that in 1097 men from many shires were 'sorely oppressed' in building a wall round the Tower. Its position is not indicated, but it must have been erected to replace the earthen bank and ditch on the north and west sides of the original enclosure. These Flambard now had to negotiate. He managed to overcome them, and once outside, was met by his friends, who were waiting for him in a boat (it was thought wiser to avoid the wooden bridge across the river, where London Bridge is now). On reaching the further bank, Flambard rode to the coast and took ship for Normandy. An alarm had been raised in the Tower, but by then he was well away.

By a pact said to have been made by Rufus with his elder brother Robert, Duke of Normandy, Robert was to succeed him as King of England. In this expectation Robert had mortgaged Normandy to Rufus to raise money for a Crusade and had only just returned from the Holy Land. Flambard now had little difficulty in persuading him to assert his claim. An army for the invasion of England was quickly assembled and crossed to Portsmouth, where the Norman malcontents in England were expected to rally to Robert's standard. But he received very little support; Henry, with his English subjects unanimously behind him, drove his brother's forces back, and Robert had to abandon his claim to the English throne. Further signs of plotting forced Henry to cross the Channel with a large English army, and after a decisive victory at the Battle of Tinchebrai in 1106 he won the duchy of Normandy from his brother, who was brought to England and held as a prisoner for the rest of his life. Thus had Flambard played a part in an odd reversal of events, leading to the conquest of Normandy by England.

Many years later Flambard was allowed to return home, but he was taken off the work on the Tower. Restored to his see, he was given leave to finish the cathedral in Durham, a great and noble monument to his skill as an organizer and his flair for architecture.

The man who took over the care and maintenance of the Tower was a Norman baron named William de Mandeville. He was appointed Constable and was in fact the son of the Tower's first Constable. He found that much had to be done, for in the twenty years since its completion the White Tower had suffered a great deal of damage from devastating storms and earthquakes.

CHAPTER FIVE

The Treacherous Constable

On Henry's death in 1135 his daughter Matilda succeeded as Queen. She had been married at the age of twelve to Henry V, the Holy Roman Emperor; after his death in 1125 she had married Geoffrey Plantagenet, Count of Anjou and Maine, from whom the Plantagenet kings of England were descended.

The barons, however, disputed her right to the throne, for hereditary accession was not automatically recognized at that time. Had her brother William been alive, his right to the crown might have been accepted, for Henry I had ensured that the barons did homage to the boy. But he had been drowned in the wreck of the 'White Ship' off Barfleur in 1120. The Council, which had replaced the old Saxon Witan and consisted chiefly of Norman bishops and barons, declared that a woman was unfit to rule; then, exercising their right to elect a ruler from the royal line, they selected Stephen, the son of Henry I's sister and grandson of William the Conqueror.

Stephen accepted with alacrity. He crossed over at once from Boulogne, was enthusiastically received in London and was crowned King at Westminster in 1135. Matilda, refusing to accept the Council's decision, rallied her supporters and plunged the country into a civil war, which dragged on until 1142, the barons changing sides as it suited their interests.

At Whitsun in 1140, at a time when Matilda appeared to be gaining the ascendancy, King Stephen took refuge in the Tower with his wife and his entire court. The news was increasingly depressing, and to ensure the loyalty of the new Constable, Geoffrey de Mandeville, son of William, the previous holder of that office, Stephen ennobled him as the Earl of Essex.

As long as Stephen remained in the Tower he was secure. But tempted after some weeks by encouraging reports to resume the war against Matilda, he was captured at Lincoln and taken in chains to Bristol. Essex, still in the Tower as Constable, immediately changed sides to escape Matilda's vengeance. But London would not accept Matilda as Queen; the people found her high-handed and haughty. She unwisely refused to honour the concessions granted to the city by her predecessors. At the first sign of their hostility she fled, and eventually reached Normandy.

To make sure that she in her turn did not take refuge in the Tower, the Londoners instantly laid siege to it to dislodge Essex. Many of them had served in the militia and had their own bows and arrows, catapults, spears, lances and mallets. But without battering-rams and mobile siege-towers (the lofty wooden battlements of which gave security to the archers), a speedy surrender was unlikely. The attacks were answered with a sustained hail of arrows and missiles from the windows and battlements of the White Tower. It was obvious that the Tower's garrison would have to be starved into surrender.

Essex, who was still in the Tower, took stock of his resources and saw that the provisions and munitions were inadequate for a lengthy resistance. So he decided to break out. With a large detachment of the garrison as escort, he marched through the Tower's gates and made his way from London to Fulham, where he arrested the Bishop of London although he was in no way responsible for the belligerent attitude of the Londoners. Eventually Stephen defeated and captured Essex and stripped him of his authority. Once again Essex adroitly changed sides. He vowed he would be loyal to Stephen in future; and the King was deluded into forgiving him and even restored him to office as Constable.

Essex's promise of loyalty soon proved to be

Seal of King Stephen. (By permission of the Trustees of the British Museum)

worthless. On discovering that the Constable was in constant communication with Matilda, Stephen ordered his immediate arrest. But Essex managed to get out of the Tower with a body of armed men and began to lay waste the countryside to the north of London. In an uncharacteristic burst of energy, Stephen brought in a large number of foreign mercenaries who captured Essex at St Albans. He was charged with treason and threatened with hanging, but after being dispossessed of his castles at Saffron Walden and Pleshy—and

once again of his position as Constable—he was allowed to go free. He and his followers continued to terrorize the countryside around Cambridge until he was killed by an arrow in a skirmish near Mildenhall, in Suffolk.

John Leland, the sixteenth-century antiquary who made a close study of old English documents, states that Essex constantly added to the fortifications of the Tower, but whether this was done while he served Matilda or Stephen is not quite clear; the records give no details of the work done.

Matilda's son Henry was now twenty years old. He had inherited from his Plantagenet father, Geoffrey of Anjou, a large section of France including Normandy, which had refused to accept Matilda as ruler, but had been conquered by Geoffrey Plantagenet. By enticing and marrying Eleanor of Aquitaine, the gay, clever wife of King Louis VII of France, who was twelve years older than himself and the greatest heiress in Europe, the young Henry acquired Gascony and Auvergne and thus gained control of more than half France. In 1153 he landed in England with a powerful army and soon transformed the situation. Large numbers of his mother's supporters rallied to his support. The country was tired of the chaos and anarchy it had suffered for eighteen years, and Henry's forces continued to grow rapidly.

After suffering defeat at the battles of Malmesbury and Wallingford, Stephen offered to meet Henry and at Winchester accepted him as his heir. A few months later, on Stephen's death, his young conqueror, only just twenty-one, ascended the throne as King Henry II.

CHAPTER SIX

Becket and the Tower

The next notable master of the Tower was the famous Thomas Becket, the new King's chief minister who became Archbishop of Canterbury and was murdered in Canterbury Cathedral. Of Norman parentage but born in London, Becket was serving in the household of the Archbishop of Canterbury when he was singled out for his brilliant work on diplomatic missions and appointed Chancellor by the young King in 1155. Though older than Henry by fifteen years, he soon became his sovereign's closest friend. In addition to his duties as Chancellor, Henry also made him Constable of the Tower in 1161 and so he became responsible for the care and upkeep of the fortress. No details are available of the work he did there, and in less than a year, on being appointed Archbishop of Canterbury, he gave the job up.

In 1171 the sum of £21 (equivalent today to about £1000), was spent on the repair of 'the King's houses' in the Tower, probably buildings erected near the White Tower for the King to live in; it is thought that Henry I may have put them up as an alternative residence, something more private and personal than the vast royal apartments in the White Tower, but we cannot be sure. Henry II is believed to have added a kitchen, a bakery and a gaol to the existing buildings. However, the 'King's houses' are not mentioned in the only contemporary record of that reign which survives. What we do know is that these houses were later converted into a magnificent Palace by Henry III.

In 1172 a further £60 was spent by Henry II on various other repairs. Some years later lead was bought to cover the roof of St John's Chapel and timber was brought from Yorkshire to replace some of the great beams in the roof and floors of the White Tower. In all, £200 (today £10,000) was spent on the Tower by Henry II.

In the great-grandson of the Conqueror England again found a strong King. Henry II had inherited both his vigour and his genius as an organizer, and was to be one of the greatest kings England has ever had. Squat, fair-haired and freckled, he was powerfully built and had a will of iron. He worked ceaselessly and tirelessly and exhausted all who worked with him. 'From the very early morning,' one of them has recorded, 'you will see men running as though they were distracted, horses rushing against horses, carriages overturning carriages, players, gamesters, cooks, confectioners, morris-dancers, barbers, courtesans and parasites making so much noise, and in a word such an intolerable, tumultuous jumble of horse and foot, that you would imagine that the abyss had opened and Hell poured out its inhabitants.'

Resolved to restore order after the chaos of the preceding reign, he planned also to develop the work begun by his great-grandfather. William had set out to secure the safety of the country. The coastal defences were strengthened by the erection of castles; and the estates confiscated from the English thegns were distributed among the Norman barons, but their holdings were small and scattered so that, while they could overawe potential attackers, none would be powerful enough to fight the King. Only on the marches (as the borders were called) of Wales and Scotland were men on whom he could wholly rely given extensive lands on which they built their own castles; they were required to prevent any incursions by hostile 'savages' beyond. The highest offices in the Church were also given to the Normans so that the English priests and bishops should be held in check.

The Conqueror's son William Rufus strove to

carry on the work, but his brutality and avariciousness were believed by many to have been the true cause of his mysterious death while hunting in the New Forest, described at the time as an accident. Henry I's aim was to placate the supplanted Saxons who still formed the larger part of England's population; he promised at his accession to restore the laws of Edward the Confessor and to abolish the oppressive practices of his brother's reign—a promise which led to the arrest and imprisonment of Flambard.

Henry II's great ambition was to see that justice was meted out impartially to all his subjects; to this end he travelled continually about the country, taking with him his entire court, his judges and his clerks, the wagons laden with rolls and records bumping behind them along mile after mile of unmade roads and grass tracks.

There were at that time a number of courts at which cases were tried—two of these, the shire and the hundred courts, were presided over by officers appointed by the King. There were also a large number of minor courts where justice was dispensed by the barons or their stewards: these varied greatly according to local custom and the prejudices of the officials. In addition, there were the Church's courts.

Henry strove to bring all the different forms of justice under his own control. To begin with, he transferred to the royal courts all criminal cases such as murder, robbery, rape, arson, larceny and the harbouring of criminals. He gradually introduced professional judges, men unconnected with the Church (the earlier legal officials were clerics) and had them specially trained. In order to attract civil actions from the lower courts, he gave the people the right to appeal to him, and to this end he developed the jury system which had been introduced into England after the Conquest. But at this time the jurors were only witnesses; they gave evidence from their own personal knowledge of what had happened. Henry II broadened the scope of the jurors' responsibilities and out of this evolved the system of trial by jury which spread from England all over the world. He also set up a permanent judicial tribunal in London out of which the two great courts of King's Bench and Common Pleas later emerged. But since distances were great in those days and the roads unsafe, Henry also sent travelling justices all over the country—on assizes as this is now called—and thus not only expedited justice but drew still more litigation away from the private courts into the royal orbit. These were considerable reforms and

have endured for more than eight centuries. They helped also to draw the whole of England under the control of the King. Henry was also concerned to establish a good relationship between the people and the Crown. He sent home the foreign mercenaries brought to England by King Stephen. Next he dealt with the barons. During the stormy years of Stephen's reign many of them had raised large private armies and were not above fighting private wars, and filching land from each other as well as from the Crown. Henry forced them to give back the land they had acquired and limited the size of their personal armies. And he offered them the opportunity of paying a tax called scutage (shield money) instead of supplying armed men for the King's service. The ecclesiastical landholders, who did not wish to serve in the field, were already paying this tax, and it both suited the barons and reduced their immediate military potential, while Henry was able to use the money to hire and train professional 'regular' soldiers who were attached to him by oaths and service, whereas those provided by the feudal barons in war time were first and foremost the barons' men.

The Church he found more difficult to curb. Its influence was overpowering. At every turn one was aware of its presence and authority. In every town and every village the steeples rose alike above the hovels of the poor and the halls of the rich. The great abbeys with sculptured stone and stained-glass windows dominated the countryside, providing music and drama which the poorest could enjoy and pageants in which they could participate. The lives of the people, restricted as they were by the concept of feudal service, were further regulated from birth to death by the demands of the Church and the observance of its rites. Clerics formed the country's educated class, the members of the professions, and thus exercised great influence on the rule of the King and the barons. But Henry was gradually changing that by training men of ability who were not churchmen.

The Church's separate ecclesiastical courts were in recurrent conflict with those of the State, for some of their punishments were comparatively light. Even for violence the only penalty imposed was penance, and the severer spiritual penalties such as excommunication served neither as checks nor as deterrents. Henry demanded that priests found guilty of criminal offences should be deprived of their status and handed over to the secular courts for punishment, but this the Church refused to concede; and the right of appeal, it held, was not to the King but to the Pope. Over this argument and the implicit wider question of the supremacy of State over Church there was a deadlock which even Henry dared not break by force, and centuries were to pass before it was finally settled.

The possibility of a solution presented itself on the death of the Archbishop of Canterbury in 1162. By appointing Becket, his friend and Chancellor, as Archbishop, Henry combined the highest secular and ecclesiastical appointments in one man. But a startling change occurred in Becket. He resigned his position as Chancellor, abandoned his embroidered cloaks and rich furs for the simple black robe of a monk, and even took to washing the feet of beggars every day. Far from modifying the rights of the Church courts, he used his authority to extend them. The King's protests were brushed aside and his orders were defied.

The removal of Becket became imperative but since the appointment could not be revoked, there was only one way of undoing what had been done. It is unlikely that Henry seriously contemplated murdering him, if only because he was aware of the political inexpediency of such an act. However, on Becket's return from France in 1170, whither he had fled in 1164, he enraged the King by his excommunication of the bishops who had taken part in the coronation of his heir Prince Henry. In a burst of fury the King exclaimed, 'What a pack of fools and cowards have I nourished in my house that not one of them will avenge me of this turbulent priest.' His words were taken literally by four of his knights, who set out forthwith to Canterbury and murdered the Archbishop.

Henry's final years were disturbed and saddened by the revolt of his sons. His marriage to Eleanor of Aquitaine, who bore him five sons and three daughters, ended when the lovely Rosamond Clifford became his mistress and ultimately the mother of three more sons. Eleanor had been imprisoned in England from 1173 to 1185, and on her release went back to France. She had, as we know, been married to Louis VII of France, and had left him for Henry; it was not so much her

Henry II with his Archbishop, Thomas Becket, and four knights, from a fourteenth-century manuscript of his laws. (By permission of the Trustees of the British Museum. Cotton MS Claud. D.II.70, fol. 70)

going that distressed the French King as the transfer of her vast French possessions to the English Crown. His son Philip Augustus (Philip II), claiming that the murdered Becket had appeared to an ecclesiastic in his dreams and begged for Philip to avenge his death, responded now by giving Henry's sons his most eager support in their rebellion.

Henry had planned to set out on a Crusade to the Holy Land, but his failing health prevented it. On his death-bed he is said to have begged Richard, his eldest surviving son, to take on this task. Richard knelt penitently on the floor, said a fervent prayer and took immediate steps to honour his father's dying wish.

CHAPTER SEVEN

The Tower and Magna Carta

Alien in dress and belief to their Western opponents, the Saracens were often accused of breaking faith in peace agreements. In this fourteenth-century manuscript of the Chroniques de France, *Crusaders encounter unarmed Saracen leaders whose followers nonetheless bear spears and brandish scimitars. (By permission of the Trustees of the British Museum. MS Royal 16.G.VI, fol. 442r)*

Richard I was thirty-one years old when he came to the throne. In appearance he was quite unlike his father; the chronicles tell us that he was tall, golden-haired and blue-eyed. He was a poet and musician, and used to divert himself during campaigns by playing the lute and singing songs of his own composition. He had been engaged in fighting from the age of fifteen and had proved himself to be a great and gallant warrior. He was to devote the greater part of his life to fighting and he was in England for no more than ten months of his ten years' reign.

Richard's mind was so set on the Crusade that instead of taking up his new responsibilities as King, his thoughts were fixed entirely on raising money for his campaign against the infidels in possession of Jerusalem and other sacred places in the Holy Land. It was only as a result of his father's admirable organization of England's 'civil service' that there was an effective administration during his long absences. He put the highest offices in England and Normandy up for auction, sold royal lands, extorted feudal dues, released the Scottish King William the Lion from his vassalage in return for money, sold charters to a large number of towns and boasted that he would have sold London if he could find a buyer.

He brought his mother Eleanor of Aquitaine back to England to supervise the government of the country but placed the actual control in the hands of William Longchamp, Bishop of Ely, a man whom he knew he could trust. He also made him Constable of the Tower of London.

Longchamp was a Norman of humble birth descended from a French serf; he was small, swarthy and a cripple, but his energy was boundless. Despite the depletion of the Exchequer by Richard's call upon it for his Crusades, Longchamp spent enormous sums of money in strengthening the fortifications of the Tower. In the very first year he spent as much as £2881 (equal in present terms to about £144,000). Obviously so vast a sum of money must have been for some major work, but the relevant Pipe Roll (the audited accounts of the Exchequer) does not give details. What is known from recent excavations, however, is that Longchamp extended the Tower westwards. For this, the ditch on that side had to be filled in. He took in enough land to double the area of the Tower. On the west and the north sides he built a new wall, not of earth but of masonry, as surviving sections show, and extended his wall along the river bank, possibly all the way to join the Roman wall, although only a section of it stands today, running from the Bell Tower (which he built at the western limit of his wall) to the Bloody Tower gateway. Payments were made for the purchase of stone and lime, and recent excavations reveal that Purbeck marble was used for the plinth of the Bell Tower and this length of wall. On the west and north sides beyond the wall he made a new ditch (where Mint Street now runs) 'hoping,' we are told, 'that the water from the Thames would flow through it.' But the chronicler Matthew Paris tells us that the attempt to flood the ditch was unsuccessful, presumably because the sluices were unable to retain the water at low tide.

Longchamp may also have built the Wardrobe Tower about halfway along the Roman wall, using the existing mural bastion for this purpose. In the years 1192 and 1193 he spent a further £100 (approximately £5000 today) on fortifying the Tower with mangonels (a new type of military engine for hurling larger stones than could be shot by catapults) and a number of other weapons of defence which are not detailed in the records.

Assault on a walled town in Crusader times. The attackers use stone-hurling machines and scaling ladders, and are repulsed by crossbow bolts and long-handled pikes. The surrounding pictures show the everyday activities which continued as best they might during the disturbance of battle. From a thirteenth-century manuscript of the Chevalier au Cygne, *an early French epic. (Bibliothèque Nationale, Paris, Service Photographique. MS Fr. 12558, fol. 143v)*

These elaborate and costly precautions were taken when it was discovered that the King's younger brother John was plotting to seize the throne. Before setting out for the Holy Land, Richard had nominated as his heir his four-year-old nephew Arthur, the son of his brother Geoffrey, who was older than John. To placate John, Richard heaped titles and estates on him and allowed him to draw the revenues of a large number of counties in the Midlands and the west of England. As soon as Richard's back was turned, John set up his own court and a rival administration which challenged the authority of Longchamp. With his own large body of armed followers John paraded the country, and all who were against Longchamp flocked to his side. He also got in touch with King Philip Augustus of France, who had gone on the Crusades with Richard but had returned home after a quarrel. The plan was for John to seize the Tower while the French King sent an army to invade England.

Longchamp's activities, encroaching as they did on the city's boundaries, had enraged Londoners. They complained to the Council, most of whom strongly resented a man of Longchamp's humble birth being left in control of the kingdom and put in authority over them. His overweening ambition and his abuse of power in advancing his relatives set everyone against him. The chronicler William of Newburgh states that 'The laity found him

more than king, the clergy more than Pope, and both an intolerable tyrant.'

Meeting while Longchamp was away at Windsor, the Council charged him with a series of 'tyrannous acts'. Longchamp at once set out for London with a large body of troops. The Council retaliated by sending out a powerful force to prevent his reaching the capital. He managed to circumvent them and got through to the Tower. There he was instantly besieged by the Council's forces, who were soon joined by John's private army.

The siege, the second the Tower had to suffer, lasted many days. Faced with this powerful dual opposition and aware that his work on the Tower's defences were not yet complete, Longchamp gave up his attempt to defend it and fled. He slipped out of the Tower disguised as a woman, made for Dover Castle, and after a brief stay there, crossed over to France; from there he sent messages to the Holy Land to inform Richard of the startling developments and urging him to return home with the greatest possible speed.

John's troops now entered the Tower. With the fortress under his control, he proclaimed himself the 'Chief Governor of the Kingdom'. Richard promptly despatched to England Walter of Coutances, Archbishop of Rouen, who was with him on the Crusade, with orders to take over the Tower as the new Constable.

Richard abandoned the fruitless siege of Jerusalem and set out for England. Shipwrecked in the Adriatic during the voyage, he decided to cross Europe by land and adopted a disguise to evade capture, but was recognized, seized and secretly imprisoned in a remote castle. An attractive legend, which may well be based on fact, states that Richard's faithful minstrel Blondel travelled from castle to castle with his lute, playing his master's favourite melodies until at last he got a responsive answer from Richard.

During Richard's imprisonment, which lasted more than a year, King Philip had encouraged John in his efforts to seize the English throne by informing him that his brother was dead, but now the Holy Roman Emperor revealed that Richard

The statue of Richard I in Old Palace Yard, Westminster, outside the Houses of Parliament. Sculpted by Baron Marochetti, it was praised by the contemporary Edinburgh Review *as 'the noblest equestrian statue in England'. (Graphic Photo Union)*

Although King John ultimately became estranged from his barons, he had generously permitted them to share the sport on his estates. Here he hunts deer, in an early fourteenth-century manuscript. (By permission of the Trustees of the British Museum. Cotton MS Claud. D.II.70, fol. 133)

was his prisoner and demanded £100,000 for his release. This was twice the annual revenue of England at the time and in today's value equivalent to more than £5 million, but the barons, the Church and the people of England, preferring Richard's reputation to John's intrigues, readily subscribed the bulk of this enormous sum and Richard was allowed to return home.

On his arrival he was given a most enthusiastic welcome. Generous by disposition and eager to return to the east, Richard forgave his brother's duplicity, though ample evidence was available to justify his sending John to the Tower. Richard was killed in France in 1199, at the age of forty-two, besieging a small castle for a treasure it was said to contain.

John was by no means certain of the succession. His nephew, Arthur of Brittany, had a far stronger claim to the throne; and although Richard had, on his death-bed, nominated John as his heir, the decision in fact rested with the Council, and the barons were not disposed to accept him. Only the powerful influence of William Marshal, Earl of Pembroke, finally swayed the balance. 'Mark my words, Marshal,' the Archbishop of Canterbury warned him, 'you will never regret anything in your life as much as this.'

John was the youngest of Henry's sons, and certainly the most hated although he was his father's favourite. On hearing, as he lay dying, that John too had risen in rebellion against him, Henry had cried, 'Is it true that John, my very heart, whom I have loved before all my sons, has deserted me?'

A little over five feet tall, John is described as being sallow, with sly slanting eyes, given to maniacal rages and insatiably avaricious. During his seventeen troubled years on the throne almost his entire inheritance in France was lost: all that was left was the distant and unruly province of Aquitaine. England's close link with Europe, which had endured for more than a century, was all but severed. Even the Conqueror's duchy of Normandy was lost. Yet modern scholars have come to accept him as an able, if unpopular administrator.

During the many ruinous distractions abroad and the acute disturbances at home, John appears not to have spent much time in the Tower of London, but he gave a great deal of attention to its strengthening. Meticulous though he was in reorganizing the increasingly complex administration of the country and the systematic ordering of the Chancery and the Exchequer, details are lacking as to what was done in the Tower. The records we have show that he spent £450 on it, but the figure would certainly have been higher if the Pipe Roll for the year 1212–13 had not been lost, for the Close Rolls (the Chancery Rolls of only temporary value, the seal of which could be broken) show that much work was done in the Tower at that time. It is believed that the Bell Tower, which was begun by Longchamp, was now completed. The recurrent sieges of the Crusades had greatly advanced Western knowledge of siege warfare and defensive structures; and Longchamp had already begun to put these lessons into operation. John carried on the work. He is also said to have 'repaired the King's houses' and to have deepened Longchamp's ditch on the north side. We do know that in 1214–15 he spent £12 (about £600 now) on building a wall between the Tower and the city of London. This wall, which does not survive, is thought to have been just an outer boundary which was pulled down during the extensive work done in the next reign.

The Tower figured in John's life recurrently and fatefully. According to some accounts and in particular that of the nineteenth-century biographer Agnes Strickland in her many-volumed *Lives of the Queens of England*, he was involved in 1214 in a desperate infatuation with Maud, the daughter of Lord Fitzwalter. John had already been married twice. After discarding his first wife, he had taken as his second a fourte-year-old French heiress, Isabella of Angoulême, who was the bride-elect of another man and who became the mother of John's heir, Prince Henry.

29

Finding Maud Fitzwalter unresponsive despite his persistent entreaties, John had her kidnapped from her parental home at Dunmow in Essex and imprisoned her in the White Tower, hoping thus to break her spirit and make her more amenable to his advances. Her father attempted to rouse the people to help in rescuing her, but failing to raise a revolt, he fled to France with his wife and the rest of his family. Meanwhile John continued his courting at the Tower, but Maud still resisted him. Enraged by her obstinacy, he arranged for a poisoned egg to be served to her for breakfast. She died after eating it.

On receiving news of her murder, the grief-stricken Lord Fitzwalter returned at once to England. His chances of gaining support were now considerably enhanced by the mounting hostility towards the King, due in part to his interference in the rights and privileges of the barons and given a further cause by the discovery that John's nephew Arthur had been killed at his orders.

At the same time John was involved in a bitter struggle with the Pope over the appointment of Stephen Langton as Archbishop of Canterbury. Unlike his predecessors, Langton was an Englishman by birth, a great scholar and author of the hymn 'Veni, Sancte Spiritus'. Refusing to allow Langton to take up his office or to set foot in England, John billeted his mercenaries in Canterbury, confiscated the property of the monks of the cathedral, and drove them out of the country. The Pope retaliated by excommunicating John, and in 1208 imposed an interdict on the entire country. The consequences for the people of England were catastrophic. At a time when the life hereafter provided almost the only solace for the hard life of the peasants, all the churches were closed, marriages could only be celebrated in church porches, sermons were preached in the churchyards and the dead were buried in unconsecrated ground. The deeply religious susceptibilities of the people were outraged, but John remained completely indifferent. It gave him the gratifying opportunity of raiding the monasteries and seizing their immense wealth. If a robber murdered a priest, the King shrugged it off with the words, 'Let him go. He has only killed one of my enemies'.

These conflicts had been going on for some years before John, with his coffers overflowing, felt that something must be done to allay his unpopularity. As a first step he decided to make his peace with the Pope. He submitted as a penitent and knelt at Dover to receive the papal legate. The excommunication was lifted and John prepared now to meet the barons. He began by blaming them for the loss of his French territories. Had they come to his aid, he said, all might have been saved. The war resulting in the loss of these territories, as the barons were only too well aware, had been caused by John's insistence on marrying the bride-elect of Hugh, Lord of Lusignan, the heiress Isabella of Angoulême, which gave him the reversion of that important French territory. Hugh appealed for help to King Philip, who tried to arrange a reasonable settlement. When John failed to comply, the French King confiscated Aquitaine, Poitou and Anjou and sent his forces to occupy Normandy. Thus one after the other the French dominions were lost, and those English barons who held lands on the other side of the Channel found they had to pay homage and render service to the French King.

John, resolved now to win back these lost territories, imposed heavy taxes on the barons. Twice a capital levy was inflicted on them. Those unable to pay were cast into prison; their lands were seized and heavy fines were demanded for their release and the return of their estates. A great many fell deeply into debt to meet these demands. John sold heiresses to low-born foreigners and compelled widows who were wards in Chancery (that is, women under the age of twenty-one for whom the Chancery court acted as guardian) to marry against their will or pay a crippling fine. His wealth in time filled all his castles. He had barrels laden to the brim with silver marks and chests filled with vast quantities of jewellery and precious fabrics. He set up a department of State known as the Wardrobe, where some of the jewels and rich raiments were kept as his personal possessions; his son Henry III was later to move them into the Wardrobe Tower. Part of the money was used for hiring foreign mercenaries; many of the mercenary captains were made sheriffs, and were thus enabled to blackmail property-owners by bringing false accusations against them.

The barons decided it was time to put an end to this intolerable persecution. While ostensibly on a pilgrimage, they met towards the end of 1214 at Bury St Edmunds and formed a pact. Stephen Langton, Archbishop of Canterbury, strove all that winter to reach a peaceful settlement between them and the King, but John was shifty and evasive. It was at this moment that Lord Fitzwalter returned from France to avenge the murder of his daughter. He was Lord of Dunmow and hereditary holder of Baynard's Castle, the tower built by William the Conqueror; a contemporary describes him in the *Histoire des Ducs de Normandie et des Rois d'Angleterre* as 'one of the foremost barons of England and one of the most powerful'. There rallied to his side Geoffrey de Mandeville, Earl of Essex (grandson of the turncoat Essex of Stephen's reign), Henry Bohun, Earl of Hereford, Robert de Vere, Earl of Oxford, together with others from the great families of Clare and Bigod. They marched on London and the gates of the city were eagerly opened to them by the Mayor and the leading citizens. They then seized the Tower.

It was their plan to hold the Tower until John yielded to their demands. To enforce this they set out for Windsor, where the King was staying. John, finding his position precarious, finally decided to yield. He sent a messenger to the barons, who had by now reached a meadow at Runnymede with their squadrons of horsemen. On the memorable morning of 15 June 1215 they saw a small cavalcade approaching. At its head was the King, accompanied by Langton and the papal legate. The cavalcade dismounted and the King declared his readiness to accept the barons' terms. Thus was the seal set to Magna Carta (the Great Charter). The King swore that no free man (which meant, in the main, the barons) would be imprisoned or dispossessed save by process of law and the just judgement of his equals. Property necessary for a man's livelihood could not be taken from him; even the villains had to be protected against ruinous and unlawful exactions. And it had also been agreed that the 'Great Council' would be summoned before any new tax could be granted.

The barons knew that the King could not be relied on to fulfil these solemn undertakings. So they held on to the Tower. If given the chance, they realized, John would lose no time in setting aside the Charter and wreaking vengeance on them. He had in fact already sent a message secretly to the Pope denouncing the barons as rebels and traitors, and had also begun to raise additional mercenaries in Europe. By the end of August, a very few weeks after the granting of Magna Carta, the King received letters from Rome annulling it and releasing him from his oath; the mercenaries he had been recruiting on the Continent had already begun to arrive in England.

Civil war, inevitable now, finally broke out. The barons, with the Tower in their possession, promptly got in touch with the King of France; declaring that it was their resolve to depose John, they offered the throne to the Dauphin Prince Louis, the French King's heir. Though he was the husband of John's niece, Blanche of Castile, Louis responded at once to their appeal. Three contingents of the French army landed in the Thames estuary and Louis himself arrived shortly afterwards with a large body of knights: John's fleet had been unable to stop them. On the invitation of the barons and the Mayor of London they made their way to the Tower where, amid the wildest scenes of joy, Louis set up his court. He was to remain in occupation of the Tower for a year—the only time in its history that it has been under the control of a foreign power.

John avoided battle and withdrew, but Prince Louis's forces went on to Windsor and besieged the castle. There were risings everywhere in the country. The rebel barons in the north of England obtained the support of the King of Scotland. In the west, Llewellyn the Great, the ruler of north Wales, came to their aid. Almost every town was hostile to the King.

John, with his great band of mercenaries, took the war to East Anglia, where he burned and destroyed manors and churches and abbeys. The common people suffered from the cruelty and callousness of both sides. In October 1216, while John's baggage train was crossing the Wellstream estuary into Lincolnshire, it was engulfed in the quicksands. He lost all his carts and wagons and everything they contained—the royal crown, the coronation regalia, a vast quantity of jewels, dozens of gold and silver goblets, ornamental plate and candelabra and rich garments looted from the monastic houses. John was safe on the Lincolnshire side, but, suffering from dysentery brought on by over-eating and drinking, he was borne away in a litter and died shortly afterwards at the age of forty-eight.

With the crowning of his nine-year-old son as Henry III at Gloucester (a gold circlet was used in place of the lost crown), the war ended. Prince Louis withdrew his court from the Tower and eventually returned to France with his forces.

CHAPTER EIGHT

Henry III Expands the Tower

A great deal of information has survived about the work done on the Tower of London during the fifty-six years of Henry III's reign. Not only was the original plan, approved by William the Conqueror a hundred and fifty years before, vastly altered, but even the improvements and extensions of Longchamp and John were found to be quite inadequate. The bitter experience gained during the loss of Normandy, when fortress after fortress on the frontier fell to the French invaders, was turned to good account by the three regents appointed to rule England during Henry's minority. It had been seen only too clearly that very few of the castles were able to withstand a prolonged siege, and the development of siege-craft now made the reconstruction of all existing fortresses essential.

The plan was to use the White Tower as the centre, expand to the east, west and north, and build a high wall beyond fortified by powerful mural towers, with a wide moat beyond the wall. This, of course, involved taking in land on which there were dwellings, and compensation had to be paid to those who were displaced.

The work was begun in 1220, when Henry III was thirteen years old. When he grew older, the King showed a keen personal interest in the work and supervised the operations himself. Indeed, he developed a great passion for building and has left for the wonder and admiration of posterity the lovely cathedral at Salisbury, the magnificent edifice which replaced the Westminster Abbey of Edward the Confessor, and many other beautiful and impressive buildings.

To begin with, the regents repaired 'the King's houses' which stood south of the White Tower. The obscure origin of these buildings has already been mentioned; who built them and whether they were in fact being used as a royal residence we do not know. Now, for the first time, some light is shed on them. The Great Hall and the King's Chamber are particularly mentioned. In 1220 building work began on the new towers along what is now the Inner Wall and one of these, the round Wakefield Tower, had a chapel and chamber 'next to the King's Hall towards the Thames'. Henry often lived in 'the King's houses' and was continually improving and enlarging them. In 1230 a new kitchen was built and a year or two later the Great Hall underwent extensive repairs, amounting almost to rebuilding. The details are maddeningly sparse. We have no idea of the size or shape of the Palace Henry III was erecting south of the White Tower and backing on to the Inner Wall, at that time still lapped by the waters of the Thames. In 1234 the exterior of the Hall and Great Chamber were whitewashed. Four years later the interior of the Queen's Chamber on the east (built during, or possibly even before, the reign of Henry II) was 'whitewashed and painted with false pointing and flowers' but after two years 'they were wainscoted and painted with roses'. The King's 'Great Chamber' was redecorated at the same time and provided with new wooden window-shutters painted with the royal arms.

Year after year the reconstruction and decoration of the Palace went on—a new 'sausery' for storing salted meat was built 'large and fair' between the Great Hall and the kitchen in 1241 and a large pentice (passage) leading to the kitchen entrance. Some years later, in 1246–7, new 'privy chambers' (lavatories) were constructed for the King and Queen; to accommodate the Queen's privy it was found necessary to build a new turret. In 1256–7 the 'great wardrobe' of the Palace was roofed with lead; it would have been on the upper floor alongside the King's Chamber

The Great Hall in Stokesay Castle, Shropshire, which is thought to have been built in a similar style to Henry III's Palace in the Tower. The Castle probably dates from the time of Edward I, who granted Laurence de Ludlow a licence 'to strengthen his mansion with a wall of stone and lime, and to crenellate, or embattle, the same'. (National Monuments Record)

—indeed all the royal living quarters must have been above the ground floor, which would have been occupied by guards and retainers. The advantage afforded by the new Wakefield Tower being built next to the King's Chamber was soon utilized, for a door was cut through which the royal family could enter and leave the Palace with privacy and make their way down the tower's staircase to the postern gate leading to the King's Steps on the river. The expense was considerable, we are told, but the exact figures are not available.

The Palace no longer stands, but it must have been very similar to Stokesay Castle in Shropshire, which was built at this time. There would have been a large timber-roofed Great Hall, with a fireplace in the middle of the room so that all could sit round it and only a hole in the centre of the roof to let out the smoke. All the other rooms would have opened off it and they may all have had glazed windows. The Palace was provided with its own defensive walls and towers. The wall on the west which ran northward from the Wakefield Tower had arched recesses on the inner side, each pierced with a loophole. It was defended at the northern end by Coldharbour Tower, which spanned the gap between the end of the wall and the White Tower; to reach the Palace (save for the King's private access), this well-guarded gate had to be negotiated, as well as the White Tower. On the eastern side the en-

closure was completed by the Roman wall, and the Wardrobe Tower, built on Roman foundations before 1200, perhaps by Longchamp, bridged the gap between that wall and the White Tower.

The Wardrobe, a name originally given to a closet off a bedroom, was where the King and the wealthier nobles kept their clothes, furs, silken robes, jewels, plate, more costly furniture and other valuables, as well as their money. The King had an enormous room for this purpose in each of his residences, strongly built and well-guarded —the word 'wardrobe' is derived from the French *garde-robe*. He also kept there his arms and armour, diplomatic papers, State records, charters and chapel ornaments. For safety, the greater part of the contents of these rooms was taken from castle to castle when the King toured the country and even formed part of his baggage train when he went to war. King John had his crown, his jewels, clothes and money with him when the ship transporting them was sunk, and he lost everything. His son Henry III took the costly contents of his wardrobe to France and pawned his crown and regalia to raise money for the troops.

It was Henry III who separated all his own personal funds from the State Exchequer and set up a department for this purpose known as the Wardrobe. The taxes collected for military needs were transferred to the Wardrobe, which paid the wages of the archers and the armourers: this section eventually became known as the Ordnance department. Because of the often heavy losses while the Wardrobe was being carted from town to town, the Wardrobe Tower was used as a depository for the Crown Jewels, the personal finances of the King, his valuable clothes, ornaments and furniture, as well as the State papers. Later the records were moved to the Wakefield Tower, and in 1360 Edward III separated the Ordnance section from the Wardrobe.

Much later in Henry's reign the Roman wall on the east was pulled down and the Palace was extended: this and the new wall beyond it took in a large slice of land that belonged to various institutions. Compensation had to be paid to the Master of St Katherine's Hospital and the Prior of Holy Trinity, Aldgate, amounting to £166 2s 10d. The Palace extension provided a separate small hall and chambers for the Queen and a large garden on the east which was known as the Queen's Garden.

The new enclosing wall (later to be the Inner Wall) was placed much further out, but Henry completed little more than two sides of it. Vast quantities of lime were bought, and a new quarry was opened at Reigate in Surrey to provide ample supplies of stone. Immense purchases were also made of other building materials, such as timber, lead and Purbeck marble, five ship-loads of which were brought in barges from Dorset. Along the section of the wall facing the river, Henry built the Bloody Tower gateway: the tower above it was added by Richard II. Though originally called the Garden Tower because a garden adjoined it on the other side, it became so associated with tragedy and suffering in the succeeding three and a half centuries that from 1597 it has been known as the Bloody Tower. The only rectangular tower, it was built above the archway of the large watergate, which had a drawbridge and two portcullises. The walls of the Bloody Tower are of ragstone rubble (that is to say of rough, unsquared ragstone*) with freestone dressings. It has three storeys; much of the interior was altered during the next century. There are a few prisoners' inscriptions on the walls. The Wakefield Tower, then known as the Record and Hall Tower because of the records stored there, has only two storeys and the lead-covered roof has a battlemented parapet. The rooms on both floors are octagonal and have deep embrasures with arrow-loops in almost all of them. This tower was used occasionally as a prison.

Apparently not much work was done at this stage on the Roman wall along the river front, although where a bastion marked its junction with the Roman wall running northwards Henry built a new and more substantial tower, the Lanthorn Tower—it was destroyed by fire in 1788 and was rebuilt a little to the north of the old site. He did, however, build a wall running eastwards from this point and marked the outward corner with still another tower—the Salt Tower, the fourth tower along this wall. The Salt has a rounded exterior and two square turrets, one on the north, the other on the west. Its walls are of ragstone rubble with vertical bands of ashlar. There are three storeys: the room on the ground floor is of irregular pentagonal shape, with five splayed embrasures, each with an arrow-loop. From the passage leading to this room a door leads to the stair turret; a small room with a barrel-vault marked with chamfered cross-ribs has been built into the thickness of the wall. The

* There is a glossary at the end of the book explaining these terms.

The portcullis mechanism in the Bloody Tower. (Ministry of Public Building and Works)

room above has an original stone fireplace with a joggled lintel carried on shaped corbels and capped by a moulded string-course, above which rises a pyramidal stone hood. From this room a pointed doorway leads to the parapet walk. The room on the top floor is similar in size and shape and has rather larger arrow-loops. Prisoners' inscriptions can be seen on the walls.

The enclosing wall now ran northwards, in a line parallel to the earlier Roman wall pulled down to extend the Tower. Henry built three further towers along it—the Broad Arrow, the Constable and the Martin, at which the wall turned westward and carried three more towers—the Brick (only partly finished by Henry), the Bowyer and the Devereux.

The Broad Arrow has a rectangular room on the ground floor and three embrasures with pointed heads. This room was used as a prison and has inscriptions on the walls. The Constable Tower, which resembles it in some respects, was not used as a prison. The Martin Tower now has three storeys and stands on a base of a completely different style. The shape of the tower is an irregular circle, flattened at the points of junction, and there are two rectangular turrets. The Brick Tower also has three storeys. The Bowyer Tower has only two; its base is solid and incorporates a portion of the Roman wall. The ground floor has only one room with three original embrasures: two now have modern windows, but the third retains the original arrow-loop. The Devereux Tower at the corner, also of two storeys, is in shape an irregular circle with a circular staircase turret on the southeast side. The lower storey has a stone vault which is in two bays: the northern

35

bay has three chamfered ribs meeting in the middle, the southern has four chamfered ribs, all of Caen stone.

We do not know if any work was begun on the fourth wall enclosing the Tower on the west side. Where certain important details are missing from the records, this is thought to be due to the fact that, with the King in personal control of the building activities, the instructions were often given verbally instead of in writing. We know, however, that a 'noble gateway' was built by the King 'at great expense' and that it fell as if struck by an earthquake. The site of this gateway is not recorded in any contemporary document, but it is likely to have been on the site of the Beauchamp Tower, which was erected in the next reign as the main land gateway into the Tower. Henry's gateway appears to have been dedicated to Thomas Becket and bore his name and is so referred to by contemporary chroniclers. Stow, writing later, tells us that it collapsed shortly after it was built, and that on being re-erected, it fell again exactly a year later, on 23 April, St George's Day. Many took this as a sign of Becket's disapproval. One of the Tower chaplains declared that he had seen the ghost of Becket standing by this tower, wearing the mitre and the vestments of the Archbishop of Canterbury; and that it collapsed as he struck it with his crozier. It was long thought that this was a reference to the present St Thomas's Tower above Traitors' Gate and part of the Outer Wall, but that was built many years later by Edward I. The collapse of Henry's gateway is believed to have been caused by the fact that it was built on land reclaimed from Longchamp's ditch. The tower did not suffer a second collapse a year later; that fall was of a nearby wall, which also stood on part of the reclaimed ditch. It was not unusual for towers to collapse, as the records of other parts of the country show.

Henry had a new moat dug beyond the Inner Wall, running along three sides of the Tower. It will be recalled that Longchamp had trouble with the sluices of his ditch. Henry's moat was wider, deeper and much further out, and he brought in a Flemish expert on dykes, Master John le Fossur, to deal with the hydraulic problems. His new sluices were found capable of retaining the Thames water even at low tide.

These massive building operations went on throughout his reign. The cost continued to mount frighteningly but the exact total cannot be ascertained as the surviving accounts are incomplete. However, we know that from time to time Henry ran into difficulties and the pace was slackened. One year the King's entire income from the city of London was made over for the payment of the work being done in the Tower, and still it was not enough—the King had to borrow money from his brother Richard of Cornwall to meet outstanding bills. Strict instructions were given to the Constable and the Keeper of the King's Works to exercise the most rigid economy and to salvage and use all timber and lead and rubble from the fallen tower and wall.

CHAPTER NINE

Other Improvements in the Tower

Henry III's activities in the Tower were not confined to the extensive strengthening of the defences and the reconstruction of the Palace. He also put in hand many other improvements. A number of additional granaries were built to enable the Tower to withstand a long siege. Obviously with so many more towers the garrison had to be increased and fresh quarters had to be provided for the archers and men-at-arms, armouries for their weapons and new blocks of stables for the knights' horses.

The White Tower was whitewashed both inside and out in 1240, and 'the leaden gutters through which rainwater showered from the top' were 'carried to the ground' so that 'the newly white-washed walls may in no wise be injured by the dropping of rainwater'. A timber gallery was constructed at the top of the White Tower on the side facing the river in order that the archers and the men with catapults and stones should be able to see the bottom of the walls and shoot down any invaders who had got as far as the base of the building; presumably similar galleries already existed on the other three sides.

The Chapel of St John inside the White Tower was also whitewashed all over and stained-glass was put into three of the windows—one depicting the Virgin and Child, another the Holy Trinity, and the third St John the Evangelist. This is the first evidence of glass being used in the Tower, though the wealthier Romans in England had glass in their windows and the Saxon King Edwin put glass in the windows of a church he built in York. The cross and beam over the altar of St John's Chapel were painted 'with good colours', and two 'fair images' were made of St Edward offering the ring to St John and placed in the Chapel. It was also decided that the chaplain should in future be paid: he was to receive fifty shillings a year, as well as his vestments, a chalice and other things necessary for saying Mass.

Then in 1255 Henry had an Elephant House built at the west end of the Tower because King Louis of France had just sent him an elephant as a gift. Nearly a century and a half earlier, Henry I had started a park of wild beasts at Woodstock in Oxfordshire and these were now transferred to the Tower. Among them were three leopards, which had been presented by the Holy Roman

The Tower elephant with its keeper Henricus de Flor, drawn in 1255 by Matthew Paris. Between the elephant's legs is a Latin inscription telling the English reader unfamiliar with such beasts that the size of the man may be taken as a guide to that of the animal. (By permission of the Master and Fellows, Corpus Christi College, Cambridge. CCCC MS 16, fol. iv.a)

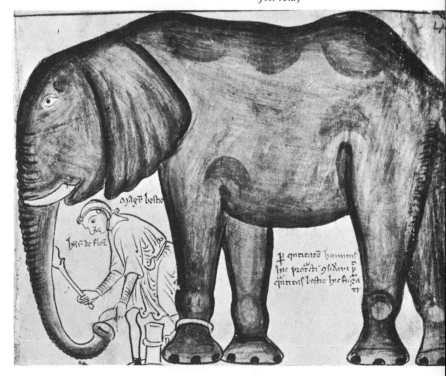

Emperor Frederick—three leopards were featured in the English King's coat of arms. The size of the building was specified by Henry: it had to be forty feet long by twenty feet wide. Surprisingly, he told the sheriffs of London to carry out this work and pay for it; he added that it should be 'made in such a fashion and of such strength as to be fit for other uses when required'.

This was the beginning of the London zoo. Soon other animals arrived as gifts—first a lion, then a Norwegian bear, which was provided with a long chain so that it could fish from the river. The Elephant House was partitioned into sections for these animals and the 'public were allowed to come and see the Royal Menagerie'. They gaped in wonder at the elephant, for no such animal had been seen in England since the invasion by the Roman Emperor Claudius 1200 years before, when elephants were used as 'tanks'. Matthew Paris tells us that the public 'flocked together to see this novel sight'. The elephant died three years later and was buried in the grounds of the Tower.

By the northwest corner of the enclosing wall stood the Chapel of St Peter ad Vincula. It was originally much larger, with two chancels (one to St Peter, the other to St Mary), two roods and several altars, but it had been neglected and had fallen into a sad state of disrepair. Henry III restored and embellished it. In 1240 he ordered the Chapel to be 'roofed without delay' and large glazed windows inserted. 'The chancel of St Mary in the church of St Peter and the chancel of St Peter in the same church' must, he said, be 'well and decently brushed and plastered with lime', and two 'large and handsome stalls' be 'made for our own and the Queen's use, and be painted'. Overhead was a 'great painted beam' bearing a Crucifix with Mary and John. An 'image' was made of 'St Christopher carrying Jesus and set up in the church' and two pictures were painted 'of the blessed Nicholas and Katherine and set before the altars dedicated to those saints'. Images of other saints were also placed in the church, and two fat cherubim 'with a cheerful and joyous countenance' were introduced, 'standing on the right and left of the great cross in the said church'; and 'one marble font with marble pillars, well and handsomely wrought'. Bright stained-glass was put into the windows.

One wonders what safeguards were adopted to ensure the security of the Tower during these

(left) *A king instructs his masons, one of whom holds the implements symbolizing his craft—the T-square and callipers;* (right) *building in progress. From a manuscript of Matthew Paris. (By permission of the Trustees of the British Museum. Cotton MS Nero D.I, fol. 23v)*

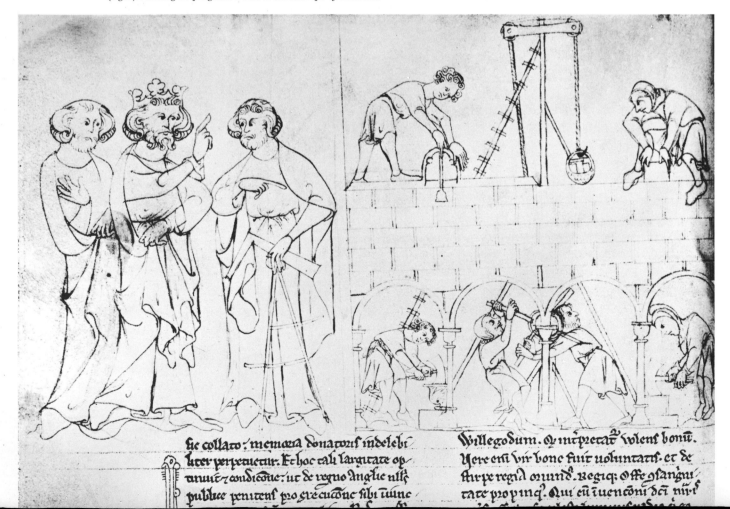

(Right) The Arras medallion commemorating the arrival of Constantius Chlorus, Caesar of the West, in Britain (c. AD 296) to put down a rebellion against Diocletian. Behind the suppliant figure of London ('LON') is a building which may represent the Roman fortress of London, the Tower's predecessor by some 800 years. (Peter A. Clayton)

(Below) From its earliest days the Tower, like all fortresses, was associated with the making and storing of weapons and armour. The tournament scene below shows some of the elaborations on the theme of protection which could be produced for display. Each knight's highly decorated mail is exactly matched by the accoutrements of his horse, while helmets are adorned by anything from a pair of horns (far left) to a complete swan's head. (By permission of the Trustees of the British Museum. MS Harl. 4431, fol. 150)

*Miniature from the poems of Charles Duke of Orléans,
who was captured at Agincourt and lodged in the White
Tower for a quarter of a century. Against a panorama
of London Bridge, the Thames and the spires of city
churches, a sectional view of the Tower contains scenes
from the Duke's long imprisonment. Robert Louis
Stevenson's description of this picture is quoted on
page 88. (By permission of the Trustees of the British
Museum. MS Royal 16.F.II, fol. 73)*

*(Opposite) The Palace built by Henry III and his
successors in the Tower no longer exists, but its
furnishings may have resembled those in this fifteenth-
century hall. We see little actual furniture, but an
emphasis on brilliant fabrics. The high-backed chair of
state stands beneath a fine canopy; the form (left
foreground) and the low-backed settle are both draped,
as is the buffet, or plate cupboard, projecting from the
rear wall. Rich stuffs cover the walls and floor.
(Bodleian Library, Oxford. MS Laud Misc. 751,
fol. 127)*

lexandre
fist sumptu
eusement
mettre en
sepulture
les gens de guerre quil auoit
perdu en chassant le roy daire
et distribua .xiiii.m. mars

aux aultres compaignons
de son armee dont la plusprt
des cheuaulx fut prinse · et
mesmes ceulx qui demoure
rent par la payne et grant
challeur se mortfondirent ·
Toute la peccune quon auoit
deuant assamblee de la cite

(*Above*) *Yeomen Warders being reviewed by the Governor of the Tower. All wear ceremonial dress; the Chief Yeoman Warder (with his back to the camera) carries his mace bearing a silver model of the White Tower. In the background is the Queen's House. (Ministry of Public Building and Works)*

(*Left*) *The ceremony of the keys takes place every evening at 10 p.m., when the Chief Yeoman Warder, escorted by a sergeant and three men, locks the Tower's three main gates for the night. On his return, the following exchange with the sentry takes place:*

Sentry: *Halt, who comes there?*
Chief W: *The keys.*
Sentry: *Whose keys?*
Chief W: *Queen Elizabeth's keys.*
    (*The guard present arms and the Chief Warder takes off his bonnet.*)
Chief W: *God preserve Queen Elizabeth.*
Guard: *Amen.*

The keys are then deposited in the Queen's House. (Fox Photos Ltd) continuous building operations, spread out over fifty-six years. There must at no time have been fewer than four or five hundred workmen there, the bulk of them unskilled casual labourers who drifted from town to town seeking work and were often engaged only on a temporary basis. No doubt the whole site was well-guarded, including the numerous huts put up on the fringe for the smiths to sharpen tools and beat out iron clamps, and for the carpenters, glassworkers and painters. There were also lime-kilns (possibly out of doors), and by 1258 cement had been brought into use, made by mixing wax, pitch and resin in a molten state. The casual labourers, some of whom were women (who carried stones and earth and helped with ditch-making at half the cost of male labour), were to be found in swarms along the old Roman roads, jostled by pilgrims, prostitutes, monks, strolling players, vagabonds, thieves, artisans, merchants, barons and their ladies on horseback, the King's justices on their way to assizes, and sometimes the King himself, with an escort of twenty-four archers and followed by four-horsed carriages, which, though curtained and brightened with tapestries and embroidered cushions, were as cumbrous and awkward as carts.

Both Henry and his Queen, Eleanor of Provence, took an enthusiastic interest in building and re-decorating. Old castles were renovated; bare walls were marked out in squares and painted with flowers, unpaved, rush-strewn floors were carpeted; chairs were redesigned and decorated with leatherwork.

A devout Christian, Henry revered the memory of Edward the Confessor, after whom he named his heir. In 1244, shortly after the consecration of St Paul's Cathedral in the city of London (after its destruction by fire in 1666, this was replaced by the present Wren structure) Henry completely rebuilt Westminster Abbey. The style he adopted was inspired by the cathedrals erected at Amiens and Rheims by his cousin, the saintly King Louis IX and son of the Prince Louis (Louis VIII) who occupied the Tower in John's reign. For some years the sombre massive round-arched architecture of the Normans, which had prevailed in England for nearly two centuries, had been giving way to the delicate, elegant grandeur of the Gothic style. Henry's Abbey is a masterpiece of Gothic architecture: to him we owe the mosaic-paved ambulatory with its many lovely chapels and the raised theatre for the coronation of the

St Paul's Cathedral, London, as it looked in medieval times. Originally built in the twelfth and thirteenth centuries, it subsequently received a new spire which towered 489 feet above ground level, dominating the London skyline, until it was struck by lightning in 1561 and replaced by a square tower. (National Monuments Record)

kings of England.

The gay coronation processions from the Tower to Westminster Abbey were initiated by Henry. He was himself crowned twice: the first time when he came to the throne as a child of nine, a solemn but simple ceremony in Gloucester Cathedral; the second on his marriage to Eleanor of Provence in 1236, when he was twenty-nine and she only fourteen. This was an elaborate and impressive event. The procession started from the Tower and the chroniclers write of it with glowing enthusiasm. 'London was so full of noble gentry and folk from the country, and with players and sundry that she could scarcely contain them within her capacious bosom . . . The streets were delivered from dirt, mud, sticks and everything offensive.' The crowds cheered excitedly as the King and Queen emerged from the Tower, possibly using Henry's new land gate, and rode slowly to the Abbey through streets hung with tapestries.

The marriage was a very happy one. The Queen was beautiful and Henry remained both devoted and faithful, an unusual quality in kings at that time. They shared the same tastes and enthusiasms. Henry was in many ways a pleasing husband, with his fine features (save for his long nose) and most impressive head. He was sincerely religious, hearing three masses every day, and when the priest raised the sacred bread of the sacrament, he always kissed the priest's hand, which even the saintly Louis IX of France thought unnecessary. But Henry's behaviour was at times marred by certain characteristics inherited from his father John, who was shifty, unreliable and self-centred. Henry could on occasion be quite unscrupulous, and would resort to subterfuge to get his own way.

Apart from these failings, which were to be the cause of many grave difficulties in the course of his reign, he had numerous admirable qualities. Born in Winchester, he rejoiced in the fact that he was English rather than European, and unlike his forebears, he spent almost his entire life in England. But his devotion to his mother's foreign relatives and later to the family of his Provençal wife eventually led to an upheaval that all but cost him his throne.

The Normans had begun by now to identify themselves with the English. For generations they had spoken French among themselves but English with their tenants, and for some years the cases tried in their courts had been in English. However, the marriage of each King with a Continental princess had kept up the foreign links. This influence was accentuated when Henry III's mother, who was still very young when King John died, married the French bridegroom from whom John had snatched her, and their numerous progeny were brought up with her son Henry, whose own marriage with Eleanor of Provence led to the infiltration of further numbers of foreign relations into England. Members of both these groups were given the highest offices in the land. One uncle became the Earl of Richmond, another was made Archbishop of Canterbury. A half-brother was made the Earl of Pembroke, another became Bishop of Winchester and adviser to the King. Simon de Montfort, a Gascon who had married Henry's sister, was also given a hand in affairs of State, with important results, as will be seen presently.

The country was extremely prosperous, more so than it had ever been before. Trade was expanding: for years there had been a brisk demand for beautiful things such as silks, fine closely-fitting chain mail in place of heavy hauberks of leather with their metal scales, furs from Scandinavia, timber from the Baltic and wine from France and Spain. More recently the import of spices had begun to reach enormous proportions. Ginger, cloves, pepper, cinnamon and nutmeg were needed to make preserved meat more palatable, for with little on which to feed livestock in winter, most were slaughtered in September and the meat salted or smoked for consumption during the cold months. England exported honey, herrings, corn and an immense quantity of wool, which was bought by the Flemish merchants and manufactured into excellent fabrics. The English merchants were rich; new towns began to spring up and the middle classes became increasingly important. The barons, protected by Magna Carta, which was confirmed again and again in the early years of Henry III's reign, had never enjoyed such affluence. The Church was also fantastically rich. Only the King's revenues suffered continuous depletion as a result of his extravagant building projects.

There followed two serious clashes with the barons. The first occurred in 1234, when the King was found to be resorting to his father's device of enlarging his personal revenue by heavy taxation without consulting 'the national and noble born men of England', on which the Charter had insisted. In the battle that ensued the King's forces were defeated, but the barons refrained from exacting vengeance and for some

England's prosperity largely depended on her wool trade with Flanders, where weavers produced fine cloth from English yarn. This twelfth-century miniature illustrates the work of wool production: on the right, the shepherd tends his flock, while on the left preparations are made to set up a loom for weaving. From the Canterbury or Eadwine Psalter. (By permission of the Master and Fellows, Trinity College, Cambridge. MS R.17.1)

years all seemed to go well. Then, urged by his foreign advisers, Henry began to hanker for the recovery of the French territories lost by his father. There followed costly and unfruitful expeditions. After borrowing money recklessly at exorbitant rates of interest, Henry faced ruin. He summoned his Council of barons, which by now was sometimes referred to as the Parliament, and told them frankly of his inability to meet his heavy debts. They arrived armed, but left their swords at the door—a practice that survived as a tradition for centuries.

The King and his heir, known as the 'Lord Edward', having no choice, swore to accept and abide by their advice. Henry was told to abandon his Continental ambitions and dismiss his foreign advisers. Parliament, the barons insisted, must meet regularly three times a year. A permanent executive council, chosen by Parliament and the King (in effect, a Cabinet) must be set up to advise the King, and all officers of State including the Chancellor and the Treasurer must be accountable to it.

For a time this was adhered to and then, like his father, Henry asked the Pope to free him from his promise. Anticipating trouble, he moved a garrison of foreign mercenaries into the Tower of London and sent the Queen there for safety.

The barons, with the support of the Londoners, promptly laid siege to the Tower. One can imagine the feelings of the Queen, who had come to the Tower as a bride of fourteen and had since spent many happy years there, to find herself now at thirty-eight besieged by her husband's subjects. Would the King be able to rescue her before the barons succeeded in their mining operations and made her their prisoner? She decided not to give them the chance and made plans to slip out furtively at nightfall, travelling up the river by barge to join her husband at Windsor. But 'sundry Londoners,' the records state, 'got together to the bridge under which she was to pass, and not only cried out to her with reproachful words, but also threw mire and stones at her, which she was constrained to return'; this suggests that she picked up the stones and the mire—as well as decaying vegetables and rotten eggs, according to another chronicler—and hurled them back at her assailants. At any rate she was forced to return to the Tower.

Meanwhile Simon de Montfort, realizing that the country needed a strong ruler, decided to take decisive action against Henry. At first regarded as an ambitious adventurer, he had been unpopular for most of his thirty years in England, but of late many of the barons and especially the new

41

middle classes had begun to appreciate his firmness and his uprightness of character. His main strength lay in London and the counties to the south and east. The King had a powerful following in the north and among the barons on the Welsh border. Moreover, by proclaiming his resolve to help the poor, who were not represented in Parliament, Montfort obtained considerable support from the populace throughout the country.

On 14 May 1264 his army met the King's at Lewes in Sussex. The royal forces were heavily defeated and both the King and his heir Prince Edward were made prisoners. The administration of the country was taken over by Montfort, who ruled 'in the name of the King'. In the following January he enlarged Parliament by summoning to it not only the barons, the bishops and the more important abbots and two knights elected by each county, but also two representatives from each of the larger towns; it was the first time the townsmen were given the right of having a say in taxation. By this important and significant change, Parliament was given a democratic direction which survived Simon de Montfort's defeat and death in the bloody Battle of Evesham later that year: having been granted his full freedom after the Battle of Lewes, Prince Edward had gathered a fresh army and obtained

overwhelming support from the barons on the Welsh Marches.

On regaining control, Henry exacted his revenge for the humiliation inflicted on the Queen by the Londoners. The Mayor and Sheriffs of the city were arrested and imprisoned, and all the receipts from the shops and houses on London Bridge (a stone bridge was built in 1176 to replace the old timber one) were given to the Queen, who henceforward enjoyed a considerable annual revenue. The papal legate was put in control of the Tower as Constable.

Once again the Tower was besieged, this time by the Earl of Gloucester, the champion of the Londoners. In spite of a long and gallant defence, it would have fallen had not the King arrived in the nick of time with his troops. A large number of Jews had taken refuge in the Tower to escape their persecutors, and it was largely through their assistance and their great bravery, it is said, that the Tower was able to hold out.

During his long reign of fifty-six years, one of the three longest in the history of England, Henry III spent a great deal of time in his comfortable Palace in the Tower. While in residence on one occasion, he led a proud procession of prelates and courtiers to the Tower Wharf to receive a phial that was reputed to contain some drops of Christ's blood. This precious relic of the Passion, sent to the King by the Patriarch of Jerusalem, was taken ceremoniously to St Paul's Cathedral, where it was exhibited to the congregation for veneration; it was then taken to Westminster Abbey, and after a three days' ceremony, brought back to St Paul's and enshrined in a golden reliquary on the High Altar.

Since Flambard was incarcerated in the Tower in the preceding century as its first famous prisoner, there were apparently none of distinction until this reign, though there must have been many of less consequence whose names have not come down to us. There is no evidence of any foreign prisoners of war having been held there for ransom. Until the reign of John, before his Continental possessions were lost, such prisoners were incarcerated in the castles in Normandy or brought to Corfe Castle, near the south coast of England; but in the succeeding centuries a great many were put in the Tower—indeed during the reign of Henry's son Edward I prisoners of various types were brought there by the hundred.

Henry III was responsible for the imprisonment of two prominent persons in the Tower. The first of these was Hubert de Burgh, who had served three kings faithfully and with the utmost loyalty —Richard I, his brother John, and now Henry III. He was descended from the Conqueror's half-brother Robert of Mortain and was thus by birth a member of the royal circle. As a soldier, he was engaged in King John's Continental wars which led to the loss of Normandy. It was in his keeping that John had placed his nephew Arthur, but he refused absolutely to carry out John's orders that the young Prince should be blinded and castrated. This episode, based on the records of Ralph of Coggeshall, has been immortalized by Shakespeare in his play *King John*.

ARTHUR: ... Hubert, if you will, cut out my tongue,
So I may keep mine eyes: O, spare mine eyes ...
HUBERT: I will not touch thine eye
For all the treasure that thine uncle owes:
Yet am I sworn and I did purpose, boy,
With this same iron to burn them out.
ARTHUR: O, now you look like Hubert. All this while
You were disguised.
HUBERT: Peace; no more. Adieu.
Your uncle must not know but you are dead;
I'll fill these dogged spies with false reports:
And, pretty child, sleep doubtless and secure,
That Hubert, for the wealth of all the world,
Will not offend thee.

As we know, Arthur was eventually murdered, and although Hubert had no part in it, because of his continuing loyalty to John he bore the stigma of this crime until the end of his life. His brilliant defence of Chinon in 1204, when almost the whole of Poitou had passed into French hands, and his naval victory over the French in the Straits of Dover after John's death, when the Dauphin Louis, who had occupied the Tower for over a year, was forced to withdraw from England, were heroic achievements. He accompanied John to Runnymede for the sealing of Magna Carta and was one of the three regents during the minority of Henry III. He was also for a time Constable of the Tower.

When Henry came of age, Hubert was at the height of his power. He was strongly opposed to the young King's plan to reconquer the lost French possessions and was nearly stabbed to death by the enraged monarch when he failed to provide enough ships at Portsmouth to take the expeditionary force across the Channel. This gave Henry's foreign relatives the opportunity to undermine Hubert's authority and in 1231 the blow fell. He was accused of embezzlement, and a number of other charges were soon added. He was stripped of all his offices, and in fear of his life took sanctuary in a chapel in Essex; but a troop of soldiers sent by Henry dragged him from the steps of the altar, bound him with ropes and placed him 'upon a miserable jade, with his legs tied under the animal's belly and thus ignominiously conveyed him to the Tower'. He was loaded with irons and subjected to every hardship and insult, but it is not known where he was lodged, whether in a dungeon of one of the new towers or in the vaults of the White Tower.

The Bishop of London's threat to excommunicate all concerned with the violation of the sanctuary caused Henry to return Hubert to the sacred refuge from which he had been dragged. But this did not protect him from further persecution. The King placed guards round the chapel and instructed them not to allow any food to be brought to him.

After many days of suffering and despair, Hubert emerged voluntarily from the chapel and was instantly seized by the guards. A blacksmith was fetched to put iron fetters on him. But the blacksmith, Matthew Paris records, on discovering who it was, said, 'Inflict whatever judgement you will on me, for as the Lord liveth, I will sooner die any kind of death than put fetters on him. Is not this the faithful and valiant Hubert who hath often preserved England from ruin by foreigners and hath restored England to the English?'

Hubert was eventually taken back to the Tower and was held in solitary confinement there for months. In 1234 he was granted a full pardon and most of his estates were restored, but he never recovered his old position of favour at court.

The other prisoner of importance during this reign was Griffith, son of Llewellyn the Great, ruler of north Wales. During Henry's war with the barons, Llewellyn had seized his opportunity to encroach on the neighbouring territories, and in the fighting that followed his eldest son Griffith and his grandson Llewellyn were both captured and taken to the Tower. They were imprisoned in the former royal apartments at the top of the White Tower, where Flambard had been a prisoner. Hearing of Flambard's successful escape, Griffith decided to adopt the same plan. Stow tells us in his *Annals* that Griffith, 'having in the night made of the hangings, sheets and etcetera, a long line, he put himself down from the top of the Tower. But in the sliding, the weight of his body, being a very big and fat man, broke the rope, and he fell on his neck, and broke his neck withal; whose miserable carcase, being found in the morning by the Tower Wall, was a most pitiful sight to behold: for his head and neck were driven into his breast, between the shoulders. The King hearing thereof, punished the watchmen, and caused Griffith's son, that was imprisoned with his father, to be more straitly kept.'

After the victory of his son Edward and the death of Montfort, Henry continued to rule the country for another seven years, always with the support of Parliament as constituted by Montfort. He died at the end of 1272, and the longest reign of the Middle Ages closed in peace.

CHAPTER TEN

Edward I's Massive Concentric Fortress

Henry's heir was in his thirty-third year when he succeeded to the throne as Edward I. Two years before his father's death he had set out on a Crusade, and he was at Acre in the Holy Land recovering from a wound inflicted by an assassin when the news of his accession was brought to him. A further two years were to pass before he reached England. Despite his absence, his succession was not disputed, for he had distinguished himself in warfare during his father's final battles with the barons and his clemency towards the vanquished had won the respect and admiration of all.

Indeed, his right to the throne was unassailable. He was descended from Alfred the Great as well as from William the Conqueror; England had been ruled by his ancestors for four hundred years. The barons acclaimed him with unfeigned enthusiasm. 'The government of the realm has devolved by hereditary succession,' they proclaimed. Thus for the first time hereditary right was recognized as replacing the old method of election.

It was Edward's plan to make the Tower of London a great concentric fortress, far more formidable than any other fortress in Europe. The project is believed to have taken shape in his mind during the last years of his father's reign, when control of the kingdom was largely in his hands. He began the work within a few days of his return from the Holy Land. First he ordered a careful survey of the condition of the Tower and the repair of all dilapidations and damage caused by the two sieges. The work was entrusted to Master Robert of Beverley; it took nine months to complete and cost £173 9s 4d.

In the following year he embarked on his massive scheme, which occupied no less than ten years, 1275–85. To begin with, he completed his father's western wall facing the city of London, from the Bell to the Devereux Tower. This necessitated the demolition of a gate opened by his father halfway along the wall and the Beauchamp Tower was erected in its place. Then he ordered the construction of an enclosing Outer Wall running at a distance of thirty feet or so beyond Henry III's Inner Wall. This involved undoing some more of his father's work. Henry's extensive ditch, on which the Flemish dyke expert Master John le Fossur had worked less than forty years before, had to be drained and filled in, and a new and much bigger moat was constructed, a hundred feet wide in parts, beyond the Outer Wall. This new enlargement of the Tower encroached still further on St Katherine's Hospital on the east side and the tenements of many of the poorer Londoners, who had to be found accommodation and to all of whom compensation had to be paid.

A great deal of land was reclaimed from the river, not only for the new Outer Wall and the moat, but also for a new Wharf built beyond it. Edward opened two new entrances to the Tower. One entrance was from the Thames, and dominated by a tower of immense span—St Thomas's Tower—which straddled the moat; under it is Traitors' Gate with its enormous portcullis. This superseded the Bloody Tower, until now the main water-gate. The other entrance was by land on the west side, with a causeway across the moat leading to a barbican (by the Elephant House) and onward to the Middle and Byward Towers.

The new moat took six years to complete and the wages paid to the workers alone during those years totalled £4150 (today well over £200,000). To this had to be added the cost of the heavy timbers for shoring, piles and palisades, the purchase of tools and the wages of a fresh dyke

Traitors' Gate, view from the river side. The approach was originally connected to the river, and was accessible only by boat. (Ministry of Public Building and Works)

expert brought from across the Channel, Master Walter of Flanders, who was engaged for nineteen weeks to supervise the early stages of the work, and who returned when the moat was nearing completion to bring in the water, apparently from one of the London watercourses nearby. Edward sold all the earth that was dug out; being excellent clay, it was avidly bought by the London tilers.

On the three landward sides of the Outer Wall no towers were built. Along the southern or river wall Edward built three in addition to St Thomas's—the Byward, the Well and the Develin Towers. It is possible that he extended the wall further eastward to the Iron Gate, but this is not certain, though there undoubtedly was a gate at both the eastern and the western end of the wall, and at both these points water-mills (possibly tide-mills) were erected, which were worked by the sluices of the moat beneath them. To the west, where the Lion Tower barbican was

constructed by Edward at the outer sweep of the moat, there was 'a stone wall below the mill towards the town to keep the water in the moat'.

The accounts for these ten years of building and expansion (1275–85) were checked and approved by Giles de Oudenard, who is described as 'Keeper of the Works' (equivalent to Clerk of the Works today). In charge of the actual construction was the master-mason Master Robert of Beverley, who died in 1285; associated with him in the work until 1279 was Brother John of the Order of St Thomas of Acre. The total cost of these works amounted to £21,000, which in today's terms would be more than £1 million; and the area of the Tower of London now covered eighteen acres, as it still does today.

Edward had now achieved the major part of his plan, but plenty of work still remained to be done. First the Tower had to be made impregnable. There had been important changes in the art of warfare and new methods of assault had to be

46

reckoned with. In the past, battering rams had been used to smash the walls and force an entry. But now there were great new siege engines, such as the mangonel, which had a pulley for projecting large stone missiles, and the trebuchet, an even more formidable engine of attack, equipped for hurling into a fortress not only heavier missiles, but also the carcases of dead horses—an early form of germ warfare. Edward's moat helped to keep the enemy and their new weapons at a safe distance and the double row of walls with their guardian towers multiplied the obstacles: if one was breached, there was another to contend with, and even in the innermost enclosure there were cross-walls. Armoured infantrymen and steel-clad horsemen were now supported by well-disciplined groups of infantry armed with a new weapon, the long-bow, which had a greatly extended range and a deadly accuracy compared with the cross-bow previously used, as Edward was himself to demonstrate in his Scottish campaigns. The garrison of the Tower was once again greatly increased and still more barracks were put up to accommodate the additional troops and administrative offices.

But Edward did more than attend to the defences of the Tower. He was responsible for the Mint being established there: a separate section was provided for it in the western Outer Wall at a cost of £729 17s 8½d.

The Palace was also given attention. As we have seen, Henry III had extended and given a unity to the 'King's houses' built at various times against the Inner Wall, and had greatly embellished them. Now his son set men at work on the chambers of the King and Queen, the Great Hall and the Small Hall. The Queen's chapel was painted and 'a new chapel' was built 'next door to the Small Hall.' All the living rooms now had tiled floors and were comfortably furnished. The Queen's Garden, we know, was to the east; the position of the King's Garden is not clear, but we are told that it had vines growing in it. All this was within the innermost enclosure; and to reach the Chapel of St Peter ad Vincula, the King and Queen would have had to go through the powerfully guarded gate in Coldharbour Tower, cross what is now known as the Parade Ground and walk along Tower Green. But the Palace itself had two chapels. St Peter ad Vincula, already reconstructed by his father, was demolished and completely rebuilt by Edward between April 1286 and April 1287; the cost of this was £317 8s 3d.

On St Thomas's Tower he appears to have lavished much care. Lead was bought for the roof and later for the roofing of the three turrets of the large room facing the Thames. Wooden partitions were then erected inside this room, and there is a reference to thirty-four *fenestre currentes*, apparently of wood. Glass was later put into the windows, some of it coloured with figures; tiles were bought for the floor and timber and iron for the 'Great Gate'. The painting of the carved stone images 'above the large room facing the Thames' is referred to and also the provision of timber for the water-gate and large hinges for the gates.

Now let us look at the King himself. Edward was of immense height—he towered above his contemporaries and his long legs earned him the nickname of 'Longshanks'. He had a fine noble head, of which his father was so proud that he had it carved in stone above a capital in the north transept of Westminster Abbey. His hair, golden and abundant, turned white in later years. His eyes, we are told, were dark and bright, 'like a dove's when he was pleased, but in his anger fiery as a lion's'. He had inherited his father's slight droop of the left eyelid (his grandfather John had it too) and he stammered occasionally, but he overcame this impediment and became a most effective speaker. A superb horseman, he loved hunting and hawking and his skill in tournaments was outstanding. He filled his court with minstrels and players, had a keen sense of humour and loved practical jokes.

At the age of fifteen he married Eleanor of Castile, the daughter of Ferdinand III, King of Castile and Leon, who won back Seville and Cadiz from the Moors. Eleanor herself had accompanied her husband on his Crusade, and it was her devotion and care that saved his life after the assassin's attack with a poisoned dagger at Acre. Strikingly attractive, her hair worn in long, dark tresses, she was gentle in manner and supplied a calm and placidity which Edward lacked. Throughout her life Edward remained devoted to her. When she died in his arms thirty-six years later, he wrote, 'My harp is turned to mourning, in life I loved her dearly, nor can I cease to love her in death.' The grief-stricken King accompanied his wife's body on its long journey from Nottingham to London, and at every resting place he later erected a cross in her memory: one of these stands in the forecourt of Charing Cross railway station. They had thirteen children, seven of whom survived.

On returning from the Crusades, Edward fol-

Cross erected at Northampton by Edward I, in memory of his Queen, Eleanor of Castile. (National Monuments Record)

lowed the precedent of his father and set out from the Tower for his coronation at Westminster Abbey. The streets of London were hung with tapestries, the conduit in Cheapside ran with wine, and money was flung by the handful to the cheering multitude. The festivities were kept up for a full fortnight. Food was provided for the crowds: the King bought 400 oxen, an equal number of sheep, pigs and wild boars, and no less than 20,000 fowls. When the knights dismounted to kneel before their sovereign in Westminster Hall, instead of tethering their horses, they let them loose for the mob to seize and take away as gifts.

A quarter of a century later, on Edward's remarriage, there was a second coronation. The new Queen Margaret, daughter of Philip III of France, spent the preceding night in the Tower, but the revelry was not so prolonged.

Throughout the thirty-five years of Edward's reign the Tower was filled with prisoners. Prominent among these were a large number of Jews. No doubt there were Jews in England before the Norman Conquest, but the more settled conditions brought about by the strong rule of the Conqueror led to their arrival in considerable numbers. A great many foreign merchants came too and set up in London and other towns because of the increased trading opportunities with Europe. Unaffected by the Church's edict that no Christian should lend money on interest, the Jews became the country's sole moneylenders. Tradesmen and craftsmen, artisans and landowners, as well as noblemen and at times even the King himself, called on them to meet pressing obligations. Often the interest was high. Goods, and occasionally land, were given as surety and if the loan was not repaid the Jews inevitably profited.

Gradually resentment began to develop against them. From the actual debtors it spread to the poor who laboured with small return, and from the towns it spread to the country. The Jews were regarded as an alien people, who dressed differently, talked both French and English with strange accents and took no part in the Christian ceremonies which regulated the life of the ordinary citizen. This growing anti-Semitism was fanned by the belief that the Jews had crucified Christ. Prejudice and ignorance heaped a host of other crimes upon their unfortunate heads. They were said to slaughter Christian children for the ritual sacrifice at the Passover, a belief that persisted despite the lack of any confirmatory evidence. They were accused of witchcraft, and from time to time were attacked by the townspeople, who seized their goods and often murdered them. An appalling massacre marred the coronation of Richard Coeur de Lion. The Jewish elders who had brought gifts for the King were set upon outside Westminster Abbey and killed; there were similar incidents in Lincoln, (King's) Lynn and other parts of the country, the worst atrocities

48

occurring in Yorkshire.

To prevent the recurrence of such incidents, the Jews were made to live in separate walled sections of the towns called the Jewery—a part of the city of London is known as Old Jewry to this day. Richard, like his predecessors, had disapproved strongly of these tragic anti-Semitic outbreaks, for the Jews were a considerable source of profit to the Crown, which extorted large sums of money from them in taxes and fines. Henry III, as we have seen, allowed them to move into the Tower of London to escape their persecutors. However, in the reign of his son the royal attitude changed. While on his Crusade, Edward had borrowed heavily from Italian bankers who ignored the Church's ban, and they soon began to come in and settle in England. The Jews were thus no longer indispensable, and they were now ordered to wear a distinguishing yellow badge.

In 1278 Edward caused all the Jews in England to be arrested on the charge that they were clipping the coins of the realm. Actually the coins used at the time were often clipped into halves and quarters when change was required in smaller values; but the Jews were accused of paring off the edges and thus reducing the amount of metal in the coin. As a safeguard, Edward had new dies cast and moved the Mint into the Tower.

Six hundred Jews were imprisoned in the White Tower's dank and rat-infested vaults. Popular feeling had, no doubt, contributed to the adoption of such stern action against so large a number; as it happened, the Pope had that very year issued a strong condemnation of usury. After being held in the Tower for some months, 267 of the Jews were taken out and hanged. In succeeding years the Jews in England were repeatedly subjected to fresh and humiliating restrictions until in 1290 they were finally banished from the country, only certain highly skilled physicians being exempted. Not until Oliver Cromwell became Protector four centuries later were the ports again opened to them.

CHAPTER ELEVEN

The King of Scotland and the Great Wallace as Prisoners

Edward I had many great qualities. He had inherited the tremendous administrative capacity of his great-grandfather Henry II as well as Richard Coeur de Lion's dedication. He was ready, despite his strong desire to maintain peace, to go to war to adjust a wrong if he found that there was no other solution. And, like Richard, he had a readiness to forgive and to show magnanimity.

He had learned the art of government from his father Henry III and had personally led the royal forces in the battles against Simon de Montfort. But he had a love for order and reform which Henry lacked. He saw the immense advantage of the parliamentary system as reshaped by Montfort, and realized that only by bringing in the middle classes as a counterpoise to the nobility and the Church could the old feudal system dominated by the barons be effectively undermined.

If Henry II was a great lawgiver, Edward far surpassed him. He began by building on the foundations laid by his ancestor. Like Henry II, he decided to see for himself what was required, and set out immediately after his coronation on the first of many tours. He took with him the entire court of the King's Bench—judges, attorneys, pleaders, clerks and a great cavalcade of law officials. The journeys were tedious and uncomfortable. He travelled across muddy tracks, through fog, rain and snow, the wagons lumbering behind, laden with documents, files and parchment rolls. The King discovered that many of the sheriffs took bribes, while others put their unfortunate victims into wooden cages or cast them into noisome dungeons, to the peril of their health and their lives, if the fines imposed upon them were not paid.

Like his saintly cousin, the great French King Louis IX, Edward resolved to give the people his protection and to see that justice was done. He issued a series of statutes revising the law, cleared up obscurities and removed what was inessential. This resulted in a general acceptance of the law in an age when 'might was right' and in this respect put England ahead of every other country in Europe. At that time there was, of course, no police force. Edward insisted that every village and small town must provide a nightly 'watch and ward' group drawn from a rota of householders, whose duty it was to challenge, and if necessary arrest, every suspicious traveller. 'If any such passing strangers do not allow themselves to be arrested,' stated the royal ordinance, 'then the watch shall pursue them with the whole township and neighbouring townships with hue and cry from township to township until they are taken.' He developed and expanded the jury system and appointed justices of the peace. Edward's reforms earned him a place in history as 'The Lawgiver'. Much of what he did still survives and to this day forms part of the legal fabric in England and many other countries.

He tried hard to avoid war. He abandoned, for example, any thought of recovering the lost dominions in France and put up with considerable provocation from his cousin King Philip III of France. He even surrendered the fortresses of his one remaining province of Gascony as a token of his submission. But when Philip tricked him by adding the province to his own dominions, Edward had no alternative but to fight.

The campaign was delayed by disorders in Wales and in Scotland which could not be ignored. Those regions, forming as they do an inseparable part of the island over which he ruled, had to be brought under firm control. Most of Wales was administered by the Marcher barons, whose estates had been granted by the early Norman kings. Some had greatly extended the original holdings, and by now they had possession of the whole of south and central Wales. These vast regions had been colonized, and powerful castles had been erected to protect them. The overlordship of the English King was acknowledged but the barons were allowed to have their own private armies to keep at bay the fierce unconquered tribes who dwelt in the wild, mountainous and mainly barren northwest. Their chieftain Llewellyn the Great, taking advantage of the troubled conditions in England during the previous reigns, had ravaged the lands and burnt

the castles of the Marchers. He had annexed two-thirds of Wales, but in the fighting that followed in Henry III's reign it had been lost again. His eldest son Griffith, as we saw, was captured and taken to the Tower, where he died while trying to escape. Griffith's son, also named Llewellyn, was now the ruler of the northwest corner of Wales, on the condition that he did homage to the English King for this territory.

Having conferred upon himself the title of Prince of Wales, Llewellyn not only declined to pay homage to Edward, but entered into a treaty of marriage with Simon de Montfort's daughter. Edward decided that no security was possible

Caernarvon Castle, the traditional setting for the investiture of the Prince of Wales, as it would have looked in medieval times. Edward II is said to have been born in the Eagle Tower (right foreground), but this is unlikely to be true since the building of the Castle was only begun c. 1285. Reconstruction drawing by A. Forestier. (Mansell Collection)

until Llewellyn was brought to heel. After a series of fiercely fought battles the 'Prince of Wales' surrendered and swore fidelity; but on being allowed to return home, he went back on his pledge. In the renewed fighting Llewellyn was killed and his severed head was sent to the King, who ordered it to be crowned with ivy and paraded through the streets of London for all to see. It was then taken to the Tower and fixed on a pike above the White Tower, where Llewellyn had been a prisoner with his father Griffith. His brother David fought on, but in 1283 he was betrayed by his own countrymen and executed; his head was set up beside his brother's on the Tower. The title of Prince of Wales was annexed by Edward and bestowed upon his eldest son, who was born at Caernarvon in 1284. It has ever since been the principal title by which the heir to the English throne is known.

Trouble in Scotland followed, and war soon broke out. At that time Scotland had a population of less than half a million. There were few fertile plains or valleys in that narrow rocky mist-sodden land, and only a sprinkling of small towns where the traders were mostly English and Flemish immigrants, importing wine and honey, salt, oil and spices. Like the Welsh, the people were lawless raiders of cattle and sheep. For centuries Scotland had been an independent kingdom, but its recent kings had married English princesses and nominally the country was under England's suzerainty. In 1295, just as Edward was preparing once again to recover Gascony, John Baliol, King of Scotland, entered into an alliance with France, and the following year marched his troops across the border.

Edward retaliated at once. He summoned the most comprehensive Parliament yet assembled 'to meet the dangers that threaten'. The two Robert Bruces, father and son, Baliol's rivals for the throne, gave Edward their complete support. A vast army was assembled by Edward for the conquest of Scotland. After the capture of Edinburgh Castle, Baliol surrendered; he and his son were sent to the Tower along with other Scottish prisoners. Their strange clothes caused the Londoners to gape in astonishment and derision.

Baliol was imprisoned in the Banqueting Hall of the White Tower and enjoyed special privileges much as Flambard had done. He brought his own chaplain, an assistant chaplain, two chamberlains, a tailor, a pantler, a butler, a barber, his horses (we are not told how many), a pack of hounds and

The Coronation Chair in Westminster Abbey, made in 1300 for Edward I. The Stone of Destiny can be seen in its base (National Monuments Record)

a huntsman: one wonders what hunting he was able to do within the confined area of the Tower grounds. The sum of 17s a day was allowed for his maintenance, but this was cut down by an Order in Council and the number of his entourage was also reduced; the huntsman was sent away, as well as a page, one of the chamberlains, two greyhounds, ten beagles and one of the horses. The cost of his luxurious imprisonment was borne by the English King, who was able to recover the sum spent and a great deal more from the confiscation of Baliol's personal estate. After some months, the Pope interceded for his release. Edward pardoned Baliol and provided him with a home in England and a pension.

After despatching Baliol to the Tower, Edward continued his march into Scotland, penetrating further than any army had done since the time of the Romans. He took the Stone of Destiny from Scone Abbey and sent it to London where it still forms part of the coronation chair in Westminster Abbey, just as after his Welsh campaign Edward had sent back King Arthur's iron crown to be laid on the high altar of the Abbey.

But Edward's problems in the north were far from over. As soon as he again turned his attention to recovering Gascony, a new leader arose in Scotland—William Wallace, a man of gigantic stature, linked neither by blood nor marriage with the Scottish royal house. Wallace's following was a ragged horde, but his magnetic personality attracted many of the great Scottish lords, including the young Robert Bruce. His brilliance as a military leader made him a formidable opponent.

Wallace's soldiers, clad in animal skins and armed with home-made spears and axes, went into battle with their rations of oatmeal and dried lentils on their backs. At Stirling Bridge in 1297 Wallace won a resounding victory and crossed into England. Edward abandoned his campaign in France and marched north at the head of a large army—the armoured cavalry now supported by the newly-formed infantry of Welsh archers, recruited by the Marcher barons and armed with the deadly long-bow.

Despite Wallace's brilliant strategy, he was heavily defeated at Falkirk in July 1298. He managed to keep up a sporadic resistance for another eight years but finally, in 1305, he was betrayed and taken prisoner near Glasgow. At his trial in Westminster Hall he was sentenced to be hanged, drawn and quartered; he was placed on a hurdle, dragged four miles to the Tower, and then at Smithfield 'he was hung in a noose and after-

wards let down half living, his privates cut off and his bowels torn out and burnt'. His head was stuck up on London Bridge for all who passed by, on land or water, to see. But to the ordinary people of Scotland he was already a legend and Robert Burns's famous *Scots wha hae* is still sung in his glory.

The death of Wallace, however, did not see the end of Edward's troubles in Scotland. In March 1306 Robert Bruce was crowned King at Scone, and Edward at once took up the challenge. Bruce was twice defeated in the campaign of that summer and was forced to take refuge on the island of Rathlin, where he is reported to have had his famous encounter with a spider. He returned to Scotland the following spring, and Edward again set out for the north. But the King was now too old and weak to ride or march and had to be carried in a litter. He died at Burgh-by-Sands in July 1307, and Scotland remained unpacified.

The last years of Edward I's reign were years of severe economic strain. Taxation was increased repeatedly and there were sharp rises in the export duty on wool and leather. But the prosperity of the country was only temporarily impaired. Trade with Italy was expanding fast. Silks, dyes and spices were bought from the merchants of Venice, Genoa and Pisa who had opened up the caravan routes to the Far East. (This was the time of Marco Polo's famous journey to China.) Larger ships were being built, for since the introduction of the compass, which the Arabs and Chinese had used for years, they no longer had to hug the coast when the sun and stars were hidden by clouds; and the increasing knowledge of geometry, which also came from the East, was leading to the production of more reliable land maps and sea charts. The Universities at Oxford and Cambridge were by now well-established; and at about this time, Roger Bacon, a scientist at Oxford, is reputed to have invented gunpowder, which was to revolutionize the art of warfare.

London was growing fast, though neither John Baliol nor William Wallace would have seen much of it on their humiliating progress through the city. Its population, then around 50,000 or so, was spilling beyond the walls into Fleet Street and the newly formed suburbs at Clerkenwell and Saint Clement's Well, where the waters were 'sweet and wholesome and multitudes went there on summer evenings to take the air'. Within the old city wall, with the massive Tower at the eastern end, the thatched timber houses were small but comfortable, with larger stone houses by the river for the nobles. Many had gardens planted with trees and a lovely new scented flower, the rose, which also came from the East; smaller gardens grew vegetables for the market. At this time there were more than a hundred churches in London, some of which also ran schools for boys.

There was great excitement, the chronicler FitzStephen tells us, when 'upon the river's bank, near where the wine is sold from ships and wine-cellars, a public cook shop' was opened, the first of its kind in London. 'There every day according to the season, you may find dishes roast, fried and boiled, fish great and small, the cheaper meat for the poor, the more delicate for the rich, such as venison and birds both big and little. If friends, weary with travel, should of a sudden come to any of the citizens, and do not want to wait hungry till fresh food is bought and cooked, [they come here;] a great crowd of knights and foreigners at whatever hour of night or day.' And the many who came to London, whether for trade or to visit their friends and relatives, could find varied diversion: cock-fighting, bull- and bear-baiting in the winter, wrestling and archery in the summer; and every Sunday in Lent after the midday dinner 'young gentles rode out on war-horses with lance and shield' to take part in jousts and tournaments.

King Edward and his Queens (Eleanor until her death in 1290 and Margaret after 1299) often stayed at the Palace in the Tower. Once during the King's absence on a Scottish campaign, while Queen Margaret, who had been married for barely a year, was staying there, Edward was greatly concerned to hear that a smallpox epidemic had broken out in London. To safeguard the Queen's health, he ordered that 'no petitioner from the city should presume to approach the Tower lest the person of the Queen be endangered by the contagion being brought from the infected air of the city'. She stayed there till the following spring, when she joined the King in Yorkshire.

At no time during the reign of Edward I was the Tower without prisoners. In 1303 the King's officers went into Westminster Abbey and arrested the Abbot, forty-eight Benedictine monks and thirty-two others, described as 'inferior persons', and brought them all to the Tower on a charge of 'robbing the Treasury of £100,000'—equivalent to nearly £5 million today. The King's treasures, including the Crown Jewels, had always been kept in the Abbey; in the preceding reign Henry III had removed the crown and sceptres to the Tower, but the rest of the royal regalia had remained in Westminster. It was now found that the room in which they were kept had been broken open and the entire contents had been stolen. The Abbot and the other eighty were tried by the King's justices. They were found guilty of negligence, but not of theft. Who the real culprits were was never discovered. But the Crown Jewels have been kept in the Tower ever since.

A little earlier some of the justices themselves were brought to the Tower as prisoners, including Sir Ralph de Hengham, Chief Justice of the court of King's Bench (which itself used to be in the Tower but was removed after Magna Carta to Westminster Hall), and Robert Lithbury, the Master of the Rolls. They were charged with 'criminal partiality in the discharge of their offices'. They were held in the Tower for some time, then tried and heavily fined. 'Hengham had to pay 7000 marks'—a mark was 13s 4d—and was discharged; Adam de Straton, Clerk to the Court, was fined 30,000 marks for acquiring 'marks old and new, besides jewels without number and precious vessels of silver, which were found in his house, and a King's crown', believed to be the one lost by King John off Lincolnshire. After their discharge, an order was issued that henceforth no one connected with the courts of justice 'should take any fee or gift of any man, except only a breakfast or suchlike present'.

In the closing year of Edward's reign all the members of the Order of Knights Templars were imprisoned in the Tower. This international religious and military order had been established in 1118 to protect pilgrims on their way to the Holy Land. The Knights had acquired great wealth and were accused of robbery and murder, profligacy and the practice of vices 'of the most shocking description'. When they refused to confess, they were put to the torture, for which purpose a chamber was set up in the vaults of the White Tower, equipped with the necessary implements. The Order was suppressed at the Council of Vienna in 1312 and its wealth and possessions given to the Knights of St John of Jerusalem.

When Edward died in 1307, he begged his son to carry his bones at the head of the army until every Scot had surrendered, but his feckless, pleasure-loving heir paid no heed to this dying wish. The body was brought back to London and buried in Westminster Abbey on 27 October.

CHAPTER TWELVE

The Queen's Love Affair in the Tower

Events in the Tower during the reign of Edward II were at once unusual and startling. The impressive setting, magnified and made impregnable by the King's father and grandfather, was to be the stage for a sordid intrigue between the Queen and a prisoner, which led to humiliating and tragic consequences for the King and the country.

The new monarch, who was twenty-three when he came to the throne, had none of the qualities of his strong-willed father. Although of immense height and powerful physique, his character was weak and immature. In manner he was effeminate, he dressed foppishly, delighted in frivolity and was incapable of decisive action.

A few months after his accession he went to Paris to marry Isabella, the twelve-year-old daughter of the King of France. His true affections, however, had from his early youth been centred on a handsome young Frenchman called Piers Gaveston. This arrogant, penniless adventurer had been banished from the country by Edward I in 1307, but he returned to England for the new King's coronation and carried the crown of St Edward in the procession in the Abbey. He was 'so decked out', wrote a chronicler, 'that Piers Gaveston more resembled the God Mars than an ordinary mortal'.

Much as he disliked the rigours of campaigning, in 1314 Edward took up his father's struggle with the Scots; but his half-hearted efforts were to have disastrous consequences. Bruce's small following had grown into a considerable army, and he was fortunate in having as his lieutenant the brave and audacious James Douglas, whose father William had been imprisoned in the Tower and had died there in 1298. The two armies met on 24 June at Bannockburn, three miles southeast of Stirling. The battle was long, confused and extremely bloody, but finally the English were driven from the field leaving behind at least 10,000 dead. The immense booty captured by the Scots included the entire English royal regalia, a great quantity of jewels, costly ecclesiastical vestments, worth in all more than £200,000 and equivalent to many million pounds today. It took four years for England to recover from the blow.

Meanwhile Edward's disregard of the terms of Magna Carta had angered the barons, and once again the country faced civil war. To avoid a conflict, the King moved his court to Newcastle, but the barons pursued him. The Queen was captured and Edward's favourite, Piers Gaveston, hated by the nobles for his arrogance and his lewd behaviour, surrendered and was beheaded shortly afterwards. The King soon found a new favourite to take his place—Hugh Despenser, a self-seeking young baron of the Welsh Marches, whose father was already at court. Both were extremely unpopular, and some of the other Welsh Marcher lords, taking the law into their own hands, invaded and laid waste their lands. One of these assailants was the young Roger Mortimer, who was to play a vital and tragic role in the life of Edward II. Ordered by the King to withdraw, they marched instead on London and, quartering their troops on the outskirts, warned the King that if he did not get rid of the Despensers, they would choose a new monarch. After some hesitation the King gave in and the rebel lords dispersed.

In 1321 the Queen was grossly insulted by one of their supporters. She had been on a pilgrimage to the tomb of St Thomas Becket at Canterbury. On the way home, with darkness descending, she sought shelter for the night at Leeds Castle in Kent. Not only was hospitality refused by Lady Baddlesmere, the owner, but the Queen and her retinue were attacked and driven from the gates. Six members of the royal party were killed, and

the Queen had to fly for safety. The King's troops were despatched to besiege Leeds Castle, and the garrison was starved into surrender. Lady Baddlesmere was arrested and sent to the Tower and the castle's constable was hanged. This is the first recorded instance of a woman being imprisoned in the Tower.

The presence of the King's favourites naturally imposed a great strain upon his relationship with the Queen. Two children, however, were born of the marriage; the heir to the throne, also called Edward, was born in 1312, and ten years later the Queen, while living in the Palace in the Tower, gave birth to a daughter who was known as 'Joan of the Tower'. The royal apartments at that time were in such a bad state of disrepair that the rain seeped through the roof on to the beds, drenching the Queen and the baby Princess. The Constable, John Cromwell, was dismissed for not seeing to its proper repair and thus endangering the health of the royal mother and child. The baby Princess was betrothed at the age of seven to Prince David, the five-year-old heir of Robert Bruce, King of Scotland.

Encouraged by his success against Lady Baddlesmere, Edward II set out in pursuit of the

Seal of Isabella of France, Queen of Edward II. (By permission of the Trustees of the British Museum)

rebellious Welsh Marcher lords. In 1322 he captured Roger Mortimer and a number of others in a border skirmish and locked them in the Tower. Charged with treason and sentenced to death, Mortimer asked if he might be allowed to see the King. On being told that Edward was not in London he asked if the Queen, who was then living in the Tower, would be kind enough to see him.

Queen Isabella granted his request. Mortimer's strong, handsome features, elegant bearing and charm made a great impression on her. She promised to intercede with the King and managed to get the death sentence commuted to life imprisonment; but the King insisted that Mortimer must remain a prisoner in the Tower. Isabella sent for Mortimer to tell him what she had achieved; further meetings followed, and in time he became her lover. The illicit intrigue, which went on for months, was doubtless conducted in the royal apartments in the Tower. How the meetings were contrived we do not know. For the Queen to take a serving-maid into her confidence would not have been enough. As a prisoner Mortimer was guarded with a vigilance which the authority of the Queen alone could not have relaxed; for the new Constable stood in awe of the King's displeasure, which had descended on his predecessor for neglecting to repair the royal apartments. The records do not indicate in which of the towers Mortimer was imprisoned. It is possible that he was confined in one of the dungeons of the White Tower and that the Queen made use of the former royal apartments there for their secret meetings. What is known, however, is that Mortimer was planning to escape from the Tower and to this end he decided to get his supporters outside to start a rebellion, besiege the Tower and make the King their prisoner. Messages were smuggled out, no doubt with the Queen's connivance, but the King got wind of it and Mortimer was again sentenced to death. This time the Queen induced two prominent ecclesiastics to intervene. They pleaded with the King and were able to obtain from the weak and irresolute monarch yet another remission of the death sentence.

Mortimer now turned his thoughts once again to escaping; for nothing could be achieved until he was free. His escape obviously required the Queen's fullest co-operation, for it is clear from the records that her quarters in the Palace were used for the escape. Mortimer had first to be transferred to the Palace; so the Queen bribed

Gerald Alspaye, the Constable's valet, to drug his gaolers.

The escape took place on the night of 1 August 1324. After creeping through a hole into the kitchen, Mortimer climbed up the spacious chimney and out on to the roof of the Palace, alongside the Wakefield Tower. Working his way across the ledge of the roof, he reached the Bloody Tower and let himself down to the ground with the aid of a rope ladder. He negotiated the Outer Wall and the moat, finally reaching the King's private postern gate on the river, where a boat awaited him. He crossed the river and rode through the forests of Sussex and Hampshire to the Solent, where he took ship to Normandy and eventually reached Paris. The Constable of the Tower, Stephen de Seagrave, was arrested and imprisoned for 'conniving in the escape'.

In 1325 the Queen crossed to Paris herself. She used as her excuse the quarrel between France and England over Gascony, all that was now left of the English dominions in France. Her brother had succeeded to the French throne in 1322 as Charles IV, and the papal nuncio, no doubt at the Queen's prompting, suggested to Edward that his wife would be the best person to plead with her brother for a final settlement, to which the King agreed. When Isabella reached Paris she took the dramatic events one vital step further. She wrote and asked her husband to send their son Edward over in order that he might do homage to the French King for Gascony.

With the arrival of the thirteen-year-old heir to the throne of England she possessed her trump card. She now defied her husband quite openly. A large number of English exiles soon began to gather round her, and the fact that Mortimer was among them inevitably caused a scandal. The Pope sent her a sharp protest, but the Queen ignored it. Taking Prince Edward, she and Mortimer went to Holland and made their plans for the invasion of England. Isabella saw the Count of Hainault, a province of the Netherlands which was an important market for English wool, and proposed a marriage between her son and the Count's twelve-year-old daughter Philippa in return for ships and an army with which to invade England. The terms were accepted, and the Queen and her lover sailed across the Channel in September 1326, taking Prince Edward with them. Inviting the people to support the heir to the throne instead of his father, who was generally unpopular, the Queen received an enthusiastic response. A large number of discontented barons, including the King's cousin the Earl of Richmond and his half-brother the Earl of Kent, rallied to her support: they felt it was the only way permanently to drive out the ruthless and avaricious Despensers. The Queen's progress was triumphant and her forces gathered strength as they went, another of the King's half-brothers, the Earl of Norfolk, soon throwing in his lot with them.

Now it was the turn of Edward and the younger Despenser to take refuge in the Tower. From there they issued a series of proclamations calling upon the people to rally to the defence of the country, and rewards were offered for Mortimer's head. But since the people were unresponsive, the King thought it wiser to leave the Tower and flee to the west of England.

Mortimer set out at once for Gloucester, where his army was augmented by the Welsh Marcher barons and those of the north. Bristol, where the elder Despenser had taken refuge, was soon captured and he was executed. A few weeks later the King and his favourite were taken prisoner. Young Hugh Despenser was hanged 'fifty feet high' and the King was taken under guard to Kenilworth Castle.

Parliament was then summoned in the name of the King's heir and met in Westminster Hall, where the representatives of the realm listened to accusations against their King. He was charged with incompetence and with giving office to men whose evil advice had led to the neglect of the country's needs. The Members were then asked if they wanted the King or his heir to be their ruler. As only four voted for the King, the young Prince was brought in and was greeted as the new monarch.

By law the King was required to agree to his own deposition. Accordingly, a parliamentary delegation went to see him at Kenilworth; by threatening to crown his wife's lover instead of his son, they forced him to abdicate, and the new King was proclaimed as King Edward III. His father, aged only forty-three, was hustled from dungeon to dungeon until, after being mocked at Berkeley as a madman and made to wear a crown of plaited straw, he was brutally murdered in September 1327 on the instructions of Mortimer and with connivance of the Queen. Such was the terrible end of the first English Prince of Wales.

Mortimer returned to the Tower of London with the Queen, and there was merrymaking and feasting in their honour. The new King, being a

Head of the alabaster effigy of Edward II on his tomb in Gloucester Cathedral. After Edward's murder, he was unofficially canonized by his son, and the tomb became a centre for pilgrims. (A. F. Kersting)

minor, was not yet able to assume full sovereignty; in effect he was the prisoner of Mortimer and his mother, who ruled in his name.

This unforeseen development naturally aroused the anger of the barons. The favourite of the late King had been replaced by the favourite of the Queen, a man whom they regarded as a regicide and a usurper. In 1328 Mortimer assumed the coveted title of Earl of March, thus elevating himself above all the other Marcher barons, and he continually enriched himself by seizing the estates of others. Aware of the growing antagonism towards him, Mortimer arranged the execution of the late King's half-brother Edmund, Earl of Kent, as a warning to potential rebels.

It was time, the barons decided, to put an end to Mortimer. The boy-King, who was subjected to the utmost humiliation, would, they felt, be glad to be rid of his mother's lover. In October 1330 Parliament met at Nottingham. The Queen and Mortimer were lodged in the castle, access to which could be gained by way of a secret passage under the moat. Through this passage, guided by two of the King's officers, a body of armed noblemen made their way into Queen Isabella's private apartments. There they found Mortimer

undressing to go to bed. Despite the Queen's entreaty, 'Have pity on gentle Mortimer,' they seized him and sent him in irons to the Tower, the scene of the first act of this tragedy. He was tried by his fellow peers and condemned to death. He was then dragged through the streets on an ox-hide to the common gallows at Tyburn and hanged.

Queen Isabella survived him by twenty-eight years and spent her time at Castle Rising in Norfolk to which her son had confined her. She died in 1358 and her body was later brought to London for burial. At the same time another funeral procession, with the body of her daughter Joan, who had been born in the Tower, also drew into London. The two Queens were buried together in Grey Friars Church.

For some years not much was done in the way of additions or extensions to the Tower. Edward II was, however, responsible for two important improvements. The Outer Wall on the south or river side was made 'broader and higher' from St Thomas's Tower towards St Katherine's Hospital, that is to say as far as the Develin Tower and the Iron Gate. Its total length was $412\frac{1}{2}$ feet and the construction was carried out by Master Walter of Canterbury, mason, in 1324–25. This completed the work begun by Edward I. The four towers of the Inner Wall on the east side, the Salt, Broad Arrow, Constable and Martin Towers, were also repaired and crenellated, and the work was entrusted to Master Thomas de la Bataille. During the troubles in 1313 Edward II had also made a feverish attempt to strengthen the Tower defences. He set up five springalds (engines for throwing heavy missiles), constructed a barbican and brattices towards St Katherine's, had the ditches cleared, made a new gate in the 'great arch' of St Thomas's Tower and put in two new portcullises.

This siege picture, from an early fifteenth-century manuscript, shows some of the methods of assault against which the Tower was repeatedly re-fortified, even by such unwarlike rulers as Edward II. In front of the tents to the right is a springald, the immediate forerunner of the cannon (right foreground). The invention of gunpowder and subsequent development of artillery rendered the walled castle obsolete. (Bodleian Library, Oxford. MS Bodl. 264, fol. 22r)

CHAPTER THIRTEEN

Prisoners from the French Wars

In the new reign the Tower was recurrently filled with prisoners brought back from Edward III's victorious campaigns in France; and the yield in ransoms was richly rewarding. But until the death of Mortimer, the young King was himself held in the Tower in semi-captivity. As the kingdom could only be ruled in his name, his captors went through the mockery of conferring upon the fifteen-year-old boy the necessary dignity of the monarch; in his name they concluded the humiliating Treaty of Northampton which acknowledged Bruce as King north of the Tweed. The treaty included the betrothal of Edward's sister Joan to the young heir to the Scottish throne who succeeded as King David II in 1329.

On coming of age at eighteen, Edward resolved to restore the dignity of the Crown, which had been brought into such squalid disrepute, first by his father, and then by his mother and Mortimer. He was admirably equipped for the task. Endowed with both shrewdness and strength of character, he was further blessed with a most engaging personality. His fine looks, his youth, his charm, his skill in the tournament, his chivalrous manner, so much in accord with the recently revived legend of King Arthur, invested him with a magnetic appeal.

The Tower soon received King Edward's attention. He began by issuing orders that the gates, walls and bulwarks must be guarded 'with all diligence, lest they be surprised by the King's enemies'. The gates, he insisted, must be kept shut 'from the setting till the rising of the sun'. Some years later, on returning unexpectedly at night from the Continent, he found the Tower so laxly guarded that it could not possibly have held out against a sudden attack. He immediately arrested the Constable and a number of his officials. The Lord Chancellor, who had overall responsibility for the Tower's security, was also arrested and thrown into gaol.

The fabric of the Tower had in general been much neglected by Edward II, and a complete survey was ordered by Edward III; the estimate of the necessary repairs amounted to £920 3s 4d; to this were added supplementary recommendations for the repair of two towers at a cost of £710, and the partial rebuilding of the Wharf in stone at £180 13s 4d. Thus the total estimate amounted to £1810 16s 8d, equal today to close on £100,000. It is not possible to identify all the items in the survey, but work was certainly done on the Palace during these years and on various walls.

A certain amount of detailed information is available about the Wharf. We learn, for example, that Richard le Waller was entrusted with making a 'wall' thirteen perches in length 'from the Water-gate to the postern beneath the King's Mint'—that is to say from Traitors' Gate to the postern by the Byward Tower. This was an extension of the earlier section of the Wharf built from Petty Wales, which lay beyond the western confines of the Tower enclosure, to the Byward Tower; neither of these sections was built of stone. Not until later in Edward's reign, in 1365–6, were large quantities of ashlar and other stone purchased; a mason named Maurice Young was then paid £24 for making sixteen perches of the Wharf. Presumably it was at this time that a large part of the old earth and timber Wharf was rebuilt in stone.

Throughout his reign Edward III gave the Tower his constant attention. He continued the work begun by his father of heightening and strengthening the river side of the Outer Wall and carried on the heightening and crenellating of the section which ran west from St Thomas's Tower to the postern at the Byward Tower. Thomas de Dagworth and Simon of Dorset, masons, were entrusted with this task in 1336. Three years later, in 1339, the south Inner Wall between the Bell and the Salt Towers was also reinforced and crenellated. Edward then built two cross-walls, one on each side of St Thomas's Tower, running northward from the Outer to the Inner Wall. These flanked one if not two sides of the Bloody Tower gateway and provided far greater security for the Inner Ward, to which that gateway gave access.

It appears that for some years Edward III used as his private bedroom not the King's Chamber which opened off the Great Hall in the Palace, but the room on that floor in the Bloody Tower. However, in 1335 he moved to a new room at the eastern end of the Palace, and a few years later, in 1340–1, built a gate in the Inner Wall between this room and the Salt Tower, and a water-gate in the Outer Wall with the Cradle Tower to protect it.

The Cradle is an attractive and architecturally distinctive tower. Two storeys high, it is built of ragstone rubble with Reigate stone dressings; the roof is lead-covered. The middle section forms the gateway and has lodges on either side. The gateway has an original two-centred and moulded outer arch with a portcullis (of which only the slot remains) and a segmental-pointed rear arch; this section of the building projected into the moat. On either side are arched recesses of varying width; and there is a two-centred archway on the north part with single-light windows with cinque-foiled heads. The gate-hall has a doorway in each of its side walls and a lovely little stone vault, the ribs of which spring from moulded corbels, two carved with rabbits. The chief mason employed for building the gate in the Inner Wall, the Cradle Tower and the postern was John of Leicester.

Edward III, who had been betrothed by his mother at the age of fourteen, was married to Philippa of Hainault in 1328 and moved into the Tower shortly afterwards. He was critical of the conditions in the Palace, finding that there were not enough servants to attend to his and the Queen's comfort. She was pregnant at the time and presently gave birth to a daughter—the second royal birth in the Tower—but unhappily the child, named Blanche, died in infancy.

Though the marriage was an arranged one, it proved to be a most fortunate union. Philippa was beautiful and her excellent upbringing and education gave her an understanding of and taste for the fine arts which led her to patronize artists and scholars. Froissart, the renowned chronicler, was a countryman of hers and served for some years as her secretary. Her distinctive choice of clothes set the fashion, bringing in short, tight-waisted dresses one year and long, wide dresses the next.

The Tower was often the royal couple's home. They lived there in the Palace, which now had a great many apartments opening off the Great Hall on the first floor; the ground floor was used by the servants and the guards. The chamber to the east of the hall was the King's bedroom. The nobles also slept in that room on rush mats on the floor; the King's bed, a four-poster, was curtained to provide privacy. It was usual to sleep naked; but in the King's chamber the nobles slept in their everyday clothes. The Queen maintained a similar routine in her personal large hall and chamber in the adjoining apartments, no doubt varying it when the King visited her. There were quite a number of lavatories, with seats, and the drainage was taken through pipes into the river. There were no bathrooms. A large wooden two-seater tub, bound with iron bands, was brought into the chamber and filled with hot water when required, which was about once a month; the King and Queen, like the baron and his lady in their own homes, generally bathed together so as not to waste the hot water. The tub, like the four-poster bed, had curtains to provide privacy in a room that was constantly filled with people.

When the King and Queen were not in residence, the rooms were bereft of furniture. The tapestries, used partly for decoration but chiefly to keep out draughts, were packed in chests as were the linen and cutlery; the tables were folded and strapped together—in fact everything save the large beds, the massive tables and heavy chairs was despatched in advance to the next royal lodging.

The King's constant residence in the Tower and his wife's love of beautiful things were responsible later in the reign for the employment at the Tower of Henry Yevele, the most famous architect of his day. Yevele, known as 'the King's Mason', worked for both Edward III and Richard II, doing splendid work at Westminster Hall and Westminster Abbey. He was appointed 'disposer of the King's works pertaining to the art of masonry' in the Tower.

Yevele was paid twelve pence a day, not a princely sum even when translated into present terms, but he was paid this for 365 days' work a year—which would be less than £20 a week today. He reconstructed the Bloody Tower and added the vaulted gateway in which the bosses in the form of lion's masks are a striking feature. The archway has two inner bays, covered with tierceron vaulting. He also put in a heavy new portcullis, weighing two tons; it required thirty men to raise and lower it. The warder in charge of this portcullis, of the drawbridge and all the Tower gates at the time was John O'London, the first warder to be mentioned in the annals.

Edward III ruled firmly but with due regard to the exercise of justice. 'Our affairs and the affairs of our realm,' he stated in his instructions to sheriffs and other officials throughout the country, 'have been mismanaged in the past to our damage and dishonour and that of our kingdom and to the impoverishment of our people. We wish all men to know that in future we will govern according to right and reason as is fitting our royal dignity, and that the matters which touch us and the estate of our realm are to be disposed of by the common counsel of the magnates of our realm and in no other manner.' His resolve, he stated, was to rely at all times on the co-operation of Parliament. He planned to heal, to be conciliatory and to make concessions so that trade might flourish and the financial strength of the nation might be fully restored.

Edward was painfully aware of two humiliating agreements made by his mother and Mortimer. The first of these was the 'Shameful Treaty of Northampton' with the Scots; this had dispossessed a large number of English barons who owned land in Scotland, and Edward's demand for their restoration had been ignored. The other galling memory was the pact made by Isabella with her brother Charles IV of France, which deprived the English King of two-thirds of his remaining French possessions by legalizing what had in fact been illegally seized. Anger over these capitulations was outspoken and widespread. But Edward knew that any attempt at adjustment would mean war with one or both countries and his exchequer was too depleted to support it.

He did however encourage the attempt of Edward Baliol, heir to the Scottish King who had been Edward I's prisoner in the Tower, to recover the throne so arbitrarily seized by the Bruces. When Baliol's army set out in 1332, Edward sent with him several hundred of his famous archers. The forces of the boy-King David were defeated at Dripplin Moor and

Baliol was crowned King at Scone. In gratitude he restored Edward's overlordship of Scotland and transferred to him the important border town of Berwick. But the Scottish patriots resented this and within two months they had driven out Baliol and repossessed the town.

This forced Edward's hand. He now marched north with a powerful army and laid siege to Berwick. When the Scots tried to relieve the town, Edward's archers with their long-bows wrought havoc among the Scottish pikemen mounted on moorland ponies. Bannockburn was avenged at Halidon Hill. Edward lost only one knight, one man-at-arms and twelve archers. Baliol became King once more and this time transferred a large area of southern Scotland 'to the Crown and kingdom of England'. The boy-King David was smuggled out of the country and took refuge in France with his Queen, Edward's sister Joan, in the hope that with help from that country, which was always ready to support the Scots, his fortunes might one day be restored.

From France Edward wanted nothing but the return of his lands, and he tried hard to come to a friendly settlement. But discussions had gone on for years between the two royal cousins without anything being achieved. The French King was determined to hold on to everything he had and if possible absorb the rest as well. War thus became inevitable, and because of Edward's immense popularity, the barons and the knights, the merchants and the burgesses of the towns readily voted funds for the campaign. There was even a grant from the Church. This generous support came in response to a shrewd move by the King, who published details of his negotiations with France and his repeated attempts to reach a peaceful settlement. So that the whole country should be informed, he had it read out in every county court.

Another factor that helped him enormously was the wool trade. Wool, the principal English export, was bought chiefly by Flemish towns, which had become prosperous by weaving it into excellent cloth. The Flemish merchants and townspeople were strong in their support of England; the nobility, on the other hand, favoured France and were constantly obstructing the wool trade. In this Edward saw his opportunity, and in 1336, by placing an embargo on the export of all wool, he brought about a serious crisis in the Netherlands. The people rose against the aristocracy and appealed to England for help. Edward responded and thus began the Hundred Years' War with

France, from the battlefields of which streams of prisoners were to flow to the Tower of London.

In that year, 1337, England was strong. The keen interest of the King and the constant activity of privateers in the Channel had both helped to produce a first class navy. The army too was a powerful and efficient fighting machine. The old method of raising troops by feudal levy had been abandoned and Edward had established a force of specially picked men recruited for their hardiness and skill and paid well for their services. They were professional soldiers, ready to serve anywhere all the year round without being recalled home for the harvest.

The army was composed in the main of mounted knights armoured in chain mail, supported by groups of highly trained archers, equipped with the long-bow, the new weapon of deadly accuracy. Its effective use by the Welsh archers had caused Henry III to adopt it, and his son Edward I had made it the principal weapon of his army. Six feet high, the bowstrings drawn back to the ear for shooting, the long-bow could propel a shaft two hundred and fifty yards, a range unmatched for five hundred years by any infantry weapon, including firearms. The arrow could penetrate the armour of the mounted knight and his saddle, burying itself in his horse. Shot through an oak door four inches thick, the head of the shaft stood out a hand's breadth on the other side. By rapid and continuous shooting, a company of archers could annihilate a cavalry attack. Supported by a considerable transport for their arrows, maces, axes and other implements, these archers always

planted a heavy iron-pointed stake in the ground in front of them, as an obstacle for charging horses, before opening fire. This formidable new arm of warfare, unsuspected abroad even by England's nearest neighbours, provided an ascendency that was fully exploited in the Hundred Years' War with France.

The long-bow also had its place in the Tower of London, where it was not only used by the garrison for the defence of the fortress but manufactured in the Tower workshops.

Edward assembled his expeditionary force in the Cinque Ports, where the English navy was ready to escort it across the Channel. Following a victory over the French fleet off Sluys, the long-bowmen were brought into play; shooting from the ships at long range, they cleared the shores and covered the landing of the English force.

The cost of the series of campaigns that followed far exceeded Edward's anticipation and he had to resort to pawning his crown and even betrothing his ten-year-old heir, Edward Prince of Wales (later known as the Black Prince), to one of the princesses of Brabant to raise more money. Only three of his great victories need be noted here because of their rich harvest of prisoners for the Tower. The first of these was at Crécy in 1346. The Black Prince, then only sixteen years

Shooting at butts with long-bows. Drawing after a miniature in the Luttrell Psalter, c. 1340. (Radio Times Hulton Picture Library)

old, distinguished himself by his brilliance and courage. The French army ceased to exist; among their dead, lying in immense piles on the battlefield, were 1500 knights and 10,000 soldiers. An ally of the French King, the great warrior King John of Bohemia, now fifty years old and blind, was in command of the French advance guard and charged with the reins of his bridle tied to those of the knights on each side of him. He was killed, and both Edward and his heir attended this valiant soldier's funeral. The plume of ostrich feathers on the dead King's helmet was given by Edward to his son and has ever since formed part of the insignia of the Prince of Wales.

The English army then marched on to Calais: its capture was important because it was the port nearest to England and also because the English wool exports passed through it *en route* to the looms of Flanders. In a message to the Constable of the Tower, Edward asked for every available cannon to be despatched to him. At that time the cannon was an elaborate form of cross-bow, with a mechanism for shooting arrows with heavy iron heads or in some cases large iron bolts—an effective weapon for a siege. Gunpowder had only recently been introduced. While it is possible that Edward's cannon at Calais fired stone balls with the aid of gunpowder, there is no clear evidence as to which type of cannon was sent from the Tower, or if in fact the Tower had a sufficient supply of gunpowder-fired cannon.

Naval vessels crossed from England to blockade the sea approaches to Calais, and Edward settled down with his cannon, his knights and men-at-arms, 30,000 men in all, to starve the citizens into surrender. After a siege which lasted almost a year the town surrendered, and was to remain in English hands for nearly two centuries. The captain of the defenders of Calais, John de Vienne, and a number of burghers and knights came out bareheaded and barefooted and surrendered the keys of the city to Edward. He sent them to be interned in the Tower.

Ten years later, in 1356, the English under the Black Prince met King John II of France and his army at Poitiers. The young Prince proved himself to be a great commander, and although his troops were heavily outnumbered, his victory was complete. The French King was taken prisoner, as were his younger son Philip, an archbishop,

Ancient type of cannon which fired a bolt instead of a cannonball. From a miniature in the treatise of Walter de Milemete, De nobilitatibus, sapientiis et prudentiis regum, *c. 1327. (By permission of the Governing Body of Christ Church, Oxford. MS 92, fol. 70v)*

thirteen counts, five viscounts, twenty-one barons and nearly two thousand knights. They were all brought to England and put into the Tower. The streets of London were hung with flags and banners and the air was filled with cheers, rising above the ringing of the church bells, as the procession of prisoners went past. The French King, treated with respect and courtesy, was mounted on a white charger with the Black Prince riding beside him on a small black palfrey. Behind came the aldermen and wardens of the city, followed by hundreds of liveried guildsmen.

The French King and Prince Philip occupied the royal apartments on the top floor of the White Tower. Young King David of Scotland, who was a prisoner there at the time, had to be moved out to make room. As we have seen, when Edward III restored Baliol to the Scottish throne in 1333, David and his Queen took refuge in France. But eight years later, taking advantage of Edward's Continental involvement, David returned to Scotland. In 1346, at the instigation of King Philip VI of France, father of John II, he invaded England, but was defeated and taken prisoner at the Battle of Neville's Cross, just west of Durham. Also captured with him were the Earls of Sutherland, Carrick, Fife, Monteith and Douglas, all of whom were brought under heavy escort to the Tower, where the King was received with honour by the Constable, Sir John Darcy. Now, after ten years, he was moved from the White Tower to Odiham Castle in Hampshire; some months later, on paying a ransom of 100,000 marks, equal to nearly three million pounds today, he was allowed to return to Scotland.

The royal French prisoners were granted every possible comfort during their stay in the Tower. Edward demanded an enormous ransom for their release—300,000 crowns for the King alone—and in order to prevent His Majesty escaping, an iron grille was fixed on the window of his chamber. This grille, made in the forge in the Tower by the chief smith, Andrew le Fevre, weighed 210 pounds, the cost of which was met by the Treasury. It took three and a half years for the French to raise the money for their King's

ransom, and even so it was paid in instalments; but after the first payment King John was allowed to return home. His son, however, was still held as a prisoner. Given temporary leave to visit his wife, the young Prince broke his parole, whereupon the French King honourably surrendered himself to the English. This time he was housed in a castle in Lincolnshire, where he lived in great luxury until his death a few months later.

Raising money to pay the royal ransom so beggared the French exchequer that for several years all their silver coins were replaced by leather discs with a small silver stud in the centre. The other high-ranking French prisoners, the Counts of Eu and Tankerville and many other nobles brought to the Tower after the siege of Caen, together with three hundred burghers, had to raise their own ransom money.

Every English knight was allowed to keep the ransom paid for his prisoner. Thomas Holland, a member of an obscure Lancashire family, received such a substantial sum for the Count of Eu that he claimed the hand in marriage of the beautiful Princess Joan, known as 'the Fair Maid of Kent', the King's cousin. Holland had secretly married her when she was twelve, but had been afraid to reveal it when the King gave her in marriage to the Earl of Salisbury. But his immense wealth now enabled him to secure from the Pope an annulment of the later marriage; Joan was acknowledged as his lawful wife. At the same time Holland was made Earl of Kent—a romantic outcome of an imprisonment in the Tower. The loot from these campaigns was so enormous that there was hardly a woman in England without some jewel, ornament, or fine linen brought back by the ordinary soldiers.

Dedicated as Edward III had always been to the legend of King Arthur and his chivalrous

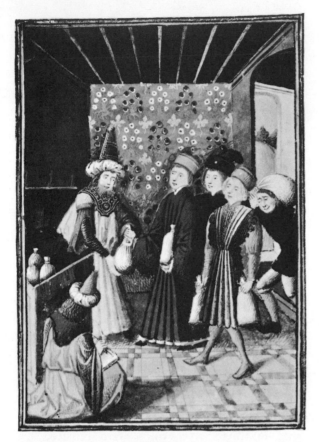

The practice of ransoming exalted prisoners was not confined to Western Europe. This miniature from Froissart's Chronicles *shows the ransom of the Count of Nevers, who was captured by the Turks at the Battle of Nicopoli in 1396. (By permission of the Trustees of the British Museum. MS Harl. 4380, fol. 118)*

knights of the Round Table, he had for some years nursed the thought of having a Round Table of his own and founding an Order of Christian Chivalry. This he finally achieved on his return from Crécy, when he established the Order of the Garter, dedicating it not to King Arthur but to the patron saint of England, St George. The first members of the Order were the King and twenty-six of his most eminent knights. As its emblem he chose a lady's garter which had been dropped by accident at a ball at Calais by his cousin Joan, mentioned above. Picking it up, the King gallantly wound the blue ribbon of the garter round his own leg, remarking '*Honi soit qui mal y pense*' ('Evil be to him who evil thinks'), and these words are still inscribed on the badge of the Order.

During these years of warfare all Europe was swept by a terrible plague known as the Black Death. It appears to have entered Europe through the Crimea, where silk-traders from the caravan route to China had taken refuge from Tartar horsemen. The infection was carried by ship to various ports in Europe and was eventually brought to Weymouth. From there it spread rapidly and claimed vast numbers of victims in London and as far north as Yorkshire. The death rate was appalling: it is estimated that nearly half the population of the country, which then numbered about four to five million, died of the disease. The greatest havoc was in the towns, where the streets were narrow and completely without drainage. The corpses were flung into hastily dug pits. Processions of the clergy went barefoot through the streets praying for the curse to be lifted. Crops were left to rot in the fields. The courts of King's Bench and Common Pleas ceased to meet and church bells were no longer rung. In London about thirty thousand people are said to have perished. In the Tower many craftsmen died, among them the King's mason William Ramsey and his brother John. After the Plague had abated, Thomas of Gloucester was appointed the new Warden of the Masons at the Tower to re-start the building there.

In the years that remained of Edward III's reign nearly all that had been won in France was lost and he himself declined into senility. Many must have wondered what went wrong, how it was that after such impressive victories the greatest military power was made to suffer defeat after defeat. The Black Death had taken an appalling toll of life and wealth; and the war, though triumphant, had plunged England into crippling debt. The ransoms were paid intermittently. In France, defeat had brought chaos, but the behaviour of the English troops, especially the mercenaries, vast numbers of whom stayed in France to terrorize the countryside and rob the people, roused such intense hostility that the French King was able to muster and train a fresh army which eventually succeeded in expelling the invaders.

By 1360 Edward controlled one-third of France as a result of his early victories; he was left in the end with only Calais in the north and Gascony along the west coast, running from Bordeaux to Bayonne; almost the whole of Aquitaine had gone. The Black Prince, one of the outstanding military leaders in his youth, had to retire from the field and return home a sick man, leaving the command to his younger, less competent brother John of Gaunt, so named because he was born in Ghent. In 1361, to the dismay of his parents, the Black Prince married his cousin Joan of Kent, only six months after the death of her husband Thomas Holland; for this a dispensation had to be obtained from the Pope. Thus Joan became the mother of the next King of England, Richard II, for the Black Prince died a year before his father.

On the death of Queen Philippa after a long and happy married life, Edward took as his mistress his wife's lady-in-waiting Alice Perrers and lived with her in doting dependence until his death in 1377 at the age of sixty-five.

Effigy in gilt copper on the tomb of Edward the Black Prince in Trinity Chapel, Canterbury Cathedral (the Prince died on Trinity Sunday, 1376). Part of the inscription, in Old French, is humorously resigned:

> *And if ye should see me this day,*
> *I do not think, but ye would say,*
> *That I had never been a man,*
> *So much alter'd now I am.*
>   *(A. F. Kersting)*

CHAPTER FOURTEEN

Angry Peasants March on the Tower

The immense, sombre, terrifying Tower, with armed men at every gate, archers at the windows and watchers on the ramparts, centre of the nation's strength and coveted prize of every struggle for power, was to witness a succession of strange and startling events during the reign of the ten-year-old boy, often referred to as 'Richard of Bordeaux' because he was born in that city, who became King in 1377 as Richard II.

It began with the joyous event of his coronation. The child-King, who was living at the Palace of Sheen, was escorted to the Tower on the day after his grandfather's death and stayed in the fortress for three weeks while the necessary arrangements were being made at Westminster Abbey. The chronicler Holinshed has described the coronation most vividly. Blond, clad in white robes and looking 'as beautiful as an angel', he wrote, the young King rode out of the Tower attended by a vast retinue of knights and nobles. The houses were hung with tapestry and the fountains and the conduits once again flowed with wine.

Appointed to rule as Regent during the King's minority was John of Gaunt, recently made Duke of Lancaster after taking over the estates of his wife, the heiress Blanche of Lancaster: dukedoms were unknown in England until the reign of Edward II. He had taken over command of the army in France from his brother the Black Prince, in an attempt to retrieve the lost territories; in this he had failed dismally. He had also been responsible for the conduct of affairs in England during his father's last years, but his administration had earned him considerable unpopularity. The heavy taxation, though inevitable, was bitterly resented. The country was utterly exhausted and faced bankruptcy.

When he summoned the first Parliament for three years in the last year of Edward's reign, John of Gaunt found the representatives in an angry mood. The Commons dominated the proceedings. In 1343 the seventy-four knights from the shires and the two hundred representatives from the towns had taken the vital decision to form their own separate assembly. Hitherto they had sat with the Lords, but now they moved into another hall of assembly—the Painted Chamber of the Palace of Westminster, and there formulated their own business procedure. A Speaker was appointed to voice their complaints (the title remains, but the Speaker now acts only as chairman). Thereafter they only entered the chamber of the Lords to expound their deliberations. At John of Gaunt's Parliament it is recorded that the Speaker, 'standing with his followers before the nobles, whereof the chief was John Duke of Lancaster whose doings were ever contrary', denounced the mismanagement of the war and the oppressive taxation, demanding an account of the expenditure. John of Gaunt was furious. 'What do these base and ignoble knights attempt?' he cried. 'Do they think they be kings or princes of the land?' The Black Prince, borne in a litter to the meeting from his death-bed, gave his complete support to the Commons. After his death, suspecting that John of Gaunt had designs on the throne himself, the Commons insisted that 'the noble child Richard of Bordeaux come before Parliament so that the Lords and Commons might see and honour him as the true heir apparent to the realm'. Thus was the succession secured for Richard II before the death of Edward III.

Trouble of a very different kind developed in the first years of Richard's reign. There was widespread discontent, chiefly among the serfs. Although they were not actually slaves, and could not be bought or sold as individuals, they were tied to the land they cultivated and could not leave it without the consent of their overlord. For a certain number of days each week they had to work for the lord; the rest of the time they might work for themselves. If they or their children left, they could be pursued and brought back in chains; but if they joined the Church or, having escaped to one of the larger towns, contrived to live there for a year and a day, they were beyond the lord's reach.

This system had begun to break up. The drift to the towns, where the former peasant could work and earn money for himself, generally as an artisan, had gone on for years and was greatly accelerated after the Black Death. With the tragic loss of so large a section of the population, vast tracts of the countryside had to be left uncultivated. There was an enormous shortage of labour. Prices rose steeply, but every effort to obtain higher wages by those who still worked on the land was fiercely resisted by landowners who did everything in their power to enforce their ancient rights and recover escaped workers. There was rioting in many parts of England. Agitators stirred up the crowds at the fairs on market day and were joined by hundreds of priests who strongly disapproved of the high-handed attitude of the Church, which was the largest landlord in England. The most violent upheaval took place in the counties around London. One of the wandering priests, John Ball, preaching on the text 'When Adam delved and Eve span, who was then the gentleman?' was arrested and thrown into gaol.

In May 1381 the peasants of Kent massed together and marched up the valley of the Medway to Maidstone, where they chose as their leader Wat Tyler, a former soldier of the French wars who had since earned his living by highway robbery. In addition to his brilliance as a mob orator he possessed considerable skill in organizing and disciplining the excited throngs around him. Marching on the local gaol, he swelled his following by releasing the prisoners, among whom was John Ball.

Twenty thousand strong by now, the peasants set out for London. In a proclamation Wat Tyler stated their aims. They owed allegiance to none, he declared, except King Richard; and they were resolved to remove the traitors around the King and to root out and destroy all the lawyers and officials who had corrupted the country. The fourteen-year-old King was staying at Windsor, but moved to the Tower with his chief advisers and was joined there by his mother and her ladies. Meanwhile the Mayor of London was busy strengthening the guards at the gates in the city walls.

Tyler's great army of rebels spent the night at Blackheath. Another band of insurgents from Essex camped in the suburb of Whitechapel, a mile from the eastern walls of London. Inside the city sympathy for the rebels was strong among the apprentices and labourers.

After sacking Rochester Castle, Tyler had sent its Constable to see the King and arrange a personal interview. The Constable's children were held as hostages and it was made clear that if the request was not granted the children would be killed.

The next morning the King and his chief ministers set out in five barges from Tower Wharf and crossed the river to Greenwich. They found the insurgents assembled under two great banners of St George. The young King and his ministers, including the Archbishop of Canterbury, waited in their boats while the rebels celebrated Mass. When it was over, Richard tried to speak to them, but his words were drowned by angry shouting. With difficulty he was able to say, 'Tell me what you want now that I have come to talk to you.' But the rebels seemed in a menacing mood, and after a time the boats pulled away and returned to the Tower.

The two rebel groups then made for London, where the gates were opened for them by sympathisers. As they surged through the narrow streets, they encountered religious processions praying that there would be no violence. Their chief purpose was to get food, for they had eaten little during their long march. Food and ale were provided by the poor people living in the slums. Once the hunger of the rebels was appeased, many thousands of them set out for the Savoy in the Strand, the home of John of Gaunt, which lay a mile beyond London's western wall. Gaunt was not there and his servants fled as they saw the crowd approach with lighted torches. Plundering had been forbidden by Wat Tyler, but the contents of the house—beds, rich tapestries and costly furniture—were flung out of the windows and the house itself was set on fire. At that time Fleet Street, just outside the city wall, was the favourite walk of Londoners. All the shops and houses along that street were burned to the ground.

The great body of rebels camped for the night in the open spaces around the Tower, some on

Tower Hill, others on St Katherine's Wharf just east of the Tower. Inside the fortress, the King presided over a meeting of his Council. They debated anxiously what their next move should be. With the rebels in possession of London, the King and his ministers were now virtual prisoners in the Tower. From one of the turrets of the White Tower the young King had seen more than thirty fires blazing in various parts of the city and beyond. In the southern and eastern counties the rebels seemed to be in complete control, and the trouble appeared to be spreading in other directions.

The Tower garrison consisted of six hundred men-at-arms, archers and armed guards. In the nearby London residence of Sir Robert Knollys, a great soldier dedicated to the service of the Crown, there were a further hundred or so archers and men-at-arms; and it was thought that loyal Londoners might be able to provide a few hundred more. But the Earl of Salisbury, who was with the King in the Tower, advised against their trying to break out. Although very few of the rebels had armour, fighting in the narrow streets and lanes with mallets and axes and shooting arrows from windows and rooftops would give them a great advantage because of their numbers. After much discussion, it was finally decided that the King should go out and talk to the rebels in the Mile End fields, to draw the crowd away. The Archbishop Simon Sudbury, who was also Chancellor, and the Treasurer Sir Robert Hales, both of them marked men, would then be able to leave the Tower and cross the Thames to safety, together with young Henry Bolingbroke, the son and heir of John of Gaunt.

The King readily agreed to do this. A proclamation was read out from the walls of the Tower and the King, accompanied by those members of his Council who were not anathema to the rebels, rode out through the Bulwark Gate. The crowds were wildly excited and followed them to Mile End. But many stayed behind to keep an eye on the Tower; so that when the boat with the Archbishop and the other two men put out from the water-gate, they were forced to go back.

At Mile End the multitude knelt before the King, the son of their revered hero the Black Prince, crying, 'Welcome, our Lord King Richard. We will have no other King but you.' Richard promised to grant all their demands. Serfdom would be abolished, he said, and all holders of land under that system would in future be full tenants, paying a modest yearly rent of only fourpence an acre. He also promised a general pardon if they would return quickly to their homes. Froissart records that his words 'appeased well the common people'.

Wat Tyler then told the King that the people 'will that you suffer them to take and deal with all the traitors who have sinned against you and the law'. The King promised that all 'as could be proved by process of law to be traitors' should have due punishment. This did not appear to satisfy Tyler or the leader of the Essex rebels, for while the King was still with the grateful, cheering crowd, they crept back to the Tower, where a large body of their adherents were still watching the gates. The two leaders bluffed their way in and the others swarmed into the Tower after them. They broke into the royal apartments, terrified the ladies of the court, seized and kissed the King's mother, and hacked the rich embroideries of her bed to pieces. The King's bed was overturned to see that no one was concealed under it, and much pillaging was done throughout the Palace. The Wardrobe Tower was ransacked. There is a reference to John Ludewyk or Lowick, the Keeper of the Privy Wardrobe within the Tower, having built a new house towards the end of Richard's reign. It was erected very close to the White Tower, and was probably put up to provide greater security for the Crown Jewels. Later the Jewel Tower was built for the safe keeping of the royal regalia.

Simon Sudbury and Sir Robert Hales, expecting death, had gone into St John's Chapel in the White Tower to pray. The Archbishop had just received the Treasurer's confession and was administering the last rites when the mob burst in and dragged them out to Tower Hill, where both were beheaded. The Archbishop's head was then stuck on a pike, crowned with a mitre and borne through the streets of London.

When told of this, the King refused to return to the Tower but went instead to Baynard's Castle. All that night there was tumult and rioting in the capital; many were murdered, especially among the Flemish merchants, more than a hundred and fifty of whom were said to have been slain.

Richard decided to make another bid for peace the next morning. Many thousands of the peasants had already returned home, but he saw Tyler and the other more violent leaders in the cattle market at Smithfield, just outside the city walls. The King had about two hundred retainers with him, all wearing armour under their robes. With them

Wat Tyler is struck down at Smithfield by the cutlass of Mayor Walworth. From a miniature in Froissart's Chronicles. (*By permission of the Trustees of the British Museum. MS Royal 18.E.I, fol. 175*)

was the Lord Mayor of London. The contemporary chronicler Anonimalle records that Tyler 'came to the King in a haughty fashion, mounted on a little horse so that he could be seen by the commons, and carrying in his hand a dagger'. After seizing the King's hand and shaking it 'forcibly and roughly', he called for a flagon of water and rinsed his mouth out. The Mayor, William Walworth, after he had 'reasoned with his violent behaviour and contempt in the King's presence, arrested him'. Tyler thereupon thrust at the Mayor's stomach with his dagger, but it merely struck the armour. The Mayor then drew his cutlass, a scuffle ensued and Tyler was killed.

Uncertain what the rebels' reaction would be, the King rode fearlessly across to them, as might have been expected from the son of the heroic Black Prince, and said, 'I will be your leader. Let him who loves me follow me.' The effect was dramatic. As he swung his horse towards the north and made for the open country, the crowd followed. On hearing of this, Sir Robert Knollys assembled his archers and, supported by the better disposed citizens of London, set out to rescue the King. They found him in Clerkenwell Fields talking with the rebels. Knollys's men encircled the crowd, and a troop of heavily armoured knights forced their way through the multitude to the King's side. There was no resistance from the rebels, who slowly dispersed.

The King and his government retracted everything they had promised to the rebels. Far from being granted a free pardon, the insurgents were pursued, ferreted out and executed; numbers vary—Froissart says 1500 were hanged or beheaded, others say not more than a hundred and fifty perished. It was not until December, six months after the Peasants' Revolt, that a general pardon was given to those remaining. To the end of his reign many believed that the King's Council was alone responsible for exacting such vengeance; but the records show that the King personally attended the trials that meted out such harsh justice. Jack Straw, Tyler's lieutenant, was executed; so was John Ball the preacher. Just a week after the Smithfield meeting, when a delegation of peasants saw the King and asked for the charters he had promised, his answer was that as the pledges had been extorted by force, they counted for nothing. 'Serfs and villeins you are and so you shall remain,' he said.

We must remember that Richard was then little more than a boy. It was not long, however, before he began to assert himself and dismiss his old advisers. Tall, fair, handsome, rather effeminate, with his young, good-looking and quite worthless favourite Robert de Vere, Earl of Oxford, at his side, he was nevertheless happily married, though childless. He selected as his heir a descendant of his father's younger brother, Lionel Duke of Clarence, Edward III's second son. Lionel's only child Philippa had married Edmund Mortimer, great-grandson of that Roger Mortimer who was Queen Isabella's lover in the Tower. But the Mortimers were not to succeed to the throne; Richard himself was forced to abdicate in favour of Henry Bolingbroke, son of Edward III's third son John of Gaunt.

CHAPTER FIFTEEN

Richard II Abdicates in the Tower

Richard II, like his great-grandfather Edward II, loved beautiful things and actively encouraged the arts. The poet Chaucer, author of the *Canterbury Tales*, was Clerk of the King's Works and often supervised the building and repairs at the Tower, where he had an office from July 1389 to September 1391. He was also employed earlier by Richard on diplomatic missions, and he was granted a pension on his retirement. Chaucer's presence at court led to the marriage of his sister-in-law Katherine Swynford to John of Gaunt as his second wife. At Richard's request, another poet named John Gower, a friend of Chaucer's, wrote a long poem called *Confessio Amantis*, consisting of tales and meditations on love: it is the earliest collection of tales in the English language. The work of Henry Yevele, the brilliant architect of Edward III and Richard II, was by no means confined to the Bloody Tower gateway and Westminster Hall. Other examples of his skill are the tombs in Westminster Abbey of Edward III and of Richard II and his first Queen, Anne of Bohemia.

But Richard had another side to his character which is less appealing. He was assertive and dictatorial, and his rule eventually became a blatant despotism which led to recurrent trouble. In 1387 the lords of the Council, led by the King's uncle, Thomas Duke of Gloucester, took up arms against him. De Vere attempted to oppose them but was defeated at Radcot Bridge, in Oxfordshire, and fled overseas. The victorious barons then laid siege to the Tower of London, resolved to depose Richard as his great-grandfather Edward II had been deposed, but Henry Bolingbroke restrained them. The siege was raised to enable the two sides to arrive at a settlement. They met in the Council Chamber in the Tower. Gloucester insisted on taking over the

The chronicler Froissart presents his book to Richard II, his patron. From a miniature in the Chronicles. (*By permission of the Trustees of the British Museum. MS Harl. 4380, fol. 23v*)

government of the country himself. The King was forced to accept his terms. Parliament was summoned and unhesitatingly gave Gloucester its full support. Many of Richard's unpopular ministers had fled; those who remained were executed. Among them was Sir Simon Burley, the King's aged tutor. He was handed over to the sheriffs of

73

London at Bulwark Gate, taken by them to Tower Hill and beheaded—the first recorded official execution on that site.

Two years later, Richard was in full control again. Biding his time, he eventually revenged himself on those who had driven de Vere from the country. In 1394 the Queen died. The Earl of Arundel arrived late at Westminster Abbey for her funeral, and Richard struck him across the face, drawing blood. The clergy angrily rebuked the King for thus polluting the sanctity of Westminster Abbey as Canterbury Cathedral had been polluted by the murder of Becket. Arundel was later arrested and sent to the Tower. Gloucester's turn came next. He was arrested, imprisoned for a time in the Tower, then smuggled out through Traitors' Gate, taken to Calais and there murdered by the King's agents.

To give his despotism an air of constitutional

The Traitor's Gate, painted by David Scott. Usually the Tower victim's last sight of the outside world, for Thomas Duke of Gloucester it provided only an illusory escape. (Scottish National Gallery)

authority, Richard made a show of relying on Parliament. But he packed the assembly with his own supporters. He overawed both the electors and the elected: the election rooms were filled with archers and other troops wearing the King's livery, all others being forbidden to carry arms. The Parliament thus elected met in a specially built wooden hall, open at the sides, with archers standing all round ready to shoot at a signal from the King. With power thus completely in his hands, the country was at his mercy. The unlimited scope for taxation and confiscation led him to embark on a life of unprecedented luxury and extravagance.

The end came rapidly. Anxious to get his

74

cousin Henry Bolingbroke out of the country, Richard banished him on a trifling pretext—a personal quarrel between Henry and the Duke of Norfolk. On the death of John of Gaunt, Richard confiscated all the Lancaster estates. As the new Duke of Lancaster, Henry returned at once to England to claim his inheritance. He brought with him only a few personal friends, but found that the entire country was eager for a new leader, and rallied round him in massive support. At first Henry made it clear that it was not his intention to depose the King. But as the number of his supporters continued to increase, a clash became unavoidable. Richard, who was in Ireland putting down a rebellion, hurried home only to find that his uncle, Edmund Duke of York, whom he had appointed Regent in his absence, had given up any thought of a fight. The King thereupon surrendered.

Henry made him ride behind as his prisoner through the streets of London to the Tower, and on 29 September 1399, in the Council Chamber of the White Tower, Richard surrendered the throne to his cousin. The dramatic ceremony took place in a highly charged atmosphere. Both men had been together in that chamber during the troubled days of the Peasants' Revolt of 1381—eighteen years earlier—when the young Richard rode out from the Tower to face Wat Tyler and his rebels. Now Richard stood beside the empty throne, wearing his crown and long flowing robes, his figure slim, his face still handsome but lined by time. He addressed the assembled lords, prelates, knights and judges in these words: 'I have been King of England, Duke of Aquitaine, and Lord of Ireland; crown and heritage I clearly resign here to my cousin Henry of Lancaster; and I desire him, here in this open presence of you all, to take this sceptre.' He then took off his crown, saying, 'Henry, fair cousin and Duke of Lancaster, I present and give to you this crown and all the rights dependent on it.' This poignant scene Shakespeare has immortalized in deeply moving lines:

You may my glories and my state depose,
But not my griefs; still am I King of those.

Richard was finally taken to Pontefract Castle in Yorkshire and kept in a dungeon under strong guard. Three months later, a group of barons who supported him plotted a counter-revolution. It failed, but it sealed Richard's fate: no rallying point could be left for the discontented.

Richard II resigns crown and kingdom to his cousin Henry Bolingbroke. (Bibliothèque Nationale, Paris, Service Photographique. MS Fr. 2646, fol. 368)

How Richard died, whether of grief, according to the official statement, or by violent means, remains a mystery to this day. His body was brought back to London and kept in the Tower for one night. It lay in state before the altar in St John's Chapel, with the face exposed, so that all could see that he was dead.

Richard had often stayed in the Tower, living in the Palace which Henry III had decorated with such loving care, while his Queen, Anne of Bohemia, resided in the adjoining Queen's lodgings. After Anne's death, these were occupied by Richard's second Queen, seven-year-old Isabella, daughter of the mad King Charles VI of France. There had been many splendid tournaments there, and sometimes Richard would ride out to the jousting in Smithfield, leading a stately procession which included the Queen and the entire court. Less pleasant were the occasions when he had to deal with his uncle the Duke of Gloucester, with the Earl of Arundel and later the

Earl of Warwick, all of whom had played a prominent part in the conspiracy against his favourite, de Vere.

Gloucester, as we have seen, was smuggled out of the Tower through Traitors' Gate and murdered in Calais. Warwick, after dining with the King in the palace of the Lord Chancellor overlooking the river, was arrested as he rose to leave and taken to the Tower in a barge. Imprisoned in the tower which still bears his family name of Beauchamp—possibly in the sombre semi-octagonal room on the second storey, though his inscription is not among the many on the walls—he was released a year later, when Henry Bolingbroke became King. Warwick's life had been spared only because he had distinguished himself in the French wars under Edward III and Richard feared public indignation.

Arundel, taken to the Tower as a prisoner a little earlier, as we have seen, pleaded not guilty and offered to prove his innocence by the old feudal test of 'ordeal by battle'; this Richard refused to allow. As he was led out to the scaffold on Tower Hill, Arundel asked that the cords binding his hands be loosened, so that he might distribute such money as he possessed to the people who had come to see him die. We are not told whether the request was granted. Walking beside him were his son-in-law the Earl of Nottingham and his young nephew the Earl of Kent. Arundel turned to them and said, 'It would have been more seemly of you to have absented yourselves from this scene. The time will come when as many shall marvel at your misfortunes as you do at mine.' His prophecy was fulfilled not long afterwards.

CHAPTER SIXTEEN

The Ceremony of the Bath

In October 1399 Henry IV spent the night before his coronation in the Tower, as so many of his predecessors had done; but he introduced a ceremony that was to be kept up for some centuries. He conferred the Order of the Bath on forty-six of his followers whom he had singled out for knighthood. The custom was not new, but the ceremony was preceded on this occasion by the knights actually being given a bath. In the hall adjoining St John's Chapel on the second floor of the White Tower, forty-six bath tubs were set out, each with a luxurious canopy above it. The baths were filled with warm water and all the knights were made to get into the tubs. It is thought that, in an age when baths were not common, some kings did not relish coming too close to the men they were about to knight.

While they were in their tubs, King Henry entered at the head of a procession of priests and nobles. Going up to each of them in turn he made the sign of the Cross on the candidate's back and knighted him with these words: 'You shall honour God above all things; you shall be steadfast in the faith of Christ; you shall love the King your Sovereign Lord, and him and his right defend with all your power; you shall defend maidens, widows and orphans in their rights, and shall suffer no extortion, as far as you may prevent it; and of as great honour be this Order unto you, as ever it was to any of your progenitors or others.'

The King, the nobles and the priests then withdrew. The new knights got out of their tubs and were dried by their attendant squires. They were then escorted to forty-six beds, each hung with costly draperies; in these they rested for a time. When the curfew bell was rung in the Bell Tower, the knights rose, donned the long brown robes of monks and walked in procession to the adjoining chapel of St John. They knelt and prayed before

The Chapel of St John the Evangelist in the White Tower. Here the new Knights of the Bath kept night vigil before receiving their swords from the King on the morning of his coronation. (Ministry of Public Building and Works)

the high altar with the light of the candles flickering on their helmets, shields and armour, hung up on the walls. The knights remained in meditation throughout the long, cold October night, and at the end of the vigil each knight placed a lighted taper and a penny on the altar: the taper was for God, the penny for the King. Then they walked across the courtyard to the Palace to receive their swords from the King.

By now the coronation procession had begun to assemble. The chronicler Froissart provides a vivid description of it. 'The Duke of Lancaster [King Henry] left the Tower this Sunday after dinner, on his return to Westminster; he was bare-headed, and had round his neck the order of the King of France. The Prince of Wales [the future Henry V, now aged eleven], six dukes, eighteen barons accompanied him, and there were knights and other nobility, from 800 to 900 horse in the procession. He passed through the streets of London, which were all handsomely decorated with tapestries and other rich hangings; there were nine fountains in Cheapside and other streets he passed through, that ran perpetually with white and red wines. The whole cavalcade amounted to 6000 horse that escorted the Duke from the Tower to Westminster.' Some accounts say that the deposed King Richard was still in the Tower at that time and may even have seen the procession set out, for he was not removed to Pontefract Castle until after the coronation.

Henry IV's accession was the fulfilment of John of Gaunt's personal ambitions. Though the descendants of Lionel Duke of Clarence had a superior claim to the throne, Henry certainly enjoyed the support of Parliament; once again election replaced primogeniture. But the by-passing of the senior line sowed the seeds of the terrible Wars of the Roses, which were to cause havoc and suffering for the next eighty-six years and the tragic death of many rival contestants for the throne.

In the fourteen years of his reign Henry displayed many fine qualities of kingship. He was able and tolerant and, despite the wrongs to which he had been subjected, he avoided reprisals. From the outset he relied upon the support of Parliament, ruling 'by common advice, counsel and consent'. In consequence a further great advance was made in Parliament's rights: they not only voted the taxes, but insisted on knowing how the money was spent.

But things were by no means easy for Henry, and trouble was not long in coming. Although the country as a whole rejoiced at having him as King, highly placed supporters of Richard who found themselves in eclipse lost no time in plotting the new King's overthrow, and there were risings in various parts of the country. The Earls of Kent and Salisbury, the first to move, were attacked and put to death by the people of Cirencester. The Earl of Gloucester and Lord Lumley suffered similarly at Bristol. Sir Thomas Blount and twenty-nine other knights and squires were dealt with as brutally at Oxford.

When the Earl of Huntingdon, Henry's brother-in-law, joined the Bishop of Carlisle and some others in a fresh conspiracy, Henry claimed them as his prisoners and they were sent to the Tower. After five days Huntingdon was executed without trial and his head was stuck up on London Bridge, already crowded with the heads of other victims. The Church intervened on behalf of the Bishop; after a long imprisonment in the Tower, he was transferred to the custody of the Abbot of Westminster. A year or so later, Richard II now being dead, the Abbot of Winchelsea and Friar Roger Frisby were brought to the Tower with seven other monks for writing and circulating 'railing rhymes, malicious metres, and taunting verses against the King' with intent to rouse and incite the people to rebellion. They were implicated in a plot to put Sir Roger Clarendon, an illegitimate son of the Black Prince, on the throne. All were condemned to death. They were taken from their 'vile' cell in the Tower by cart to the gallows at Tyburn, where Marble Arch now stands. There they were hanged in the full view of the public as a warning and an example.

The next move was made by Edward Duke of York, son of John of Gaunt's brother Edmund of York. Both he and his father had helped Henry to attain the throne; but he was now drawn into a scheme concocted by his sister-in-law Anne Mortimer. Henry had in his care and strict custody Anne's brothers, the two Mortimer heirs of Lionel Duke of Clarence—Edmund, fifth Earl of March, who was seven, and his younger brother Roger. As members of the senior line, their claims to the throne were superior to Henry's own. With the assistance of their uncle Sir Edmund Mortimer they were to be taken from Windsor to Wales, where the young Earl was to be proclaimed King. The plot was discovered, however, and the Duke of York arrested and imprisoned in Pevensey Castle; he was later released.

Trouble with Wales followed. Sir Edmund

Mortimer's father-in-law, Owen Glendower, a descendant of Llewellyn the Great, seized the opportunity to start a rebellion. Welshmen flocked to his standard, even those employed in England, and others who were students at English universities returned home to support him. The revolt soon reached considerable proportions and it was feared that France and Scotland would join in and overthrow the newly established Lancastrian dynasty. Henry had to act promptly. At a battle in Monmouthshire, Glendower's son Griffin was taken prisoner, together with a number of other Welsh leaders; they were all brought to the Tower.

The war against Glendower continued nevertheless, and it was soon followed by an outbreak of trouble on the Scottish border. The two great rebel leaders in the north were the Earl of Northumberland and his son, known as 'Hotspur' because of his fiery temper. They had been Henry's staunch supporters and had helped him to the throne. But Hotspur was also an uncle by marriage of the young Earl of March, and with his father he now swung to the support of Glendower. However, his opposition was shortlived; he was killed in July 1403, in a small battle at Shrewsbury. In 1405 Northumberland rebelled again, failed once more and had to flee to Scotland. Hotspur's son joined his grandfather, and was for some years maintained by the Scots in

honourable captivity.

The King, though only in his forties, had begun to decline in health: he suffered from heart trouble and fainting fits. His son Prince Henry, just turned twenty, took control of the two wars and by his skill and brilliant leadership brought both to a successful conclusion.

Another prisoner of importance brought to the Tower was Prince James of Scotland, the son and heir of King Robert III, who was to be the ancestor of the Stuart Kings of England. He was not taken in battle, nor was he a hostage of war. The Prince, only nine years old at the time, was on his way to France for his education and was seized when his ship, running into bad weather, was driven ashore at Flamborough Head in Yorkshire in 1406. He was placed in the Tower, not as an honoured guest in receipt of courtesy and hospitality, but as a prisoner, together with his tutor the Earl of Orkney and his other attendants. It is said that when the news of this cruel treatment reached King Robert in Scotland he died of a broken heart. The boy thus became King James I of Scotland while in captivity—yet another King to be imprisoned in the Tower. He was kept there for two years and was then moved to Nottingham Castle, where he was a prisoner for a further sixteen years. Not until a ransom of 60,000 marks had been paid, in the reign of Henry VI of England, was King James released.

CHAPTER SEVENTEEN

Henry V Imprisons 'Falstaff'

The Tower of London had by now begun to play a new role as a substantial money-earner for the Exchequer. Its income, derived from the ransoms of prisoners of war, was to be considerably enhanced after Henry V inherited the throne from his father and embarked on his triumphant campaigns in France.

As we have seen, the Prince of Wales took over the reins of government while his father was still alive. Shakespeare views him as nothing but a frivolous reveller before he came to the throne, but this seems doubtful, for the calls made on him during his father's decline reveal his deep seriousness of purpose and clear understanding of statecraft. He never shirked his duties, whether on the field of battle or at the Council table. Indeed, so impressive were his varied talents, that those who worked with him during these years, especially Henry IV's three Beaufort half-brothers, sons of John of Gaunt's second marriage, urged the young Prince to persuade his father to abdicate and let him assume the full responsibility of government. This so enraged Henry IV that he instantly removed his son from his position of President of the Council and dismissed from office all who had supported the idea. The dying King had nearly two years still to live. Unable to walk, scarcely able to sit on a horse, he continually gabbled about going on a Crusade. In March 1413, while at prayer in Westminster Abbey, he had a stroke and died.

These two lost years, following his dismissal from responsibility, may well have been spent by 'Prince Hal' as 'a diligent follower of idle practices, much given to instruments of music, and fired with the torches of Venus herself'; certainly some of the contemporary chroniclers on whom Shakespeare drew held this opinion. On Henry V's accession, however, the mantle of responsibility was donned again and the air of authority at once assumed.

The new King, now twenty-five, tall, oval-faced, long-nosed and ruddy-complexioned, immediately moved into the Tower, travelling in great state; he rode through London with 'a great rout of lords and knights'. There was to be no delay in his coronation, he said; it was fixed for 9 April 1413, barely a fortnight after his father's death. The arrangements were made briskly. On the night before the traditional procession to Westminster Abbey, the new Knights of the Bath were assembled in the large hall alongside St John's Chapel and the young King carried out the ceremony of knighting precisely as his father had done, making the sign of the Cross on the back of each knight while he lay in his bath.

Before the night vigil had ended, there was a severe snowstorm. Adam of Usk records that snow 'fell upon the hill-country of the realm and smothered men and beasts and homesteads, and drowned out the valleys and the marshes in marvellous wise.' In London the wind blew fiercely and by dawn the entire city was white. Snow lay thick in the streets and on the low rooftops as the King and the long impressive procession of nobles, bishops and knights on horseback ploughed through it. The cheering thousands, gathered at the windows, on the slippery rooftops and in the streets, wondered what interpretation could be put upon this strange occurrence. Was it an omen for good or evil? Did it signify the blessing or the wrath of God?

There were, of course, sections of the community who had not been well disposed towards the young Prince during his father's lifetime. They consisted chiefly of churchmen who strongly

The worldliness of monasteries is exemplified in this illuminated initial of a cellarer monk drinking from one of his casks. From a thirteenth-century health manual of Aldebrandius of Siena. (By permission of the Trustees of the British Museum, MS Sloane 2435, fol. 44v)

disapproved of his early sympathy with a religious group known as the Lollards. This group aimed to carry out the reforms advocated thirty years earlier by the Oxford divine and preacher John Wycliffe, who denounced the great wealth of the Church, the worldliness of the monks and the clergy, and called for a campaign of purification. Such criticisms had been made for nearly two centuries by the Franciscans and other medicant friars. Wycliffe, pointing out that 'Christ during His life upon earth was of all men the poorest', advocated that all tithes paid to the Church should be used for the maintenance of the poor. His doctrines were condemned by the Archbishop of Canterbury; Wycliffe himself was brought to trial before the bishops in St Paul's Cathedral in 1377, and his followers were severely censured and ordered to recant. The Church's resolve to stamp out the menace was shared by the rich barons and merchants, who feared that popular criticism might soon be directed against their own wealth.

The Lollards went underground for a time, but the movement continued to spread, finding support among parish priests, artisans and craftsmen and in time even among the middle classes and numerous members of the gentry. It had many adherents in Kent, in the Midlands and the counties along the Welsh border. Eventually a joint assault upon the Lollards was launched by the Church and the great nobles, who declared that the movement was a threat to the whole fabric of society. Its members were branded as heretics because some of them had unwisely declared that the Host lifted at Mass was a dead thing, 'less than a toad or a spider'. Severe laws were passed against the Lollards, and their martyrs were brought to the Tower by the cart-load. Those who refused to recant were burnt at St Paul's Cross in front of the Cathedral. Henry IV's Archbishop of Canterbury, Thomas Arundel (brother of the Earl of Arundel whom Richard II had executed), was the fiercest opponent of the Lollards, and it is said that Henry V, at his coronation on that icy, snow-swept day, refused to allow Archbishop Arundel to crown him.

But not long afterwards Henry felt it was the King's duty to be 'the chief defender of the Holy Church'. This sudden reversal of policy brought cruel, even tragic consequences to many, and especially to one who had been the King's friend and boon companion, Sir John Oldcastle, depicted in Shakespeare's plays as 'Falstaff'. The date of Oldcastle's birth is not certain but he was a relatively young man at this time and not the aged figure we see on the stage, certainly not more than thirty-five—or about ten years older than the King. He was the son of Sir Richard Oldcastle of Herefordshire and met Henry, then Prince of Wales, while serving in the Welsh campaigns. He won the Prince's admiration and esteem, and was subsequently put in command of a section of the army the young Prince Henry sent to France. Oldcastle was later elected to Parliament. On marrying Joan, the heiress of Cobham, he was translated to the Upper House as Lord Cobham.

Oldcastle joined the Lollards in Herefordshire, where the group had a great many adherents. In 1410 the churches on his wife's large estate in Kent were laid under an interdict for unlicensed preaching, and three years later, a few days before Henry IV's death, Oldcastle himself was accused of heresy; but his close friendship with the new King prevented any action being taken against him. Not long afterwards a book belonging to Oldcastle was found in a shop in Paternoster Row in London—it was considered distinctly incriminating. The discovery was reported to the King, but he still insisted that no action should be taken. Instead, he sent for Oldcastle and urged him to give up his association with the

The first page of the Acts of the Apostles in Wycliffe's English translation of the Bible. The Lollards hoped to discourage abuses in the Church by bringing the teaching of God directly to the people, unhampered by ecclesiastical ceremony. (Mansell Collection)

Lollards. Oldcastle refused, saying that while he was prepared to place his entire fortune at the King's disposal, he could not give up his religious beliefs.

Henry hesitated no longer. The Church must be allowed to take action. A royal writ was issued for Oldcastle's arrest. He was seized in his castle at Cowling in Kent and was taken to the Tower. Tried by the ecclesiastical court in September 1413 (six months after Henry became King), he was convicted as a heretic. His fate was now sealed; the decree was that he must be bound to the stake and burned outside St Paul's 'for the good of his soul'. However, the King, still anxious to help him, ordered that no action should be taken for forty days: possibly he still hoped to persuade Oldcastle to recant.

During that time of waiting, the prisoner managed to escape. He may have been confined in the Beauchamp Tower, for it was sometimes referred to as the Cobham Tower. How he got out of it and eventually out of the main fortress is not known. The Church dignitaries, furious that their victim had eluded them, declared that the escape was accomplished with the aid of the Devil. From the records 'the Devil' appears to have been a London parchment-maker named William Fisher. It is known that after Oldcastle's escape, Fisher hid the fugitive for a time in his house in Smithfield. Fisher was arrested and hanged, but by then Oldcastle had escaped again. It has never been discovered what cunning plan was evolved by Fisher or how many of the guards were bribed (it is, of course, possible that some of them were Lollards, as Fisher himself undoubtedly was). Somehow he was spirited from his dungeon, smuggled across the heavily guarded inner enclosure of the Tower, then taken through the Bloody Tower gate, over the Outer Wall and across the wide water-filled moat. It is thought that the King connived at his escape.

But if Henry was disposed to be lax, Oldcastle certainly was not. Once out of London, he went furtively about the country furthering a Lollard plot to seize the King and his brothers during a Twelfth Night celebration at the King's palace at Eltham in Kent, which Edward II had once given to Queen Isabella. Oldcastle had to act swiftly, for he did not escape until the end of October and Twelfth Night was only a few weeks away. It was his purpose, according to general belief, to abolish the monarchy and set up a Commonwealth, as Cromwell did two centuries later.

The plot was worked out with meticulous care. A group of Lollards were to go to Eltham as mummers on Twelfth Night and carry out their plan during the revels. Earlier that day, in preparation, they moved into a house bearing the sign of 'The Axe without Cripplegate'. However, the plot was revealed to the King by a carpenter. Henry immediately left Eltham with his brothers, the Archbishop of Canterbury and others of his retinue. Orders were issued for the gates of London to be closed, and at ten o'clock that night Henry set out from Westminster Palace with a large body of armed men and hid in the woods near St Giles's Fields, where the Lollards were to assemble to await the arrival of the mummers from Eltham. Meanwhile a group of the King's men raided 'The Axe without Cripplegate' and arrested the conspirators. As soon as the Lollards had gathered in St Giles's Fields, Henry and his men-at-arms sprang out of the woods and seized them. Some were killed, others captured and taken to the Tower. Oldcastle once again managed to escape. Hiding in villages and woods, he made his way by stages to his native county of Herefordshire on the Welsh border, and though a continuous search was carried out, he succeeded in evading capture for close on four years. Again and again his pursuers came very near to seizing him. He was known to be in St Albans, hiding in a peasant's cottage, but he got away before his captors could reach him. He reappeared in Pontefract and once again evaded the net. During these years of pursuit, Oldcastle never missed an opportunity of hatching fresh plots to dethrone Henry. He was closely involved with a group of Scottish insurgents whose leader claimed to be King Richard II.

Eventually Oldcastle's hiding place at Welshpool, in Wales, was discovered, and a body of armed men under the command of Lord Charlton of Powys closed in on it. There was a struggle, and Oldcastle was 'sore wounded ere he would be taken'. He was brought to London and once again imprisoned in the Tower. The charges against him now were far more serious, for in addition to heresy he was accused of treason, and was duly condemned to death. He was taken to St Giles's Fields, where his Lollard followers had assembled for the Twelfth Night plot, and was there hanged and then burnt, 'gallows and all'.

When Shakespeare's play *Henry IV* was first performed, he was portrayed under his real name of Oldcastle; later, because of his family's objections, this was altered to Falstaff.

CHAPTER EIGHTEEN

The Exalted Prisoner from Agincourt

Apart from maintenance and repairs, no major work appears to have been carried out at the Tower of London during the reign of either Henry IV or Henry V. About this time the Wharf was replaced by a stone structure, but it is apparent from the records that the work was carried out by stages and spread out over a long period. We have seen how Edward III extended the original earth and timber construction and provided for its partial rebuilding in stone in 1365–6. A quarter of a century later, in June 1389, when Richard II was King and Geoffrey Chaucer was Clerk of the King's Works, the section stretching eastwards from the water-gate to beyond St Katherine's was rebuilt. It is likely that a still further extension of the Wharf beyond the eastern section of the moat to a small tower (of which no details are available) by the Iron Gate, was begun, and possibly completed, by Henry IV or Henry V. This 'small tower' was apparently put up as an additional guard at the eastern exit, where the Develin Tower already stood. Though there are no details, it is known that Henry IV had a new drawbridge made 'beneath the tower called the Garettoure next the gate towards St Katherine': the word 'garetta' was then used to describe a small turret. From time to time the moat was drained and cleaned— a necessary task since the drainage of London was emptied into it; but even so part of the sediment remained and the stench was often overpowering.

Alterations were carried out to the various residential buildings erected by Edward III. One of these was for the chaplains, built near the Chapel of St Peter ad Vincula. Another was for the Constable; for its windows 105 feet of glass were purchased, 'worked with fleurs-de-lys and borders of the King's arms'. Particulars survive of the expenditure on some of these repairs carried out by the two Henrys, but the frequent changes of the names of the various towers make it difficult to identify them today.

The development of gunpowder and cannon during the fifteenth century greatly reduced the defensive strength of the Tower; it was consequently much more a prison than a fortress, and its dungeons were brought into the fullest use. This trend began under Henry IV, and was accentuated in the succeeding reign.

Like his father, Henry V regularly consulted Parliament. No law, he declared, would be passed without its assent. All the liberties of the Church, of the barons and of the towns were confirmed. A policy of wide and generous conciliation was adopted, untempered, as it had of necessity been in his usurping father's reign, by savage repression, but calculated to prevent all further uprisings. He began by granting a general pardon. The King had already restored the Mortimer estates to his cousin the Earl of March; now the Earl was invited to court. Henry negotiated with the Scots for the release of Hotspur's son and reinstated him as Earl of Northumberland; it was also he who brought the body of Richard II back to London to be buried in Westminster Abbey.

A soldier by instinct and upbringing, Henry realized that the surest way of resolving difficulties at home was by embarking on a war against France. For some years England had not been involved in any Continental entanglements. France had ceased to be a menace. Since the French King Charles VI was feeble-minded, his younger brother Louis, Duke of Orléans, had taken over the government of the country. But the murder of Orléans in a Paris street, instigated by the King's cousin the Duke of Burgundy, had

*Late fifteenth-century iron cannon in the Tower Armouries.
Equipped with rings for lifting and for being secured to its
bed, this example has an exceptionally large fore-sight and
a calibre of 6 in. (Ministry of Public Building and Works)*

led to war between the two factions. Burgundy appealed to England for help, but Henry, then Prince, could send only a small contingent. He now agreed to come to Burgundy's aid provided that he was recognized as the rightful King of France. He based his claim on his descent from Isabella, the Queen of Edward II, who belonged to a senior branch of the French royal family. Burgundy unhesitatingly gave him this assurance.

Henry summoned the Council of State and Parliament, and received their fullest support. Success, they saw, would bring an ample reward, both from the annexation of territory and from an expansion of trade. The House of Commons voted abundant financial aid.

The preparations for the war were long and thorough. Henry reorganized the navy, not only by taking over and arming privately owned ships, but by building a number of 'great ships' and about 1500 smaller vessels. The army was specially picked and trained. Long-bowmen formed its backbone, reinforced by 2500 knights in armour, each with his men-at-arms. In all, about 10,000 fighting men sailed from Southampton on 11 August 1415. The young Earl of March, now aged twenty-two, went with the expedition, for just before it embarked, a plot had been discovered to murder the King and his brothers and place the Earl on the throne.

Crossing the Channel, the King and his army landed at the mouth of the Seine. He needed a base on the coast and found Harfleur ideally suited for the purpose. He had come prepared to lay siege to the town, with miners, carpenters and numerous engines of attack as well as artillery. It is almost certain that these cannon were fired by gunpowder, for in the forty years or so since the Battle of Poitiers, continual efforts had been made

to replace the mechanically fired cannon by this new method, and by now enormous cannon were being made. There was an iron foundry in the Tower, and other, possibly larger, cannon were being made in foundries in Sussex. They were cast in small tubular sections and linked together by bulky bands that stuck out like ribs. That was the finished article; when required for firing, it was mounted on stout iron trestles, one at each end. At a much later date the cannon were given wheels.

Henry V took with him to Harfleur twenty-five 'master gunners' and fifty 'servitor gunners', the master being the captain of the gun and the others forming a team of two for each cannon. It would appear from this that the number of cannon shipped to Harfleur was twenty-five. The tradition persists, and there is a basis of truth in it, that when the French Dauphin heard that Henry V was getting ready to invade France, he sent the English King a gift of tennis balls. Henry's reply was, 'I shall soon bandy him some London-made balls that will rip the roof off his hall and batter his walls to the ground.'

Harfleur was strongly fortified, with walls and a moat and two towers on each side of the entrance (though it was by no means as strong as the Tower of London); the land around had been flooded to keep the attackers at bay. The sun was hot and the soggy ground became a fever-bed. Dysentery soon broke out among the English forces. Henry encircled the swamp with troops; bringing his guns into position, he ordered his brother, Humphrey Duke of Gloucester, to keep up a continuous bombardment. After two months Harfleur surrendered, and the banners of St George and England fluttered above the gates of the town. The sick and the wounded, numbering many thousand, were taken to the waiting ships and sent back to England, together with a large number of hostages who were imprisoned in the Tower of London.

With his army severely depleted by sickness, Henry considered his next move with care and caution. He decided to march along the coast to Calais, which had been in English hands for half a century. For most of the way he was unmolested, but near Agincourt he found the French army across his path, barring the way ahead. It was a formidable force, outnumbering his by nearly four to one. One of his officers, bemoaning that there were idle men enough in England to adjust the odds, was rebuked sharply by Henry: 'Wot you not that the Lord with these few can overthrow the pride of the French?' Shakespeare records this in unforgettable words. In his play *Henry V*, the Earl of Westmoreland says,

O that we now had here
But one ten thousand of those men in England
That do no work today!

The Battle of Agincourt, with the English on the right, under the banner of St George. The artist has depicted long-bowmen in both armies, but in fact the range and onslaught of the English arrows took the French by surprise and contributed largely to their defeat. (Bibliothèque Nationale, Paris. Photo Falquet)

to which Henry replies,

If we are marked to die, we are enow
To do our country loss; and if to live,
The fewer men, the greater share of honour.

The English troops, aware of the possibility of their complete annihilation, were quiet on that fateful eve of battle, but all night long the French held high revelry and diced for the hostages that would be theirs.

Early the next morning, 25 October 1415, St Crispin's Day, Henry V donned his royal cloak decorated with leopards and lilies and went among his men mounted on a small grey horse. Upon his helmet was a richly jewelled crown. When he returned, he dismounted and ordered his entire cavalry to dismount too. Then, after waiting in vain for the French to attack, he gave his order in a loud clear voice, 'In the name of Almighty God and St George, Avaunt Bannerer!'

It had rained heavily for the last ten days, and the sodden land between the two armies had been reduced to a quagmire by the French baggage train. But the sun came out that morning and the day was bright and clear. Henry had no intention of being taken prisoner; he realized that the ransom would cripple England's finances. There was just a chance of winning, and that chance he

was prepared to take. He moved his long-bowmen forward; as was their custom, they drove their heavy iron-pointed stakes into the ground a few yards in front of them, in case the French cavalry decided to charge. They then released volley after volley of their deadly arrows.

The French cavalry charged the archers, and the arrows continued their devastation. The French horses sank into the quagmire and the armoured knights toppled down in great heaps, the dead and the wounded piled upon each other in appalling confusion. The archers then slung their bows behind them, drew from their belts their axes and iron-shod mallets and closed in. Vast numbers of prisoners were taken.

Then suddenly, while the hand-to-hand fighting went on, the French camp-followers broke into the rear of the English lines and attacked the royal baggage train, stealing the King's crown, the Great Seal and such other loot as they could find. Henry, thinking that a fresh French force had begun to attack from the rear, decided he could take no chances and ordered that all the French prisoners must be put to death. The English knights hesitated, for every prisoner represented a huge ransom. The King, brooking no delay, sent two hundred of his own guards to carry out the slaughter. Only the most exalted members of the French nobility were spared. The Battle of Agincourt lasted less than three hours, and ranks as the most memorable victory ever won by an English army.

Henry resumed his march to Calais and returned to England with 1500 prisoners. Among them was the French King's nephew, Charles Duke of Orléans (son of the murdered Duke Louis), the Duke of Bourbon, the Counts of Vendôme and Eu, and Marshal de Boucicault. Among the dead left on the battlefield were the great D'Albret, Constable of France, three dukes, many counts, about three hundred barons and knights and about five thousand French men-at-arms, mostly of noble birth. Of the English army only the Duke of York, the Earl of Suffolk and about a hundred and fifty archers and men-at-arms were killed.

Arriving at Dover, Henry went straight on to London, and rode through the crowded, cheering streets with his prisoners and the spoils of victory. He insisted on wearing just a plain dress and refused to allow his 'bruised helmet and bended sword' to be borne in the procession 'lest they should forget that the glory was due to God alone'. The King and his chief prisoners went into St Paul's, where fourteen bishops sang the *Te Deum*. He then left for his Palace at Westminster. The prisoners were taken to the Tower, where the Duke of Bourbon, the Marshal and a number of other prisoners were to die in captivity.

But by far the most important of those brought back from Agincourt was the Duke of Orléans. Aged only twenty-four, he was one of the joint Commanders-in-Chief of the French army. He was rescued from among the heaps of dead and dying on the battlefield, and his wounds, according to one account, were so serious that he was fortunate to be still alive. He was given medical treatment and brought to the Tower. His younger brother Jean of Angoulême was also taken prisoner. His captor was Sir Richard Waller, lord of the manor of Groombridge in Kent; he was taken to Groombridge Place where he was confined under a strong guard in a nearby house on the estate. But the Duke of Orléans, the King insisted, must be held as a prisoner of the Crown, no matter who his actual captor had been. An enormous ransom was demanded for his release, and since it could not be raised for some years the Duke remained as a prisoner in the White Tower for a quarter of a century.

One reason for Henry's concern was the Duke's nearness to the French throne, which the English King himself claimed. Charles of Orléans had married his cousin Isabella, daughter of Charles VI of France and widow of Richard II of England; he was only fifteen at the time of the marriage and she, two years his senior, had brought him a dowry of half a million francs. Henry IV had tried to prevent the marriage, as he would have liked the link with England to be maintained and doubtless thought of his own heir as her bridegroom. Eventually Henry V married her younger sister Katherine. Isabella died three years after her marriage to the Duke of Orléans, leaving a daughter aged two.

By temperament the young Duke was quite unsuited to a military life. He was chiefly interested in literature and spent his time as a prisoner writing poems, many of which were later published. Some of these were written in English, and the great critic George Saintsbury comments, 'They exhibit something of the smoothness of versification not uncommon in those who write, with care, a language not their own.' But the bulk of his work consists of hundreds of short poems written in French and it is obvious from their content that many were written in the Tower. 'He is a capital example,' adds Saintsbury, 'of the cultivated and refined—it may almost be called the lettered—chivalry of the last chivalrous age, expert to the utmost degree in carrying out the traditional details of a graceful convention in love and literature . . . His best-known roundels—those on Spring, on the Harbingers of Summer, and others—rank second to nothing of their kind.'

A magnificently bound copy of these poems was given by King Henry VII of England to his bride Elizabeth of York on their marriage at the end of the Wars of the Roses in 1485. The book has a beautiful illumination in colour, in lovely blues, reds and gold with only the White Tower painted white, depicting in chronological perspective almost the entire history of the Duke of Orléans's imprisonment in that building. Robert Louis Stevenson describes this picture: 'It gives a view of London with all its spires, the river passing through the old bridge, and busy with boats. One side of the White Tower has been taken out, and we can see, as under a sort of shrine, the paved room where the Duke sits writing. He occupies a high-backed bench in front of a great chimney: red and black ink are before him, and the upper end of the apartment is guarded by many halberdiers, with the red cross of England on their breasts. On the next side of the Tower he appears again, leaning out of the window and gazing on the river. Doubtless, there blows just then "a pleasant wind from out the land of France", and some ships come up the river, "the ship of good news". At the door we find him yet again, this time embracing a messenger, while a groom stands by holding two saddled horses. And yet further to the left, a cavalcade defiles out of the Tower; the Duke is on his way at last towards "the sunshine of France".'

The Duke had to wait for his release until November 1440—twenty-five years after the Battle of Agincourt—by which time Henry VI was on the throne of England. Orléans was extremely well treated. Not only was he kept in great luxury in the Tower, but from time to time he was taken out hunting or hawking at Windsor, Pontefract and elsewhere, always, of course, with a very strong guard around him. But despite the respect and honour paid to him, the Duke chafed incessantly against his imprisonment. He was released on the payment of 80,000 *saluts d'or*, equal to about £50,000 then and to about a million pounds now; and that was not all, for he had to sign an agreement to pay a further 140,000 crowns later to complete his ransom. The Duke of Burgundy had by then patched up a peace with France, and on his release Orléans married Burgundy's niece Mary of Cleves (a relative of Henry VIII's wife, Anne of Cleves); her enormous dowry enabled Orléans to pay the rest of his ransom money. A further sum was required for his brother Jean, who was held for all those years as a prisoner at Groombridge.

What the Duke felt about his stay in the Tower is on record. Speaking after his release at the trial of the Duke of Alençon, he said, 'I have had experience myself, and in my prison of England, for the weariness, danger, and displeasure in which I then lay, I have many a time wished I had been slain at the battle where they took me.'

CHAPTER NINETEEN

Joan of Arc Plans the Duke of Orléans's Rescue from the Tower

Henry V reigned only nine years. Seven years after Agincourt he was dead. He had conquered all Normandy, held sway over the whole of northern France from Brittany to the Netherlands, and had even taken Paris; he also had Gascony in the south, which England had never lost. On his marriage to Katherine, the daughter of Charles VI of France, he was proclaimed Regent of France during Charles's lifetime and successor to the French throne; the Dauphin was disinherited. In 1422, while engaged in a campaign to hold what he had won, Henry died of a strange 'malady'; many people believed that he had been poisoned. He was only thirty-four. His son, an infant only nine months old, was proclaimed Henry VI of England; seven weeks later, on the death of his French grandfather Charles, he became King of France as well.

Troubles had been mounting in the last years of Henry V's reign and they were not lessened by the accession of a child. On his deathbed Henry had appointed his two brothers as Protectors: John Duke of Bedford, to rule over France, and Humphrey Duke of Gloucester, to rule over England. Bedford, a fine administrator, carried on with the work Henry had begun there as Regent.

But although the succession of the infant English King was not challenged by the Parisians or the Burgundians, to loyal and patriotic Frenchmen everywhere the Dauphin Charles was now Charles VII, the true King of France and the focus of their national aspirations. He had full control of all the territory south of the Loire except Gascony, and it was obvious that war between the English King of France and the Dauphin was inevitable. To the Dauphin's standard flocked large numbers of Scots, for the alliance between Scotland and France had never faltered. The Scottish King, James I, captured

Henry VI, in a contemplative attitude which was typical of his gentle, unassuming personality. From an early sixteenth-century window in the Chapel of King's College, Cambridge, Henry's own foundation. (Ramsey and Muspratt)

89

Joan of Arc is brought before the Dauphin at Chinon. Medieval illuminators frequently depicted her in woman's clothes, but on this occasion she is known to have worn male attire. From the contemporary Chroniques de France *by Monstrelet, c. 1428. (By permission of the Trustees of the British Museum. MS Royal D.VIII, fol. 7)*

with his tutor while on the way to France, was still a prisoner in the Tower, and Henry V had brought him to Paris to witness his marriage to Katherine. It was not till 1424, two years after Henry V's death, that King James was finally released. The enormous ransom of 60,000 marks paid for his release was intended to cripple Scotland's national Exchequer. By way of ensuring his loyalty to England, Henry VI's guardians made his release conditional on his marrying an Englishwoman. This the young man was quite prepared to do, for he was already in love with Lady Joan Beaufort, daughter of the Earl of Somerset and granddaughter of John of Gaunt. They were married in London in what is now known as Southwark Cathedral.

The situation in France was greatly worsened by the behaviour of Henry V's other brother, Humphrey Duke of Gloucester, who was Protector in England. A self-indulgent and acquisitive man, he enraged the Duke of Burgundy, England's most powerful ally in France, by invading Hainault and marrying Burgundy's niece Jacqueline of Holland and Hainault, who had already been betrothed to the Duke's cousin.

When he grew up, Henry VI proved a weak and

pathetic figure, in complete contrast to his father. From his French grandfather Charles VI he had inherited a strain of madness and was interested only in dedicating his life to piety. His uncle the Dauphin Charles was not unlike him in many respects; the eleventh child of the mad Charles VI, he too was weak and devoted to religion. More than anything he dreaded the battles with the English that seemed to go on endlessly. To his aid came an unknown peasant girl, who was to win renown as Joan of Arc. The daughter of a farmer on the edge of the Vosges forest, she had spent her youth serving wine to travellers in the town of Domrémy. Urged by the voices of saints in the woods to go and lead her country's forces to victory, she made a perilous journey across France and was taken to see the Dauphin.

The belief that she was guided by supernatural powers made a tremendous impact not only on his court but on his troops. Dressed in male attire and armour, she rode at the head of a French force to relieve the town of Orléans, which the English had surrounded. The bastard half-brother of the Duke of Orléans (still a prisoner in the White Tower) contrived to get her into the town, and she herself led the storming party against the English. The bastilles, or blockhouses, built by the English around Orléans fell one by one and the town was relieved. She now urged the Dauphin to march on Rheims to be crowned King of France. Dangerous though the venture was, he obeyed; his coronation was solemnized in the country's traditional setting. One of her most cherished ambitions was to free the Duke of Orléans from the Tower of London, for she believed that only he could rid France of the English conqueror. The Almighty had selected the Duke for this task, she said, and she was herself prepared to cross the Channel and rescue him; but she was restrained from making

the attempt. When Orléans returned to France, Joan of Arc had been dead for nine years.

With the crown securely on his head, the Dauphin lost interest in Joan. He was now the anointed King of France and the Archbishop of Rheims's warning that the girl was nothing but a hysterical fanatic fell on receptive ears. Inadequately supported in her attempt to relieve Compiègne, near Paris, Joan was captured by the Burgundians and sold to the English for the sum of 10,000 livres.

The English had attributed all their troubles of the preceding twelvemonth to this girl's alleged witchcraft, and they were now resolved to establish that Charles VII had won his crown not with the help of God but with that of the Devil. In December 1430 Joan was taken to Rouen to be tried for witchcraft and heresy. The French King did nothing to rescue or help her. When condemned to be burned unless she recanted, Joan broke down and 'confessed' that her visions were delusions and that she had sinned by wearing man's dress and shedding blood. Four days later she withdrew her confession and insisted that the voices were real. On 30 May 1431 she was burned at the stake in the market place at Rouen.

The Hundred Years' War between England and France, which had begun in the reign of Edward III, nevertheless dragged on for another twenty years, by which time Henry VI was thirty. It ended with the loss of almost all the English possessions in France, including Gascony, which the kings of England had held for three hundred years. All that remained was the town of Calais.

This brought to an end the flow of French and other Continental prisoners to the Tower. In future the prisoners were chiefly Englishmen; the Wars of the Roses provided an ample harvest, with most tragic consequences to the nobility and almost all the members of the royal family.

CHAPTER TWENTY

Execution at Sea

Interior of King's College Chapel, Cambridge, looking west. Begun by Henry VI and completed under the Tudors, the Chapel measures 289 by 44½ ft. and is 80 ft. high. The vaulting, by John Wastell, was completed in 1515. (National Monuments Record)

In 1429, when Henry VI was a child of eight, he was taken in the traditional procession from the Tower to Westminster Abbey to be crowned; a few months later he was crowned again, this time in Paris as King of France.

At first he showed a precocious interest in affairs of State and from the age of fifteen regularly attended all meetings of the Council. But he was no match for his uncles and great-uncles who dominated it. Gentle by nature, he tried again and again to bring about a compromise between the rival factions in the Council, but was not strong enough to exercise his influence. They treated him as a devout simpleton and he soon began to turn his attention to other things. Before he was twenty he had founded both Eton College and King's College, Cambridge.

Fierce rivalries now began to develop between the two branches of John of Gaunt's family, descendants of his two marriages. Henry IV was Gaunt's son by his first marriage to Blanche of Lancaster. Henry V and his brothers John of Bedford and Humphrey of Gloucester now represented this branch of the Lancastrians. The other branch consisted of the three illegitimate sons of John of Gaunt borne by Katherine Swynford, wife of Sir Hugh Swynford and sister-in-law of the poet Chaucer. The eldest of these sons was twenty-three by the time their parents were married, and they were then legitimized by their cousin Richard II and yet again by their half-brother Henry IV. Uncles of Henry V and great-uncles of the boy-King Henry VI, they bore the family name of Beaufort.

Humphrey of Gloucester, Protector of England while his brother Bedford ruled France, was fiercely opposed by the most powerful of the Beauforts—Henry, Bishop of Winchester, who had been appointed Chancellor at the early age of twenty-six by his half-brother Henry IV and had served his nephew Henry V in the same capacity; he was in consequence a most important member of the Council. After Henry V's death he persistently and vigorously opposed his nephew Gloucester; the Protector, though an able administrator, was self-indulgent and notorious for his many love affairs. But the Londoners liked and supported Gloucester, as indeed did most of the townspeople of England, because though a great landowner himself, his sympathies were with the traders. For some years the export of raw wool from England had been stopped because looms had been set up in the country; and only as manufactured cloth was it allowed to be exported. This trade was largely in the hands of English merchants. Beaufort, a man of immense wealth, on the other hand, supported the foreign traders. A conflict was inevitable and it soon developed. In 1424, while Gloucester was absent on the Hainault expedition, Beaufort, fearing an outbreak of rioting between the English and foreign traders, instructed the Lieutenant of the Tower, who was also the Deputy Constable, to strengthen the Tower's defences and increase the guard. When Gloucester returned to England, on the instructions of Beaufort he was refused admission to the Tower.

Furious at this rebuff, Gloucester, no longer Protector after the King came of age, decided to bide his time. He did nothing all that summer, but at the Lord Mayor's banquet at the Guildhall on 29 October 1426, he informed the newly elected Mayor that Beaufort had assembled a large body of archers and men-at-arms at Southwark, just across the river, and advised him to take immediate precautions to prevent an attack on London.

All that night a strong guard was kept on London Bridge, and when Beaufort's men tried to enter, their way was barred. The archers and men-at-arms attempted to force their way through but 'all London,' the chronicler records, 'rose with the Duke of Gloucester against the Bishop'. The Londoners were about to cross the river, seize Beaufort and bring him back as their prisoner when the Archbishop of Canterbury intervened and made peace between the two factions.

The matter was then brought before Parliament. There Gloucester accused Beaufort of treason, specifying that he had at one time plotted to murder Henry V. Unable to answer the charges satisfactorily, Beaufort retaliated by accusing Gloucester of neglecting to garrison the Tower.

The outcome was the defeat of Beaufort. He resigned from his position as Chancellor and made a show of being reconciled to Gloucester. But that unfortunately did not end the quarrel between uncle and nephew, which continued for some time, first one scoring, then the other.

If the issue had been confined to bickering within the family, the country might have been spared the consequences, but the nobles soon began to range themselves behind the two contestants and the situation took on a broader and more dangerous aspect. By now the war in France had ended. Disillusionment and anger were sweeping through England at the loss of so great an empire won by so tremendous a sacrifice of both life and wealth. The staggering victory of Henry V at Agincourt and his vast conquests had all been cast away, and the country's hostility was centred on Beaufort and his chief lieutenant the Duke of Suffolk, who had negotiated the peace with France. The soldiers back from the French wars were eagerly enrolled by the nobles in their private armies, each distinguished by its own livery. Not for one moment would a strong king like Henry II or Edward I, and least of all Edward III, have tolerated this. Henry VI, weak and ineffective, was no more than a shuttlecock between the rival Lancastrian factions.

In addition, there was a branch of the royal family with an even stronger claim to the throne than the Lancastrians—the house of York, which until now had for the most part been quiescent and co-operative. In order to follow the course of the Wars of the Roses it is important to separate the two strands of this tangled skein. Edward III had seven sons, of whom five survived. As we have seen, the eldest was the Black Prince, whose son became King as Richard II. When the childless Richard was deposed, however, it was in favour of Henry IV, son of Edward's third son John of Gaunt, bypassing the Mortimer descendants of Edward's second son Lionel Duke of Clarence. The fourth son was Edmund Duke of York; by the marriage of his younger son Richard to Anne Mortimer, Lionel's great-granddaughter, the York family inherited the Mortimer claim to the throne. (See family tree on p. 94.)

It is interesting to see that the descendants of that Roger Mortimer who was the lover of Queen Isabella in the Tower were now the legitimate heirs of Edward II, whom Mortimer is believed to have murdered.

So far, although others had pressed its claim, this senior line had done nothing to assert itself.

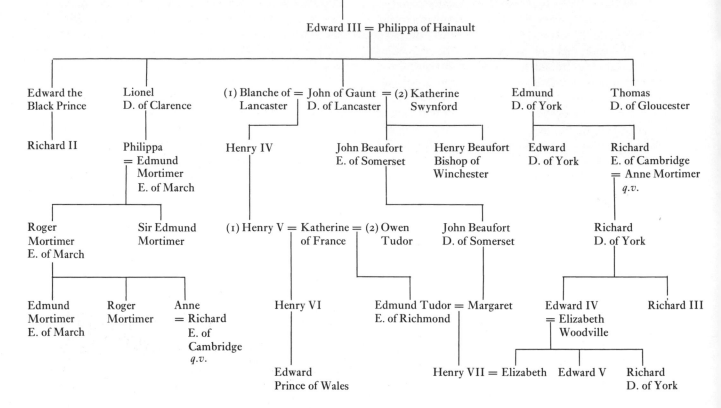

Houses of Lancaster and York in the Wars of the Roses

Its head was Edmund Mortimer, fifth Earl of March, who had served with Henry V in the French wars. His cousin (or possibly his uncle) Sir John Mortimer was one of Henry V's naval captains, and was involved in a plot in 1421 to assert Edmund's right to the throne; the plot was discovered and he was sent to the Tower. In the following April, like his ancestor Roger, he escaped, together with Thomas Payne, the secretary of Sir John Oldcastle (Falstaff), who had been a prisoner there for some years. Sir John Mortimer was soon recaptured and was eventually taken back to the Tower. To dispose of him finally, one of the Lieutenant's servants was instructed to urge him to escape again, and the attempt was made two months later. Sir John got out of his cell and made a dash for Tower Wharf where he found the guard waiting for him; in the ensuing struggle he was badly wounded. Once more in the Tower, he was accused by the Lieutenant's servant of plotting to raise an insurrection in Wales and of seeking help from the French Dauphin. At his trial at the Guildhall he was

found guilty of wilful escape, but this was altered to high treason by Parliament and Sir John was taken from the Tower and hanged at Tyburn. By now Henry VI was King, and in 1423 March was appointed Lieutenant of Ireland to keep him out of the way. There he died in 1425. The Mortimer inheritance passed to Richard Duke of York, son of his sister Anne. He was only a boy at the time, but his importance was enhanced by the fact that he was also the ward of the powerful Humphrey Duke of Gloucester. The ageing Henry Beaufort, now a Cardinal, was ready to challenge them both. For a while he bided his time but in 1435 Gloucester's brother, John Duke of Bedford, died; the Cardinal decided that Gloucester must now also be disposed of.

In 1441 the Beauforts wreaked a strange vengeance on Gloucester, striking through his wife Eleanor Cobham, who had previously been his mistress for many years. She was charged with conspiring to take the King's life by sorcery with the intention of placing her husband on the throne. Arrested with her were the Canon of

94

Westminster, Thomas Southwell, and two priests who were accused of helping her to make a wax figure of Henry VI so that it would waste away when exposed to heat and the King would then die. Imprisoned in the Tower, she was later tried by a special commission appointed by the Beauforts, found guilty and ordered to walk barefoot through the streets of London for three days as a penance. She was then sent to the Isle of Wight in perpetual banishment. Gloucester, powerless to help her, withdrew from public life and started the Oxford University Library, the nucleus of which was the very valuable collection of books he had brought back from the Louvre in Paris.

Now the Cardinal called to his aid William de la Pole, Duke of Suffolk, once a soldier and more recently the able administrator who had been sent to France in 1444 to arrange the marriage of the twenty-three-year-old Henry VI with Margaret of Anjou, the penniless niece of the King of France. The Hundred Years' War dragged on, and parts of France still remained under English sovereignty. Suffolk, backed by Beaufort, secretly agreed that as part of the marriage settlement the whole of the province of Maine would be transferred by Henry VI to the girl's father. This northern province had for centuries been the home of the English Plantagenet kings, and it was one of the most fertile of the French provinces.

Falconry, one of the Devonshire hunting tapestries made in Tournai between 1425 and 1450. This detail may represent the courting of Margaret of Anjou by Henry VI's proxy Suffolk. The lady on the white horse may be Margaret *herself: her dress and harness are ornamented with the letter 'M' (for Marguerite) and her collar is patterned in daisies (marguerites). (Victoria and Albert Museum)*

Beaufort realized that when the secret leaked out, the people, already enraged by the great loss of territory in France, would rise against him and would rally round Gloucester as their leader. So Gloucester had to be removed at once.

A meeting of Parliament was called. Gloucester, leaving his books, arrived to attend the session and was immediately arrested. Five days later it was announced that he had died of a paralytic stroke. Not for a moment was the country prepared to believe that its idol, the brother of their victorious King Henry V, had died a natural death. The English were convinced that he had been murdered, and accusing fingers pointed unhesitatingly at Suffolk, who had succeeded Beaufort as Chancellor and was known to be the main agent of Beaufort's villainies. The Cardinal himself died six weeks later, but Suffolk remained, and a vast number of people, peers as well as commoners, were far too devoted to Gloucester to let the matter rest there. The murder, if it was murder, was an act of grave folly, for with Gloucester dead, his ward young Richard of York inevitably stepped into his place.

When it was learned that Maine had been given away, Suffolk was doomed. Parliament was summoned and the Commons, through the Speaker, petitioned the King. Suffolk was charged with treason, accused of taking bribes to release the Duke of Orléans from the Tower, of surrendering Maine, and of betraying secrets to the French. He was then removed to the Tower.

His friends appealed to the King. Grateful for the devoted bride Suffolk had found for him, Henry released him after a short confinement; but, unwilling wholly to disregard the decision of Parliament, he banished Suffolk from the country for five years. Suffolk sailed from Ipswich for Calais in April 1450, but was intercepted off Dover by some warships led by the *Nicholas of the Tower*. He was taken off in a boat and brought before the master of the *Nicholas*, who received him with the words: 'Welcome, traitor!' The *Nicholas of the Tower* was attached to the service of the young Duke of Exeter, Admiral of England, Constable of the Tower of London and son-in-law of the Duke of York.

The captain and officers tried Suffolk on the very charges brought in his impeachment, which suggests that the warships had been sent for the express purpose of seizing him. He was found guilty and condemned to death. A description of his execution, written three days later, appears in one of the *Paston Letters*: 'And in the sight of all his men he was drawn out of the great ship into the boat, and there was an axe and a stock, and one of the lewdest of the ship bade him lay down his head that he should be fairly ferd [dealt] with, and die on a sword; and took a rusty sword and smote off his head with half a dozen strokes, and took away his gown of russet, and his doublet of velvet mailed, and laid his body on the sands of Dover: and some say his head was set on a pole by it.'

CHAPTER TWENTY-ONE

Henry VI a Prisoner in the Tower

Events now moved briskly. On 31 May 1450, within a few weeks of Suffolk's execution, a rebellion occurred in Kent. It recalled to many the Peasants' Revolt under Wat Tyler, which had also broken out in Kent less than seventy years earlier. The leader this time was Jack Cade, who claimed that his real name was John Mortimer. The demand again was for the removal of the King's 'evil counsellors' (chief of whom, until their deaths, were Beaufort and Suffolk), with these particular additions: the punishment of those concerned in Gloucester's death and in the loss of the French possessions.

For some years there had been grave and growing distress in many parts of the country. The prolonged war on the Continent had led to ever higher taxation and a constant rise in prices. In the towns the facilities given to foreign traders by Beaufort and Suffolk had cut deeply into the business done by the English, and foreign craftsmen and artisans had been arriving in large numbers and taking away work from skilled native craftsmen. In the country districts the land had suffered from severe frost, followed by bad harvests. The price of corn rose sharply; 'men ate more beans, pease and barley than ever was eaten before'. Farm wages were reduced, and the workers left their employers to go to the towns, although there was little employment to be found.

Cade's followers began their march on London in an orderly fashion, but the King, unlike Richard II, did not go out to talk to them; instead, on the advice of his Treasurer Lord Say, he sent a large body of armed men to attack and scatter them. The Archbishop of Canterbury and other court officials instantly protested, realizing that the rebels had the sympathy of a great many people, including highly placed squires and even peers. The King agreed to hold back his troops

for the time being, and the Archbishop and his brother the Duke of Buckingham rode out at once to Blackheath to talk to Cade. They learned that the rebels merely wanted 'to have the desires of the Commons in Parliament fulfilled' and that Lord Say and some of the King's other advisers should be removed.

The Archbishop promised to intercede with the King, but Henry flatly refused to abandon Say and his other ministers and sent his troops to deal with the rebellion. Cade's men now left the open heath, took to the wooded country around Sevenoaks, and later managed to cross London Bridge and enter the city of London. The Tower was attacked, but the rebels were driven off by the garrison. When Buckingham insisted that unless the King gave way many members of his own royal bodyguard would go out and join Cade, Henry had Lord Say and other ministers imprisoned in the Tower as a placatory gesture.

This was not enough for Cade, whose men were by now in occupation of London. Say's trial was demanded, and when nothing was done, the Londoners were 'right wroth'. When the trial was at last being arranged, they induced the Lord Mayor of London to let Cade and a number of his followers into the Guildhall to see that their wishes were carried out. As soon as Lord Say and the others were led in, Say turned to the judges and demanded his rights: that he should be tried only by his peers. At this the rebels lost patience. They seized Say and dragged him off to Cheapside, where, without any pretence of a trial, they cut off his head. The other ministers were dragged to Whitechapel and beheaded also.

Cade then withdrew his forces to Southwark, but a great many of his followers remained in London where, in defiance of his orders that no citizens should be molested or their houses

London Bridge, from Hollar's panorama of the city. (By permission of the Trustees of the British Museum)

pillaged, they ran through the streets rioting and robbing. The Londoners, who had begun by siding with the rebels, were by now disgusted with their disregard of justice, their high-handed execution of Lord Say and his associates, and their indiscriminate pillaging. They appealed to the Lord Mayor to call on the garrison of the Tower to quell the rebellion. There followed fierce fighting on London Bridge which lasted all through the night; many were killed, and the houses and shops on the bridge were set on fire.

On the intervention of the Archbishop of Canterbury, who had taken refuge in the Tower during the rioting, a free pardon was granted in writing by the Chancellor to 'John Mortimer' and his followers. At this the rioters dispersed.

But like the promise made by Richard II to Wat Tyler, it was not kept. The King's officials pointed out that a pardon granted to 'John Mortimer' could not apply to Jack Cade, and a reward was offered for his capture. He was mortally wounded at Heathfield on 12 July 1450, and a large body of soldiers was sent out to round up his followers; a great 'harvest of heads' was reaped, according to the chroniclers. In

command of the King's troops was the Duke of Somerset, nephew of the late Cardinal Beaufort and now head of that branch of the Lancastrians. When Henry VI rewarded him by making him his chief minister and giving him control of all the armed forces of England the breach between the two families was completely healed. But almost at once a petition was sent in by the Commons for Somerset's removal. It was his military incompetence, they insisted, that had led to the loss of Normandy. The King ignored their appeal.

This was the starting point of the Wars of the Roses. Somerset was widely disliked throughout the country, and many now looked to the head of the rival royal line, the Duke of York, who had demonstrated his skill as an administrator while Lord Lieutenant of Ireland. His fine character had also made a great impression: he was virtuous and upright and had exercised his powers with justice and restraint. As the only other direct male descendant of Edward III, he was looked upon by many as Henry's natural successor, since the King was still childless after five years of marriage. But when a Member of Parliament named Young demanded in the House of Com-

98

mons that the Duke should publicly be proclaimed the heir to the throne, he was arrested and sent to the Tower.

In 1453 the King lost his reason. He recognized no one, his speech was incoherent and for fifteen months he was completely incapacitated. His sickness led directly to the downfall of the incompetent Somerset. The Queen, who had given birth to a son in October, leaned towards Somerset chiefly to keep York out; he had one further advantage from her point of view—he had no following in the country and was wholly dependent upon the King. But with the King's illness came the moment for decisive action. The Duke of Norfolk, nephew and ally of the Duke of York, petitioned the Council for Somerset's removal, and after some debate this was agreed; in December Somerset was arrested and sent to the Tower and the Duke of York took over the administration as Protector.

He soon brought about a remarkable change in the condition of the country. Disturbances were vigorously suppressed. Even his own supporters were punished with conspicuous impartiality and his moderation was marked by the inclusion of many royalists in the Council and by his resolve not to be vindictive towards Somerset.

All this came to an abrupt end at Christmas 1454, when the King suddenly regained his sanity. York ceased to be Protector and the Queen, her position strengthened by the birth of her son, took control in the name of the King and immediately released Somerset from the Tower.

On relinquishing his post, the Duke retired to Yorkshire, accompanied by many of his faction. Summoned to attend a meeting of the Council, he not unnaturally felt that, with the Lancastrians now in control, there was a risk of his suffering the same fate as Gloucester. So he assembled a force of three thousand armed men and set out for London, having despatched a letter to the King declaring his loyalty and asking for an audience.

The King, who had already left London accompanied by Somerset and the Lancastrian party, never received the letter, and on 22 May 1455 the two forces came face to face at St Albans. Thousands more supporters were on their way to join York, but before they reached him the battle had been fought. The numbers were equally matched, but by using both cannon and archers York won an immediate advantage. Somerset was killed and his son captured. The King was slightly wounded and took refuge in the house of a tradesman and the battle ended in half an hour

with the complete defeat of the royalist forces. This was the first battle of the Wars of the Roses, so-called because the Lancastrians had a red rose as their emblem and the Yorkists a white rose.

After the battle the Duke of York went down on his knees before the King and expressed his complete loyalty and devotion. He then escorted Henry in state through the streets of London and immediately called a meeting of Parliament. He and his friends were re-appointed to the Council, and Parliament cleared the slur on Gloucester's memory by proclaiming that he had been the King's 'faithful liege' right up to the day of his death. Shortly afterwards Henry's insanity returned. Once again Parliament appointed York as Protector; but a few months later Henry recovered, and the Queen instantly asserted herself and dismissed York from the Council.

For some years there was an uneasy truce, disturbed from time to time by risings in various parts of the country calling for York's return. Efforts were made to bring about a reconciliation between the two sides, and in London a remarkable demonstration of friendship took place when the two groups escorted the King in an impressive procession to Westminster, Queen Margaret walking beside the Duke of York, followed by Lancastrian and Yorkist lords in equal pairs. But with the young Prince of Wales now standing between York and the crown, an eventual showdown was inevitable.

The Queen was well aware of the position, and in view of her husband's mental state, she herself made ready for the conflict. Born a Princess of France, she had a combativeness and courage that have rarely been equalled. Nothing would deflect her from her resolve. Her devotion to her husband was unwavering and she was preparing to fight both for his security and for the heritage of the son she had borne him.

During the lull Richard of York, partly for his own safety, returned to Ireland and resumed his duties as Lord Lieutenant. Meanwhile his nephew Richard Neville, Earl of Warwick, later to be known as 'the King maker', decided to take the initiative on his behalf. Appointed Captain of Calais by York when he was Protector, Warwick suddenly returned to England with a great force of armed men and marched on London, intending to seize the Tower and proclaim his uncle Richard King. But the Queen acted swiftly. Her supporters Lords Hungerford and Scales moved into the fortress and strengthened the garrison.

When Warwick learned of this, he decided to

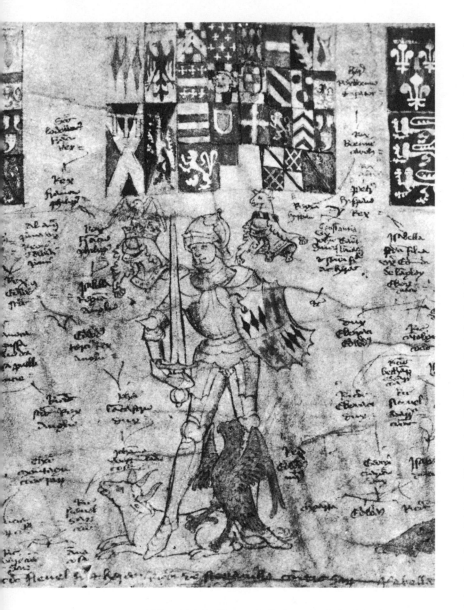

Warwick 'the King maker', from the Roll of the Earls of Warwick by John Rous. (College of Arms)

London at the head of his troops and made straight for Westminster, where he took up residence in the Palace and claimed the throne as his rightful inheritance.

To avoid further bloodshed, a pact was made by the two sides. It was agreed that Henry VI should remain King until the end of his life and that Richard of York should then succeed him. But the arrangement took no account of Queen Margaret, who was by no means prepared to see her son's inheritance disposed of in this manner. She and the Prince of Wales were still free, living at Harlech Castle, and she determined to fight on. She spent the next four months assembling her forces. On 30 December 1460 she won an astounding victory at Wakefield. York was killed, and his eldest son Edward, aged eighteen, became the new Duke of York. The slaughter was appalling. Those who had not fallen in battle were savagely beheaded after it. The Earl of Salisbury, York's brother-in-law, was captured in flight and beheaded. The heads of Richard of York, of his second son, Edmund Earl of Rutland, also killed in the battle, and of Salisbury were set up over the gates of the city of York.

A savage vendetta followed. Young Edward of York's fury led to swift reprisal. Nor was the Queen idle. She assembled a great force of northern lords with their men-at-arms and had a considerable contingent from the Scots, always ready to join in any action to the detriment of the English.

Edward struck first. He moved his army westward to meet the Queen and on 2 February 1461, only a month and three days after the disaster at Wakefield, he engaged her forces in battle at Mortimer's Cross, near Ludlow, and won a decisive victory. Once again there was great slaughter both during and after the battle. Among the prisoners executed that day was a Welshman named Owen Tudor, who had joined the retinue of Henry V's widow Queen Katherine. They are reputed to have been secretly married; certainly they had two sons whom Henry VI acknowledged as his brothers. The elder son, Edmund, married Somerset's daughter Lady Margaret Beaufort and was raised to the peerage as the Earl of Richmond. It was their son, then aged only five, who eventually became King Henry VII, the founder of the great Tudor dynasty.

The Queen was now concerned only with rescuing her husband from the Earl of Warwick. She hurried south and on 17 February encountered his army, and the captive King, at St Albans.

avoid a head-on collision, although he need not have worried: however well Hungerford and Scales might have strengthened the garrison, there was a 'lack of victual' in the Tower and it was quite unable to withstand a long siege. Ignorant of this, Warwick marched his army to Northampton, where he gained an easy victory over the royalist forces. The King was found 'sitting alone and solitary' in his tent. As after St Albans, the victors knelt, affirmed their loyalty to him and escorted him back to London. On learning of the victory, York crossed quickly to England. Holding his sword high, he rode into

Warwick's army was completely defeated and he was lucky to escape with his life. The King was found sitting under a large tree, where he had watched the outcome of the battle with evident satisfaction.

With both armies away, London had been left defenceless, and Parliament was prepared to grant the victors anything they demanded. Edward of York, who had been hurrying to London after Mortimer's Cross, arrived first, went straight to St Paul's Cross and announced his right to the throne. From there he proceeded to Westminster Hall and took the oath before the Lords; then, putting on the royal robes, he sat on the throne and was proclaimed King Edward IV.

The Queen, with Henry in her possession, was determined to go on fighting to the end. Unwilling to give her any respite, Edward rushed north to deal with her. The two forces met at Towton in Yorkshire, where a battle was fought in a blinding snowstorm. The wind drove the snow into the eyes of the royalist army and greatly helped the range and speed of the Yorkist arrows. After six hours of furious fighting the issue was still undecided, when the hand of York was greatly strengthened by the arrival of the Duke of Norfolk with a fresh body of men. In the end the Queen's army was utterly defeated. Thousands were killed in the battle, and those of the leaders who survived were later put to the sword. The Queen managed to save Henry's life and took refuge with the Scots.

King Edward now returned to London and took up residence in the Tower. Henry VI had greatly improved the Palace before the troubles started. He loved its isolation and seclusion and had doubtless planned to spend much of his time there. In 1443 alterations were begun. New and possibly larger windows were put in on the south side of the Great Hall, high enough for the King to see the river beyond the two lofty defence walls. In the following year a new kitchen was put in, 'with divers other chambers and buildings of office'. A new drawbridge was installed at one of the Tower's entrances, and the residence of the Keeper of the King's Lions was reconstructed and enlarged.

Edward was received at the Tower gates with great pomp and was ceremoniously escorted to the Palace. Three months later, on 29 June, he was crowned King in Westminster Abbey. On the night before the coronation he gave a lavish banquet in the Tower; following the custom of his predecessors, he knighted thirty-two of his followers. Among them was his younger brother Richard, then nine years old and later to become King Richard III: he was made not only a Knight of the Bath but also an Admiral. The chronicler Fabyan states that the new knights of the Bath 'were arrayed in blue gowns with hoods and tokens of white silk upon their shoulders'. They rode with the King the next morning in the traditional procession through the streets of London to the Abbey.

The new King was six foot three in height and strikingly handsome. His contemporaries describe him as pleasure-loving and much addicted to the company of pretty women. Many were the scandals about his *affaires* with the wives of city merchants. But Edward IV, though not yet twenty, had outstanding qualities. That he was a leader endowed with great military skill had already been demonstrated; he now proved to be a subtle and skilful administrator, though ruthless and often unscrupulous. His rule soon became a despotism. The exercise of strong control had, of course, become imperative owing to the breakdown of Henry VI's government, the lawlessness of the nobles and the general state of disorder throughout the country. Highway robbery flourished; there was recurrent rioting and endless affrays between the townsmen and the foreign settlers and traders; at sea piracy was rife.

Edward's initial move was to secure his possession of the crown; for both Henry and his son, now eight years old, were still a danger. Henry and all his supporters, living and dead, were adjudged guilty of high treason. More than a hundred and fifty were sentenced, the dead to the confiscation of the estates they had left, the living to death. Attention was given to the defences of the Tower. The garrison was strengthened. On the river bank emergency bulwarks were constructed of empty pipes of wine filled with sand.*

Nothing, however, was likely to deter Queen Margaret. In addition to her powerful army, which had won its last engagement at St Albans, she had two formidable foreign allies. One of these was France, which was ruled by a member of her own family; Charles VII died in 1461 and was succeeded by his son Louis XI, a cousin of Margaret's. The other was Scotland, which had for centuries worked in close alliance with France against England. For her husband's and her son's rights, Margaret was prepared to go to any

---

* A pipe of wine was a large cask which usually held 105 imperial gallons.

lengths. She surrendered the border town of Berwick to get help from the Scots, and mortgaged Calais to the King of France. In 1462 her great army of French, Burgundian and Scottish troops landed in the north of England and seized the three strongest castles in Northumberland.

Edward marched north at once. To support his troops he sent his newest and finest artillery by sea. The guns wrought havoc on the stout embrasured walls and the castles surrendered, unable to withstand the onslaught. To ensure peace, Edward was magnanimous. He forgave the Queen's supporters and even gave one of them, the young Duke of Somerset, a high position.

But the Queen refused to give in, and the war went on. In the struggle that followed, Edward was betrayed by some of those he had pardoned, and this was followed by a return to the savagery and slaughter that had marked the earlier stages of the war. In 1464, three years after Edward's accession, the pathetic figure of Henry VI was seen at Clitheroe in Lancashire. He was seized and brought to London as a prisoner. There he was placed on a small sickly horse, his legs tied to the stirrups with leather thongs; a battered straw hat was put upon his head and a placard on his back with insulting words scrawled upon it, and thus he was led through the streets of the capital. He was made to circle the pillory three times and was finally brought to the Tower. A vast crowd followed him to Tower Hill, jeering and shouting insults as he was led through the massive gates and across the three drawbridges.

(*Right*) *Grotesque helmet, the only surviving piece from a parade armour made by Conrad Seusenhofer at Innsbruck in 1511–14 and presented to Henry VIII by the Holy Roman Emperor Maximilian I. In the Tower Armouries. (Ministry of Public Building and Works)*

(*Below*) *Blued foot-combat armour with gilt decoration in the form of leafy sprays and flowers, from a set of twelve made at Augsburg in 1591 by Anton Peffenhauser. They were intended as a Christmas present to Christian I of Saxony from his wife the Electress Sophia, but Christian died in September of that year. Formerly in the Royal Armoury, Dresden, and now in the Tower. (Ministry of Public Building and Works)*

Early seventeenth-century armour decorated with blued and gilt bands, traditionally but erroneously believed to be that of Henry, son of James I and Prince of Wales. French or Italian work; in the Tower Armouries. (Ministry of Public Building and Works)

Close helmet from a parade armour made c. 1540–50 and later presented to Henry, son of James I. The armour is embossed and damascened in gold; it is sometimes called the 'lion' armour because the embossing takes the form of lion masks. French or Italian work; in the Tower Armouries. (Ministry of Public Building and Works)

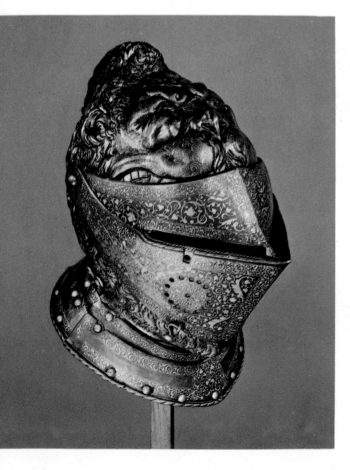

(*Above*) *Coronation regalia in the Tower. St Edward's Crown, made for Charles II, is thought to have replaced that of Edward the Confessor. The Rod of Equity and Mercy with the dove, symbolizing the monarch's function as guardian of his people, lies across the Royal Sceptre, denoting kingly power; in the head of the latter is the largest of the four 'Stars of Africa' cut from the Cullinan diamond. The Sword of State, made for George IV, betokens knightly duty; on the jewelled pommel and scabbard are the English, Scottish and Irish national emblems. The 'ring of kingly dignity', made for William IV, bears a sapphire set with the Cross of St George in rubies. The gold 'bracelets of sincerity and wisdom' were made for Elizabeth II. The oldest pieces, the Ampulla and Spoon, are both used in the anointing; they were restored for Charles II, but the Ampulla may have been used by Henry IV, and the Spoon was perhaps made for King John. (By permission of the Controller of Her Majesty's Stationery Office. Crown Copyright reserved)*

(*Left*) *The coronation of Elizabeth II in Westminster Abbey, 2 June 1953. The Queen wears the Pallium Regale, or pall of gold. On her head is St Edward's Crown; in her left hand she holds the Rod of Equity and Mercy, in her right the Sceptre; she wears the Ring on the third finger of her* ʳⁱght *hand. (Fox Photos Ltd)*

The Imperial State Crown, made for Queen Victoria in 1838 and remade for George VI in 1937. It is worn by the Sovereign on the return from the Abbey after the coronation and for certain state occasions. Prominent among the jewels is the 'Black Prince's ruby', said to have been given to that prince by Pedro the Cruel in 1367, and later worn by Henry V in his coronet at Agincourt. Below it is the second largest of the 'Stars of Africa'. Beneath the finial in the centre are the four long pearl drops traditionally known as 'Queen Elizabeth's earrings', although no evidence connects them with the Tudor Queen. (By permission of the Controller of Her Majesty's Stationery Office. Crown Copyright reserved)

Crown made for Queen Elizabeth the Queen Mother, containing the famous Indian diamond named the Koh-i-Noor (Mountain of Light). Its history goes back to the thirteenth century; it is believed to bring good luck to a woman who wears it, but bad luck to a man. (By permission of the Controller of Her Majesty's Stationery Office. Crown Copyright reserved)

CHAPTER TWENTY-TWO

The Coronation of Elizabeth Woodville

Henry was confined in the Wakefield Tower, where later visitors were to come from all parts of the world to see the Crown Jewels and the other royal regalia. He had for company only his faithful dog and a pet sparrow; and for reading the two books he had asked for were brought to

The great curve of the Wakefield Tower, with the Bloody Tower gateway to the left and the overhead bridge to St Thomas's Tower. (Ministry of Public Building and Works)

him—the Bible and his breviary. A chaplain was assigned to conduct the services in the adjoining offertory, and from time to time Henry was allowed to receive a few visitors. He did not seem to mind either his indignity or the loss of his comforts. 'So long as I can have the Sacrament,' he said, 'I am not worried about the loss of my earthly kingdom.'

A few months after the fallen King was brought to the Tower, there was feasting and revelry in the Palace in honour of a new Queen. Soon after Henry's capture, Edward had married Elizabeth Woodville, but the marriage had been kept secret because the bride was a commoner; the aristocracy expected the King to make a suitable dynastic match. Elizabeth was the widow of Sir John Grey, a Lancastrian who had been killed fighting for Henry VI against Edward. There were two sons of that marriage, and she and her sons were, of course, liable to suffer the severe penalties imposed by Edward on all Henry's supporters. The King met her when seeking a night's shelter at her uncle's castle; impressed by her beauty and well aware of his

Edward IV, Elizabeth Woodville, their family and courtiers. From the frontispiece to the Sayings of the Philosophers *by Elizabeth's brother Lord Rivers. (By permission of the Archbishop of Canterbury and the Trustees of Lambeth Palace Library)*

own power of fascination Edward had sought her favours, but Elizabeth refused to yield. The ban against her family was promptly removed, but she still remained obdurate until finally, abandoning prudence and a plan for an advantageous alliance with the French King's sister, Edward asked her to marry him. For five months their marriage was kept secret; when at last it could be revealed, Edward arranged for his Queen's coronation.

As was customary, she spent the preceding night in the Tower amid scenes of feasting and revelry. By now Edward had also raised the status of her family. Her five brothers, seven sisters, two sons and her father were all given high rank or married into the nobility. Thus eight new peerages came into the family, one for her father, another for her brother Anthony, a third for her elder son and the rest through five brothers-in-law. Since there were only sixty peers at that time this was considered excessive. One of her brothers, aged only twenty, was married to the eighty-year-old Dowager Duchess of Norfolk. Others were given office: Elizabeth's father, now Earl Rivers, was made Treasurer of the realm.

On the morning of her coronation, her dazzling beauty set off by her magnificent gown of 'bawdkin satin' and a multitude of glittering jewels, Queen Elizabeth was carried by eight noblemen in a covered carriage slung on poles which was then harnessed to six white ponies. The throngs at the Tower gates cheered with wild excitement as the procession emerged and began to thread its way through the city's narrow streets; the houses were hung with tapestries and women fluttered their kerchiefs from the windows.

The Earl of Warwick, King Edward's cousin and barely a dozen years his senior, was far from pleased. Until now he had played a leading role in the Yorkist organization, had planned the battles and distinguished himself in them; he and his Neville kinsmen had ruled the country while Edward frolicked and flirted. It was generally believed, with ample justification, that it was to Warwick's initiative that Edward owed his throne. The marriage had completely undermined Warwick's carefully laid plans for an alliance with the French King's sister, which was the only way to stop the abundant aid that was being given by the French to Queen Margaret. Though angry and apprehensive about the consequences of Edward's folly, Warwick did nothing for the moment. But four years later, when Edward married his sister Margaret to Charles the Bold, Duke of Burgundy, who was at loggerheads with the French ruling house, Warwick decided that it was time to act. He knew that the nobility of England hated the exaltation of the Woodville family and feared that disaster would overtake their own estates if by France's help Queen Margaret succeeded.

Edward could not be allowed to remain King, and Warwick decided to undo what he had done. He got in touch with Edward's younger brother, George Duke of Clarence, pointing out that not he but a son of the Woodville marriage would be the successor to the throne. While Clarence brooded on this, a marriage was secretly arranged for him with Warwick's elder daughter Isabel. Then, with Clarence's concurrence, a rising was started in the north and at the same time the House of Commons was roused into protesting against the arbitrary and despotic government of the country.

Edward hurried north to quell the rebellion. Warwick and Clarence had meanwhile gone to Calais and brought back the garrison to England. They were received with tremendous enthusiasm as they marched through Kent to London. Before Warwick could join the northern lords, the issue was decided. King Edward was defeated and taken prisoner. The Queen's father Lord Rivers and her brother John Woodville, also captured, were beheaded. Edward promised most solemnly to mend his ways and was set free on agreeing to pardon all those who had taken up arms against him.

But a very few months later, in March 1470, on the pretext of suppressing a rebellion in Lincolnshire, Edward assembled his army and charged his brother Clarence and his cousin Warwick with treason. Both fled to France, where Queen Margaret was staying with her father, and made a pact with her for the restoration of Henry VI to the throne. The pact was sealed by the betrothal of Margaret's son the Prince of Wales, who was now seventeen, to Warwick's younger daughter Anne. To allay Clarence's uneasiness about his chances of succeeding to the throne, it was arranged that he should be next in succession after the Prince of Wales had become King.

The next move was to secure the release of Henry from the Tower and make him King again. The Tower officials had received no instructions from King Edward. On the morning of 5 October 1470, aware that the tide had turned against him, they opened the gates to admit Warwick's brother the Archbishop of York and Bishop Wainfleet and conducted them to the Wakefield Tower and into the presence of King Henry, who had been a prisoner there for six years. They found him engaged in prayer. He was ill clothed, 'nor so cleanly kept as beseemed such a personage'. Henry was unwilling to return to the throne, but despite his resistance, they brought him out on to the Green by the Chapel of St Peter ad Vincula where a throng of nobles and prelates awaited him. Thus escorted, he was borne in triumph, 'mute as a calf', through the streets of London, while the crowds gaped in wonder. He was then taken to Westminster and proclaimed the rightful King.

Meanwhile Edward had fled to Holland, where his brother-in-law the Duke of Burgundy at first refused to help him. Clarence now found the arrangement made for the succession quite unacceptable, got in touch with his brother and promised to fight on his side. This brought Edward hurrying back to England. Warwick's forces were gathering against him, but at the eleventh hour Clarence came to his brother's aid with 'a considerable army'. A fierce battle was fought on 14 April 1471 at Barnet, just outside London. Warwick was killed and Edward became King again.

During Henry's six months on the throne, Queen Margaret had not been with him. She only returned from France with the Prince of Wales on the day of the Battle of Barnet. When Edward learned that she was on her way to Wales, he tried to overtake her and a desperate battle was fought at Tewkesbury on 4 May. The Prince of Wales, not yet eighteen, fought with a vigour and courage that his grandfather Henry V would have admired, but was killed, calling in vain for help from his treacherous brother-in-law Clarence. His mother was captured and taken to the Tower. Being a woman, she was spared the savagery visited on the men in the battles of the Wars of the Roses. She was kept in captivity for eleven years until ransomed by King Louis XI in 1476.

Henry VI had been captured at the Battle of Barnet and taken back to the Tower. Only a very few of his followers escorted him across the fateful drawbridge. He was there when his wife and their daughter-in-law Anne of Warwick, Princess of Wales, were brought to the Tower after the Battle of Tewkesbury. But they were not allowed to see each other. That same day, 21 May 1471, Edward IV rode into London in triumph; and on that night, according to Stow, Henry VI was murdered: he could not be allowed to live and again be used as a tool for the dethronement of Edward. But no evidence survives to establish how Henry died. What is clear is that he died while at his devotions in the little oratory in the Wakefield Tower. This 'foul midnight murder' was said to have been the work of Edward IV's youngest brother, Richard Duke of Gloucester, later King Richard III, the hunchback or 'crouch-back' as history has labelled him. A number of chroniclers were convinced that Richard was the murderer. Polydore Virgil said, 'The report is that Richard, Duke of Gloucester, killed him with a sword.' According to John Morton, Bishop of Ely, 'He slew with his own hand King Henry VI, as men constantly say.' Dr Warkworth's chronicle, written between 1473 and 1500, stated, 'Henry VI was put to death on May 21, on a Tuesday night between eleven and twelve' and mentioned Richard's part in 'this dark deed'. Among others of this view were Hall, Grafton, Holinshed, Rous, Sandford and de Commines.

Henry VI was the first English king to die in the Tower. His body was taken to St Paul's in London, where it lay 'with his face open' (un-covered), and 'it bled profusely', says Dr Warkworth. It was then carried to Blackfriars Monastery by the river, placed in a barge at night and taken to Chertsey Abbey for burial. Monks followed the corpse in accompanying barges, singing dirges as they rowed up the river.

On the anniversary of his death, the two institutions which Henry piously founded—Eton College and King's College, Cambridge—always place flowers in the Wakefield Tower oratory: lilies from Eton, white roses from Cambridge.

Queen Margaret and the Princess of Wales did not know that Henry had died. When they learned of it some days later there were lamentations, so loud and heart-rending that the sentries around the Tower could hear them, and even the people in the streets beyond the Tower walls are said to have heard them crying.

CHAPTER TWENTY-THREE

The Princes in the Tower

Edward now felt safe. There were no longer any rallying points for his enemies. In 1470 the Queen had presented him with an heir, who was given his father's name of Edward, and another son was born two years later. The succession appeared to be secure.

The King planned carefully for the years ahead. Law and order were essential. Since so many of the leaders on both sides had been killed in the many battles or slaughtered afterwards, it was no longer difficult to break up the standing armies of the nobles. Everything Edward could do to win the goodwill of the people was done. Trade was encouraged. The merchants flourished. Taxation was kept to the minimum. Even literature enjoyed the stimulus of the King's interest. In 1476 Caxton set up his printing press at Westminster, and many of the early chronicles so painstakingly compiled in various towns were passed to him to be translated and printed. Malory's *Morte d'Arthur* and Chaucer's *Canterbury Tales* were among the other books to come from his press. Writers began to work on plays and developed the dramatic form which Shakespeare was to bring to perfection in the next century.

But Edward was not prepared to forgive Clarence for supporting Warwick, despite Clarence's having crossed over and fought on his brother's side at the crucial moment. The patched-up peace between them was no more than a formality. The treachery still rankled. Edward's youngest brother, Richard Duke of Gloucester, now aged twenty-six, was accorded all his favours. He was given positions of trust and high office; the extensive estates of the Earl of Warwick in the north were made over to him, and he became one of the richest men in the land. Clarence, who was married to Warwick's elder daughter Isabel,

The Wife of Bath's Prologue to her tale. From Caxton's edition of Chaucer's Canterbury Tales, *c. 1490. (By permission of the Trustees of the British Museum)*

107

protested strongly, claiming that the entire inheritance should have been his. And when he learned that Richard was planning to marry Warwick's other daughter Anne, the widow of the Prince of Wales, Clarence hid her in his London house disguised as a kitchen-maid. But with the help of Edward, Richard managed to get her away and marry her.

Clarence was so enraged that he began to flout the authority of the King on every occasion. Whether he was also plotting Edward's overthrow is not certain, although that is the accusation on which he was arrested and imprisoned in the Bowyer Tower in January 1478. Parliament, hitherto ignored by the King, was summoned for the sole purpose of hearing the charges and passing judgement on his brother. Their verdict was a foregone conclusion. 'Not a single person uttered a word against the Duke but the King, not one made answer to the King but the Duke.' The death sentence was pronounced and its execution was left in the hands of the King. A few days later it was reported that Clarence had died in the Tower. He was said to have been drowned in a butt of malmsey wine. This was doubted then and has been disputed since. How Clarence really died has never been discovered, but it is obvious that Edward did not want the execution of his brother to be carried out in public.

Edward himself, who had both lived and played hard, died quite suddenly in April 1483 at the age of forty, the penalty of debauchery, it was said. There were no doubts about the succession. His elder son, now twelve, was proclaimed King as Edward V. The boy was at Ludlow on the Welsh border, staying with his mother's brother, the second Earl Rivers, and they set out at once for London.

The control of the Council was in the hands of the Woodville faction, including the Queen's two sons by her previous marriage, Thomas Grey, Marquess of Dorset, and Richard Grey. Dorset was told to go to the Tower and make sure that it was well guarded, since the King's treasure was lodged there. But also on the Council were Richard of Gloucester, the new King's other uncle, and his friends Lords Hastings and Stanley. That Richard would be Protector during the King's minority was inevitable, but the appointment had not yet been made. He was in Yorkshire when the King died, and he too now set out for London. When he reached Northampton, the King's escort of two thousand horsemen were about ten miles ahead. Rivers stopped the

cavalcade and, together with his nephew Richard Grey, went back to Northampton to greet the Duke of Gloucester, who had with him the Duke of Buckingham, one of his staunchest supporters. Rivers and Grey were amicably received and were given dinner at an inn, but the next morning they were arrested.

Gloucester then left with the Duke of Buckingham to join the young King, who had been waiting with his entourage at Stony Stratford. The commanders of the royal escorting cavalry were instantly arrested. Forcing his way into the King's presence, Gloucester informed the startled boy that his uncle Lord Rivers was plotting to take over the government. The boy, frightened and bewildered, burst into tears. When his mother learned what had happened—Edward IV had established a post service as a means of rapid communication—she hurried out of the Palace of Westminster and took sanctuary with the monks in the adjoining Abbey, taking with her the young King's brother, nine-year-old Richard Duke of York, and her other children. A hole was cut in the wall between the two buildings, and through this such personal belongings as could be transported were brought to her.

Gloucester and the King arrived in London a few days later. Edward was lodged in the Bishop's Palace at St Paul's, and Richard ordered the postponement of the coronation, the date of which had already been fixed. It was now 4 May. Within eight weeks the boy-King was deposed, and eleven days later Gloucester was crowned as King Richard III.

Let us now trace this rapid sequence of events. First, Richard was appointed Protector by the Council, whereupon the Woodville party, led now by the Marquess of Dorset, instantly fled. Then Richard suggested that the twelve-year-old King should be moved to the Tower. The Council did not dare object, and he was taken there on 19 May. True, it provided a comfortable residence in which the King could live and be adequately protected, but the guards were under Richard's control.

Three weeks later, on 10 June, Richard wrote asking his friends in the north to bring as many armed men as they could muster to London, as 'the Queen, her blood, adherents and affinity . . . daily doth intend to murder and utterly destroy us and our cousin the Duke of Buckingham and the old royal blood of the realm.' Sir Richard Ratcliffe hastened south with four thousand men, stopping on the way only to behead Richard's prisoners, the young King's relatives Lord Rivers

Richard III, by an unknown artist. (Reproduced by gracious permission of Her Majesty the Queen)

and Richard Grey.

On the morning of Friday 13 June a meeting of the Council took place in the Council Chamber on the top floor of the White Tower. Richard arrived at nine o'clock. Sir Thomas More, drawing on a contemporary account (probably Bishop Morton's) and writing some years later, describes a dramatic scene. The meeting apparently began quite affably. Addressing Bishop Morton, Richard said, 'My lord, you have very good strawberries in your garden at Holborn. I pray you let us have a mess of them.' Shortly after the Council began its discussions, Richard asked to be excused and left the chamber. He returned between eleven and twelve in a very different mood. 'What punishment,' he demanded, 'do they deserve who conspire against the life of one so nearly related to the King as myself and entrusted with the government of the realm?'

The members of the Council looked at him with astonishment. At length Hastings said, 'They deserve the punishment of traitors.'

'That sorceress my brother's wife and others with her,' Richard added, 'see how they have wasted my body with sorcery and witchcraft.' At this he bared his arm, which was shrunken and withered.

He next referred to Jane Shore, who had been the mistress of Edward IV for many years, but after his death had been taken over by Hastings. His scathing attack on her and his angry penetrating glare made Hastings speak again. 'Certainly if they have done so heinously they are worthy of a heinous punishment,' he said.

'What?' cried Richard. 'Dost thou serve me with "ifs" and "ands"! I tell thee they *have* done it, and that I will make good upon thy body, traitor.'

At this he brought his fist down heavily on the table and guards who had been concealed in the passage built within the walls of the Council Chamber rushed out, crying 'Treason!' They seized Hastings, the Archbishop of York, Bishop Morton and some others. As the prisoners were being led out, Richard told Hastings to prepare for instant death. The guards took him into the yard behind the White Tower and, forcing his head down on to a log of wood that some carpenters had left lying by the Chapel of St Peter ad Vincula, struck it off with an axe. Hastings, hitherto a friend of Richard's, had been hostile to the Woodvilles, but recently, disapproving of some of Richard's actions, had begun to detach himself from the Protector. The Archbishop and the Bishop were taken to Wales and there imprisoned in Brecknock Castle. One of the others arrested, but later set free was Lord Stanley, third husband of Margaret Beaufort and thus stepfather of the future King Henry VII.

Three days later Richard sent the Archbishop of Canterbury to Westminster Abbey to persuade the Queen to give up her other son, the nine-year-old Duke of York, on the grounds that it would be more companionable for the two brothers to be together. The Council, purged by Richard of those who might not be ready to co-operate, even contemplated using force if she refused. Thus the Queen, despite her gravest fears, had no option, and both the sons of Edward IV were now in the Tower under the supervision and control of their uncle Richard. Neither of the Princes ever left the Tower again.

Richard's next move was to bar them from any

possibility of inheritance by branding them as bastards. For this he employed Dr Ralph Shaw, brother of the Lord Mayor of London, another ardent supporter. Taking as his text 'Bastard slips shall not take deep root', Dr Shaw delivered his sermon at St Paul's Cross just outside the cathedral on 22 June. He attacked the marriage of Edward IV to Elizabeth Woodville. Edward, he declared, had already been betrothed to Lady Eleanor Butler and so was not free to marry Elizabeth; moreover, the marriage ceremony was performed in an unconsecrated place and was therefore no marriage at all. The children were consequently illegitimate, and the crown was Richard's by right. At this point Richard, who was waiting for the cue, rode past accompanied by the Duke of Buckingham. The congregation merely looked at him with astonishment. According to Sir Thomas More, 'They stood as if turned into stones for wonder of this shameful sermon.'

No further time was lost. Two days later in the Guildhall, where the Mayor had assembled the citizens of London, the Duke of Buckingham entered with a band of his retainers and urged the assembly to call on Richard to assume the crown. An eye-witness records that the Duke was so well rehearsed 'that he did not even pause to spit'. There was no response when the Duke had finished speaking save from his own retainers, who threw up their caps, crying 'King Richard!'

Parliament met the next day, proclaimed that Edward IV's children were illegitimate and petitioned Richard to accept the crown. On the following day he was enthroned in Westminster Hall as King Richard III and was crowned on 6 July.

His coronation procession, like all the others, started from the Tower. Richard travelled in great state down the river, and for two days and nights before it, he made the Tower the scene of magnificent pageantry and celebrations. The excitement and revelry must, of course, have been heard by the two young Princes, who had to be moved out of the King's Palace when Richard took up his own residence there. They were possibly lodged in the Wakefield Tower alongside the Palace, but it is much more likely, as was the general belief, that they were in the Bloody Tower just beyond it. Richard's wife also travelled to the Tower by boat and had arrived there a few days before him.

For his coronation Richard dressed himself in 'marvellously rich' attire. An account still in existence states that he wore 'a doublet of blue cloth of gold, wrought with netts and pyneapples, with a stomacher of the same, lined (with) oon ell of Holland clothe, and oon ell of busk . . . and a longe gown for to ryde in, made of eight yards of p'pul velvet, furred with eight tymbres and a half and thirteen bakks of ermyn, and four tymbres, seventeen coombes of ermyns, powdered with 3300 of powderings made of boggy shanks, and a payre of short spurs with gilt.' The Queen's robes were just as magnificent. In the Venetian archives of the Frari there still exists this record: 'sixteen yards of the finest lace of Venice—from Burano—for the coronation robes of Queen Anne of England'. The order for the lace was given to a Venetian merchant five months earlier, when Edward IV was still alive. The procession was of immense splendour. In the cavalcade rode three dukes, nine earls, twenty-two barons and a great number of knights and squires. They were attended by four thousand horsemen.

The ritual in the Abbey was punctiliously observed. The Archbishop of Canterbury (Cardinal Bourchier) placed the crowns on the heads of Richard III and his Queen, until recently the wife of the Prince of Wales, Henry VI's heir. They were anointed with oil and received the Sacrament. A great banquet was given afterwards in Westminster Hall. It was all very impressive, but many people, including those who watched the solemn ceremonial in the Abbey and later attended the festivities, began to feel qualms of conscience about the brutal manner in which Richard had attained the throne. The contemporary *Croyland Continuator* records that he soon 'fell in great hatred of the more part of the nobles of his realm, insomuch that such as before loved and praised him and would have jeopardied life and goods with him if he had remained still Protector, now murmured and grudged against him in such wise that few or none favoured his party, except it were for dread or for the great gifts that they received of him. By means whereof he won divers to follow his mind, the which after deceived him.'

Among those who turned away from him was the formerly devoted Duke of Buckingham. In Buckingham's custody in Wales was Bishop Morton, who had been arrested during the Council meeting in the White Tower. Buckingham and his captive now joined forces and together they resolved that, above all else, the two Princes must be rescued from the Tower. When news of this was brought to Richard by his spies, no time was lost in getting rid of his nephews.

CHAPTER TWENTY-FOUR

The Murder of the Princes

The exact date of the death of the Princes in the Tower is not known. It is said to have occurred between 7 and 14 August, that is to say about a month after the coronation. What is certain is that the Princes were not seen again by their guards after the month of July 1483. Nor does

(left) Richard Duke of York, and (right) Edward V, from the Royal Window in the north transept of Canterbury Cathedral, given by their father Edward IV in commemoration of the marriage of Margaret of France to his ancestor and namesake Edward I. (Nicholas Servian: Woodmansterne Ltd)

one know precisely what happened.

The account of the chronicler Grafton is corroborated by that of Sir Thomas More. Some scholars argue that More could not have known the facts as he was only five years old when they occurred. Had he been fifty it is unlikely that much could have been discovered of a secret so closely guarded. Confessions made later, after Richard was dead—and they could hardly have been made while he lived—enable us to piece together what apparently happened, but even this is disputed by those who have sought to clear Richard III of any responsibility for the crime. Some apologists go so far as to say that the Princes were murdered by King Henry VII. Winston Churchill firmly rejects this. 'We are invited by some,' he writes, 'to believe that they languished in captivity, unnoticed and unrecorded, for another two years, only to be done to death by Henry Tudor.'

Thomas More's narrative of what happened is also regarded as suspect because he wrote it under the Tudors, who were of course anxious to enhance their popularity by denigrating Richard; it has even been said that More was willing to write a lying record rather than offend King Henry VIII. This accusation completely ignores the deeply religious convictions, the honesty and inflexibility of this saintly man, who was prepared to, and did, suffer imprisonment in the Tower and death rather than express his approval of this same King Henry VIII's marriage to Anne Boleyn, as will be described in a succeeding chapter. There can be no doubt that More believed in Richard's guilt.

According to the contemporary chroniclers and Sir Thomas More, Richard was on his way to Gloucester when he made the decision that the Princes must be murdered. He sent a special messenger named John Green to the Constable of the Tower, Sir Robert Brackenbury, with orders to kill them. When the messenger arrived, Brackenbury was at prayer in St John's Chapel. Because he had come from the King, Green was taken to the Chapel. Brackenbury rose from his knees and read the message. Indignantly he refused to take any part in 'so mean and bestial a deed'.

On the messenger's return with this reply, Richard, who was at Warwick Castle by this time, shouted angrily, 'Whom should a man trust when those I thought would most surely serve at my command will do nothing for me?' A page who overheard this mentioned that Sir James Tyrell

could always be relied on. The King went straight away to see Tyrell, a former companion in arms and now Master of his Horse. He found Tyrell asleep, roused him, and told him to set out at once for London, giving him a warrant instructing Brackenbury to deliver the keys of the Tower to him for one night.

Brackenbury, though doubtless suspecting what the order meant, reluctantly complied. Tyrell then went to the Bloody Tower, where local tradition within the Tower itself states that the Princes were confined, and talked to the gaolers. One of them, a man named Miles Forest, indicated his readiness to assist and Tyrell got his own groom John Dighton to help him. When Forest and Dighton entered, the Princes were asleep. They pressed the pillows against the faces of the children and held them there until the boys were dead. Then Tyrell went in to see that the King's instructions had been faithfully carried out.

The bodies of the Princes are said to have been buried in some earth under a corner of the adjacent Wakefield Tower, but later a priest in the service of the Constable dug up the bodies and buried them secretly 'in consecrated ground'. No one knew where this was, for the priest refused to speak and his secret went with him to his grave. Two centuries later, in the reign of Charles II, the skeletons of two boys whose apparent ages fitted those of the murdered Princes were found amid the rubble on the collapse of the staircase leading to St John's Chapel. King Charles ordered the royal surgeon and some skilled antiquaries to examine the skeletons. They were satisfied that these were the skeletons of King Edward V and his brother the Duke of York. On this the King had them placed in a marble urn and reburied in Henry VII's chapel in Westminster Abbey, with a Latin inscription which lays full blame upon their uncle Richard III. An exhumation and further examination in 1933 corroborated the report of King Charles's unbiased authorities.

The murderers were certainly handsomely rewarded by Richard. Tyrell was appointed Governor of the town of Guisnes near Calais and was also presented with land in Wales. Forest was given a post at Baynard's Castle and after his death his widow was granted a pension. Dighton was made bailiff of Aiton in Staffordshire and also received a pension. Even Green, Richard's first messenger, was not forgotten: he was given the Receivership of the Isle of Wight; and all four received a general pardon 'for all their former crimes' under King Richard's royal hand and seal.

Tyrell, arrested in Henry VII's reign for another crime in no way connected with this, confessed while in the Tower under sentence of death. He described in detail the part he had played in the murder of the Princes and named the others who were implicated. Dighton is also said to have confessed later.

However Richard's apologists may try to clear him of complicity in this murder, the fact remains that so long as the Princes lived, his position on the throne remained insecure: they provided a rallying point for those who wanted to get rid of him. He must have realized that it was not enough to brand them as illegitimate; according to some authorities he even went so far as to state, while his mother was still alive, that both his elder brothers, Edward IV and Clarence, were the offspring of her unfaithfulness—a false and cruel libel on a woman of noble birth who was greatly respected. It should be remembered that one of the Princes had already been proclaimed King Edward V. The younger Prince, the Duke of York, had been married at the age of six to the heiress Anne Mowbray, the Duke of Norfolk's daughter; after the death of the Princes Richard confiscated not only the property of the two boys but also that of Anne Mowbray. Many years later this was restored by the Tudors to her aged great-aunt Lady Margaret Mowbray.

It is possible to argue that Richard III may not have been as black as he was painted by his enemies and that no jury today could possibly find him guilty of the crime. How could they after five hundred years, with all the witnesses dead and all the clues destroyed? At best they would return the verdict used in the Scottish courts—'Not proven'. But it is hard to clear Richard of complicity as an accessory. He put the Princes in the Tower, and as King he had full responsibility for their safety there. The guards were under his absolute control. Had the Princes' escape been contrived, when they would have been far more dangerous to him, some steps would certainly have been taken to find them. Had they been murdered in the Tower by others, would the King not have set up a full enquiry and visited the extreme punishment on the assassins?

Nothing in fact was done, and it is not surprising that the general public began to wonder what had become of the young Princes, a speculation which anticipated Sir Thomas More's account by thirty years, and was current while Richard was still alive and on the throne and the Princes had been dead only a very few weeks.

The Tower was like a town. There was a large garrison there which lived in barracks and drilled daily on the parade grounds. Guards were mounted on the turrets and ramparts. There was an Armoury and a vast body of workers: masons, carpenters, plumbers, glaziers, painters, smiths in the iron foundry, store supervisors in charge of the granary, keepers of the animals in the zoo and the skilled workers in the Mint. They would certainly have seen the Princes in the royal gardens while they lived in the Palace, and the guards would have known of their whereabouts after they had been moved to the Bloody Tower: food had to be taken to them, and they might even have been seen playing or taking exercise on the ramparts.

There was a constant traffic of guards and workmen going to and from the Tower. When the Princes were no longer about, these people would have talked, not only inside the Tower but to their relatives and friends outside it, wondering what had become of the boys. In this way rumours must have reached their unhappy mother, Queen Elizabeth Woodville, who was still in sanctuary at Westminster Abbey.

There then arose a popular demand for the Princes' release which was soon followed by rumours of their death. It confirmed their poor mother's persistent fears and 'she swooned and fell to the ground and there lay in great agony, yet like a dead corpse. When she came to her memory again, she wept and sobbed and filled the whole place with her pitiful sorrow. She beat her breast, and tore her fair hair, calling on her sweet babes by name. Then kneeling down she cried on God to avenge her.'

'The English people who lived at the time,' writes Winston Churchill, 'and learned of the events day by day formed their convictions two years before the Tudors gained power.' Such explanations as Richard III was able to offer were disbelieved and totally rejected. The vast majority of the people of England were convinced that Richard had used his position as the Protector of the boy-King Edward V to usurp the throne and then to do away with him and his younger brother; 'for which cause,' states the *Chronicles of London*, 'King Richard lost the hearts of the people.' The murder was referred to as a definite fact in the States-General in France in January 1484, only five months later.

Richard's closest associate, the Duke of Buckingham, responsible, as we have seen, for the initial and vital moves that raised Richard to the throne, was himself a member of the royal family, descended from Edward III's fifth son, Thomas Duke of Gloucester, and from the Beauforts on his mother's side. After the murder of the Princes, Buckingham, who was planning to rescue them from the Tower, turned completely against Richard III and gave his full support to his cousin Henry Tudor, Earl of Richmond, with a view to helping him gain the throne.

Henry Tudor, as we have seen, was the grandson of Katherine of France, widow of Henry V, and Owen Tudor; their son, Edmund Earl of Richmond, married Lady Margaret Beaufort, great-granddaughter of John of Gaunt. (See family tree on p. 94.) Henry Earl of Richmond was the only male member of the royal house of Lancaster still alive, other than Buckingham, who was linked with it through his mother and grandmother. To strengthen Henry's position, Buckingham tried to arrange a marriage between him and Elizabeth of York, the eldest sister of the murdered Princes, who was still with her mother in the Abbey; Buckingham felt it would serve the additional purpose of bringing peace to England by uniting the two rival houses of Lancaster and York.

From childhood Henry had had an uneasy life. As the son of a half-brother of Henry VI, he was inevitably involved in the struggle that raged round that unfortunate king. For seven years he was beseiged in Harlech Castle. At the age of fourteen he managed to get out and escaped to Brittany, where he had been living ever since. He was now twenty-seven. When Buckingham raised the standard of revolt to bring him to the throne, Henry set out from Brittany with a group of English nobles who had joined him in his exile, but was prevented by a storm from reaching England. The rebellion failed, and Henry returned to Brittany. Buckingham, who had gone into hiding, was betrayed on the offer of a rich reward, and was beheaded by Richard.

It was now of vital importance for Richard to dispose of Henry. He tried to tempt the Duke of Brittany with an immense sum of money into surrendering the fugitive, but his offer was refused; a second bribe, offered to the corrupt Treasurer during the Duke's illness, nearly succeeded, but Henry left Brittany just in time.

Elizabeth of York, eldest daughter of Edward IV and Queen of Henry VII, from her tomb by Torrigiano in Westminster Abbey. (Warburg Institute, London)

Richard could do nothing now but wait until Henry made his next attempt. Meanwhile he strove to win the utmost support from the people of England by demonstrating that he was a good and just king. Many admirable measures of enlightened reform were passed. Parliament, so long in abeyance under his brother Edward IV, was recalled. By endowing new religious foundations and giving the fullest possible patronage to learning, Richard sought to win over the Church. He was generous towards those in distress and magnanimous towards the less dangerous of his opponents. But the murmurs against him, especially in the south of England, continued to grow, and more and more Englishmen of birth and standing crossed the Channel to join Henry.

Richard was stricken in January 1484 by the death of his only legitimate son, and a few months later his wife also died. The rumour now began to spread—so much was Richard detested—that he had murdered his wife in order to marry his niece Elizabeth of York, selected by Buckingham as a wife for Henry Tudor. There is not the slightest evidence that Richard's wife was murdered; but, though he denied publicly that he had any intention of marrying his niece Elizabeth, some colour was given to its possibility by his friendly overtures towards the girl's mother, the dowager Queen Elizabeth, whom Richard had of late always referred to as 'Dame Elizabeth Grey'. He now suggested to her that they should be reconciled. A solemn deed was drawn up and witnessed by the Lords Spiritual and Temporal as well as by the Lord Mayor and aldermen of London, promising 'on his honour as a King', to provide maintenance for her and to arrange suitable marriages for her daughters. Whether because she was tired of living in the cramped conditions of the sanctuary or because she was thinking of the future of her daughters, Queen Elizabeth at last left the monks' quarters in the Abbey and was received by Richard with great ceremony. Rich dresses were bought for her and her daughters, and the stigma of bastardy on the children, so recently proclaimed in public, was forgotten. If Richard had thoughts of this incestuous marriage, papal dispensation would have had to be obtained, but it is equally likely that he wanted to make sure that the girl did not escape from sanctuary and marry Henry Tudor; indeed, he had already encircled the Abbey with his troops.

Meanwhile Henry was again preparing to cross to England with his forces, which included French troops but numbered in all no more than 2000 armed men. He sailed from Harfleur on 1 August 1485 and landed at Milford Haven. With the support of the Welsh gentry his troops soon swelled to 5000 men.

When news of this reached the King in Nottingham, he assembled his forces and set out for Leicester. He had an army of 10,000 well-armed and disciplined men to deal with Henry's ill-assorted, hastily gathered force. Chief of Richard's supporters were the Duke of Norfolk and the Earl of Northumberland. Of the support of Sir William Stanley, who had a following of 3000, Richard was not so sure, and Sir William's brother Lord Stanley was married to Margaret Beaufort. Richard therefore seized Lord Strange, the son and heir of Lord Stanley, and held him hostage as surety for the Stanleys' loyalty.

Henry's forces were now just outside Leicester at Market Bosworth, and the battle was fought at Bosworth on 22 August 1485. Richard, mounted on a great white charger and wearing his crown, addressed his troops with a tremendous display of confidence. 'Dismiss all fear,' he said. 'I assure you this day I will triumph by glorious victory or suffer death for immortal fame.' He then sent a message to Lord Stanley to warn him that if he did not join in the battle his son would be instantly executed. Stanley's reply still rings down the centuries. Proudly he said, 'I have other sons.' The order for Lord Strange's execution was given, but it was not carried out by the officers in charge.

When the battle began, the Earl of Northumberland's force looked on without taking any part in it. Lord Stanley crossed over with his men and joined Henry. At this Richard shouted 'Treason! Treason!' dismounted and, drawing his battle-axe from his belt, plunged into the fight, intent on killing Henry himself. He got as far as the standard bearer and slew him. Sir William Stanley's men now turned on Richard's army. Fighting desperately, Richard fell at last, severely wounded, and his battered crown rolled off his head into a hawthorn bush. It was picked up by Lord Stanley and placed on Henry's head, while he was proclaimed King Henry VII.

Richard was the last of the Plantagenet kings, who had ruled England for more than three hundred years. Henry founded the Tudor dynasty, which provided the Tower with an almost incessant flow of prisoners; a great many of them, bearing noble and exalted names, perished there.

CHAPTER TWENTY-FIVE

Henry VII's Queen Dies in the Tower

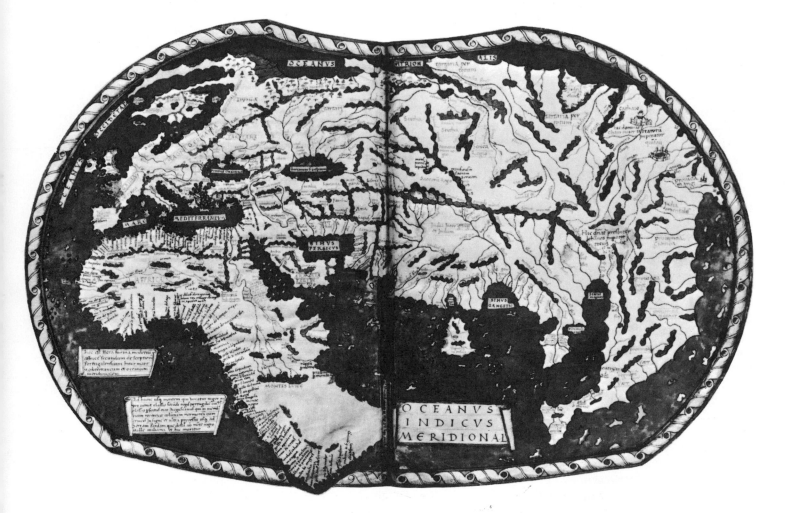

The discovery of America in 1492 revolutionized the concept of the Western world, previously centred on Europe and the Mediterranean. This map shows the known world before that date, with Spain at the westernmost limit; the wealth of the Americas gave her new consequence and became a dominating factor in European politics. (By permission of the Trustees of the British Museum. MS Add. 15760, fol. 68-9)

The accession of Henry VII marks the end of the Middle Ages and the beginning of a new era which, with the inevitable developments and adjustments of time, has endured to the present day. The old familiar frontiers of the world began to vanish and it grew bigger and bigger as the explorers set out in ships to open up new routes to the East, the source of Europe's most coveted luxuries. The voyages of the Portuguese navigators, hugging the endless coast of Africa as they tracked southward, and presently the voyage of Christopher Columbus, seeking a westward course across the Atlantic, led to a complete alteration of all existing charts and maps, and to the discovery that the world was round, and fabulous wealth could be had for the seeking. The future was filled with glorious, richly rewarding opportunities. Men began to look ahead instead of back to the vanished civilizations of Greece and Rome, and were ready to carve up new, unappropriated continents.

Portugal and Spain, being first in the field, reaped the initial harvests. During the five centuries their country was occupied by the Moors, the Spaniards had been seeking to drive out the infidel by a succession of holy wars. Their successes were small; they quarrelled too much among themselves. They held but a fraction of Spain— the kingdom of Castile at the northwestern tip jutting out on to the Atlantic, a strip by the Pyrenees called Aragon, and alongside it the small county of Barcelona. The Moors ruled the rest of the country from their capital Cordova. Portugal was no more than a third the size of Castile. The Moorish capital possessed all the luxuries of civilized life. There were nine hundred public baths. The streets were paved with stone, had beautiful arcades and sparkled with fountains. But in time the Spaniards succeeded in driving out the Moors; and, in 1492, the year Columbus discovered America, Granada, the last important Moorish state, was conquered, and the joint Christian rulers, Ferdinand of Aragon and Isabella of Castile, uniting by marriage two Spanish royal lines, were able to raise the country to undreamed-of importance as wealth began to flow in from the Americas. Henry VII of England fixed covetous eyes on a marriage between his heir Prince Arthur and Katherine, daughter of Ferdinand and Isabella.

Henry was only twenty-nine years old when he won the throne of England on the field of Bosworth. His appearance was not particularly prepossessing. He was large-nosed, tight-lipped and had dark, almost lashless eyes. His bony face was sallow. In height he was a little above average. He was amiable by disposition, careful by instinct, and extremely shrewd, yet capable of cruelty in his determination to prevent a recurrence of the tragic upheavals that had rent the country for so long. He was fortunate in that many possible rivals to the throne were dead and the heavy slaughter in and after each battle had removed their most powerful supporters.

Much had to be done to restore order. Four centuries of persistent effort by the Norman and Plantagenet kings to establish and enforce the law had been disrupted. England was still essentially an agricultural country, and had not fully recovered from the havoc of the Black Death when the Wars of the Roses broke out. On the land the sheep were abundant and on their wool a thriving industry had been established. Trade had to be encouraged and extended: wider markets were now within the reach of merchants.

Henry was in a strong position to assert himself. The barons, always a formidable check on the monarchy, had been decimated, and the new nobles were men of his own making. The lesser gentry and the townsfolk looked to him for help and got it. He was in a unique dictatorial position, with powers not possessed by any king of England since the reign of Edward I two centuries before. He faced pitfalls, as we shall see, but by his skill contrived to keep the crown upon his head for twenty-four years and was able to pass it on to his son when he died.

His first visit to the Tower was made shortly after his arrival in London. It was marked by a scene of unique pageantry, outstanding in the city's history. In the long procession the nobles of Lancaster and York rode together, two on each horse, as an indication to all of the amity that now prevailed between the two factions. Only the Earl of Warwick, the ten-year-old son of the Duke of Clarence, whom Richard III had branded as illegitimate and had imprisoned in Yorkshire, was not in the procession; Henry VII had him moved to the Tower to keep him out of the reach of plotters seeking a rival claimant to the throne.

All Richard III's other personal prisoners were released. One of these was Sir Henry Wyatt, who had been confined in a dungeon of the Tower for two years. It is recorded that 'a cat came one day into the dungeon unto him, and, as it were, offered herself unto him. He was glad of her, laid her on his bosom to warm him, and, by making much of her, won her love. After this she would come every day unto him divers times, and, when she could get one, bring a pigeon.' Wyatt had complained to the warder about his food, and now asked, 'If I provide it will you cook it for me?' The warder said he would, so Wyatt gave him these pigeons and they were prepared for him. Henry VII made Wyatt a member of the Privy Council and later appointed him joint Constable of Norwich Castle together with Sir Thomas Boleyn, father of Anne Boleyn. A portrait of Wyatt, painted in his days of great prosperity, shows the faithful cat with a pigeon in its claws, offering it to Wyatt through the grated bars of his cell.

On 28 October 1485 at a meeting in the Council Chamber on the top floor of the White Tower, the new King rewarded those who had supported him at Bosworth. Among them was Lord Stanley, who was made the Earl of Derby and thus became the ancestor of the present earls of that name.

The coronation which followed was a simple affair, entirely unimpressive, for Henry contended that money should not be spent on lavish display until the finances of the country had been put in order. Following precedent, however, on the night before he created twelve new Knights of the Bath in the apartment adjoining St John's Chapel, with all the ceremony established by his predecessors.

The plan for uniting the rival royal lines by a marriage between Henry of Lancaster and Elizabeth of York was now fulfilled. The wedding took place in Westminster Abbey in January 1486, five months after Bosworth, and as a wedding present Henry gave his bride the very lovely illuminated volume of poems written by the Duke of Orléans while he was a prisoner in the Tower. In the following year Henry had Elizabeth crowned Queen in a special ceremony at the Abbey. The pageantry this time was much more magnificent than at his own coronation. The Queen was brought to the Tower by river from the Palace of Greenwich. Her richly decorated barge was escorted by a large number of other barges, all of them 'freshly furnished with banners and streamers of silk'. Henry waited on Tower Wharf to receive her when she landed.

The next day the Queen, tall and beautiful, apparelled in cloth of gold and damask and a mantle of ermine, with her fair yellow hair hanging down her back with a caul of gold over it, and on her head a circlet of gold richly garnished with precious stones, was borne in a litter, also covered with cloth of gold and damask. She reclined on large pillows of down covered in cloth of gold as she was taken to Westminster Abbey through the narrow, winding streets of London. All the houses were hung with tapestries, and the streets were lined with members of the livery companies and with children, 'some arrayed like angels and others like virgins, to sing sweet songs as her Grace passed by.'

Henry's right to the throne, questionable on the grounds of heredity but secured by right of conquest, was confirmed by Act of Parliament, which defined specifically that 'the inheritance of the crowns . . . rest, remain and abide in the most royal person of our new sovereign lord Henry VII and the heirs of his body lawfully coming.' A challenger with no lawful claim to the throne himself, a baker's son named Lambert Simnel, aged only ten, appeared in the year of the Queen's coronation. He was described by contemporary writers as a comely youth, 'not without some extraordinary dignity and grace of aspect'. The rumour had recently got about that the two Princes in the Tower were still alive, and a young Oxford priest called Richard Symonds took Simnel under his care to teach and train him with a view, it is said, to passing the boy off as the younger of the Princes and thus procuring for himself the Archbishopric of Canterbury. But while Simnel was being taught the manners and behaviour of a young prince, a fresh rumour began to spread that the young Earl of Warwick had died in the Tower; Symonds felt it would be easier to pass Simnel off as Warwick. The project was believed to have the support of John de la Pole, Earl of Lincoln, son of Richard III's sister the Duchess of Suffolk and selected by Richard as his heir; he was a grandson of that Duke of Suffolk who was executed in the Channel and whose body was laid on the sands at Dover.

Henry VII called a meeting of the Council, at which the Earl of Lincoln was present, to discuss what steps should be taken to unmask the impostor. It was decided that the real Earl of Warwick should be brought out of the Tower and shown to the people. Immediately after the meeting, Lincoln fled to Flanders. Warwick was duly paraded through the streets of London so that the passers-by should see and talk with him.

Before long Lincoln turned up in Ireland, where it was thought that the masquerade had a better chance of success. There the old feuds carried on from generation to generation had recently taken on the current labels of Yorkist and Lancastrian. Young Simnel was smuggled into Ireland, welcomed by the so-called Yorkist leaders and crowned in the cathedral in Dublin as King Edward VI in the presence of Lincoln. The Dowager Duchess Margaret of Burgundy, sister of Edward IV and of Warwick's father Clarence, was doubtless aware of the deception, but she nevertheless accepted Simnel as her nephew, the intention being to substitute the real Warwick, or even Lincoln, after Henry VII had been dethroned. The Duchess sent over two thousand German soldiers to assist the conspirators; after the coronation in Dublin, these troops, together with some poorly armed Irish forces, crossed the Irish Sea to Lancashire.

King Henry immediately set out with an army of well over six thousand men. The forces met in battle at Stoke-on-Trent. Lincoln and most of his followers were killed; Simnel and his tutor, the priest Symonds, were taken prisoner. Symonds was sent to the Tower, but, recognizing that Simnel was only a tool, Henry refused to punish him. He was given a post in the royal scullery, where he served for many years.

Another imposter was Perkin Warbeck, who was about the same age as Simnel. His real origin is disputed. He was said to be the son of Jehan de Werebecque, a waterman of Tournai, in Flanders, but many believed him to be the son of Duchess Margaret by the Bishop of Cambrai, and this seems to have been confirmed later by the Emperor Maximilian, who had married Margaret's stepdaughter Mary, heiress of Burgundy. The impersonation this time was not of Warwick, who was known to be alive, but of the Duke of York, the younger of the two Princes murdered in the Tower, who certainly could not be produced.

Warbeck had been brought up in Antwerp and had worked as a domestic servant in the household of some well-placed families. In 1491 he went to Cork as the servant of a Breton silk merchant. In his confession later, Perkin said that many took him to be of noble birth when they saw him dressed in the silks of his employer. At that time he could hardly speak English. But he was most carefully trained in the succeeding years, was taken on a tour of the Continent and was received in most places as the lawful King of England. In July 1495, supplied with men and ships by Maximilian, he sailed for Kent. On landing, his men received short shrift from the peasants and fishermen, and Warbeck made off with remarkable rapidity for Ireland. He tried to land at Waterford, but failed there too and fled to Scotland.

The Scottish King James IV was not well disposed towards Henry VII, though he later married Henry's elder daughter Margaret; he accepted Warbeck and offered to help him. Marriage to a Scottish lady of noble birth would, he felt, be of considerable advantage, and so he married the imposter to his own cousin Lady Katherine Gordon, the Earl of Huntley's daughter. To equip him suitably for his role, James gave Warbeck an allowance of £1200 a year, a handsome income at that time.

An invasion of England was launched, but it was repulsed by the English northern earls, and Warbeck set out on his wanderings again, accompanied now by his wife, who bore him two children. After trying Ireland once more, again without success, he crossed to Land's End and was joined by some disaffected Cornishmen. At Exeter he fled on seeing Henry's troops approach and surrendered at Beaulieu in Hampshire. Henry sent him to the Tower, but took his wife into the household of the Queen.

Henry felt that imprisonment was not enough and insisted on Warbeck confessing his imposture in public. First he was paraded through the streets of London, ridiculed and mocked by the spectators. Then he was taken to New Palace Yard in Westminster, where he was placed in the stocks and had to read out his confession in the presence of his wife. A few days later this was repeated in Cheapside.

During his two years in the Tower, Warbeck contrived to communicate with the young Earl of Warwick, which could hardly have been achieved without the help of their warders. The plan of the two young men, both twenty-five now, was to murder the Constable of the Tower, Sir John Digby, and seize the keys. Once out of the Tower, Perkin Warbeck was to claim the crown for himself. Warwick was quite content, it was said, if Warbeck as the new King restored to him the confiscated estates of his father.

The plot was discovered. Warbeck was taken to Tyburn and hanged; Warwick, being a member of the royal family, was executed on Tower Hill in 1499. He had spent fourteen years of his life in the Tower and was found to be so fuddled at his trial that, as one chronicler put it, 'he could not discern a goose from a capon'.

Sir William Stanley was accused of supporting Warbeck. This was a startling charge, for he had swung to Henry's side at Bosworth. It is possible that he was dissatisfied with the rewards he received from the King. The evidence against him was slight, apparently based on a single remark. Asked if he was for Warbeck, his reply was that if Warbeck was in fact the young Duke of York he would never put on his armour and fight against him. Sir William was confined in the White Tower, tried by the Council and executed on Tower Hill.

With the pretenders out of the way, Henry was able to realize a hope he had been assiduously pursuing for some years: the marriage of Prince Arthur to Katherine of Aragon, daughter of Ferdinand and Isabella of Spain. The negotiations had been going on through a diplomatic service which Henry had established soon after coming

to the throne—the first on such an extensive scale in Europe. But while there were other claimants to the throne, the Spanish rulers had the gravest doubts about the Tudor king's ability to hold it. With the last of them now removed, Ferdinand and Isabella finally gave their consent and in October 1501 the bride arrived in London for the wedding.

To mark the occasion Henry arranged an elaborate programme of festivities for which he and the Queen moved into the Palace in the Tower. There were daily banquets and tournaments. The marriage was solemnized with great splendour at St Paul's. The royal couple were

A Tudor dynastic picture: Henry VII and Elizabeth of York (background) with Henry VIII and Jane Seymour. Copy made by R. van Leemput in 1667 of a painting by Holbein commissioned in 1537 for the Privy Chamber,

Whitehall Palace. The original was destroyed by fire in 1698. (Reproduced by gracious permission of Her Majesty the Queen)

little more than children, Prince Arthur being fifteen and Katherine just a year older. But within five months Prince Arthur died. In the midst of his great grief King Henry did not lose sight of the need to maintain the link with Spain, and planned to marry the widow to his second son Henry, who was now his heir. The boy was only ten years old so the marriage had to wait, and did not finally take place until the Prince ascended the throne seven years later as King Henry VIII. Meanwhile Katherine remained in England.

Advantageous marriages were sought for all Henry's children. This formed an essential part of his foreign policy, for he hoped to secure peace for England by establishing closer ties with powerful countries in Europe. In 1502, the year Prince Arthur died, Henry married his elder daughter Margaret to King James IV of Scotland, as a result of which union the Stuarts were to ascend the throne of England a hundred years later. A younger daughter, Mary, was later married to King Louis XII of France, son of the Duke of Orléans who had been a prisoner in the Tower.

Henry VII spent much time in the Tower and, when in London, preferred to live in the Palace there. After the Battle of Bosworth he formed a personal bodyguard known as the Yeomen of the Guard, and a section of it has been in the Tower ever since. In February 1503 the Queen, now in her late thirties, gave birth to a daughter in the Tower. This was the third royal child to be born in the Tower. All of them were girls: the others were Joan, daughter of Edward II and Isabella, and Blanche, daughter of Edward III and Philippa of Hainault. Henry's daughter was named Katherine; she died in infancy. Nine days after the child's birth the Queen died in the Tower; her brothers had been murdered there by Richard III, she died in the comfort and luxury of the Palace.

It was a shattering blow for Henry, for the couple were deeply devoted to each other. He never married again, though from time to time he contemplated doing so for reasons of State. He had his wife's body embalmed 'with gums, balms, spices, sweet wine and wax', and the next day,

Sunday 12 February, it was carried from the State bedroom to St John's Chapel in the White Tower, which was hung with black brocaded silk and crepe. There it was placed on a bier surrounded by five hundred tapers in tall candlesticks. For three days masses were celebrated every morning by a succession of priests; in the evenings *De Profundis* and *Miserere* were chanted. The Queen's body was taken from St John's Chapel to Westminster Abbey 'in a carriage covered with black velvet, with a cross of white cloth of gold . . . and an image exactly representing the Queen was placed in a chair above in her rich robes of State . . . and at every end of the chair knelt a gentlewoman usher by the coffin, which was in this manner drawn by six horses, trapped with black velvet'.

The hearse was followed by groups of officials and ladies-of-honour. At every crossing the funeral cortège was met by priests and choirs from the various city churches, carrying banners and chanting. At the corner of Fenchurch Street thirty-eight women, representing the years of the Queen's life, wearing white dresses and wreaths of white flowers, came to pay their respects. Children dressed as angels with golden wings sang dirges along the route. At the door of every house and at the windows the residents stood with burning tapers. The Queen was buried in Westminster Abbey where the attractive tomb by Torrigiano, the celebrated Italian artist, marks her grave.

During the twenty-four years of his reign Henry VII acquired a reputation for avariciousness. He was careful with his money and accumulated enough wealth to make him the richest prince in Christendom. But he also spent money generously, indeed lavishly, on causes which he felt deserved his support—the hospital of the Savoy, for example, and the magnificent chapel at Westminster which bears his name, where both his wife and he are buried. The recumbent effigies on the tomb present a good likeness, for the features were modelled from contemporary portraits. Henry died in April 1509, six years after his wife, and was succeeded by his son Henry VIII.

CHAPTER TWENTY-SIX

Henry VIII's First Victims

The reign of Henry VIII was to witness the erection of many new buildings in the Tower and to see a change in the type of prisoners brought there.

The new King was only eighteen when he came to the throne; he was tall, strong, blond and handsome, with a light-hearted manner and a wide range of accomplishments as athlete, scholar, linguist and musician which made him one of the most popular kings ever to succeed to the throne of England. It is said that, being a younger son, he had been destined to enter the Church—certainly his knowledge of theology was considerable—but naturally on the death of his brother Arthur in 1502 this idea was abandoned, and his education was broadened to benefit to the full from the growing development of the Renaissance.

From the early years of his reign, Henry showed his interest in women and in hunting (he was, after all, the grandson of Edward IV) and only gradually was he drawn into politics. Meanwhile, the men his father had put at the helm of State continued to rule as the Council. The Council had been unpopular for some years, chiefly because of the severe extortions of two brilliant lawyers, Edmund Dudley and Sir Richard Empson, who had formulated the financial policy of Henry VII, aimed at procuring for the King as much wealth as possible. It was estimated that they brought him no less than £4,500,000, much of it by charging innocent people with crimes they did not commit and obtaining money from them on the promise of stopping legal proceedings. As Henry VII lay dying, aware that without his protection these ministers might be exposed to the wrath of the people, these two tax-collectors assembled their friends to discuss what should be done.

Henry's death a month later led to their own, for one of the very first moves made by the Council after the accession of Henry VIII was to arrest them and throw them into the Tower. If ever two men were unfairly imprisoned there these were the two, for the fruit of their extortions was retained by the new King. And since popularity for the new reign was what the Council sought, they decided to make the gesture even more palatable to the country: Dudley and Empson must be executed. The law, however, did not impose the death penalty for extortion or, in the words of the charge, for 'tyrannizing over the King's subjects as collectors of taxes'. So the charge was changed to 'constructive treason' and the assembling of their friends for a discussion just before the old King's death was interpreted as 'an armed conspiracy to overthrow and murder' the new King.

While the two men awaited their trial, Dudley tried to escape from the Tower with the help of his brother, but was caught and taken back to his cell. He then thought of a different plan: he wrote a treatise called *The Tree of Commonwealth* and dedicated it to the King. It stressed the advantages of having monarchy, and he hoped that the King would be both flattered and inspired by it. But Henry never read it, and Dudley and Empson were executed on Tower Hill in 1510. Dudley's son and grandson were to suffer the same fate, as we shall see.

During the months they were in the Tower, Henry was busy with his own plans. In June 1509 he married Katherine of Aragon; she was twenty-three, he was eighteen. Then he arranged for their joint coronation. The King and Queen came to the Tower by river with an escort of decorated barges, as Henry VII had done, but in this instance the trumpets blared and the cannon thundered a greeting. The usual ceremony of creating Knights of the Bath followed that evening, and the next day Henry and Katherine rode out past the Lion Tower and through the Bulwark Gate.

Young though he was, Henry VIII soon began to assert himself, and succeeded in establishing an unprecedented degree of autocratic authority. When we consider the fate of those of his predecessors who tried to assert themselves and failed—John who was forced to grant Magna Carta, his great-grandson Edward II who was deposed and murdered, Richard II who was also deposed, Henry VI who was imprisoned in the Tower and murdered there, Richard III whose supporters broke away from him and rallied round Henry Tudor—we are amazed that Henry VIII should have been able to silence all opposition and achieve what even the shrewd and assertive Henry II had failed to do when he quarrelled with Becket.

Henry VIII succeeded because he had no effective opposition: all the powerful barons were either dead or too young to assert themselves. The only Lancastrian left was his grandmother Lady Margaret Beaufort, now Countess of Derby; and the last heir of the House of York, the Earl of Warwick, had been executed by Henry VII in 1499. Moreover, the country was prepared to put up with much for the sake of peace and a well-

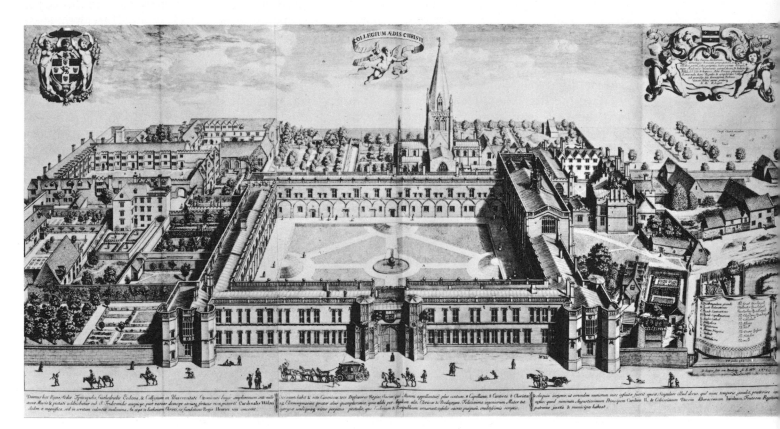

Christ Church, Oxford, originally founded in 1525 by Wolsey as Cardinal College and refounded seven years later by Henry VIII. View from David Loggan's Oxonia Illustrata, *1675. (By permission of the Trustees of the British Museum)*

regulated life. Henry's imprisonments in the Tower and executions involved only a few; the rest of the people remained unaffected and were happy to be able to bring up their children without running into a battle in the nearest market town and to share in the prosperity resulting from the country's expanding trade.

Like his father, Henry VIII gave power not to the old aristocracy but to men who owed their advancement solely to their own ambition and the favour of the King. Thomas Wolsey, for example, was the son of a butcher in Ipswich, and Thomas

123

Cromwell and Sir Edward Walsingham were of equally humble birth. The latter was descended from a cordwainer in Gracechurch Street in London and became Lieutenant of the Tower in 1525; he was the father of Sir Francis Walsingham, the famous statesman of Queen Elizabeth's reign. The change in the administration had been attempted before: Henry II and Edward I had both selected ministers from humble backgrounds, but the men they chose, once raised in status, tended to merge into the nobility; the de la Poles actually married into the royal family, and a descendant of one of them, the Earl of Lincoln, was close enough to the throne for Richard III to select him as his heir. But the tax-collectors Empson and Dudley received no lordly escutcheons, and the new King exercised another effective check by using the axe whenever power seemed likely to corrupt.

Thomas Wolsey, a young priest who was for a time bursar at Magdalen College, Oxford, attracted the attention of Henry VII while in his early thirties. His outstanding brilliance led to his being sent on diplomatic missions. He was also given various administrative tasks, and his handling of affairs with conspicuous success led to his being appointed to the Council by Henry VIII. Henry gave him the house in Fleet Street in which Empson had lived until his imprisonment in the Tower. In 1514 Wolsey was made Archbishop of York and a year later he became Lord Chancellor and was also made a Cardinal by the Pope.

For the next fourteen years Wolsey was in effect the ruler of England; but the credit for every success he accorded to the King. It was through his diplomatic skill that England was raised to a higher status among nations than she had ever known before. The victories of Henry II, of Edward III or even of Henry V, who conquered half France and won the French crown for his son, had not raised England to the absolute equality which she now enjoyed with the greatly expanded Holy Roman Empire (largely Germany), the now consolidated France and the new Spain.

Wolsey encouraged the youthful Henry's Continental ambitions. The French army was routed at the Battle of the Spurs in 1513, after which Tournai surrendered without a fight; and in Scotland in the same year a great victory was won at Flodden. Henry was jubilant and danced night after night 'in his shirt' in Brussels with the ladies of the court of the Emperor Maximilian, who was also ruler of the Netherlands.

As part of the peace settlement, Wolsey arranged a marriage between Henry's younger sister, the strikingly beautiful Mary, and Louis XII, King of France, a match which Henry VII had long envisaged. Mary was seventeen; Louis, at fifty-two, was thirty-five years her senior. He died three months after the marriage, and it was said that his passion for her had hastened his end. But the position England had secured remained unaffected. Louis's successor, Francis I, although already married, sought the favours of the pretty widow. According to Mary, he was 'importunate in divers matters not to my honour', and she resisted his advances. She had told Henry earlier that she would only agree to marry the 'very aged and sickly' Louis on the condition that if she survived him, she would be allowed to choose her second husband herself, and Henry well knew whom she would now choose. For some years she had been deeply in love with Charles, the handsome young Duke of Suffolk, whose rise to prominence had been rapid and romantic. His father William Brandon had borne Henry Tudor's standard at the battle of Bosworth where he was killed by Richard III himself. Charles, only one year old at the time, was taken into the household of the grateful victor and grew up with the royal children. He and Henry used to joust and tourney together and became firm friends. Henry VIII made him Duke of Suffolk in 1514, at which time there was only one duke left in England—the Duke of Buckingham. Suffolk was sent to Paris on the death of Louis XII to offer condolences to the new King. Henry made him vow before he set out that he would not marry Mary, but the vow was broken and they were secretly married in Paris.

Knowing that the secret could not be kept for long, Suffolk revealed it in a letter to Wolsey, hoping that he would use his power and influence with the King to allay his wrath. It is ironical that he should have chosen Wolsey as his go-between, for fourteen years later, when Wolsey's fall seemed imminent, Suffolk had no scruples about attacking him. His act of base ingratitude brought this rebuke from the Cardinal: 'If I, simple Cardinal, had not been, you should have had at this present no head upon your shoulders wherein you should have had a tongue to make any such report in despite of us.' At the time of Suffolk's secret marriage Wolsey interceded with the King, but the news was received 'grievously and displeasantly', he wrote and told Suffolk; and he added, 'You are in the greatest danger man was ever in.'

Hampton Court Palace, presented by Wolsey to Henry VIII in an attempt to assuage the King's displeasure. Wolsey's arms can be seen over the gate. (Ministry of Public Building and Works)

Wolsey's power of intervention and of action was considerable, and his awareness of this brought a change in both his mode of life and his bearing. In the early days of his power, though the decision may have been his, it was his habit to say 'His Majesty will do *so and so*' (until this time the Kings of England were always spoken of as 'His Grace'); later it was 'We shall do *so and so*'; eventually it became 'I shall do *so and so*.' Wolsey's palace at Hampton Court was more magnificent than any of the royal establishments. In the great banqueting hall of his London residence in Whitehall there were endless 'masks and mummeries'. His attendants were numbered by the hundred. When he rode forth, a great procession of retainers escorted him through the streets of London. His servants were obliged to go down on their knees when they served him. A peer of the realm held the basin when he ceremoniously washed his hands. He had a host of spies on whose information men were sent to the Tower, among them the chronicler Polydore Virgil. Wolsey intercepted the letters of foreign ambassadors and warned them in an outburst of fury not to put anything in their despatches without his consent.

But he served the King well. He helped Henry in the divorce from Katherine of Aragon, but he antagonized Anne Boleyn, to whom he was opposed, and this had much to do with his downfall in 1529. He surrendered everything and retired to York to fulfil his duties as Archbishop there. But he was charged with treason, arrested and taken to London for trial. Had he not died on his journey to the capital, he would have been imprisoned in the Tower, where a cell had already been prepared for him; and he would doubtless have ended his life on the executioner's block on Tower Hill.

Thomas Cromwell, who was Wolsey's protégé and eventually also became chief minister, was less fortunate. Eleven years later he was arrested, imprisoned in the Tower and executed. But let us first consider two greater and more pious men who met the same fate while Cromwell ruled.

CHAPTER TWENTY-SEVEN

Sir Thomas More

Sir Thomas More was Wolsey's successor as Lord Chancellor (which was only one of Wolsey's high offices), and it fell to him to handle in Parliament the initial legislation for Henry's divorce from Katherine of Aragon.

It has generally been asserted that Henry sought the divorce because he had become infatuated with Anne Boleyn. That he was infatuated cannot be disputed. Anne's elder sister Mary had already been his mistress; there had also been others, by one of whom he had a son. But Henry's main concern was to provide a male heir to the throne. His daughter Mary, born of Katherine, could of course have succeeded; but no woman had ruled England save Matilda, the daughter of Henry I; her succession, disputed by her cousin Stephen, had led to civil war. To have a disputed succession now was the last thing either Henry or the people of England wanted: the horrors of the Wars of the Roses were still fresh in living memory.

Only on one ground could Katherine be divorced—that she had been married to Henry's brother Arthur and had actually lived with him as his wife. This would render Henry's marriage to Katherine invalid because it was within the degree of affinity proscribed by the Church. Doubts of the legality of such a marriage had been voiced by the Pope when Henry VII asked for a dispensation, before Anne Boleyn was born. Nevertheless, the dispensation was granted and seven months after the marriage their first child, a daughter, was still-born. A year later a son was born to Katherine but lived only for three days; a subsequent son was also still-born. Further disappointments followed. The country was uneasy, and Katherine herself told her father that these unfortunate events were regarded as an evil omen in England. As early as 1514, only five years after his marriage, Henry began talking of a divorce. But in 1516 the Queen gave birth to a daughter, and hopes rose again. The delighted Henry said, 'We are both young; if it was a daughter this time, by the grace of God the sons will follow.' Unfortunately, they did not. Miscarriages occurred; physicians were sent from Spain but they were no more successful than the English doctors. In 1525, when Katherine had reached the age of forty, all hope of a further child began to vanish. Many read into this sequence of child mortality the disapproval of God, for was it not written in the Bible that he who marries his brother's wife shall be childless?

Anne Boleyn is said to have become Henry's mistress in 1529, two years after the divorce proceedings began; she was certainly pregnant before they were over. Sir Thomas More was not in favour of the divorce, but his explanation of the King's motives to Parliament was frank and explicit. He told the House of Commons, 'There are some who say that the King is pursuing a divorce out of love for some lady, and not out of scruple of conscience, but this is not true . . . The King hath not attempted this matter of will or pleasure, as some strangers report, but only from the discharge of conscience and surety of the succession of his realm.'

There was another and much more serious point of divergence between More and the King. The reform of the Church had More's full approval. He had already condemned ecclesiastical abuses, as the Lollards had done more than a century earlier. The abuses had to be eliminated; reform was essential. But his conscience would not permit him to accept the rejection of the authority of the Pope as Christ's Vicar on earth, nor that Henry should take his place as Supreme Head of the English Church.

Sir Thomas More and his household in 1527: pen sketch of a Holbein drawing, probably made for a painting to celebrate More's fiftieth birthday. More's wife, Dame Alice, *is on the extreme right, behind his eldest daughter, Margaret Roper, who is seated with a book in her hand. (Kupferstich-kabinett der Öffentliche Kunstsammlung, Basel)*

In 1532 More resigned as Lord Chancellor and returned to the house he had built in Chelsea, where he lived in patriarchal fashion with his wife and entire family: son, daughter-in-law, three daughters and their husbands and eleven grandchildren. Here he had entertained Erasmus, the Dutch theologian, the painter Holbein and other friends but, left now with an income of only £100 a year, he was forced to make severe economies. Erasmus described this household: 'There is not any man living so affectionate to his children as he, and he loveth his old wife as if she were a girl of fifteen. Such is the excellence of his disposition that whatsoever happeneth that could not be helped, he is as cheerful and as well pleased as though the best thing possible had been done.'

Henry married Anne Boleyn secretly in January 1533, but the news was not made public until Easter. She was crowned Queen with great pomp at Westminster Abbey two months later, as we shall see in a later chapter. More received a special invitation to the coronation from the King

himself, together with the sum of £20 to buy himself a new suit of clothes for the occasion. It was meant by way of persuasion, for the King knew well enough that he opposed both the divorce and the marriage to Anne. More declined the invitation and returned the money. The Act of Supremacy was passed in the following year, making Henry head of the Church. Linked with it was the Act of Succession, which vested the inheritance of the crown in the children of the new marriage. Everybody was required to take an oath to abide by these enactments. More was summoned to make his submission at the Arch-bishop's Palace at Lambeth. He was ready to accept the succession, he said, since that was a decree rightfully made by Parliament and by the government of the country; the Oath of Supremacy was another matter: it demanded the denial of his religious beliefs, and his conscience would not permit him to endorse it. He was warned that his refusal would greatly provoke the King's wrath. Even so he refused to submit; he

More's cell on the ground floor of the Bell Tower. (Ministry of Public Building and Works)

did not feel bound, he said, 'to change my conscience and conform to the Council of one realm against the General Council of Christendom'. Persuasion having failed, More was sent to the Tower.

He was taken there by boat on 17 April 1534 and confined in the Bell Tower, one of the strong towers erected to strengthen the Inner Wall by Longchamp in the reign of Richard I 250 years before. More, now in his fifty-seventh year, was placed in the large ground floor room, lofty-ceilinged and dark, for the only window was a very small one high up in the wall. He was treated most harshly. The use of pen and ink was denied him, but he managed to write to his daughter with a bit of coal. No books could be brought to him from his house, nor were any lent to him by the Lieutenant of the Tower. His only attendant was unable to read or write, yet More was made to pay 5s a week for the man's maintenance and 10s a week for his own. Most of his time was spent praying and meditating in the all but total darkness. All the letters sent to him by his wife and children were at once burnt. This More told a commission which came to interview him in his cell, for there was a constant flow of visitors who sought to persuade him to take the Oath of Supremacy.

One visitor was Thomas Cromwell, now occupying the new post of Vicar-General and Vice-gerent, or deputy of the Supreme Head of the Church. He came in April 1535. He did not visit More in his cell, but sat in the Council Chamber in the White Tower with the Clerk of the Council and the Crown lawyers around him. After changing his prison gown, More was escorted thither by the Lieutenant. He was told that his obstinate resistance would only serve to stiffen the attitude of others who felt like him and that the King would be gracious if he were prepared to conform. More replied, 'I do nobody any harm, I say no harm, I think no harm, but wish everyone good. And if this be not enough to keep a man alive, in good faith I long not to live.' That got Cromwell no further; he came a second time, but again his visit had no effect.

Thomas More was confined for more than a year. Finally allowed the use of pen and paper, he wrote a treatise on Our Lord's Passion and composed a short ode to 'Eye-flattering Fortune', uttering the warning that the fickle goddess should not be trusted.

He was brought to trial on Thursday 1 July and had to walk four miles from the Tower to Westminster Hall, where he had so often sat in judgement. For some time he had been ill, suffering from gravel, stone and pains in the chest; he leaned heavily on a staff as he went through the streets. The sight of the feeble, grey-bearded old man attracted the sympathy of the passers-by.

In the Hall sat a special commission of fifteen judges, among them Anne Boleyn's father (now the Earl of Wiltshire), her brother Lord Rochford, and the Duke of Norfolk. There was also a jury of known supporters of the King. More was told that by his opposition to the King's supremacy he had not only shown malice but had committed treason. He replied that twenty years of loyal service, royally recognized in the offices that he had held, should be sufficient to protect him from any allegation of malice against his sovereign. The jury, as expected, found him guilty, and the Lord Chancellor, Sir Thomas Audley, More's successor in that office, sentenced him to be hanged, drawn and quartered.

More left Westminster Hall, preceded by the executioner carrying his axe with the sharp edge turned towards the condemned man, as custom demanded. Sir William Kingston, Constable of the Tower and a close friend of More's, escorted him personally. They travelled down the river in complete silence, but Kingston was so overcome that he found it impossible to go further than the old Swan Pier at London Bridge: the boat went on without him. When it arrived at Tower Wharf, More's daughter Margaret Roper rushed past the guard and flung her arms about her father, kissing him and crying. He tried to comfort her, but as he turned to go, she clung to him again and he could control himself no longer; those looking on broke down too.

During the five days that remained to him More composed certain prayers that are still used in the devotions of the Catholic Church. At nine o'clock on the morning of 6 July he was led out of his cell. He had been informed that the King in his gracious mercy had decided that he should not be hanged, drawn and quartered at Tyburn, but should suffer death by execution on Tower Hill; to which he replied, 'God forbid the King shall use any more such mercy on any of my friends.'

As he emerged from the Bulwark Gate a woman hurried out of an inn with a glass of wine for him. More thanked her and shook his head. 'Marry, good woman,' he said, 'my Master, Jesus Christ, had vinegar and gall, not wine given him to drink.' Another woman pushed her way forward through the ranks of the halberdiers and asked More to return some papers she had sent him when he was Lord Chancellor. 'Wait for an hour,' he told her, 'and by that time the King's Majesty will rid me of the care I have of thy papers—and of all other matters whatsoever.' There was some booing and jeering from a crowd beyond the executioner's block; it was believed that they were hired by Anne Boleyn to show that not all the people sympathized with Thomas More but that some approved of her marriage to the King.

When he came to the structure erected for the block, More saw that it was rickety and took the Lieutenant's arm. 'I pray you, Mr Lieutenant, see me safe up, and for my coming down let me shift for myself.' He recited the *Miserere*; then turning to the executioner, he said, 'I fear my neck being so short, you will gain little credit in the way of your profession.' Carefully he arranged his long grey beard. 'Pity that were cut,' he said, 'for it hath committed no treason.' A cloth was then tied over his eyes and with a smile he went to his death. His body was taken to the Chapel of St Peter ad Vincula in the Tower and his head fixed on a pike on London Bridge. Six days later his daughter Margaret Roper claimed it.

The King confiscated such property as More still had, turned his elderly wife Lady More out of their house in Chelsea and set aside all the legal assignments for the disposal of his effects that More had made before going to the Tower. All his property was settled by Henry on his infant daughter Princess Elizabeth, who kept it throughout the many years she reigned as Queen.

In the Tower at the same time as Sir Thomas More, and on precisely the same charge, was John Fisher, Bishop of Rochester. Now a frail old man of seventy-nine, he was also made to pay for his beliefs with his life. On his way to the Tower the entire population of the city of Rochester came out into the streets to bid their beloved Bishop farewell.

He too was imprisoned in the Bell Tower, in the room above More's. There is no staircase in this Tower, access from one floor to the next only being gained by the handsome oak staircase in the adjoining Lieutenant's House which was built by Henry VIII. All Fisher's personal property was seized. His library, which he had intended to bequeath to his old college, St John's at Cambridge, was confiscated. In his dark cell, empty save for a straw bed on the floor, he suffered acutely from the bitter cold of the dreadful winter of 1534–5. In a most moving letter to Thomas Cromwell the Bishop described his plight: 'I have neither shirt nor suit, nor yett other clothes . . . but that be ragged and rent so shamefully. Nottwithstanding I might easily suffer that, if they would keep my body warm. But my diet also, God knoweth how slender it is at any tymes, and now in mine age my stomach may not away but with a few kinds of meats, which if I want [lack] I decay forthwith and fall into coughs and diseases.' At times he was left for twenty-four hours without any food at all. When the Pope learned of his imprisonment, he made Fisher a Cardinal. This infuriated the King and is said to have sealed Fisher's fate. The cardinal's red hat never reached him. In Henry's oft-quoted words, 'Before the hat reaches him he shall have no head upon which to place it.'

Cardinal Fisher was tried on 17 June 1535, a fortnight before More, and was condemned to death. On the morning of 22 June the Lieutenant of the Tower came into his cell to rouse him. He asked what the time was. When told that it was five o'clock and that his execution was to be at nine, he asked the Lieutenant if he could sleep a little longer 'by reason of my great weakeness and infirmity'. Three hours later the Lieutenant returned and Fisher got dressed with the help of an attendant. Then he was led out of his cell, the guards walking beside him. After descending the staircase in the Lieutenant's House, they crossed the yard to the Bloody Tower and passed through the gate beneath, continuing along the causeway to the Bulwark Gate. Fisher stopped here and addressed the guard: 'My masters, I thank you for all the great labours and pains which ye have taken with me today. I am not able to give you anything in recompense, because I have nothing left: and therefore I pray you accept in good part my hearty thanks.' Too weak to walk any further, he was placed in a chair and carried to the scaffold.

Fisher had been told not to make a speech to the crowd before his execution. All he said was that he had come there to die for his faith in Christ, and he asked them to pray that he would be able to face death without faltering. He then knelt down and prayed. He also offered up a prayer for the King and for England.

The executioner got down on his knees beside him and asked his forgiveness. 'I forgive thee with all my heart,' Fisher said. Then he recited the Thirty-First Psalm and the axe fell. His head rolled off the scaffold and was stuck on a pike on London Bridge, where More's head was also placed three weeks later. The two men were buried in adjoining graves in the Chapel of St Peter ad Vincula in the Tower, where they still lie.

CHAPTER TWENTY-EIGHT

Anne Boleyn

Within a year of these two executions Anne Boleyn, who had been the cause of them, was herself in the Tower awaiting execution.

She was the daughter of Sir Thomas Boleyn, whom Henry VIII created Earl of Wiltshire in 1529, and of his wife Elizabeth, daughter of Thomas Howard, second Duke of Norfolk. Norfolk's father had been killed at Bosworth fighting for Richard III, and he himself had been in the Tower for three years. His inheritance and title were later restored to him after his victory over the Scots at the Battle of Flodden in 1513.

The exact date of Anne's birth is not known, but it is generally accepted that she was born in 1507; this would make her sixteen years old at the time Henry is supposed to have become infatuated with her, but his love-letters to her, being undated, are unable to confirm this. It seems much more likely that the romance began in 1527 when she was twenty, from which time they were certainly seen in each other's company. She had soft black eyes and long raven hair which she wore loose, but the Venetian ambassador said, 'Mistress Anne is not the handsomest woman in the world. She is of middle height, dark-skinned, long necked, wide mouth, bosom not much raised.' But he added that her eyes were beautiful. She was domineering and spiteful and had a fiery temper. Her elder sister Mary had been the King's mistress for some years. Anne herself was constantly at court during her growing years and took part in the gay revels, danced tirelessly and had many suitors. According to one contemporary chronicler she was the mistress of the poet Sir Thomas Wyatt, but this seems doubtful when we read one of Wyatt's sonnets:

> There is written her fair neck about
> *Noli me tangere*; for Caesar's I am
> And wild for to hold though I seem tame.

Anne Boleyn: panel painting by an unknown artist.
(*National Portrait Gallery, London*)

It is known that Henry Percy, heir to the Earl of Northumberland, proposed marriage to her, but this was prevented by the King, who wanted her to marry Piers Butler, a kinsman of the Earl of Ormonde who later succeeded to the title; of course that was before Henry fell in love with her himself. That she did not yield at once to Henry's overtures is indicated in his letters, the originals of which are in the Vatican library. He writes, 'I trust your absence is not wilful on your part; for if so, I can but lament my ill-fortune, and by degrees abate my great folly.' And again: 'Henceforward my heart shall be devoted to you only. I wish my body also could be.'

Her link with the royal house was close. Apart from her sister's intimate association with Henry, a daughter of the Duke of Norfolk, Anne's first cousin, Lady Mary Howard, was betrothed to the King's illegitimate son Henry Fitzroy, Duke of Richmond. Anne's constant presence at court would not therefore have aroused comment until she was installed in Henry's house in August 1527. Henry's intention to divorce Katherine of Aragon was already common knowledge, though they still lived under the same roof; Katherine did not in fact move out until the summer of 1531. A few months later, Anne and Henry went together to France on a visit to King Francis, by which time Katherine was practically a prisoner. Not long after this, in January 1533, Henry and Anne were secretly married. Anne was already pregnant, and when the news of their marriage was revealed it was antedated to 14 November of the preceding year. In September 1533 a daughter was born—the future Queen Elizabeth I. It was a great disappointment to Henry that the child was not a son.

While Anne was still pregnant, the King arranged for her coronation. She was brought to the Tower the night before from the Palace of Greenwich. Travelling by boat, she was escorted up the river by the Lord Mayor of London, his sheriffs and aldermen. As at the coronation of Henry's mother, there were a large number of attendant boats, all most extravagantly decorated; some carried 'terrible monsters and wild men', others, 'dragons continually moaning and casting wild fire with hideous noises'. In other gaily bedecked barges musicians were performing on 'shalms and shagbushes'. This weird, noisy regatta arrived at Tower Wharf at five in the afternoon and was welcomed by a salute of guns fired from ships along the entire river front; this was followed by a thunderous boom from the biggest gun mounted on the Tower battlements.

Anne landed at the King's Steps, the private water-gate, and was greeted by Henry with a kiss. Taking her hand, he led her to the Palace, which had been extensively redecorated for her. There

was feasting and revelry throughout the night, and the boats lying offshore kept up their din until dawn, which must have been a strain for the five months pregnant Queen.

It was in fact only the beginning of what was to be a series of coronation ceremonies which lasted for days and has never been equalled. In the words of Froude: 'The marriage had been huddled over like a stolen love-match, and the marriage-feast had been in vexation and disappointment. These past mortifications were to be atoned for by a coronation pageant on which the art and wealth of the richest city in Europe should be poured out in the most lavish profusion to adorn.' Not until 1 June, a fortnight later, did Anne set out from the Tower for her coronation. As Henry wanted the focus to be entirely on her so that the people should see their new Queen and take her to their hearts, he took no part himself in the impressive procession through the streets of London to the Abbey. Early that morning, having created twenty Knights of the Bath as convention required, he slipped away to Westminster by boat. For the Londoners, who had hung their streets with gay silks, rugs and tapestries, in scarlet and crimson and cloth of gold, it was an unforgettable day. It was, as one chronicler recorded, 'a blazing trail of splendour'. At the street corners there were *tableaux vivants*, some representing saints and angels, others drawn from the classics which the Renaissance had begun to make familiar to the people, showing Apollo and the Nine Muses. The fountains and conduits ran all day with wine.

At the head of the procession rode the French Ambassador, representing Francis I, at whose court Anne had for a time been lady-in-waiting to the Queen—la Reine Claude, whose name is still associated in France with the greengage. He was escorted by French knights riding two by two, wearing surcoats of blue velvet with yellow sleeves, their horses adorned with blue trappings. Then came the Knights of the Bath, the bishops and abbots, marquesses, earls and barons in splendid robes. They were followed by the Archbishops of Canterbury and York, the Lord Chancellor, the Duke of Suffolk carrying the silver wand of the High Constable, the Lord Mayor of London and all the civic dignitaries in their magnificent liveries and uniforms. The Queen rode in a horse-drawn litter, decked out in white damask reaching to the ground. Seated under a golden canopy hung with bells, she wore a robe of crimson brocade covered with precious stones, and round her neck was a string of enormous pearls 'larger than big chick-peas, and a jewel of diamonds of great value', as a Spanish observer recorded. Her loose black hair fell to her hips, so that she appeared to be sitting on it, and on her head was a coronet of rubies.

The procession passed through the city, then along Fleet Street and the Strand, into Whitehall and past York Place, Wolsey's old palace in Whitehall, which he was made to give up because Anne wanted to entertain there. Her arrival at Westminster Abbey, where the King awaited her, was heralded by a blare of trumpets. According to the Spanish observer, Henry 'took her in his arms and asked her how she liked the city, to which Anne answered, "Sir, I liked the city well enough, but I saw a great many caps on heads and heard but few tongues." ' 'It is a thing to note,' the Spaniard adds, 'that the common people always disliked her.' Other chroniclers confirm this; one states that she was coldly received because the people were still faithful to 'the old Queen', as they called Katherine of Aragon.

Anne was to return to the Tower three years later, this time as a prisoner. Her haughtiness, her vanity, her bad temper, her spiteful behaviour towards her stepdaughter Mary, who was subjected to continuous humiliation and made to serve her infant half-sister Elizabeth as a maid, caused the Queen to be hated at the court. Plot after plot was hatched for her undoing, and she was soon to discover that the King, irritated by her behaviour, which he thought fell short of her dignity as Queen (she is said to have been too free and flirtatious with some of the courtiers), had found a fresh outlet for his affections in Jane Seymour, one of the ladies-in-waiting. When it began is not clear. After the birth of Elizabeth in the autumn of 1533, Anne had two further pregnancies: in 1534 she had a miscarriage and in January 1536 (a day or so after the death of Katherine of Aragon) she had a premature confinement and the child died. By now the King had small hope of a male heir from Anne. Certainly by September 1535 he had begun to take an interest in Jane Seymour, and by the following January Anne was aware that she was being 'supplanted' by one of her own women attendants, for on 'entering the room unexpectedly she was surprised to see the beautiful Jane Seymour seated on Henry's knee, receiving his caresses with every appearance of complacency'.

Contemporaries at court state that Princess Mary, who hated Anne, did everything in her power to further this new romance, in which she was assisted by Thomas Cromwell. At this time Henry was merely amusing himself with Jane Seymour, but that he was dissatisfied with the Queen there is no doubt. More and more he had been complaining of her shrewish temper and of the cruel things she said to him.

On May Day, which was then a public holiday, the King and Queen were watching a tournament at Greenwich. Suddenly, to the astonishment of all, the jousting came to an abrupt halt as Henry, who had just been handed a letter, rose from his seat in the royal balcony and departed 'with a wrathful countenance'. He got into a boat with six companions and went to Westminster, leaving the Queen at Greenwich.

The next day Anne was arrested and taken to the Tower. Her brother Viscount Rochford was arrested at Westminster at the same time and also sent to the Tower. This was the outcome of the deliberations of a secret committee of the King's Council which had been set up to enquire into certain charges against the Queen. Anne's uncle the Duke of Norfolk and her father the Earl of Wiltshire were on this committee. Their findings were communicated by Cromwell to the King in the note that was brought to him at Greenwich.

CHAPTER TWENTY-NINE

Anne's Trial and Execution

Heavily guarded, the Queen was taken by boat from Greenwich and landed at Traitors' Gate. With her were the Constable of the Tower, Sir William Kingston, Lord Chancellor Audley and Thomas Cromwell. The Lieutenant of the Tower, Sir Edward Walsingham, was waiting to receive them. She fell on her knees on the wet steps and protested that she was innocent 'of whatever I am accused'. She then begged to be allowed to see the King, but he was not there. She asked if she was to be taken to a dungeon. 'No, Madam, but to the same lodging you occupied before your coronation,' said the Constable. All she could murmur was, 'It is too good for me.' She then became hysterical, 'weeping a great pace', records the Constable, 'and in the same sorrow fell into a great laughing, and so she did several times afterwards.'

When she was calmer, he led her through the arched gate of the Bloody Tower into the Palace. As she entered she began to weep again, and throwing herself on the floor, she wailed, 'My God, bear witness there is no truth in those charges.'

In addition to her brother Lord Rochford, four other prisoners had also been brought to the Tower: Mark Smeaton, one of the court musicians, Sir Henry Norris, who had travelled from Greenwich with the King only the day before and had been taxed by Henry for his undue familiarity with the Queen, Sir Francis Weston and William Brereton. Of these only the musician admitted his guilt. For some months, or as other authorities have it, ever since the birth of Princess Elizabeth, Anne had been watched. What apparently emerged was that two courtiers, Norris and Weston, were seen at different times to have visited her in her room, and what had been overheard indicated that she had committed adultery with both of them.

The King then ordered that a group of Councillors and judges, with the Lord Chancellor at their head, should investigate the reports. They sat all one day and far into the night and found that the evidence was inconclusive. A few days after his arrest, Smeaton, whose lute-playing had been much admired by Anne—herself a skilled performer on that instrument—was charged with being the Queen's lover. It is said that Cromwell extracted an admission from him under torture, promising that his life would be spared if he confessed. Smeaton not only admitted that he had been the Queen's lover but claimed that he was not the only one, Norris and William Brereton having also been intimate with her.

On the evening of Anne's arrest, when the King's son the Duke of Richmond came to say goodnight to him, Henry burst into tears. 'By God's great mercy,' he said, 'you and your sister Mary have escaped the hands of that damned poisonous strumpet. She was plotting to poison you both.' To forget his shame he plunged into a round of gaiety. 'Sometimes,' the ambassador of the Holy Roman Empire reported, 'he returns along the river after midnight to the sound of many instruments or the voices of singers. He is out to dinner here, there and everywhere with the ladies.'

Anne had been moved by now to a small room on the first floor of the Lieutenant's House. She had as her attendants in the Tower three waiting-women, two men and a boy. Two other women selected to act as spies, her aunt Lady Boleyn and a Mrs Cosyns, slept in the room with her, while the Constable's wife Lady Kingston slept in a closet by the door of the bedroom. The Constable wrote to Cromwell constantly to keep him informed. 'I have,' he said in one letter, 'everything told me by Mistress Cosyns that she thinks meet for me to know.' The other prisoners implicated in the case, including Anne's brother Lord Rochford, who was charged with incest, were lodged in various other towers. Some of them were in the Martin Tower, at the northeast corner of the Inner Wall. All except Anne and her brother were tried on 12 May at Westminster Hall. Anne's father the Earl of Wiltshire and the entire bench of judges with one exception sat in judgement, with a jury of twelve knights. The prisoners were found guilty and sentenced to be hanged, drawn and quartered, but their execution was deferred until the trial of the Queen.

Anne's trial took place in the Tower itself three days later. The Great Hall in the Palace was specially equipped for the purpose. A raised dais was erected for the twenty-six peers who were to serve as judges; this amounted to half the entire peerage but did not include the Queen's father; her uncle the Duke of Norfolk presided. Lord Chancellor Audley, being a commoner by birth, was not allowed to sit in judgement on the Queen, but was placed beside Norfolk to give legal advice. On the other side of Norfolk sat the Duke of Suffolk. In the body of the Hall benches were provided for the other peers, the Lord Mayor of London and the aldermen, and a gallery had been built at the King's command for members of the public. About two thousand were present, among them Mrs Orchard, Anne's nurse.

The proceedings opened with a gentleman usher calling 'Anne Boleyn'. The Queen was brought in by the Lieutenant of the Tower and taken to a seat on a platform which was covered with purple velvet. She was dressed in a robe of black velvet over a kirtle of scarlet brocade and wore a small cap with a black and white feather to surmount her black hair, which was drawn up. She seemed quite composed.

Thomas Cromwell and Sir Christopher Hales opened the case for the prosecution. Anne was charged with being unfaithful to the King, with committing incest with her brother and promising to marry Norris after the King's death. She was also accused of giving poisoned lockets to Norris for the purpose of causing the deaths of her predecessor Queen Katherine and of Princess Mary. The Queen listened calmly and pleaded not guilty. Most of the original documents still exist, but not Anne's defence and cross-examination, which have been destroyed. No witnesses appear to have been called. The judges then voted, and Norfolk pronounced the sentence of

'Guilty' on his niece, saying, 'Because thou hast offended our Sovereign the King's Grace, in committing treason against his person, and here attainted of the same, the law of the realm is this: that thou shalt be burnt here within the Tower of London, on this Green, else to have thy head smitten off as the King's pleasure shall be further known of the same.' As he spoke these words he wept, and 'the water run in his eyes'. There was a gasp from the public gallery. Mrs Orchard 'shrieked out dreadfully' and Lord Percy, who had wanted to marry Anne and is said to have been betrothed to her before her marriage to the King, also shrieked and had to be carried fainting from the court. The Queen herself said nothing, but her face was a deadly white and her hair, escaping from its bonds, fell about her shoulders. She was led out by the Constable and the Lieutenant of the Tower with guards on each side. She apparently still hoped for a reprieve, for the Constable states in a letter to Cromwell that on the next day at dinner she remarked that she would go to a nunnery.

After she had left the Hall, her brother was brought in for his trial on the charge of incest. At his own examination he is said to have 'replied so well that several of those present wagered ten to one that he would be acquitted, especially as no witnesses were produced against him.' But the twenty-six peers found him guilty. On that same day he and three of the other four prisoners were beheaded on Tower Hill and buried in the cemetery by the Chapel of St Peter ad Vincula. Mark Smeaton, being of humbler birth, was taken to Tyburn and there hanged, drawn and quartered.

Anne's execution was fixed for Friday 19 May, four days later. She asked if the King would allow her to be beheaded with a sword instead of with an axe and to this Henry agreed; but as no competent executioner could be found in England, a Frenchman had to be brought over from St Omer, near Calais.

On the night before her execution she slept very badly, for the sound of sawing and hammering went on all through the night while her five-foot scaffold was being erected. This was the first execution in the Tower grounds save for the hurried execution of Lord Hastings, when a log is said to have been used as the block. Early the next morning Anne got down on her knees to Lady Kingston and asked her with tears to go and see Princess Mary and beg her forgiveness for the wrongs she had done her. Then she sent one of her attendants to ask if the Constable would be

Executioner's block and axe preserved in the crypt of St John's Chapel. The block was used in 1747 at the execution of Lord Lovat, the last Tower prisoner to be beheaded; the axe dates from about 1660. Since prisoners rarely died at the first stroke of the axe, Anne Boleyn's preference for a skilled swordsman enabled her to die with dignity as well as sparing her considerable suffering. (Ministry of Public Building and Works)

so kind as to come and be with her when she received the Sacrament. Sir William Kingston wrote of it later to Cromwell: 'At my coming she said: "Mr Kingston, I hear say that I shall not die afore noon, and I am very sorry therefore; for I had thought to be dead by this time and past my pain." I told her it should be no pain it was so subtle, and then she said: "I have heard the executioner is very good and I have a little neck"; and she put her hand about it laughing heartily.' She ate a good breakfast and then became hysterical, moaning and laughing at intervals. Sobbing on the shoulder of one of her ladies, she asked to be remembered to the maids and other servants at her childhood home at Hever Castle in Kent, and spoke of her dogs and her ponies and of Mrs Orchard.

As the moment for leaving the chamber arrived, the Constable handed her a purse containing £20 to be distributed to the executioner and his attendants. In addition to this, the records show that a fee of £23 6s 8d was paid to the executioner and a new suit of clothes was provided. The suit was black, and he wore a mask and a cap shaped like a horn.

Accompanied by the Constable, the Lieutenant and a guard, Anne went to the Green by the Chapel of St Peter. It was a bright May morning, and she had on a loose robe of grey damask with a white ermine collar. A small black hat and coif hid her hair. At her girdle she had a gold chain and cross. In her hand she held a little prayer-book bound in solid gold. Her face was flushed but her step was firm.

There was only a small group of people by the scaffold: the Lord Chancellor, Cromwell, the Lord Mayor and sheriffs, the Duke of Suffolk and the Duke of Richmond, who died a few months later at the age of seventeen and thus put an end to Henry's hopes of having him legitimized by Act of Parliament and declared his successor to the throne. The Archbishop of Canterbury, Thomas Cranmer, was also there.

The Constable helped her as she climbed the steps of the scaffold. She seemed a little dazed, but after a moment she said, 'I am not here to preach to you, but to die. Pray for the King, for he is a good man and has treated me as good as could be. I do not accuse anyone of causing my death, neither the judges nor anyone else, for I am condemned by the law of the land and die willingly.' She then knelt down and said a prayer and asked the people to pray for her. A bandage was placed over her eyes; the executioner from Calais, slipping off his shoes and drawing his long sword, which until now had been concealed in some straw on the scaffold (there was no block), struck off her head with one deft stroke. There was apparently no coffin, for her body was placed in one of the old arrow chests in the Tower. One of her women attendants lifted her severed head, covered it with a handkerchief and laid it in the chest beside her body. She was buried in the nearby Chapel of St Peter ad Vincula.

Ten days later Henry married Jane Seymour in York Place.

CHAPTER THIRTY

Cromwell's Turn Next

Four years later, in 1540, Thomas Cromwell too was brought to the Tower and executed. Like his master Wolsey he was of modest, if not humble, birth: his father was a brewer in Putney and was constantly before the manor court for failing to pay the assize dues on beer and for drinking too much of it himself.

As a young man, Thomas had served as a mercenary with the French army in Italy. After a visit to Rome he returned to London, married a woman of property and set up in business as a merchant and solicitor. We know nothing of his early legal training, but he appears to have been engaged by Wolsey as a steward in York Place in 1520, when he was in his thirties. He acted as a moneylender on the side and amassed considerable wealth. Three years later he became a Member of Parliament and was admitted to Gray's Inn. By now a confidential adviser to the Cardinal, he was employed in the dissolution of a number of the smaller monasteries, the money from which was used by Wolsey to found his famous college at Oxford, the largest and most richly endowed in the university; called Cardinal College at the time, it later became Christ Church. Cromwell supervised its building, was ruthless with the workers, and, according to gossip, readily accepted bribes. Thus his wealth grew; when his wife died childless, he made a will leaving much of what he possessed to his nephew Richard Cromwell, the great-grandfather of Oliver Cromwell, who executed King Charles I and ruled the country as Protector.

Thomas Cromwell was in his forties, square-faced, heavy-jowled and plump. He served Wolsey energetically and loyally until the Cardinal's fall in 1529 and was found in tears when he heard the news, 'which had been a strange sight in him afore', says Wolsey's secretary. Was

he weeping for his master or for himself, seeing that his own future had now become uncertain? His cunning and resource provided a speedy solution. He called on Norfolk, Wolsey's successor as President of the Council, and offered to serve him. Norfolk employed him to distribute the revenues of the fallen Cardinal to the nobles and courtiers who were finding the lavish style of Henry's court far beyond their means. Cromwell was also most useful in manipulating the House of Commons. This brought him much closer to the King, who at once detected his readiness to do as he was told rather than to advise as Wolsey had done. This soon led to Cromwell's rise in authority and influence. In 1531 he was made a member of the Privy Council. In the following year he was appointed Master of the Jewel House in the Tower, then Chancellor of the Exchequer, and finally he attained the exalted position of Mr Secretary.

He has been blamed for much that he did not do. The confiscation of the wealth of the Church was begun by Wolsey, as was also the removal of churchmen from the chief offices of State and their replacement by laymen. The granting of divorce without the Pope's sanction was Archbishop Cranmer's idea. But what Cromwell did do was to carry all the acts of the Reformation through Parliament after manipulating the parliamentary elections. He established that there should be 'no rival authority' to the King's, and thus entrenched the 'divine right' of kings which was to cause so much trouble in the next century and to lead to Charles I losing his crown and his head.

One outstanding benefit that resulted from Cromwell's activity was the translation of the Bible into English and its display in every parish church so that the people could come in and read

Thomas Cromwell, Chancellor and Secretary in matters temporal, Vicar-General and Vicegerent in matters spiritual—the architect of Henry VIII's Tudor Reformation. Painting by Holbein. (Frick Collection, New York)

it. But he was a callous and brutal man. Many nobles were arrested and sent to their deaths because they stood in the way of his plan to make the State supreme. The dissolution of the monasteries in 1536 and the confiscation of their wealth was carried out by him with ruthless efficiency. As a reward, Cromwell was raised to the peerage and made a Knight of the Garter. As we have seen, he was also made Vicar-General and Vicegerent which enabled him to act for the King in matters spiritual; in this capacity he started the registration of births, marriages and deaths.

His undoing was Henry's fourth marriage to Anne of Cleves. In 1537 Jane Seymour had succeeded in providing a male heir to the throne, but she died a few days later—to Henry's intense grief, for this was the happiest of all his marriages. Anne of Cleves was then proposed as Queen by Cromwell. Francis I of France and Charles V, the Holy Roman Emperor, who ruled over Spain, most of Germany and the Netherlands, were on the verge of forming an alliance with the Pope's blessing to launch a holy 'crusade' against the English King, who was proclaimed to be 'worse than the Turks'. Watch was kept on the Channel in 1539 for signs of the coming armada. Cleves and the adjacent regions in the Netherlands, ruled by Anne of Cleves's brother, were to Charles V what Scotland was strategically to England. Cromwell pointed out that by marrying Anne, Henry could be a thorn in the side of the Emperor. Holbein was sent to paint a portrait of her and Henry was shown a most flattering miniature which finally induced him to agree.

During Anne's journey to London, Henry went to Rochester to meet her, and his very first glimpse brought on an intense loathing. 'If I had known,' he said with disgust, 'as much as I know now she would not have come within this realm.' The marriage nevertheless took place, but Henry refused to share a bed with her. When, shortly afterwards, Francis I and Charles V fell out and the threat to England was at an end, Henry's rage knew no bounds and Cromwell's fate was sealed. He was detested by the nobility and had no friends to turn to except the King. But he continued to exercise power, unaware that the King would no longer help him.

Just before he fell from power Cromwell sent the Bishop of Chichester to the Tower and threatened to send more bishops to join him. Then quite suddenly the King struck. On 10 June 1540 Cromwell was arrested in a most extraordinary manner. Parliament was in session, and just before midday the Lords of the Council left for their dinner. As Cromwell was about to take his seat with them Norfolk stopped him, saying, 'It is not meet that traitors should sit amongst loyal gentlemen.' Cromwell turned on him in wrath and shouted, 'I am no traitor.' The captain of the guard, who was waiting at the door, now rushed in, seized Cromwell and led him away, still protesting. He was taken to the water-gate at Westminster, put into a boat full of halberdiers and rowed swiftly down the Thames to the Tower, where he was landed at Traitors' Gate. Only a few weeks before, Cromwell had been created Earl of Essex and Lord Great Chamberlain.

His arrest was a triumph for the ageing Duke of Norfolk, by now nearly seventy. He had long hated Cromwell and had fully exploited the King's anger with his minister. Norfolk possessed another trump card. His niece Katherine Howard, a girl of much more engaging beauty than Anne Boleyn, was already receiving the King's desirous glances. At a meeting of the Council, over which Norfolk presided, Cromwell was accused of thwarting the King's aims for the settlement of religion, and of saying that 'if the King and the realm varied from his opinions he would withstand them'. He was also said to be plotting to marry the Princess Mary.

While Cromwell was in the Tower, Norfolk and the Earl of Southampton went to see him in his cell. They had been sent by the King to induce Cromwell to confirm that the King was dissatisfied from the first with Anne of Cleves and had never given his full consent to the marriage.'I doubt not but that Lord Cromwell,' said the King, 'well examined, can and will declare what I said to him, since he is a person who knows himself condemned to die and will truly declare the truth.' Henry felt that Cromwell's statement would enable him to annul his marriage.

Cromwell supplied the information required and added that he knew the marriage had never been consummated; this was endorsed later by Anne herself. On this, Parliament recorded that 'the marriage was null and the King was at liberty to marry another woman'. There was no real trial, for Cromwell was not present nor was he required to send in his defence.

From his cell in the Tower he wrote to the King, 'with heavy heart and a trembling hand', begging for mercy. The letter was never answered. On 29 July, the King having got what he wanted, Cromwell was taken out through the Bulwark Gate, by which he had come so often into the Tower, and executed on Tower Hill. The headsman was apparently not very competent, for it is recorded that Cromwell died 'by the hands of him who ill-favouredly performed his office'.

CHAPTER THIRTY-ONE

Katherine Howard

On the day before Cromwell's execution Henry married Katherine Howard, his fifth wife, who was also destined for the Tower and execution. The ceremony was private but not secret. She was publicly proclaimed Queen and her name was added to the prayers in the church service.

Katherine was in her early twenties, although the exact date of her birth is uncertain. Tiny in build, she had roguish hazel eyes and auburn hair and a vivacity quite unlike her cousin Anne Boleyn's; for whereas Anne was hard, calculating and ambitious, Katherine had a gay simplicity. Henry was enchanted by her. He called her 'the rose without a thorn'. Nearly fifty now, his once tall, slender figure transformed to a gross corpulence, and walking with difficulty because of an ulcerated leg, Henry was so besotted that he could not keep his hands off her even in public.

What the King did not know was that she had already had quite a number of lovers. With her mother dead and her father an absent, impoverished aristocrat, Katherine had been brought up by her grandmother, the Dowager Duchess of Norfolk, who was extremely lax in the management of her household. She had under her care a large number of girls, most of them in their teens, who slept together in a dormitory without any supervision. Though the Duchess always locked the door at night, various young men used to climb in through the windows with food and wine, have midnight suppers, and then join in promiscuous love-making. Katherine was only thirteen at the time. Her education was neglected; she was said to be almost illiterate.

One of her lovers at this early stage was Henry Mannock, a music master who taught her to play the virginals and boasted later that she had been his mistress. Another was her cousin Francis Dereham: 'I warrant if you seek him in Katherine Howard's chamber ye shall find him there'. Twice the old Duchess beat her on discovering what was going on.

Norfolk was responsible for Katherine's presence at court. It suited him well, for as a Catholic he had been greatly distressed at the swing to Protestantism brought about by Cromwell and the marriage to Anne of Cleves. He rejoiced at Cromwell's fall and saw to it that his bewitching niece was near enough to catch Henry's eye. Katherine had been a lady-in-waiting to Anne of Cleves, who had arrived with more than a dozen of her own; Henry had sent them back, insisting that the Queen should have an English household. Before he had finished with Anne, his interest in Katherine led him to enquire if she was as good as she was lovely. Norfolk is said to have assured him that she was in every way quite irreproachable; and the old Dowager comforted herself by the thought, expressed to one or two of her intimates, that 'she cannot die for what was done before'. So the marriage was entered into in high hopes.

Katherine's past caught up with her. Dereham, who had gone to Ireland, returned suddenly and insisted that he should be given a place in the royal household; he was made the Queen's private secretary, but Katherine warned him to 'take heed of what words you speak'. Some of the old Dowager's servants turned up too. Joan Bulmer, a confidante at the time when Katherine used to receive her lovers in the dormitory, wrote to remind her of 'the unfeigned love which my heart hath always borne you', and a place was found for her too as one of the new Queen's 'chamberers'. There were others too, friends and servants, who loomed up out of the past. Surprisingly, they included Lady Rochford, the widow of Anne Boleyn's brother executed for

incest. Katherine might well have wondered what had brought her out of retirement, but with trusting simplicity she made her one of the ladies of her Privy Chamber. The cost of these servitors was £5000 a year.

Henry did not mind. He was delighted that she should want her old friends about her. With a bride so young, he began to feel younger himself; he found a fresh vigour, a burst of new and unexpected vitality. He rose between five and six in the morning and after celebrating Mass went hunting until dinner, which at that time was at ten o'clock in the morning. He told everyone that he was much better in health and he brimmed over with good humour. Jewels were poured into Katherine's lap. But, despite the minstrels, the troubadours, the banqueting and the dancing, life for the pampered Queen, though she appeared not to sense it, was full of danger. Temptations abounded. There were swarms of attractive young men, among them the elegant, handsome Thomas Culpepper, a gentleman of the King's Privy Chamber. In his late twenties, thirty years younger than the King, and possessed of considerable wealth, his social position had brought him into Henry's court. The Queen and Culpepper must have met before her marriage to the King, and they may even have been attracted to each other; whether it went any further is not known. Culpepper said later that he had 'found so little favour at her hands' before her marriage. The *affaire* between them seems to have begun eight months after Katherine became Queen. The go-between was Lady Rochford. She arranged the meetings and made sure that the coast was clear before Culpepper was admitted to Katherine's bedchamber. The *affaire* went on while the King

and Queen were on tour in the north of England and continued at Hampton Court, where their Majesties were often in residence. Despite the Queen's caution, the servants soon got to know, and they talked.

Rumours eventually reached members of the Privy Council. On All Saints' Day 1541, after attending Mass in the chapel at Hampton Court, Henry asked the Bishop of Lincoln to offer up a prayer of thanks to God for the good life he had with his present wife and hoped to continue with her. As they came out of the chapel the Archbishop of Canterbury, Thomas Cranmer, asked if the King would grant him a private interview. Once alone with the King, Cranmer said that he had heard a shameful story about the Queen and that before coming to the King he had discussed it with Lord Chancellor Audley and with the Earl of Hertford, brother of Jane Seymour. Cranmer had most carefully written everything down, and now handed the papers to the King.

It is obvious that the three men responsible for the revelation, being Protestants, were glad of the opportunity to overthrow Norfolk's powerful Catholic influence at court. The information had been brought to Cranmer by a man called Lascelles, an ardent Protestant, whose sister Mary Hall had been a servant in the house of the Dowager Duchess of Norfolk. When Katherine became Queen, Lascelles suggested that his sister should apply to be her maid, but she said quite firmly, 'No, I will not do that, but I am very sorry for her.' She then explained that the Queen was 'light both in living and in her behaviour'. When pressed to explain what she meant, Mrs Hall said that 'one Francis Dereham had lain in bed with her, and between the sheets in his doublet and hose, a hundred nights'; and further, that a man named Mannock 'knew and spoke of a private mark on the Queen's body'. This was what Cranmer had written down, 'not having the heart to say it by word of mouth'.

Henry appeared to make light of it, but immediately afterwards he ordered four members of the Council to make full enquiries. One of them saw Lascelles and his sister; others saw Dereham and Mannock and induced them to make statements. On 5 November they went to Hampton Court and placed the evidence before the King. Henry was overcome with grief. 'His heart was pierced with pensiveness, so that it was long before he could utter his sorrow, and finally with copious tears, which was strange in his courage.' The next day he saw the Duke of Norfolk and the Lord Chancellor secretly in the fields beyond the lovely gardens of Hampton Court with the Thames flowing gently past. He told them to instruct the Council to make a thorough investigation of what had really happened. Then, without seeing Katherine, he left by boat for London.

Based as it was on Cranmer's initial report, the enquiry succeeded in unravelling only what had happened before Katherine's marriage to the King. Some additional details had been unearthed. It was found that Dereham had intended to marry Katherine and was encouraged by the Dowager Duchess to do so, for she felt that since the girl was in effect an orphan without a dowry, Dereham was not an undesirable suitor. Their intimacy was no more than an anticipation of their marriage.

The King was very angry that these facts had not been disclosed to him. He sent for Archbishop Cranmer and told him to go and see the Queen. He was to point out her iniquity and inform her of the penalty prescribed by law for her behaviour —for she had injured the King and tainted the royal blood—and then he was to add that mercy would be granted her on certain conditions. Cranmer, seeing the terror on her face as he entered and thinking it wiser not to frighten the girl, began by speaking only of her unhappy husband's clemency and pity. Apparently it was his purpose to establish that she was in fact betrothed to Dereham and that her marriage to the King was therefore void. Her punishment would then be for concealment. Katherine burst into tears and denied everything. Then, aware that much must already be known, she became hysterical and confessed her past. But she denied that there was a marriage contract of any sort between her and Dereham; he had forced her to submit by using violence, she said.

After hearing Cranmer's report, Henry summoned the Lord Chancellor, councillors, peers, bishops and judges, placed the evidence before

Thomas Cranmer, Archbishop of Canterbury 1533–56: panel painted in 1546 by Gerlach Flicke, a German artist working in England. (National Portrait Gallery, London)

them and decided to send the Queen away from Hampton Court. She was moved under armed guard to Syon House, four miles away. It had been a monastery, but it was made ready and furnished modestly for her. She took some gowns and a few ladies of the court, but her jewels had by now been taken away from her.

Meanwhile further enquiries went on. Those interviewed mentioned other names. Mannock indicated that Katherine Tylney, a lady of the Bedchamber and a relative of the old Dowager, could tell other tales. Her revelations were indeed startling. She admitted that the Queen had clandestine meetings with Culpepper during her recent tour with the King. 'At Lincoln her Majesty had gone on two occasions to Lady Rochford's room, which could be reached by a little pair of back stairs near the Queen's apartment.' She had attempted to accompany her mistress but had been sent back. Another attendant, Margery Morton, spoke of other meetings at Hatfield. Lady Rochford made a clean breast of the whole thing. Meetings with Culpepper had taken place in her rooms at Greenwich, Lincoln, Pontefract, York and elsewhere over the past months. Next, Culpepper was interviewed. He had a position of great authority at the court: he was steward and keeper of many royal manors, Clerk of the Armoury as well as gentleman of the King's Chamber. He made a full confession; it was believed that this was achieved by the use, or threat, of torture in the Tower.

It is not quite clear when the torture chamber was established in the dungeons of the White Tower: it was known that torture was used by the Star Chamber, the special court of justice consisting of members of the Council and two judges which Henry VII had set up. The first mention of torture being used in the Tower was early in the fourteenth century when the Knights Templar were tortured in the vaults of the White Tower. It is next referred to in the reign of Henry VI, when the Duke of Exeter was Constable. He is said to have introduced the first rack ever used in England; it came to be known as 'the Duke of Exeter's daughter'. Another frightful implement, which seems also to have been introduced at that time was 'the brakes', used for forcing out teeth.

As the evidence against Katherine began to grow, it pointed to a suspicious familiarity between Dereham and the Queen after her marriage. Questioned about this, Dereham admitted that he had been in the Queen's private apartment more than once and that she had given him various sums of money, telling him not to talk of it. In addition an illiterate letter was found which Katherine had been foolish enough to write to Culpepper in her own hand. Translated into intelligible English, it read, 'It makes my heart die to think I cannot be always in your company. Come when my Lady Rochford is here, for then I shall be best at leisure to be your commandment.' The letter ended, 'Yours as long as life endure.' There was no doubt now about her guilt.

All the men involved were arrested and sent to the Tower. Among them was one called Damport, against whom there was but slight suspicion. To force a confession he was taken to the torture chamber and 'his teeth were forced out in the brakes', but it was finally found that he was in no way implicated and he was released. The Dowager Duchess of Norfolk, the Queen's uncle Lord William Howard and his wife, as well as the Duke of Norfolk's sister Lady Bridgewater, were also sent to the Tower for having known of Katherine's immorality before her marriage and not revealed it to the King.

The Duke of Norfolk made frantic efforts to dissociate himself from the whole unsavoury affair. He wrote to the King on 15 December 1541, 'I learnt yesterday that mine ungracious mother-in-law [she was his stepmother], mine unhappy brother and his wife, and my lewd sister of Bridgewater were committed to the Tower; and am sure it was not done but for some false proceeding against your Majesty. Weighing this with the abominable deeds done by my two nieces [Anne Boleyn and Katherine Howard] and the repeated treasons of many of my kin, I fear your Majesty will abhor to hear speak of me or my kin again. Prostrate at your Majesty's feet, I remind your Majesty that much of this has come to light through my own report of my mother-in-law's words to me . . . I pray your Majesty for some comfortable assurance of your royal favour, without which I will never desire to live.'

At the trial of Culpepper and Dereham at the Guildhall in London, the entire Privy Council and even foreign ambassadors were present. Norfolk was one of the judges, and brought his son the Earl of Surrey with him. To emphasize that he was not even remotely in sympathy with the prisoners, he continually laughed and jeered throughout their examination. The two men pleaded guilty and were condemned to be taken from the Tower and drawn through the streets of London to Tyburn, 'and there hanged, cut down alive, disembowelled, and if they still be living, their bowels burnt, the bodies then beheaded and quartered'. Both begged the King to grant them death by decapitation. This Henry finally allowed in the case of Culpepper, possibly because he had been a gentleman of the Privy Chamber; his entire wealth, however, was confiscated even before the trial. Both men were taken to Tyburn. Culpepper asked the people to pray for him, knelt and had his head struck off. Dereham suffered the entire range of penalties set out in the barbaric sentence.

Later that month, the Dowager Duchess and the other members of the Norfolk family in the Tower with her were tried and found guilty of misprision for wrongfully keeping the truth from the King. They were condemned to perpetual imprisonment and the confiscation of all their goods and possessions.

It was now Katherine's turn. She was still a

prisoner in Syon House, 'making good cheer, fatter and more beautiful than ever; taking good care to be well apparelled . . . She believes she will be put to death and admits that she deserves it,' the ambassador of the Holy Roman Empire records. She remained there over Christmas while the King was at Greenwich. For Henry there were no festivities and no music. He hunted a little, but for the most part he sat weary and disillusioned by the fire, waiting for the New Year and for Parliament to decide the fate of the Queen. The King himself attended the opening of the session on 16 January. A Bill of Attainder was brought in so that her actions should be dealt with by Act of Parliament. She was not given a chance to defend herself, but was proclaimed to be guilty of treason and condemned to death.

On 10 February 1542 the Lord Privy Seal and a group of Privy Councillors were sent to bring her to the Tower. She resisted, but was overpowered and was taken by force to the barges that were waiting by the river bank. It was a bitterly cold day. The Privy Councillors went first and Katherine followed in a small covered barge. Behind came a large boat full of soldiers under the command of the Duke of Suffolk, husband of Henry's sister Mary and grandfather of Lady Jane Grey. He was now nearly sixty. As the procession of boats passed under London Bridge, the Queen could see the heads of her two lovers, Culpepper and Dereham, displayed on pikes. Just as darkness was falling the portcullis of Traitors' Gate was opened for her. Dressed in black velvet and treated with the utmost courtesy by the members of the Council, she showed no signs of hysteria such as her cousin Anne Boleyn

had betrayed. On the contrary, having heard that with his last words Culpepper had proclaimed his undying love for her, she now declared that since the King had shown no mercy for the man she had loved, she asked for no mercy for herself.

On Sunday 12 February 1542 she was informed that her execution would take place the next morning. She asked if the block might be brought to her room so that she could rehearse how to place her head on it and her request was granted. At dawn she was led out to the Green in front of the Chapel of St Peter ad Vincula, where the scaffold on which Anne Boleyn had died had been re-erected. All around the ground glittered with hoar frost. The Councillors were present, but Norfolk was not there; his son, the poet Surrey, who was her first cousin, came instead. Katherine was by now so weak that she had to be helped up the steps of the scaffold. As she mounted, she caught a glimpse of Lady Rochford, who had been brought to the Tower a few days earlier. Katherine was able to say just a few words: 'I have sinned grievously and have full confidence in God's goodness. If I had married the man I loved instead of being dazzled by ambition, all would have been well. I die a Queen, but I would rather have died the wife of Culpepper.'

After her head was severed, her ladies came up and gathered the head and the trunk together in a black cloth. She was buried in the Chapel of St Peter near her cousin Anne. She had been Queen for eighteen months.

Some months later, Henry released the rest of the Howards from the Tower. But Lady Rochford, who claimed that she was out of her mind, was not to escape punishment by this plea: she was made to pay the supreme penalty on the scaffold.

CHAPTER THIRTY-TWO

Henry VIII's Changes at the Tower

These were by no means the only prisoners Henry put into the Tower during his reign of close on forty years. Indeed, at one time the Tower became so crowded that room had to be found in other prisons for some of his victims.

The most notable of these other prisoners was Margaret Countess of Salisbury. She was the daughter of Edward IV's brother the Duke of Clarence, who was said to have perished in the Tower by drowning in a butt of malmsey. The Countess's younger brother, the Earl of Warwick, was imprisoned by Richard III and then by Henry VII; after the impostures by Lambert Simnel and Perkin Warbeck, he was executed in 1499. Forty-two years later, his sister met a similar fate in the Tower. Her closeness to the succession could not have been regarded as a serious factor or she would have died earlier. She was, of course, the last of the Plantagenets, but she met her death because of the religious conflict which had been going on ever since Henry VIII displaced the Pope and became Supreme Head of the Church of England.

Henry's only interest was to have the control in his own hands; he was not in sympathy with the floodtide of Protestantism that had begun to sweep in. A few essential reforms he was prepared to concede, but in the main he still regarded himself as a true and staunch Catholic. The pendulum had swung towards the Protestants under Cromwell at the time of the marriage to Anne of Cleves, and then back towards Catholicism under the Duke of Norfolk and his niece Katherine Howard.

The Countess of Salisbury became involved because her son Reginald Pole was a cardinal of the Church of Rome. The trouble had begun in Cromwell's time, when Pole, not yet a cardinal, had been offered a tempting price by Henry to

Margaret Pole, Countess of Salisbury, the last of the Plantagenets: panel painting by an unknown artist.
(National Portrait Gallery, London)

support his divorce from Katherine of Aragon. He not only refused, but took refuge in Rome, where he wrote a book attacking Henry and urged the Pope, the Emperor and others to depose the English King. Of the many members of Pole's family still in England, Cromwell said, 'Those that have little offended, save that he is of their kin, might feel what it is to have a traitor to their kinsmen.' The Countess of Salisbury took the hint, immediately denounced her son as a traitor and lamented publicly that she had ever given birth to him.

For some months nothing was done, then Cromwell pounced. Members of the family and others were rounded up for being in correspondence with a traitor and were sent to the Tower. They included the Cardinal's brother Lord Montague and his cousin the Marquess of Exeter (not to be confused with the Duke of Exeter who was earlier a Constable of the Tower; the ducal title had died out by now). All these prisoners were beheaded. Another of the Countess's sons, Sir Geoffrey Pole, also in the Tower, tried to commit suicide when faced with the rack. He was released after giving incriminating details about his brother and Exeter.

The Countess's turn came later. Henry had given her a pension at the beginning of his reign, and he also persuaded Parliament to pass an Act clearing the name of her brother the Earl of Warwick. A position at court was also granted her as governess to Princess Mary. Now in her old age her entire world crumbled about her. Not only had her sons and relations been imprisoned in the Tower, but many of her friends, such as Lord Darcy, Lord Hussey, Lord Abergavenny's brother Sir Edward Nevill, the Earl of Northumberland's brother Sir Thomas Percy, Sir Francis Bygot, Sir John Bulmer and many more. They were arrested and executed for being involved in a Catholic enterprise called the Pilgrimage of Grace. Started in 1535 when the monasteries were being dissolved, it was not a rebellion, but a protest against the changes which were destroying the religious way of life as people knew it. The Lollards, who wanted reform, were sent in swarms to the Tower by King Henry V, who had once been in sympathy with their views; a century later, another Henry, professing himself to be a true Catholic, was sending to the Tower large numbers of those who wanted to preserve Catholicism. The prisoners were not taken to the Tower with blankets over their heads, but through the streets of London—a small crowded city at the time—in the full view of the public, who came out to stare at the slow procession and often jeered and shouted abuse and obscenities. Similarly, those taken for execution at Smithfield or Tyburn were drawn through the streets on hurdles or were taken in carts, as a warning to others that they too might face a like penalty.

The sixty-nine-year-old Countess was visited in her country house, questioned for twelve hours and then taken to the Tower; for her inquisitors had found a tunic with the arms of England embroidered on one side and the five wounds of Christ on the other: the banner of the Pilgrimage of Grace had been similarly adorned. She was allowed to have a maid with her in the Tower and was still there when Thomas Cromwell, who was responsible for the persecution of the Catholics, was brought in as a prisoner. She was there in fact for more than two years, suffering acutely from the cold in the winter. When she learnt of this, Katherine Howard, still only a lady-in-waiting at the court, sent the Countess some warm stockings, a pair of slippers and a furred petticoat. In May 1541, following some trouble from a Catholic group in Yorkshire, Henry decided on her execution. As she was a member of the royal family, the site selected was the green within the Tower grounds. There was no trial. She was just led out of her cell to the newly erected scaffold, but she refused to lay her head on the block. According to Lord Herbert, she tried to run away, crying 'I am no traitor,' and the executioner chased her round and round the platform with his axe, striking repeatedly at the hoary, but by now bloody head of the old woman until she submitted. The execution was clumsily carried out, for, of the three headsmen in the Tower, one, we are told, had been sent to Yorkshire for an execution and the other two had been hanged for robbing a booth at Bartholomew Fair. The Countess was buried in the Chapel of St Peter ad Vincula.

During the reign of Henry VIII extensive alterations were made in the Tower. The Palace in which the kings of England had lived for nearly four hundred years consisted by now of a number of assorted buildings erected at different times—the first, it is thought, in the reign of Henry I. The Great Hall, as we have seen, was built by Henry III and his successors continually improved and added to it. As a result, the buildings varied in design and even stood at odd angles to each other. Henry

VIII made them uniform. He rebuilt some of them and, by providing a new and continuous facade, made them into one composite structure. What it looked like, whether it in any way resembled Hampton Court which was built in the same reign, we do not know; for it was pulled down (as will be described later) and not a vestige of it remains today. We can, however, see from the site that it was twice as wide as the White Tower, for it stretched from the Wakefield Tower to the Lanthorn Tower at the southern end of the Roman wall; the Queen's garden was at the east side of the Palace.

The Chapel of St Peter ad Vincula, where so many of his victims were to be buried, also received Henry VIII's early attention. A chapel stood on this site as early as the reign of Henry I. It was re-roofed and greatly embellished two hundred years later by Henry III, who, as we have seen, put in large glazed windows, a 'great painted beam' bearing a crucifix and images of saints and cherubim. His son Edward I demolished the chapel and completely rebuilt it. Early in the reign of Henry VIII it was burnt down, and in 1515 he rebuilt the entire structure save for its northern wall, which is the only part of the original building still standing today. Henry put in the fine chestnut roof we see now, as well as the arches and the windows. There are two altars, one dedicated to St Peter, the other to the Virgin Mary, and there is a hagioscope or squint cut into the wall for the priest to peep through at the high altar.

Macaulay writes of the chapel, 'There is no sadder spot on earth. Death is there associated, not as in Westminster Abbey and St Paul's, with genius and virtue . . . not, as in our humblest churches and churchyards, with everything that is most endearing, but with whatever is darkest in human nature and in human destiny, with the savage triumph of implacable enemies, with the inconstancy, the ingratitude, the cowardice of friends, with all the miseries of fallen greatness and of blighted fame. Thither have been carried through successive ages, by the rude hands of gaolers, without one mourner following, the bleeding relics of men who had been the captains of armies, the leaders of parties, the oracles of senates, and the ornaments of courts.' We have seen quite a number of them taken there; more were to follow.

To the left of the Bloody Tower entrance into the Inner Ward, Henry VIII also built an L-shaped row of half-timbered and gabled houses, all of three storeys and attics, the chief of which was known as the Lieutenant's House, though it was later called the King's House or the Queen's House, according to the monarch on the throne. The row stretches from the space to the west of the Bloody Tower, where there was once a garden, as far as the Bell Tower, where More and Fisher and later Princess Elizabeth were imprisoned. Then the line of houses turns northwards, going almost up to the Beauchamp Tower; it was in this section that Anne Boleyn, and later Lady Jane Grey, were kept prisoner.

The Chapel of St Peter ad Vincula, rebuilt for the third time in 1515. Before the high altar are the tombs of Anne Boleyn and Katherine Howard, flanked by those of the Dukes of Somerset and Northumberland. The canopied tomb to the left of the altar is that of John Holland, Duke of Exeter and Constable of the Tower; it originally stood in St Katherine's Hospital. (Ministry of Public Building and Works)

147

CHAPTER THIRTY-THREE

The King's Armoury

Henry VIII's other work on the Tower was the erection of strong elevated mounts at various points to support the larger and heavier cannon which had come into use. The most important of these mounts may be seen today at the north-western and northeastern corners of the Outer Wall, from where the cannon could fire across the wide moat to defend the fortress from rebels attacking either from the city of London or from Whitechapel and Smithfield on the east. These two mounts are known as Legge's Mount, facing London, and Brass Mount on the other side. In addition, many towers were strengthened to support cannon and special gun emplacements were provided on the Wharf.

The Tower Armoury, with its great range of furnaces and foundries, was located by Legge's Mount between the Outer and the Inner Wall. Many of the cannon were made there, as well as iron clamps for the gun-carriages when the cannon were eventually made mobile by being put on wheels. In 1513, when Henry VII was on the throne, new foundries and workshops were opened not far from the Palace of Greenwich for the making of these large guns.

Firearms came in a year or so earlier. A few, known as 'hand-cannon', had been manufactured shortly after Henry VII came to the throne, although they did not come into general use until the reign of Henry VIII. The long-bow, however, was still retained; indeed, for more than a century bows and arrows as well as firearms were used by the troops. Breech-loading, the rifled barrel and the revolving chamber also made their appearance in Henry VIII's time.

Armour was made by skilled craftsmen and ironsmiths in the Tower workshops, which were established there in the very early years. The coat of chain mail, called a hauberk by the Normans, hung from the neck to the knees; the sleeves were loose and came as far as the elbows, and the skirt was slit at the front and the back for riding. It was made of linked iron rings sewn on to leather and had overlapping scales of iron, horn or leather sewn on to padded lozenges or squares. With it was worn a helmet with a downward guard jutting out to protect the nose. A kite-shaped shield was carried on the left arm. William the Conqueror wore chain mail at the Battle of Hastings; as the back and front of the hauberk were almost identical, William put it on back to front, as an intimation that the battle was to decide his change of status from Duke to King.

Armour of this type, with few changes (the sleeves were extended to the wrists and the stockings and shoes were also manufactured in chain mail), was worn by Richard I in the Holy Land, by his brother John and by Henry III. Edward I reinforced it with larger pieces of plate to provide greater protection from the metal-tipped arrows of the long-bow; the plates were so shaped that the arrows glanced off them, and they also safeguarded the wearer against lance and sword, mace and axe in hand-to-hand fighting. The plates grew larger and larger in succeeding years, and by the time of Agincourt most of the armour was made of plate. It was generally called 'white armour' because the metal was left bright, i.e. unpainted.

With the introduction of firearms, the armour plates became larger and thicker to resist bullets, and the weight of the armour was consequently much increased. The horse's armour too was similarly strengthened. The heavily armoured horseman had inevitably some difficulty in man-oeuvring. Lighter armour still continued to be made for tournaments and tilting and for full dress wear on State occasions. By Henry VIII's reign the skill and artistry of the craftsmen had reached a remarkably high standard, as may be seen in the splendid display of armour in the White Tower. The suits of armour worn by Henry VIII are particularly attractive and interesting. One, made for him when he was young, has a waist measurement of thirty-two inches: along the edge of the skirt is a lover's knot, linking the initials H and K in commemoration of his marriage to Katherine of Aragon. Another suit, worn towards the end of his life when he was fat, has a waist measurement of fifty-two inches and weighs ninety-four pounds. The richness of the decoration is most striking.

Though the King's armour was kept in the Palace of Greenwich, the Tower was the national storehouse for other armour and for weapons, and the Crown made repeated calls on the sheriffs of various counties for the despatch of arms. In 1341, for example, the Sheriff of Gloucestershire was ordered to 'purchase and deliver into the Tower one thousand bows; three hundred and fifty to be painted and the rest to be plain'. The price of each painted bow was fixed at eighteen pence, the plain at a shilling. The arrows cost a shilling a sheaf. Many thousands of long-bows and an enormous supply of arrows were kept in the Tower throughout the reign of Edward III and drawn on as required. Again and again, from the field of battle or from one of the Cinque Ports, while the warships waited for a favourable wind, messengers were sent to the Tower with requisitions for additional supplies of weapons or siege engines.

There is an engaging item in the records concerning swords, 'some greater and some smaller for to learn the King to play in his tender age'—the King was Henry VI, who succeeded to the throne when he was nine months old. And again: 'item a little harness that the Earl of Warwick made for the King, garnished with gold'.

The collection of armour and weapons was begun in the reign of Henry VIII. A hundred years later, when armour was no longer used, Charles II set up a museum for its display in the Tower, though it was on view there even earlier. The Armouries, as the collection is called, is in fact the oldest museum in England.

By 1542, though only fifty-one, Henry VIII was an old man, weak, ailing and enormously fat; his ulcerated leg caused him so much pain that his temper was even more ferocious than before. During the last few years of his reign, moreover,

he found himself involved in two wars.

The first of these wars was with Scotland. Learning that the continuing quarrel between the Emperor Charles V and Francis I had brought them to the brink of armed conflict, Henry seized the chance to settle an old score with Scotland.

Armour of Henry VIII as a young man, probably made at Greenwich by Milanese armourers in 1514/15, and engraved, silvered and gilded by the Fleming Paul van Vrelant, the King's 'harness gilder'. The skirt is ornamented with the initials 'H' and 'K' for Henry and Katherine of Aragon. The horse armour is Flemish, c. 1515. (Ministry of Public Building and Works)

Armour made for Henry VIII at Greenwich c. 1535, when he was in his middle forties. (Ministry of Public Building and Works)

All through his reign he had insisted that the Scots were rebels for not submitting to his suzerainty. They had, moreover, welcomed the papal order for Henry's dethronement, were incessantly intriguing with his enemies on the Continent, and had sheltered refugees from the Pilgrimage of Grace.

In an effort to achieve an amicable settlement, Henry had summoned his sister Margaret's son,

King James V of Scotland, to meet him at York for a discussion, but James refused to come. A border clash in which the English were defeated caused Henry to send a large force north under the command of the Duke of Norfolk, the now ageing hero of Flodden. In October 1542 they crossed the border. At first the English met with reverses, but in the end the Scots were utterly routed at Solway Moss. Enormous numbers were slain or taken prisoner, including some of the greatest nobles of Scotland. James V died on being told of the disaster, leaving as his successor his daughter Mary, who was only one week old. Thus did Mary Queen of Scots inherit her throne.

The struggle now was over this child. Many advised Henry to arrange a marriage between her and his heir Prince Edward, which would lead in time to a union between the two countries; but Henry wanted the throne of Scotland for himself, and Parliament endorsed his claim. The Scots, no longer in a position to carry on the war, agreed to the marriage of the infant Mary with Henry's heir, but beyond that they refused to go. Francis I came to their rescue, offering to send ships and troops to Scotland, and began negotiations for Mary's marriage with a French prince. This presented a danger that Henry could not ignore. He at once entered into a treaty of alliance with Charles V, and the two rulers jointly declared war on France.

Henry sent a detachment of English troops across the Channel, but before setting out to join them, he married his sixth wife, Katherine Parr, at Hampton Court. She was of a modest background, her father being a knight in the remote county of Westmorland. Thirty-one years old, short, plump, with attractive hazel eyes, she had been married twice before and had been widowed quite recently. Sir Thomas Seymour, the brother of Jane Seymour, had wanted to marry her but was overridden; after Henry's death he became her fourth husband.

Katherine's influence over Henry was beneficial and she achieved a reconciliation between him and his daughter Elizabeth. But even with her, his rages sometimes got the better of him. Once his fury drove him to signing a warrant for Katherine's committal to the Tower. When the Lord Chancellor arrived with a guard to take her away, the King, who had by now got over his displeasure, was found seated happily beside her. When he saw the guard, he flew into a fresh rage. Turning angrily on the Chancellor, he shouted 'Knave! Fool! Beast!' and motioned him away.

150

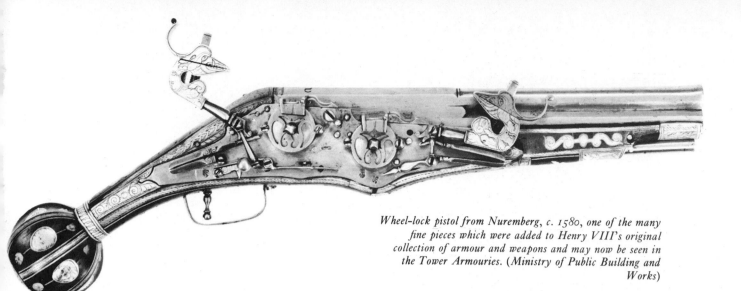

Wheel-lock pistol from Nuremberg, c. 1580, one of the many fine pieces which were added to Henry VIII's original collection of armour and weapons and may now be seen in the Tower Armouries. (Ministry of Public Building and Works)

One cannot tell what would have happened had the King lived longer, but he died three years later and his sixth wife survived him.

The King put on his armour for the last time in 1545 and crossed the Channel to lead his own army. He began by besieging Boulogne, which the Duke of Suffolk had failed to capture early in his reign. Suffolk, now well advanced in years, was brought over to try again, and this time he was successful. Boulogne remained in English hands for eight years; counting Calais, it was the second Channel port in English possession. But the Emperor soon made a separate peace with France, and Henry was left to fight on alone. War had by now broken out again in Scotland. After months of terrible strain and sacrifice (Henry mortgaged his estates and melted down his gold plate) and the landing of a French force on the Isle of Wight, Henry finally made peace. His war against Scotland had also proved a failure.

Norfolk, who had been spared when the other Howards were sent to the Tower, was now suddenly arrested, together with his son Surrey. Shortly before the execution of his cousin Katherine Howard, the young man had been made a Knight of the Garter, and had taken part in the fighting in France and in Scotland. But Henry, with his own death so near, had become deeply concerned about the possibility of trouble on the accession of his son Edward, who had a Protestant mother and was to have his mother's brother Edward Seymour, Earl of Hertford, as a Protestant Protector. The Howards were avowed Catholics, and Surrey was known to be an enemy of Hertford's. Moreover, being of royal blood (he was descended from Edward I), Surrey had imprudently gone so far as to quarter the royal arms with his own. He and his father were now charged with treason. The King himself in-

vestigated the case. Surrey was found guilty and was beheaded early in January 1547 on Tower Hill.

On the preceding day Parliament had met to deal with his father, who was now seventy-three. The Duke of Norfolk, writing from the Tower to the Lords of the Council of which he had for so long been the leading member, asked for some books to be sent him from his home at Lambeth because he could not go to sleep without having something to read. He also wanted 'some sheets to lie on' and to be allowed 'to walk in the daytime in the chamber without, and in the night to be locked again as I am now'. But the request was refused. He then sent a pleading letter to the King: 'In all my life I have never so much as imagined an untrue thought against your Majesty . . . For all the services I have rendered unto your Majesty, I implore that my accusers and I be brought before your Majesty or your Council, and then if I do not make apparent that I was wrongfully accused that I might have punishment according to my deserts.' Among his accusers was Mrs Elizabeth Holland, who had been a laundress in the service of the Dowager Duchess of Norfolk and had been Norfolk's mistress for many years.

Parliament decreed his execution and the date was fixed for the morning of 28 January 1547. In the small hours of that very morning the King died. Norfolk's execution was not carried out, but he was kept a prisoner in the Tower for six years, throughout the reign of King Edward VI, and was released on the accession of the Catholic Queen Mary, the elder of Henry VIII's two daughters.

There is no need to add further to the long list of Henry's prisoners in the Tower, which would fill many pages. Many were brought there not only each year, but each month and week.

CHAPTER THIRTY-FOUR

Lady Jane Grey

Edward VI was not quite ten years old when he succeeded to the throne. He lost no time in moving into the Palace in the Tower which his father had so elaborately redesigned and decorated.

On 31 January 1547, three days after Henry's death, which had for some reason been kept secret, Edward was proclaimed King at Westminster Hall and set out at once for the Tower, riding through the streets of London on a white horse, accompanied by his uncle Edward Seymour, soon to be Lord Protector, and an exalted company of nobles. Large numbers of mounted troops, their armour clanging, preceded and followed, while from the Tower the cannon on the mounts built by his father thundered their salute. The crowds came out and cheered their pale young King, looking so self-possessed and serious; it was a heartfelt outpouring of their relief that the savage, capricious fury of Henry VIII was at an end, though it is surprising that their horror and repulsion never found an outlet while he lived.

Having crossed the drawbridge, the new King was received at the Lion Tower by the Constable, Sir John Gage. At the drawbridge of the Byward Tower he was welcomed by Archbishop Cranmer, the Lord Chancellor and members of the Council, who escorted him to the Palace, which was 'richly hung and garnished with cloth of Arras and cloth of Estate'. There were so many lords in attendance that there was not room for them all in the Tower and many had to be found lodgings in the city outside.

The next day the Council met in the Presence Chamber (possibly the Great Hall) for the ceremony of kissing the sovereign's hand and swearing allegiance. Then the Lord Chancellor read out Henry VIII's will, made a month before

he died and signed with a trembling hand. It directed that the government of the country until Edward reached the age of eighteen should be in the hands of a Regency consisting of sixteen members of the Council. But eventually the young King's uncle the Earl of Hertford took control as Protector.

The King, Hertford and the Council remained in the Tower for some weeks. A number of ceremonies had been arranged, the first of which was the curious one of 'knighting the King'. This took place on Sunday 6 February. The Lord Mayor of London, accompanied by the aldermen, sheriffs and other city authorities, as well as the judges and the serjeants-at-law clad in scarlet robes, rode in state to the Tower and assembled in the Presence Chamber. The young King was dressed in a black cape and cap and all the courtiers wore mourning. The city fathers and judges made their obeisance, and then the Lord Protector, after reading out the declaration that it was the King's wish that he should be made a knight, took up his sword. The King discarded his mourning cape and cap and bent his head to receive the accolade. Edward then knighted the Lord Mayor and some of the judges. Ten days later there was a further ceremony of knighting in the Tower: following the precedent of Henry IV, forty Knights of the Bath were created and a number of peerages were also conferred, the chief of these being the Dukedom of Somerset on the Lord Protector.

This was the prelude to the coronation, which took place on 19 February. The King, dressed in white velvet and cloth of silver, rode out of the Tower on a horse decked with crimson trappings. The streets were gay with decorations, and there were numerous tableaux and diversions at which the King and his nobles laughed heartily. At

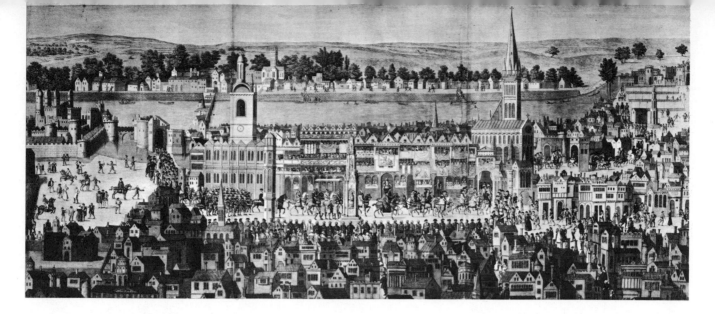

The coronation procession of Edward VI leaving the Tower on its way to Westminster Abbey. Engraving made in 1787 from a painting at Cowdray, Sussex; the original was burnt in 1793. (By permission of the Trustees of the British Museum)

Cheapside the King was presented with a purse containing £1000, so heavy that he could hardly hold it. At St Paul's a sailor slid down from the battlements of the steeple on a cable made fast to an anchor by the Dean's Gate, 'coming down as though he was flying, with his hands and legs spread out and his body gliding along the wire'. It was regarded as a 'pretty toy' to amuse the boy-King. The coronation service at Westminster Abbey was shortened because of his age.

The Protector aimed to make England a Protestant kingdom. The Mass was replaced by Morning Service and Communion; this was laid down in the first *Book of Common Prayer* which he now issued. The priests in the two main chapels in the Tower—St John's and St Peter ad Vincula—were removed, and Protestant chaplains took their place. The changes were not confined to ritual. A proclamation against the use of church ornaments led to a vandalistic attack on stained-glass and rood-screens.

The King's health being frail, the problem of the succession gave cause for continuous anxiety. If he were succeeded by his half-sister Mary, as Henry VIII had arranged in his will, there would be a sharp swing back to Catholicism, with dire consequences for the Protestants. But this was not the only problem with which the country was confronted. Henry's wars had brought the country to the verge of bankruptcy, and the war with Scotland soon flared up again. The coinage had already been debased, and Somerset had to in-struct the Tower Mint to debase it yet again. There was widespread unemployment.

Somerset was an idealist rather than a strong ruler. His handsome brother Thomas, made Lord Seymour of Sudeley in the Coronation Honours, lost no time in starting an intrigue to wrest the supreme power from the Protector. As a first step he sought to marry one of the two princesses who were the next heirs to the throne. Failing in this, he married Henry's widow Katherine Parr and also took under his care Lady Jane Grey, whose descent from Henry VIII's sister Mary, Duchess of Suffolk, gave her a claim to the succession. He then made indelicate approaches to Princess Elizabeth, at that time a girl of fifteen, while she was staying in his house. He used to slip half-dressed into her bedroom in the mornings, romp about the room with her and tickle her.

This soon became known, and it was even whispered that he had made the Princess pregnant. Somerset arrested Elizabeth's governess Mrs Ashley and her 'cofferer' Parry and sent them both to the Tower. They were later brought before the Council and revealed what had been happening. Once Somerset had the evidence he wanted, the servants were released from the Tower and Lord Seymour was arrested at his home in the Strand in January 1549. 'By God's precious soul!' he cried as the guards appeared, 'whosoever lays hands on me to fetch me to prison, I shall thrust my dagger into.' They seized him nevertheless and took him to the Tower. He was charged with treason, that is to say plotting to overthrow his brother, and was condemned to death by Parliament in an Attainder.

Shortly before his death, he bade his servant to 'speed the thing that he wrote of'. He was apparently referring to two letters he had written, one

153

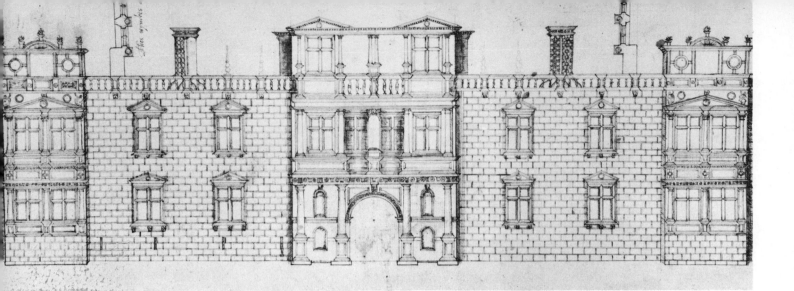

to Princess Mary, the other to Princess Elizabeth, which he had hidden in the sole of his shoe. The letters urged them to oppose the Protector, who was trying, he said, to turn the King against them in order to exclude them from the succession. The servant subsequently revealed this under torture and was hanged for having had a hand in it. Lord Seymour was executed on Tower Hill on 20 March 1549.

His brother Somerset met a similar death two years later. Unemployment was spreading and prices were rising. There was an abundance of silver in Europe, brought by the Spaniards from the mines of Mexico and Peru. In consequence, English silver shillings became more plentiful and their value fell; when debased by increasing their copper content, they were worth still less. The prices of wheat and cattle, fish and cloth were almost trebled as a result. This caused acute hardship among the poor, who were further distressed because the landlords were enclosing more and more agricultural land for pasturing sheep, to benefit from the rising price of wool. Thus the land available for growing food continually diminished.

Two rebellions broke out during 1549, one in the western counties, the other in Norfolk. Somerset suppressed the first with the aid of foreign mercenaries; but the second, started by a tanner named Robert Kett, proved more difficult to deal with and soon spread to Yorkshire and the Midlands. Kett's forces at one time numbered thirty thousand and were busy slaughtering sheep by the thousand. The mercenaries sent against them were beaten off. The rich and influential nobles on the Council turned in their rage against Somerset, and he was sent to the Tower.

Opposition to his rule had been mounting fast. The execution of his brother and the introduction

Drawing by John Thorpe of Somerset House, the Strand. To build it, the Protector demolished two churches and much private property; Westminster Abbey and St Margaret's narrowly escaped through timely bribes. (By permission of the Trustees of Sir John Soane's Museum, London. Photo: Fine Art Engravers Ltd)

of foreign mercenaries had caused considerable anger; now, his failure to deal with Kett brought things to a head. His opponents took the precaution of seizing the Tower; they removed the Lieutenant from his post and appointed a man of their own choice. Somerset promptly retaliated by warning the people in London and of the provincial towns that the Privy Council, 'of late from the dunghill', were conspiring to kill him as well as the King. His appeal was unheeded. He had been staying at Hampton Court with the King and, sensing trouble, had moved his Majesty to the greater security of Windsor. Finding that he could not hold out for long against his opponents, he finally gave himself up on the assurance that his life would be spared and his possessions left intact.

Somerset was imprisoned in the Beauchamp Tower. The nobles regarded him as much too weak to rule the country. A strong man was needed and one was available—John Dudley, son of the tax-collector Edmund Dudley who had been executed with Sir Richard Empson in 1510. He was a man of iron resolution and outstanding skill and efficiency. In the Coronation Honours distributed by Edward VI he had been given a peerage and had taken the title of Earl of Warwick; in 1551 he was made Duke of Northumberland. His handling of the rebellion was vigorous and effective; he routed Kett's forces. Thousands of rebels were killed and hundreds of prisoners were executed; Kett himself was hanged at Norwich.

Northumberland now took over the government of the country. Actuated by an insatiable ambition, he concentrated on his own advancement while still attending to the urgent need to put the affairs of the country in order. He was shrewd enough to realize that only by demonstrating that he could rule fairly and fearlessly would he be able to attain his ultimate goal. His aim was high, and he plotted unscrupulously to secure the succession to the throne for his own family. The fate of Lord Seymour, who had embarked on a similar project, did not appear to discourage him. Northumberland's scheme was to divorce his wife and marry Princess Elizabeth; but like Seymour he found this impossible to achieve. So he began to seek an easier alternative.

The young King was unmarried, had consumption and clearly would not live long. Henry VIII had specified that if Edward died childless he was to be succeeded by his elder sister Mary, and then by Elizabeth if Mary left no children. As Mary was an ardent Catholic, Northumberland was confident that he could bypass her. Who else was there apart from Elizabeth? As we know, Henry VIII had two sisters: the elder, Margaret, had a granddaughter, Mary Queen of Scots, also a Catholic. So the Duke turned to the younger line, descended through Henry's other sister Mary, whose granddaughter was the Protestant Lady Jane Grey. Northumberland's three eldest sons were already married, so he chose his fourth, Lord Guildford Dudley, as her husband, and the couple were married in May 1553. By this time the King was dying. Northumberland worked on the fifteen-year-old boy, pointing out that unless his sister Mary was set aside, the work of the Reformation would be completely undone. In any case, he argued, both Mary and Elizabeth had been declared illegitimate by Acts of Parliament. Edward, young and ill, was easily persuaded. A new settlement for the succession was made, naming Lady Jane Grey as the rightful heir. The document was signed by Edward VI and witnessed by the entire Council.

Somerset had been released from the Tower a little earlier, and there was a show of reconciliation with Northumberland, which led to the marriage of Somerset's daughter Anne and Northumberland's son Ambrose. Somerset was also restored to a seat on the Council. But the reconciliation did not last long. Northumberland learnt that Somerset was conspiring against him, had him arrested and sent him back to the Tower, charged with treasonably planning to attack and seize the Tower with a force of two thousand men. Taken from the Tower by barge at five o'clock on a dark December morning for his trial at Westminster Hall, Somerset admitted that he had collected armed men and had talked of killing Northumberland, but had later changed his mind. He was found not guilty of treason, but guilty of felony, which did not carry the death sentence. The Tower's serjeant-at-arms had brought his axe to the trial; on leaving with Somerset, he held the sharp edge of the axe away from him. The crowd, thinking that Somerset had been acquitted on every charge, cheered wildly and threw their caps into the air, many of which were lost, the chronicler Machyn tells us. This show of popularity sealed Somerset's fate, although nothing was done for nearly two months.

His arrogance, so marked throughout his life, was still evident. Messages were sent by him from the Tower to say that the 'Duke of Somerset prayeth to have: One gowne, one velvet cappe, one night cappe; two doublets; two payre of hose; three shirts; two payre velvet shoes' and so on, including tablecloths and a dozen table napkins and '£10 in money to pay for his washing, cleaning, and other necessaries'. The Duchess had also been arrested; she sent an even longer list of the apparel she required, which included a velvet waistcoat, seven plain smocks, a kirtle of black velvet, a gown of black satin, a pair of leather slippers and £20 for her washing and cleaning.

Somerset's execution was fixed for the morning of 22 January 1552. An attempt to rescue him was feared, and the Council ordered all inhabitants of London and the suburbs to stay indoors. A thousand men-at-arms were brought to Tower Hill as a precaution. Together with the garrison, they encircled the scaffold. But despite the Council's orders, the great square on Tower Hill and all the streets leading to it were thronged with spectators, pressing hard against the circle of armed men.

The Tower guard brought out the prisoner at eight o'clock. He looked strikingly handsome and, according to the records, every inch a gentleman. He was dressed as though for a State reception. He stepped boldly up the steps of the scaffold and knelt and said a prayer. Then he made a short speech: 'I am come here to die. I thank God, who might have taken me suddenly, that I was given time to remember and acknowledge him.' While he was speaking, a fresh company of soldiers, sent as an added precaution, startled both the guards and the crowd. The thought flashed through many minds that a pardon was being brought for

Somerset. It caused a great commotion. Machyn records, 'A thousand fell to the ground for fear; a hundred fell into the Tower ditch; some ran away.'

Somerset called on the crowd 'to pray together for the King's majesty'; then he drew off his rings and gave them to the executioner. Unbuckling his sword, he gave it to the Lieutenant of the Tower, Sir Arthur Davey; he removed his cloak and, after loosening his shirt collar, knelt and lowered his head on the block. The axe was raised, and all was over. He was buried close to his brother in the Chapel of St Peter ad Vincula. The Duchess was kept a prisoner in the Tower until the next reign.

Having disposed of Somerset, Northumberland concentrated on completing his plans for Lady Jane Grey's accession as Queen with his own son as King Consort. The Council, only too aware of the danger to their lives if they refused to agree, signed the necessary papers. The judges, however, refused to comply, despite the personal plea of the dying King. Northumberland confronted them in a great rage. He was so savage that the judges thought he would strike them; finally, after a written assurance had been given them by the King, guaranteeing a royal pardon if their consent was regarded later as a crime, they agreed.

Edward VI died on the evening of 6 July 1553, the anniversary of Sir Thomas More's execution. For almost a month his death had been daily expected. The doctors despaired of saving his life. They were satisfied that he was suffering from tuberculosis, but quite suddenly and astonishingly strange eruptions began to appear on his skin, his hair fell out, then his nails and finally the joints of his toes and fingers. Poison was suspected by both Catholics and Protestants; according to Machyn, no one doubted it. It was widely held that Northumberland, having arranged the succession to his satisfaction, was interested only in hastening the end. He certainly kept the death secret until all arrangements had been made to prevent Mary from becoming Queen. He wrote to her at Hunsdon in Hertfordshire to say that the King was 'sick and wished to see her'; as the boy was already dead, it seems obvious that he intended to seize her, intern her in the Tower and probably execute her on some pretext.

Some weeks earlier he had had forty pieces of cannon shipped to England from Calais. He replaced the Constable of the Tower, Sir John Gage, by an officer of his own choice, who at once began strengthening the defences and transferred cannon from various forts on the Thames estuary to the Tower. The garrison in the Tower was also greatly increased. The royal bodyguard, known as the Yeomen of the Guard and wearing the uniform selected by Henry VII, were increased in number, and were constantly drilled and exercised in the grounds to the north of the White Tower. Large supplies of fresh ammunition and firearms were also brought in and stored in the cellars of the many towers built into the Outer Wall. The workmen inside the Tower and the Londoners on Tower Hill wondered at these activities and whispered their suspicions to each other.

The moment the King died the entire Council went to Syon House at Isleworth, which Northumberland had made his riverside home, to tell Lady Jane Grey that she was now Queen. The news came as a complete surprise to her. Protesting and weeping, the sixteen-year-old girl at first refused to accept the honour. But her father-in-law, her husband Lord Guildford Dudley, and her own father, who had been made Duke of Suffolk in 1551, persisted, and eventually, with the utmost reluctance, she yielded. On 10 July, four days after the King's death, she was escorted to the State barge and, accompanied by a procession of other boats, made the journey down the Thames to the Tower. On her arrival, the cannon on the White Tower and on St Thomas's Tower thundered a royal salute.

The small, slender schoolgirl-Queen climbed the steps of the Wharf wearing a jewelled coronet and a robe of green velvet. A large number of officials, headed by the Constable and the Lieutenant, received her with deference and homage. But so strong were the suspicions against Northumberland, who was regarded by many as the King's murderer, that neither the people in the Tower nor the spectators on the river banks who saw the barges go down the river showed any enthusiasm. They 'were very silent . . . Not a single shout of welcome was raised.' Jane's husband, dressed entirely in white, walked at her side, her mother carried her train and the Council followed as she went to the Great Hall in the Palace. Now that she was secure inside the fortress, the moment had come for her to be publicly proclaimed Queen. The royal heralds climbed the ramparts of the Outer Wall. There was a flourish of trumpets. Standing at the four corners, the heralds read a lengthy document es-

tablishing Jane's right to the throne. The proclamation was repeated at St Paul's Cross in the city of London. The people were stunned and quite unresponsive. A vintner's boy who raised a cheer for Queen Mary was instantly arrested and nailed by his ears to the pillory.

Mary Tudor, the rightful heir, had set out for London on receiving Northumberland's letter, but a warning reached her from friends and she turned back and made for Norfolk, where she was confident of receiving support from the nobles. They rallied to her support, and a few days later, with an army of ten thousand, she started again for London. Northumberland, who had three hundred horsemen out scouting for her on the route she was expected to take, learned before long of her immense army. He also discovered that many of the ships he had sent to Yarmouth and other ports on the east coast had also gone over to Mary.

Meanwhile, unaware of these developments, Jane was trying to fulfil her duties as Queen. Of a studious bent, she had devoted her growing years to study and had acquired a very thorough knowledge of Greek and Latin, French and Italian, as well as of Hebrew, Arabic and Chaldee. Needlework and music were also among her accomplishments. Her first evening in the Tower was spent signing documents and letters to the Lords-Lieutenant of the various counties, commanding them to proclaim her accession. The following morning she quarrelled with her mother-in-law the Duchess of Northumberland, who insisted that Jane's husband should be made King Consort. Jane refused to agree, as no such provision had been set out in Edward VI's ruling. She was prepared, she said, to make him a Duke, but not a King.

On the next day, the twelfth, the official crown and royal regalia were brought to her from the Jewel House, but she no more than glanced at them. On the two following days she was ill, but still carried out various duties such as appointing officials. Her coronation medal was struck at the Mint in the Tower: it appears to have been made without her knowledge, for the Dudley arms are said to have been quartered with the royal arms and it bore the initials JR (Jane Regina) and GR (Guildford Rex). On Sunday the seventeenth she attended Divine Service in St John's Chapel. Alarming news of Mary's progress had been reaching the Tower every day, and by that evening the news was very serious.

Northumberland had gone out against Mary himself with several noblemen, a troop of horse and many thousands of armed followers. On reaching Newmarket he sent back a message to the Council, the members of which were all residing in the Tower and met daily in the White Tower; Northumberland complained that they had not provided sufficient forces and that his followers had begun to desert. He got as far as Bury St Edmunds but, conscious now that defeat was inevitable, fell back on Cambridge. Very early that same morning, the nineteenth, many of the Councillors had gone to see Jane's father the Duke of Suffolk, who had been left in charge during Northumberland's absence. They proposed to leave the Tower in order to ask the French ambassador for reinforcements from France to help Northumberland.

The Councillors were permitted to leave, but instead of carrying out their supposed mission, they ordered that Mary should be proclaimed Queen. They then sent a messenger to summon Suffolk from the Tower and induced him to sign the proclamation. Later that day Suffolk himself stood on Tower Hill and proclaimed Mary as the rightful Queen. He then went to see his daughter and inform her of what he had done. Jane was greatly relieved at the removal of the unwanted

Memorial to members of the Dudley family in the Beauchamp Tower. Beneath a bear and a lion supporting a ragged staff is the name of 'John Dudle', Northumberland's eldest son; in the surrounding wreath, his four brothers are represented by roses (Ambrose), gillyflowers (Guildford), honeysuckle (Henry) and a spray of oak (Latin robur, for Robert). The inscription is incomplete. (Ministry of Public Building and Works)

burden and prepared to leave the Tower, but this she was not allowed to do.

Later that same day Northumberland was taken prisoner at Cambridge. Jane was also arrested, but she was allowed to remain in the Palace, where the sound of the general rejoicing in London and in the Tower itself reached her. Her parents left very hurriedly. Northumberland and many of his supporters were brought in a few days later and were lodged in the Bloody Tower. All his sons were arrested too, including Jane's husband, who had gone with his mother to Sheen. The Duke of Suffolk and many other noblemen

were soon arrested and brought to the Tower. When her husband was taken away, the Duchess of Suffolk hurried out to intercede with Queen Mary and reached her as she was approaching London. The Duchess threw herself at the Queen's feet and begged mercy for her husband which was granted. Suffolk was released but was made to pay a heavy fine.

On 3 August Queen Mary made a triumphant entry into London accompanied by her half-sister Princess Elizabeth; it was shrewd of her to bring Elizabeth, for the people knew that it was against these two that Northumberland had been plotting. They rode together through the gaily decorated streets to the Tower, cheered all the way by the excited citizens, and as they passed through the Bulwark Gate the guns boomed their salute to the new Queen. Many of the prisoners were lined up on Tower Green, including the old Duke of Norfolk, now nearing eighty, the pro-Catholic Bishop of Winchester, Stephen Gardiner, who had been imprisoned by Edward VI, and the Duchess of Somerset, widow of the Lord Protector. As Mary approached, walking towards them hand in hand with her sister Elizabeth, all the prisoners went down on their knees. Mary was moved to tears, we are told, by Gardiner's words. She embraced each of them and released them. Norfolk's estates were restored to him and Gardiner was given a seat on the Council. Mary then took up residence in the Palace in the Tower. Lady Jane had by now been moved into the house of the Yeoman Gaoler Mr Partridge, which was in a wing of the Lieutenant's House, overlooking Tower Green.

Northumberland and his heir John Dudley were taken from the Tower a fortnight later for their trial at Westminster Hall. They were found guilty of treason for setting up Lady Jane as Queen and 'compassing Mary's destruction'. They were brought back to the Beauchamp Tower, where the Dudley inscriptions on the walls may still be seen. Northumberland lost no time in reverting to the Catholic faith and begged the Queen's permission to be allowed to celebrate Mass in St John's Chapel. Mary consented, and many London merchants and all the Privy Councillors were commanded to attend. Bishop Gardiner acted as celebrant. But it did not save Northumberland's life. The night before his execution, in a last desperate appeal, he begged Mary to spare his life so that he might 'kiss the Queen's feet'. But like his father the tax-collector he perished on the scaffold on Tower Hill, and his son Guildford, Lady Jane's husband, met the same fate a little later; thus three members of successive generations of the Dudley family suffered death under the axe.

Lady Jane, though under restriction, was treated as a guest rather than a prisoner in the Tower. Queen Mary, it seems, had no intention of executing her. Her tragic end was brought about some months later by the violent demonstrations that broke out in many parts of England following the news that Mary was to marry Prince Philip of Spain (later Philip II), a Catholic and a foreigner. Suffolk, taking advantage of this outburst of feeling, appeared suddenly in Leicester with his two brothers and a large body of retainers, and proclaimed his daughter Queen again. The rebellion was soon crushed. Suffolk was found hiding in an oak-tree, taken prisoner and brought to the Tower. A second rebellion was started in Kent in favour of Princess Elizabeth by Sir Thomas Wyatt, a man of culture and valour, grandson of the Wyatt who was fed by a cat in the Tower and son of the poet who was in love with Anne Boleyn. Denouncing the Spanish marriage, he rallied a large body of men at Maidstone and attracted many more as he marched on to London. The aged Duke of Norfolk was sent by Mary with an army to disperse them; but Norfolk was defeated, and the rabble, by now numbering many thousands, went on to Southwark, just across the river from the Tower, and opened fire on the fortress. A formidable cannonade was the response from the guns on the White Tower, the Develin Tower and St Thomas's Tower. Great damage was done to the wretched hovels of the poor people living around Southwark. Wyatt tried to cross the river at London Bridge but found the way barred. He eventually crossed at Kingston-on-Thames and marched on to London. But his men had by now begun to desert. After some fighting in the streets of London, he was seized and brought to the Tower. Among the numerous prisoners taken were two members of the Culpepper family.

Shortly after this, Lady Jane and her husband were tried for treason, pleaded guilty and were condemned to death. As they were brought back from the Guildhall to the Tower, the sharp edge of the processional axe was turned towards them. Their execution took place on 10 February 1554. Seventeen-year-old Lord Guildford Dudley, who was imprisoned in a separate tower, asked if he could say farewell to his wife, but Jane refused to see him, saying that she would find it unnerving. He was led out to Tower Hill at ten in the morning. A large crowd had gathered there, including many of his personal friends. He received the last rites from one of the Roman Catholic priests who had been brought in by Mary to replace the Protestant chaplains in the Tower, and then mounted the scaffold to his death. Lady Jane was standing at the window of her room; on seeing his body being brought back for burial in St Peter ad Vincula, she burst into tears.

Being of royal descent, Lady Jane was executed on Tower Green. There had been rumours that she was pregnant, and she was examined before being led out on that cold, misty morning. She was dressed in a simple black gown and was accompanied by her two ladies-in-waiting, with halberdiers and Yeomen of the Guard marching on each side. She made a short speech, accepting the justice of her sentence but protesting that she had been the unwilling tool of others. She then handed her prayer-book to the Lieutenant, Sir Thomas Brydges (in it she had written, 'There is a time to be born and a time to die'), and mounted the steps. Staring at the executioner, a giant of a man dressed in a tight-fitting suit of black wool and a hood, she gave way to a fit of hysterical sobbing. One of her ladies blindfolded her with a white handkerchief and as she knelt she began to grope for the block, saying 'Where is it? Where is it?' She was buried in St Peter ad Vincula near her husband.

Her father was executed a few days later, then two of her husband's brothers. Wyatt and many of his companions died some weeks later. A great slaughter followed; it is recorded that gibbets were erected in every part of the capital.

CHAPTER THIRTY-FIVE

Princess Elizabeth a Prisoner

For the first time since the troubled years of Matilda England was ruled by a Queen. She was to rule for five years, a shorter time even than her brother, and was to prove as savage as her father towards those who, chiefly for conscientious reasons, refused to accept her dictate.

It was Mary's aim to found her own dynasty. The marriage with Philip of Spain, son of the Emperor Charles V who controlled vast territories all over Europe—in Germany, Spain, the Netherlands and Naples—was arranged at the very beginning of her reign. In her infancy she had been used as a matrimonial pawn by her father and her godfather Wolsey. When she was only two years old a marriage had been arranged for her with the heir of King Francis I, and when for reasons of State this was broken off three years later, she was affianced to her cousin the young Emperor Charles, grandson of Ferdinand and Isabella of Spain. Now she was to marry his son Philip, who was eleven years her junior and a widower; he was twenty-six, she was thirty-seven.

But for this marriage (there was a betrothal ceremony in St John's Chapel with the Spanish envoy, the Count of Egmont, as Philip's proxy) Mary would have enjoyed the widest popularity. The sympathy of the country had been with her through the agonizing years of her childhood when her mother was divorced and she herself was declared illegitimate; through the long separation from her mother, whom she was not allowed to see when she was dying; through the indignity of being stripped of her title and made to serve her infant half-sister Elizabeth; through the hatred and spite of Anne Boleyn, who plotted to murder her; through the compulsion by her father to renounce the Pope—a long and appalling chapter of suffering. Her only friend during those years was the Emperor Charles V. The very

thought of the marriage, as we have seen, caused two rebellions, which she suppressed with the utmost severity; but much more was to follow when she enforced a return to the old religion and would brook no deviation.

Mary's coronation took place a few weeks after her arrival in the Tower as Queen. Lady Jane Grey was a prisoner at the time, the Spanish marriage had not yet been spoken of and the rebellions had not yet occurred. At this stage Mary was interested in winning over the people, and once again she had her sister Elizabeth at her side, which must have made many feel that her enforcement of Catholicism would not be severe since Elizabeth was a Protestant.

The two sisters went to the Tower by river on 29 September 1553. They boarded the State barge at Whitehall Stairs, and were accompanied by the Council and by many noble ladies, including the Protestant Anne of Cleves, in other barges. The gaily decorated wherries of the city companies, each flying its distinctive banner, formed part of the procession, with the Lord Mayor of London in his own barge at their head. Musicians, 'playing on sundry instruments very delectable', supplied a pleasant accompaniment.

On their arrival at the Queen's Steps at Tower Wharf, the cannon fired their salute, which would of course have been heard by Lady Jane Grey, wondering no doubt what her own fate was to be.

Two days later Queen Mary created fifteen Knights of the Bath—the first time a woman had done this; presumably there was some variation in the ceremony, for she is hardly likely to have given the accolade while they were still in their tubs! Among the new Knights was Edward Courtenay, of royal blood and a descendant of one of Henry VII's supporters at Bosworth. His father the Marquess of Exeter, as we saw, was sent to the Tower in 1538 and beheaded for corresponding with Cardinal Pole in Rome about the dethronement of Henry VIII. Exeter's son, only twelve years old at the time, had been held as a prisoner in the Tower ever since. Now twenty-seven, he was not only released and knighted, but was created Earl of Devonshire by Queen Mary. He was encouraged by this to hope that he might marry her, but finding it impossible, he thought of marrying Elizabeth and making her Queen. On the outbreak of the risings led by Wyatt and Lady Jane Grey's father in January 1554, Courtenay led the rebels in the west. When the revolt failed, he was arrested and sent back to the Tower. He

was released a year later, sent into exile and died shortly afterwards.

On the day before the coronation the Queen set out from the Tower in the traditional procession. It was led by seventy ladies on horseback dressed in crimson velvet. Behind them came the men, also on horseback, including the Councillors, the Lord Mayor and the sheriffs. Queen Mary, small and dark-eyed, her features irregular and unattractive, her hair a deep red, rode in a horse-drawn litter draped with cloth of silver. Her rich robes were edged with ermine; her caul, of gold network set with precious stones, was so heavy that she had to hold it up. Immediately

Mary I in 1553: painting by Anthonis Mor in the Prado, Madrid. (Mansell Collection)

behind came Princess Elizabeth and Anne of Cleves in an open chariot. Unlike her predecessors, Mary did not go straight to the Abbey but spent the night at Whitehall Palace—the Palace of Westminster had been extensively destroyed by fire some years earlier.

Having made use of Elizabeth on two important occasions which won for her the utmost sympathy and admiration from the crowds, Mary's attitude towards her sister now underwent a complete change. Elizabeth was sent to Ashridge in Hertfordshire, where she was kept in semi-captivity, for there was an inescapable nervousness that rebels might use her to restore Protestantism. When the two rebellions broke out in January 1554, although Suffolk proclaimed that he was fighting only for the succession of his daughter Jane and Wyatt made it repeatedly clear that Princess Elizabeth had 'no cognizance' whatever of the revolt, Mary ordered the arrest of her sister.

Three Privy Councillors were sent on 17 February with a guard of 250 horsemen to fetch her. They arrived late at night and were told that the Princess was ill in bed, but they forced their way into her bedroom. 'Is the haste such that you could not have waited until the morning?' Elizabeth asked. They replied that they had orders to bring her to London, dead or alive. Early next morning they set out with their prisoner. Being ill, she was taken in a litter, and the journey was made by short stages. It took six days, and those who saw the Princess as she went along the road, or at the inns where she rested for the night, openly showed their sympathy.

She was taken first to Whitehall Palace and there examined by the Council. Since she was not allowed to see her sister, she wrote the Queen a letter protesting her innocence, but received no reply. A fortnight later, on Palm Sunday, the journey to the Tower was made by boat. This time it was not at the Queen's Steps that she landed, but at Traitors' Gate.

Elizabeth expressed her utmost indignation at being brought there. It had been raining heavily for some days, and the rising river had flooded the landing stage. She glanced down at her feet, then at the steps awash with water and firmly refused to leave the boat. The Marquess of Winchester informed her that she had no choice. After glaring angrily at him for some moments, she at last stepped out of her covered boat into the heavy rain and said, 'Here landeth as true a subject, being a prisoner, as ever landed at these steps, and before thee, O God, I speak it, having none other friends but thee.' Then she sat down in her fine clothes on the wet stone and refused to budge.

The Lieutenant of the Tower, Sir John Brydges (brother of Sir Thomas), pleaded with her, 'Madam, you had best come out of the rain, for you sit unwholesomely.' She replied, 'Better sit here than in a worse place.' The Gentleman Usher burst into tears at this, and after scolding him for his folly she got up. The Tower Guard had been assembled to escort her. 'It is needed not for me,' she said, 'being but a weak woman.' They led her off to the Bell Tower, just beside the Lieutenant's House, where she was confined in the room on the upper floor, above the chamber which had been used for Sir Thomas More's cell in her father's reign.

Other prisoners in the Tower at that time were Sir Thomas Wyatt, being tortured to confess that Elizabeth did have a hand in his rebellion—for the Council were determined to execute her if enough evidence could be found; Henry Courtenay, Earl of Devonshire, who had been planning to marry Elizabeth; and three of Dudley's sons, including Robert, later Earl of Leicester, who was to be a favourite of Elizabeth's for many years after she became Queen. Her thoughts must often have been on her mother's imprisonment and execution in the Tower and also on her cousin Jane, for she enquired if Jane's scaffold was still standing, fearing that it might be used for her; but it had been dismantled.

Elizabeth was permitted to have two women attendants, and her own servants were allowed to bring food for her from outside; but the Constable, Sir John Gage, insisted that these servants must hand over the food to the guards at the gates and not enter the Tower themselves. This was to prevent Elizabeth having any communication with possible supporters outside. For the same reason all her linen was carefully examined after it was laundered, in case any messages were concealed in the garments. Elizabeth complained that the food, which she had to pay for, was greatly depleted by the 'rascal soldiers' before it reached her. Holinshed, a contemporary chronicler, declares that it was the Constable himself who 'had the good cheer and fared best'. Her complaints brought results; henceforward the food was delivered to her attendants intact, and arrangements were made for it to be warmed in one of the Tower kitchens (probably the Lieutenant's) before it was served.

The martyrdom of Bishops Latimer and Ridley at Oxford, 16 October 1555.

On Mary's insistence, Mass was celebrated in Elizabeth's cell every day. If this was intended to make her abandon her Protestantism and ensure that the country continued to be Catholic in the event of Elizabeth's succession, it failed. Bishop Gardiner was sent to talk to Elizabeth in her cell and bring about her conversion. His ways were devious: he had supported Henry when Mary's mother was divorced and had also approved of the King's supremacy over the Pope as Head of the Church of England. Later he became an ardent supporter of the Catholic Duke of Norfolk and it was he who charged Elizabeth with conspiracy. He paid her several visits, examined and cross-examined her, but all without avail.

Elizabeth's confinement was then made more rigorous. She was not allowed to leave her cell. When her health broke down, however, some concessions were made. She was allowed to walk on the ramparts between the Bell Tower and the Beauchamp Tower—still known as Princess Elizabeth's Walk—and occasionally she used the royal Privy Garden by the Palace, accompanied always by the Lieutenant and a strong guard. All other prisoners were forbidden 'so much as to look in her direction'. On one occasion, a boy of five, the son of one of the guards, gave her some flowers and was sternly warned never to go into the garden again when she was there. The flowers were taken away and examined in case a message from Courtenay was concealed in them.

On Saturday, 19 May 1554, after being imprisoned in the Tower for two and a half months, Elizabeth was released. She was taken to Tower Wharf and conveyed under strong guard in a large, cumbersome wherry, first to Richmond Palace and ultimately to Woodstock, where she was held captive. When the news of her release from the Tower became known, many London churches rang their bells, and years afterwards Elizabeth presented these churches with silken bell-ropes, one of which was still on view in Aldgate Church three hundred years later.

As we have seen, a number of distinguished men were sent to the Tower following the dual rebellion early in 1554, but Mary's religious severity, which brought a martyr's death to hundreds who refused to accept Catholicism, rarely involved the Tower. Of the few sent there the chief were Thomas Cranmer, Henry VIII's Archbishop of Canterbury, Hugh Latimer, Bishop of Worcester, and Nicholas Ridley, Bishop of London, who were charged as heretics. Together they were brought to Traitors' Gate within six days of Elizabeth's arrival there. They stood in their barge, shading their eyes as they took their last look at London, well aware that their fate would be death. The fortress was so full of prisoners that the three men were confined in the same cell. But they were not executed in the Tower; after being imprisoned there for ten months, they were taken to Oxford and burnt at the stake.

Religious intolerance was not the only cause of discontent. Only a few hundred people paid with their lives for refusing to accept the faith imposed on them; the rest of the country was indifferent. Three-quarters of the clergy returned to Catholicism. There was strong opposition, however, from the nobles to the idea of returning the lands they had acquired as a result of the dissolution of the monasteries; but Mary did not press this too hard. A far greater resistance was developing against the Spanish marriage, which Mary had induced a docile Parliament to accept. There were widespread demonstrations of protest. Some London boys made effigies of Philip of Spain and of Wyatt and joined them in a 'grand battle' in the streets of the capital which ended in 'the defeat and hanging of Philip'. The boys were whipped. Pamphlets were tossed into Queen Mary's kitchen. A mysterious woman's voice shouted abuse from a house in Aldersgate; the place was raided and she was put in the stocks. The punishments were mild, for the Queen was far more interested in the news that Philip was coming.

He arrived in England on 20 July 1554. The Spanish fleet brought him to Southampton Water and he was met by twenty gaily decorated barges. His bride awaited him in Winchester. There they met for the first time, and the marriage took place on the next day. They went together to Windsor, where Philip was made a Knight of the Garter and allowed to take precedence even over the Queen, which caused considerable annoyance. The French ambassador noted some weeks later, 'The Spanish King rules supreme in everything.'

The Tower was made ready for his reception, but after driving through the decorated streets of the city, the royal couple went only as far as the Bulwark Gate, where two 'giants' named Corineus Britannus and Gogmagog Albionus read a long, boring poem in Latin to the assembled English and Spanish nobles. The Tower itself paid its tribute in a more conventional way: 'It shot such peals of ordinaunce in and about every quarter thereof, and especially out of the top of the White Tower and of the Wharf, as never was heard the like in England heretofore.' A month or so later Londoners were surprised to see a string of twenty newly made well-guarded carts pass through the streets with Spanish halberdiers marching on each side. The carts, laden with chests full of silver brought back from South America, went through the three gates of the Tower and delivered the packaged wealth of the Incas to the Mint to be converted into shillings. 'It will make by estimation about £1000,' wrote one chronicler.

Later that year Cardinal Pole, whose mother the Countess of Salisbury had been accused of treasonable correspondence with him and executed in the Tower by Henry VIII, returned to England from Rome, and the country was once more made to acknowledge the Pope. At that moment, in the fullness of her joy, Mary believed that she was going to have a baby. Guns were fired and church bells were rung. But nothing came of it. The Queen was found to be suffering from dropsy.

It was not until the following year, on 25 August 1555, that the royal couple visited the Tower. Mary travelled in an open litter from Whitehall with Philip riding beside her. She had been very ill for months, and it was said that she drove through London for the people to see that she was still alive; they thought she looked 'like a ghost'. Mary and Philip did not stay in the

Tower, but went straight to the Wharf and took a barge from there for Greenwich Palace. Mary stayed all that autumn and winter alone there, for Philip had left her to join his numerous mistresses in the Netherlands. Mary inevitably heard of this and tried desperately to win him back. She pleaded with him to return. He replied that he would only do so if she had him crowned King in his own right. Some believed that the fires at Smithfield were kindled by her misery. Humble laymen were now being taken to the stake as heretics. A woman was martyred, and a heretic who had died was exhumed and burnt. Many disgusted Protestants left the country and formed exile groups abroad. Those who stayed were to become the hard nucleus of the Church of England that was to flourish under Elizabeth.

Philip, who became King of Spain, Naples and the Netherlands on the abdication of his father, the Emperor Charles V, returned to England for a few months in 1557 after an absence of nearly two years, in order to get additional support for his war against France. He and Mary visited the Tower again, coming by boat from Greenwich, and were received by the Lord Mayor of London and civic authorities, who had assembled under a canopy on the Wharf to welcome them. The cannon on the White Tower roared their welcome, which was taken up by the trumpets. But the royal couple stayed only a few hours; after a meal in the Palace, at which Philip's swarthy nobles sat beside Mary's, they left by the Bulwark Gate.

Mary of course acceded to Philip's request for military support, with disastrous consequences for England. Calais, her one remaining possession on the Continent, was lost; and, though Philip had English ships, reinforcements and money, he made no attempt to recover the town. This provoked the most bitter hatred against Mary throughout the country and when she died in 1558, ailing and disillusioned, she was said to be haunted by the loss of Calais. Refugees from that town and the neighbouring villages of Ham and Guienne settled on the edge of Tower Hill, which they called 'Ham and Guienne'; the locals soon corrupted this to 'Hangman's Gains'.

Two incidents involving the Tower marked the closing years of Mary's reign. The first was an attempt to 'seize the treasures of the Tower, possibly the regalia and the silver' as well as the money in the Mint. The son of Sir Edmund Peckham, Master of the Mint, and a member of the Throgmorton family were implicated. Their purpose was to use the wealth to overthrow Mary, but they were arrested and executed. The other event was a rising at Scarborough led by Thomas Stafford; though a grandson of Margaret Countess of Salisbury and nephew of Cardinal Pole, he had become a Protestant. The rebellion failed, and Stafford and his chief accomplices were brought to the Tower, where he revealed under torture that the King of France was behind the plot. Stafford was executed on Tower Hill, the commoners were hanged at Tyburn.

CHAPTER THIRTY-SIX

Queen Elizabeth's First Victims

Queen Elizabeth's accession to the throne brought an outburst of rejoicing all over the country. She was staying at Hatfield when she received the news of her sister's death; at once she mounted her horse and rode all the way to London with an escort led by Lord Robert Dudley, the Master of the Horse. He had been a prisoner in the Tower at the same time as herself. Along the route her reception was ecstatic. She was received at Cripplegate by the Lord Mayor of London. The capital was gay with tapestries, and there were smiling faces at the windows and on the roofs. As she entered the Tower, she dismounted and patted the earth with both her hands. 'Some,' she said, 'have fallen from being princes of this land to be prisoners in this place. I am raised from being prisoner in this place to be prince of this land.'

She stayed in the Palace in the Tower for a week. The Privy Council met every day in the Great Hall while the Queen chose her new ministers. William Cecil, later Lord Burleigh, was one of the first selected; another was his brother-in-law Sir Nicholas Bacon, father of the famous Francis Bacon, the statesman, philosopher and essayist. Dudley was also appointed to the Council. The religious policy of the new reign was discussed and formulated: the Queen made it clear that it was to be Protestantism.

Elizabeth was twenty-five years old. She was not pretty, though some chroniclers have called her so. Her nose was long and high-bridged, but she had large, expressive eyes and very attractive hands, and there was about her a strange fascination, attributed to her powerful personality and her fiery temper. She had been well educated, could speak a number of languages and had a quick brain.

Her coronation was fixed for Sunday, 15 January

'Queen Elizabeth's Salt Cellar', the oldest piece of banqueting plate in the Tower. Made in 1572, it is traditionally said to have been used by the Queen, although no records confirm this. (By permission of the Controller of Her Majesty's Stationery Office. Crown Copyright reserved)

1559, eight weeks after her accession. She left the Tower by boat early in December to make the preparations for her sister's funeral, and returned three days before the coronation travelling again by water, this time in the richly decorated State barge and accompanied by musicians who provided 'sweet music' all the way. When she set out for Westminster Abbey, the procession surpassed in magnificence anything London had ever seen before. It was in fact a pageant, of which she was of course the central figure. Seated in an open chariot elaborately carved and glittering with gold, and dressed in a lovely gown of blue velvet and ablaze with jewels, Queen Elizabeth drove through streets decked with a succession of ornate triumphal arches, each displaying a scene from history, and at the crossroads there were living tableaux of historical personages. One of these showed the Queen's mother, Anne Boleyn, holding hands with Henry VIII in happy amity. At Temple Bar gigantic figures of the legendary Gog and Magog greeted Her Majesty. In the procession with the Queen were 'barons and other nobility of the realm, as also a notable train of goodly and beautiful ladies richly appointed'. The Lord Mayor and Corporation and the city companies wore their handsome robes of fur-lined scarlet.

Quite early in Elizabeth's reign, political persecution began. Among her first victims was Lady Katherine Grey, the twenty-two-year-old younger sister of Lady Jane and one of Elizabeth's ladies-in-waiting. Being a great-granddaughter of Henry VII, she was the Queen's cousin and a possible claimant to the throne, but Elizabeth had ignored the danger she presented and added her to her entourage. What enraged her now was the discovery that Katherine had married without the royal consent, her husband being Edward Seymour, Earl of Hertford and son of Protector Somerset. It was the change in Katherine's figure that led to an angry interrogation by the Queen. When the truth at last emerged, Katherine was instantly arrested and sent to the Tower, and it was in the Bell Tower that her child, a son, was born.

Her twenty-one-year-old husband was away in Paris at the time of her arrest, but was ordered by the Queen to return at once. On arrival he was arrested and imprisoned in another of the towers; and the Lieutenant, Sir Edward Warner, had strict instructions not to permit husband and wife to see each other. They were kept under the strictest surveillance, but by bribing his gaoler Hertford was able to visit his wife, and in time she gave birth to a second son, Thomas, in the Tower. Like the first-born, he was christened in St Peter ad Vincula, where the bodies of so many relatives of both parents had been buried after their execution.

The Queen's rage now knew no bounds. The Lieutenant of the Tower was dismissed. Lady Katherine had already been married at the age of fifteen to Henry Herbert, Earl of Pembroke, who had had the marriage dissolved on the plea of non-consummation. Hertford was now fined £15,000 for corrupting a virgin of royal blood (no evidence could be found that they were married: the priest had disappeared and the only witness, Hertford's sister, Jane, had died) and for repeating the offence by having a second child.

The couple were kept in the Tower for some years. In time the rigours of their imprisonment were relaxed and they were allowed to meet. In the Wardrobe accounts of the Tower there is a list of the furniture supplied to Lady Hertford for her apartments. They include a bed 'with bolster of down', tapestry, curtains, turkey carpets and a chair of cloth of gold and crimson velvet with the Queen's arms on the back. She was also permitted to have her pet dogs and monkeys, which no doubt caused considerable damage to the bedding, the curtains and the furniture. In 1563, at the outbreak of plague in London, she was moved from the Tower but was brought back a year later; after being moved once again because of ill-health, she died, still a prisoner, at Cockfield Hall in 1568. Her husband was released in 1571 and married again. He spent thirty years trying to establish that his marriage with Katherine had taken place, but it was not until after Queen Elizabeth's death that the priest reappeared and a jury finally ruled that the marriage was legal.

Marriages of her kinswomen or courtiers always upset Elizabeth and she dealt swiftly and harshly with all involved. Lady Margaret Douglas was the next to incur her displeasure. Her mother was Henry VIII's sister Margaret, Queen of Scotland; King James V was her half-brother and Mary Queen of Scots was her niece. Some years earlier Margaret Douglas had contracted a marriage with Lord Thomas Howard, brother of the Duke of Norfolk, without the King's consent, and both were confined in the Tower; her husband died there, but Margaret was moved to Syon House and released shortly afterwards. Eventually she was restored to favour and later married the Earl of Lennox.

In 1565, while she was serving as lady-in-waiting to Queen Elizabeth, the startling news arrived that her son by the Lennox marriage, Henry Stuart, Lord Darnley, had married his first cousin, twenty-two-year-old Mary Queen of Scots, widow of Francis II of France. One could not expect Elizabeth to accept this calmly. Darnley, who was descended from Henry VIII's elder sister, had a better claim to the throne of England than Lady Jane Grey and her sister Katherine. Mary Queen of Scots had a similar claim; moreover, many English Catholics had already begun to rally behind her. It was the son of this marriage of Darnley with Mary Queen of Scots who eventually succeeded Elizabeth as King James I of England and thus established the Stuart dynasty.

Queen Elizabeth acted without hesitation, arresting Lady Lennox, who was shut in the Tower. She was not, however, treated with any severity. She was assigned a suite of the best rooms in the Lieutenant's House, which were specially decorated and furnished for her. She was permitted to have a staff of five servants—three women and two men. Lady Lennox carved an inscription above the stone fireplace in the Lieutenant's House which is there to this day: 'Upon the twenty daie of June in the year of our Lord a thousand five hundred three score and five the Right Honourable Countess of Lennox Grace commyted prysoner to this lodging for the marriage of her sonne Lord Henry Darnle and the Queene of Scotlande here is there names as do wayt upon her noble grace thys place.' Lennox was also arrested, but was not allowed to occupy the same rooms or even to dine with her. Their son's marriage did not last long. It took place in July 1565 and Darnley was murdered in February 1567, eighteen months later. He had always been intent on becoming King of England, and the marriage was designed to help him achieve this goal. His political ambition, dissolute habits and undesirable companions alienated his wife, who is said to have taken her Italian secretary David Rizzio as her lover. Darnley was a party to Rizzio's murder; later he himself was disposed of. The house in which he and Queen Mary were staying in Edinburgh was blown up with gunpowder shortly after Mary had left. Darnley survived but was strangled while trying to make his escape.

Queen Elizabeth treated the bereaved parents, who were still her prisoners in the Tower, with great compassion. She sent Lady Howard and Lady Cecil to the Lieutenant's House to break the terrible news to Darnley's mother. About an hour later Elizabeth's personal physician Dr Huick and the Dean of Westminster arrived to comfort the unhappy woman. Soon afterwards Lord and Lady Lennox were released.

Two years later, in 1572, Mary Queen of Scots was the cause of another imprisonment in the Tower. The Duke of Norfolk, grandson of the old Duke whose execution warrant Henry VIII had signed just before his death and son of the poet Surrey, who had been executed in the same year, was arrested and sent to the Tower charged with conspiring to marry Mary Queen of Scots. Mary was married to the Earl of Bothwell—young and handsome with a short red beard, bold and quite unscrupulous—who had already served a term in the Tower after his capture at Berwick a few years earlier. He had been released to go to France. On his way back to Scotland some months later, Queen Elizabeth sent ships after him, but he evaded arrest. His complicity in the murder of Darnley has never been questioned. Mary was believed to be his mistress, and his own recent marriage, one of his many matrimonial adventures, was dissolved to clear the way for his marriage to the Scottish Queen. This so enraged the Scots that there was a widespread uprising, as a result of which Mary was taken prisoner, but Bothwell escaped. Eventually Mary herself managed to escape and, crossing the border into Cumberland, appealed to Queen Elizabeth for help.

Elizabeth had been allowing English volunteers to help Mary's enemies. Nevertheless she sent messages of comfort to Mary and allowed her to stay in England. By now the Scottish Queen had been deposed in favour of her one-year-old son James. Moreover James was to be brought up as a Protestant by his uncle the Earl of Moray, who had been appointed Regent and was himself a confirmed Protestant. The fiery preaching of the Calvinist John Knox had made many converts to Protestantism in Scotland.

Norfolk, good-looking and just turned thirty, was at the head of the group of English commissioners who visited Mary to advise Elizabeth what should be done about her. During these talks Norfolk fell in love with her. She was still married to Bothwell, but she asked the Pope for an annulment on the grounds of her pre-nuptial ravishment by Bothwell, and this was granted. So the way to marriage was clear for Norfolk. He was at first confined in an ordinary dungeon in the Tower but on the outbreak of plague in London Elizabeth had him moved to one of the houses near the Palace, and he was allowed to walk in the Queen's Gallery accompanied by a guard. Two Privy Councillors, William Cecil and Nicholas Bacon, came to question him, but after a searching examination lasting many hours, they reported that they could find no grounds for a conviction.

Den VIII february werde onthalst Maria
Stuart Schots Coninginne 's ferdende Roomsch Catho-
lyck Hebbende ghesocht veel onrust ten ende te richten haer selven
mees ter te maecken van Engelant 't dwelck haer vanden raet
ofte parlement volcoomelyck werde bertoont, Anno 1587.
Metren XIII sol XIII en XIIII. &

The execution of Mary Queen of Scots at Fotheringay: contemporary Dutch drawing. 'The VIII February was beheaded Mary Stuart, Scots Queen, fervent Roman Catholic, having tried to cause much unrest, to make herself mistress of England, the which [against] her by the Council of the Parliament completely was proved.' (Scottish National Portrait Gallery)

At this Elizabeth exploded with anger. 'Away!' she shouted. 'What the law fails to do, my authority shall effect.' Her rage was so intense that she fell ill and was in bed for a week.

In the following year, 1570, Norfolk was allowed to leave the Tower but was kept under surveillance at the Charterhouse in London. Soon further incriminating evidence was found against him in intercepted letters, and after three months he was brought back to the Tower. A number of others implicated in the conspiracy were also arrested and put in the Tower: they included the Bishop of Ross, Lord Cobham, Lord Lumley and Sir Thomas Stanley.

At his trial Norfolk complained that, after being in the Tower for two and a half years, his memory was impaired by his treatment as a prisoner and so he could not answer questions; the judge brushed his objection aside. The Duke, who was not allowed counsel, pleaded that attempting to marry Queen Mary would not have affected the life or the throne of Queen Elizabeth. 'But,' said the Queen's Serjeant, 'it is well known that you entered into a design for seizing the Tower, which is certainly the greatest strength of the kingdom of England, hence it follows, you attempted the destruction of the Queen.'

He was found guilty and was sentenced to death. In February 1572 he was led out to Tower Hill by the Master of the Ordnance. As no executions had taken place for twelve years, the timbers of the scaffold had rotted and a new one had been built. Norfolk refused to be blindfolded. 'I have no fear of death,' he said. His head, severed 'with one chop by the singular dexterity

of the executioner', was shown to the assembled crowd and was buried with his corpse, after a full funeral service (not often carried out on such occasions) in the Chapel of St Peter ad Vincula.

The others implicated with him were imprisoned in the Beauchamp Tower, where their inscriptions may still be seen on the walls. Mary Queen of Scots was kept in confinement in England for nineteen years and moved from one prison to another until her execution at Fotheringay in February 1587. Elizabeth had been at a loss to know what should be done with her. She bore her cousin no personal ill-will, but could not ignore the political considerations. To help Mary to return to Scotland as Queen would involve England in war. To let her go to France would present the French with an excellent opportunity to make use of her. To keep her in England would provide the English Catholics with a rallying point for revolt. After much reflection, Elizabeth decided on keeping Mary where she could be carefully watched. Naturally there were plots, like the one which led to Norfolk's imprisonment. Mary had secretly been in touch with Philip of Spain and there were signs of preparation for an invasion. In February 1587 a plot to murder Elizabeth and rescue Mary finally led to the Scottish Queen's execution; again all the conspirators were sent to the Tower. It was the year before the Armada.

Having signed Mary's death warrant, Elizabeth wrote at the same time to her gaoler, Sir Amyas Paulet, reproaching him for not having found a way to shorten his prisoner's life. When she learned that Mary had been executed, she turned in rage on her secretary, William Davison, for sending off the death warrant at the same time as her letter to Paulet. She stormed. She raged. Declaring that Davison was responsible for Mary's execution, she signed a warrant for his committal to the Tower. The Council begged her not to vent her wrath on him, but she would not listen. Eventually his life was spared, but he had to pay a fine of £10,000 and was kept in the Tower for many years.

Elizabeth's reign, which shines across the centuries as an age of immense splendour, studded with such resounding names as Drake, Hawkins and Raleigh, Shakespeare and Marlowe, had an uneasy beginning despite the immense rejoicing at her accession. It was only by her skill and caution, her infallible gift for picking able men as her advisers and her resolve never to make an irrevocable decision that she succeeded in overcoming the turbulent political currents.

The aristocracy for the most part had Catholic leanings, but they had no intention of restoring any of the loot they had acquired from the monasteries. Nor did they want a return to a disputed succession. Year after year, until she was well past forty, Elizabeth was advised to marry and provide an heir. She saw the dangers of an unwise choice. Greatly attracted to Lord Robert Dudley, who had been made Earl of Leicester in 1564 and was constantly at her side, she saw that such a marriage would cause fierce rivalry among other, more highly placed noblemen. Her brother-in-law Philip II of Spain was another likely suitor, but he had brought disaster to England by his marriage to Mary and would undoubtedly involve the country in European affairs once more; but an absolute rejection of his advances might rouse him to active animosity. So, like all the rest, he was kept dangling.

The question of religion was another thorny problem. It was decided from the outset that the country should be Protestant and that the Queen should be Supreme Head of the Church of England. But although uniformity was sought, Elizabeth strove to avoid persecution of the Catholics. At the same time she refused to tolerate any extremist 'innovation' or 'new-fangledness' such as the Puritans sought. It was not only fanatical Protestant exiles who had fled from the Catholic rule of Mary Queen of Scots, but the Puritans within the English Church itself, who were insistent on reforms. Because of the Queen's attitude the movement went underground and formed a large and growing opposition, which met in secret, formed strong local centres and had powerful patrons with influence both in Parliament and at court. Their greatest concern was that the English crown might at any moment pass to Mary Queen of Scots, and they were resolved to defend the English Church against a papist royal supremacy.

Queen Elizabeth and Robert Dudley dancing the volta: painting by an unknown artist. (Reproduced by kind permission of The Rt. Hon. Viscount De L'Isle, VC, KG, from his collection at Penshurst Place, Kent. Photo: National Portrait Gallery, London)

Elizabeth had always been aware of this menace. After Mary's marriage in 1558 to the Dauphin, later Francis II of France, she sent a fleet to blockade the Scottish ports and prevent French reinforcements from landing; she also sent arms and even a small army to help Scottish rebels. Mary's presence in England naturally presented even greater dangers. Apart from the plots we have noted, Spanish agents were constantly trying to stir up rebellion, assassinate Elizabeth and hand the throne of England to the exiled Scottish Queen.

Among the Catholic agents who crept into England in these years were a large number of Jesuits, members of a religious order recently formed in Spain, whose avowed aim was to re-establish Catholicism in England. Many were fanatics intent upon destroying the Queen as well as Protestantism. Among the large number of those arrested the most notable was Edmund Campion. Born in London, he was educated at Oxford and took the Oath of Supremacy recognizing Elizabeth as head of the English Church when he took his degree in 1564. Two years later he welcomed Elizabeth to the university in a speech that made a great impression on her. Shortly after taking deacon's orders as a Protestant, he went to Ireland and then to the Continent where he joined the Catholic Church. In 1573 he joined the Jesuits, and returned to England in 1580 disguised as a merchant dealing in jewels, but his impetuosity and lack of discretion brought him under suspicion and he went into hiding, only emerging from time to time to preach. In 1581 his secretly printed book, *Decem Rationes*, a violent attack on the English Church, led to his arrest.

The Queen's earlier policy of tolerance had been abandoned when plots for her assassination were uncovered a year or two earlier. Campion was brought to London with a paper hat on his head bearing the inscription 'Campion, the Seditious Jesuit'. He was confined in the Tower and kept a prisoner there for some months; he was allowed no books and suffered great discomfort. To force him to reveal the names of his accomplices, he was tortured no fewer than five times with the thumbscrew in the vaults of the White Tower, and was put in the 'Little Ease' where he could neither stand up nor lie down. He and seven other Jesuit priests were tried at Westminster Hall for high treason. They were accused of 'having withdrawn themselves beyond the seas where they lived under obedience of the Pope and engaged in his design against the Queen; and that for this purpose they had now come to England to seduce the hearts of Her Majesty's subjects and to conspire her death.' Found guilty, they were sentenced to be hanged, drawn and quartered. Campion was fastened to a hurdle and dragged from the Tower through the streets of London to Tyburn, where the sentence was carried out. Three centuries later he was beatified.

This marked the beginning of Elizabeth's persecution of the Catholics, most of them Jesuit priests, which went on until the end of her reign. They were hunted down all over the country, ferreted out of priest-holes, their secret hiding places in Catholic homes, imprisoned, often tortured, and executed. But this did not stem the tide of Jesuits from the Continent. They continued to creep in, and the Queen's ministers continued to dispose of them. It is estimated that Elizabeth put to death as many Catholics in those twenty-three years as her sister Mary did Protestants in her five years of persecution.

CHAPTER THIRTY-SEVEN

Robert Devereux, Earl of Essex

The political intrigues of Elizabeth's reign reached a climax at the time of the Armada. In this 1739 engraving of a tapestry commissioned by Elizabeth's Admiral, Lord Howard, the Spanish fleet abandons the galleon Rosario *to the enemy. The English commanders are portrayed round the border.* (National Maritime Museum, Greenwich)

Elizabeth's prompt, devastating descent on anyone even remotely suspected of being an agent of Philip of Spain was based on information supplied by Sir Francis Walsingham's vast network of spies, unquestionably the best in Europe. He uncovered almost every plan hatched by Spain, and in due course learned that an Armada was being prepared for the invasion and occupation of England.

Philip was smarting from many wounds. Drake and Hawkins had been raiding and plundering the west coast of his vast new empire in South America, his rights to which had been ratified by the Pope, and also attacking Spanish harbours in Europe. English pirate ships or privateers, as they were called (they were privately owned but undertook warlike activities for the State), lay in wait for Spanish treasure-ships, homeward bound laden with gold and silver, and seized the glittering loot. The robbers kept only a part of it for themselves, because Elizabeth's agents waiting at the home port of Bristol always made sure that no dealers from London took anything away until she had her share.

This was not Philip's only grievance. In the Netherlands he ruled over a Protestant people who were being made to suffer the torture of his Inquisition. Trade with England was denied them. Their looms were made idle, which brought distress not only to them but also to the sheep farmers of England. The resulting revolt of the Dutch was actively assisted by Elizabeth as a precautionary measure to delay, and if possible prevent, Spain's expected attack on England.

In 1585 the Catholic Earl of Arundel, whose father the Duke of Norfolk and grandfather Surrey had both been imprisoned in the Tower and executed, and whose great-grandfather was in prison awaiting execution when Henry VIII died, was himself arrested and brought to the Beauchamp Tower. His name may still be seen cut into its walls in large letters, dated 22 June 1587—the year before the Armada. He spent many years in the Tower. Much of the money allowed him for his maintenance he gave to the poor, living on a miserable diet himself. By bribing the Lieutenant's daughter to leave the door open at the top of the Bell Tower, which is part of the Lieutenant's House, Arundel's wife made it possible for a priest imprisoned there to walk along the ramparts (the walk that Elizabeth herself had used for exercise) and celebrate Mass in Arundel's cell. The Mass, it was reported, was for the success of the Spanish Armada, by now on its way to England. The priest was tortured and confessed; Arundel was tried and the sentence of execution was pronounced, but it was never carried out. He died a natural death in the Beauchamp Tower in 1595.

Before the coming of the Armada the Tower was full of priests and Catholic noblemen, among them Henry Percy, Earl of Northumberland, who was most suspiciously found dead in the Bloody Tower with dagger wounds in his left breast after his servants had been removed.

Philip's Armada started for England in May 1588. Driven back by storms, it sailed again after refitting the damaged ships, and was sighted off Plymouth in the gathering darkness on 19 July. It consisted of 130 warships and transports carrying 19,000 soldiers, and there was room for a great many more who were waiting to be picked up in the Netherlands. The English fleet, inferior in size and numbers, set out to intercept the Armada. There was an engagement at dawn, but the Spaniards drew away, eager to pick up their reinforcements for the conquest and occupation of England. The English ships kept close and raked the decks of the Spanish galleons with cannon fire, killing many of the crew and demoralizing the soldiers.

When the Armada anchored off Calais to take on reinforcements, the English fleet, joined now by its eastern squadron, waited for darkness and sent eight fireships filled with explosives among the Spanish vessels. There was a succession of explosions; the Spaniards quickly cut their cables and made for the open sea. The wind bore them northward past the mouth of the Thames, and the English pursued. A fresh battle raged for eight hours. Had the English not exhausted their ammunition, no enemy vessel would have got away. What was left of the Armada made for home by rounding the north of Scotland. Not a soldier was landed and only fifty-three ships returned to Spain. A resounding victory had been won against the mighty Spanish empire.

Little more than a dozen years now remained of Elizabeth's reign. A tremendous burst of talent and energy marked these years. Spenser wrote his *Faerie Queene*, in which Elizabeth figured as Gloriana. Shakespeare began to write the first of his plays, which were seen on the stage a year or two later. Marlowe, who was only twenty-four, had his *Tamburlaine* performed in the year of the Armada. Adventurers were discovering new lands, and Walter Raleigh had embarked on his first effort at colonization on Roanoke Island off the North American mainland; the colony was christened Virginia after the Queen. Expeditions against Spain in the Azores, the Caribbean and in Cadiz went on. Drake attacked the rich city of Panama.

The Queen herself was old at fifty-five, wrinkled, bewigged, her face plastered with make-up. The great statesmen of her youth were passing to their graves—Walsingham in 1590, William Cecil, Lord Burleigh, in 1598. Her favourite Robert Dudley, Earl of Leicester, died in the year of the Armada, and his stepson Robert Devereux, second Earl of Essex, had already begun to win the Queen's favour. Having distinguished himself on an expedition to Holland with his stepfather, he was appointed Master of the Horse in 1587, when only twenty-one, and in the next year was made a Knight of the Garter.

This tall, handsome, high-spirited youth was constantly with the ageing Queen and was intolerant of all rivals, in particular Sir Walter Raleigh who was also often in attendance. Eager for foreign adventure, Devereux slipped away and joined one of Drake's expeditions against the Spaniards but was ordered by the Queen to return instantly. In 1590, again without Her Majesty's consent, he secretly married the widow of the great Sir Philip Sidney. When news of this reached the Queen, he had to face her rage; she would accept no explanation but ordered that his wife must live away from the court. Many were his intrigues with the ladies-in-waiting and her anger flared again and again, but his charm and flattery always helped him to recover the royal favour.

In 1596 Essex and Raleigh were put in joint command of an expedition against Cadiz. In the sea-fight Raleigh distinguished himself: the Spanish fleet was set on fire and the town was at the mercy of the invaders. Essex succeeded in taking Cadiz and holding it for a fortnight. On his homecoming, his popularity and his vanity knew no bounds. He was sent out again in the following year to dispose of a fresh Armada that was being assembled by Philip in a number of Spanish harbours. Instead, Essex made a dash for the Azores to seize the treasure-ships returning from South America. They eluded him, and the Armada sailed for England while his back was turned. Only the wind kept the enemy from reaching England's undefended shores. Returning empty-handed, Essex suffered the full fury of the Queen's wrath. He withdrew from the court and sent pleading letters begging for her forgiveness and favour.

In 1599 he was given one final chance. There had been recurrent trouble in Ireland. Henry VIII had assumed the title of King of Ireland but had refrained from trying to assert himself there. Earldoms were conferred on the Irish chiefs and all seemed to go well. But in Elizabeth's reign their ingrained hostility to English rule, accentuated by their attachment to Catholicism, led to recurrent rebellions. There had already been three, and Essex was now sent with the largest army ever seen in Ireland. He failed disastrously. In defiance of the Queen's commands, he made a truce with the chief rebel, the Earl of Tyrone. Returning home without his army, he forced his way into the Queen's bedchamber to make his excuses. She ordered him out of her presence. He was stripped of all his high offices and was kept as a prisoner in his own house in London, in what is now Essex Street, off the Strand.

Fuming over his humiliation, he adopted a most dangerous course: he decided to raise his own rebellion. Gathering his hot-headed friends around him, he began to correspond with King James VI of Scotland, whose help he sought. James's delay in sending the expected assistance drove the impetuous Essex to take action himself. A plan was drawn up for an attack on the court and the seizure of the Queen. When this came to the ears of Robert Cecil's spies (he had by now succeeded his father), the guards on the Palace of Whitehall were doubled.

Essex had to abandon his plan, but a new one was quickly evolved. Armed men were assembled in the courtyard of Essex's London house. By ten o'clock on the morning of Sunday, 8 February 1601, his force was three hundred strong and more continued to arrive. Within minutes of this news reaching the Palace, the Lord Chief Justice and three other members of the Privy Council arrived to see Essex. They were locked up in a room by the rebel nobleman's excited supporters, who kept shouting 'Kill them! Kill them!' Then rushing out into the Strand, brandishing their weapons, they made for the city of London, to rouse the people and capture the Tower. But Elizabeth frustrated their plans. Messengers had already been sent to tell the citizens that Essex was a traitor conspiring against the Queen; and at numerous street corners preachers urged the citizens to stay indoors, well-armed, until further orders.

By noon, Essex and his followers had arrived at St Paul's. As he went through the streets, he kept shouting that there was a plot to murder him, but no one stirred out of their houses and he received not a cheer of encouragement. When he reached Cheapside the sweat was pouring off his face, which was contorted with the realization that his exploit had failed and could end only in his ruin and death.

Detachments of the Queen's forces were by now gathering at various points, and the rebels soon found their way barred on all sides. In the skirmish that followed some were wounded, others killed. Essex made for the river, got into a boat and rowed hard for the water-gate of his house, where he barricaded himself in. Artillery was brought from the Tower and the guns opened fire. Seeing that further resistance was hopeless, Essex surrendered and was taken at once by boat to the Tower, which he entered by the Traitors' Gate. He was imprisoned in the tower just behind St Peter ad Vincula which has been known ever since as the Devereux Tower after him.

His chief supporters were also brought to the Tower; the most notable of them was Henry Wriothesley, Earl of Southampton, the literary patron of William Shakespeare. The only two books of verse published by Shakespeare were dedicated to Southampton, who is thought to be the man to whom the sonnets were addressed. Essex too was a friend of Shakespeare and *A Midsummer Night's Dream* was written in honour of his marriage.

On the eve of Essex's expedition to Ireland, Shakespeare referred to the approaching rebellion in Ireland in the Prologue to the fifth act of *Henry V* and made this prophecy of Essex's expected triumph:

> Were now the general of our gracious empress,
> As in good time he may, from Ireland coming,
> Bringing rebellion broached on his sword,
> How many would the peaceful city quit,
> To welcome him.

The Earl of Southampton was the grandson of that Wriothesley who served Henry VIII under Thomas Cromwell. He retained his power when Cromwell fell, and obtained a great deal of land around Southampton when the monasteries were dissolved. His son, the second earl, was one of the Catholic noblemen who conspired for the release of Mary Queen of Scots. The third earl, now involved with Essex, had enjoyed the favour of Queen Elizabeth. He was lavish in his patronage not only of Shakespeare but of other poets such as Thomas Nash and Gervase Markham, and was a constant supporter of the theatre.

He and Essex were tried by twenty-four peers in Westminster Hall on 19 February 1601. The prosecuting counsel was Francis Bacon, once Essex's friend and protégé. Essex, conducting his own defence, insisted that Raleigh had been plotting to murder him. From the witness-box, Raleigh denied the charge, which in any case was irrelevant. Many confessions by the other prisoners were then read out, and the verdict was never in doubt. Essex was sentenced to death. Though he bore himself well at the trial, he collapsed on his return to the Tower. He asked to see the Lords of the Council. When they came, he confessed his guilt and declared he was a miserable sinner, grovelling heartbroken before the judgement seat of God. He made wild accusations against his friends: they had lured him into it, he said. He even dragged in his sister. 'She has been among the wickedest.'

The execution took place six days later. He begged that it should be carried out in the

Robert Devereux, Earl of Essex: engraving by R. Boissard. (*Radio Times Hulton Picture Library*)

grounds of the Tower, as he did not wish to face the public. The request was granted by the Queen, who feared that there might be a public demonstration in his favour. A scaffold was erected on Tower Green, where only six others, five of them of royal blood, had been beheaded. Raleigh, as Captain of the Guard, was among those present. He stood very near the block, but hearing a murmur around him, withdrew to the White Tower and watched the execution from a window.

Essex was brought out dressed in a black cloak and hat, with three clergymen walking beside him. He mounted the scaffold and, taking off his hat, bowed to the assembled peers. Then he spoke, confessing that he had been 'puffed up with pride and vanity and had bestowed his youth in wantonness, lust and uncleanliness'. After removing his ruff and cloak, he knelt by the block in his black doublet and said the Lord's Prayer. The axe descended three times before his head was severed. The executioner then stopped and lifted it up with the salutation 'God Save the Queen!' Essex was dead, aged only thirty-three.

Southampton, also sentenced to death, was spared and imprisoned for life. On the accession of King James I two years later, he was released from the Tower and resumed his place at the court. Four of the other conspirators were executed; the rest were heavily fined. Fines had taken the place of ransoms as a source of State income.

CHAPTER THIRTY-EIGHT

Sir Walter Raleigh

Queen Elizabeth did not like staying in the Tower. Apart from her visit on her accession and again at her coronation, she avoided the scene of so many unhappy memories. The German traveller Hentzer, writing two years before Elizabeth died, luridly describes the gory heads of her victims which could be seen in various parts of the Tower. And the moat, constructed three hundred years earlier, was by now anything but salubrious. The drainage of the city of London poured into it and, although the sluices were opened from time to time to empty it into the Thames, an obnoxious smell remained. Many complained of it and of its appalling effect on their health—a further reason why Elizabeth would wish to avoid the Tower.

When in London she preferred to live in the Palace of Whitehall. Hampton Court and Richmond Palace were other favourite residences; and it was at Richmond that she died on 24 March 1603. For two years, ever since Essex's execution, she had been melancholy and lonely. She was often found sitting in the dark, 'sometimes with the shedding of tears to bewail Essex'. Ill for some weeks before the end, she summoned her Council and told them, 'I wish not to live any longer, but desire to die.' The Archbishop of Canterbury knelt beside her and began to pray. Some hours later she fell into a deep sleep from which she never awoke.

She was succeeded by Mary Queen of Scots' only child, James VI of Scotland, who became James I of England. He was thirty-seven years old and in ailing health, his legs so weak that he could hardly stand up; he had to lean on an attendant and could only indulge his passion for riding by being strapped in the saddle. He was slovenly in his dress, talked almost ceaselessly in a broad Scottish accent and always had about him one or more male favourites, whom he loaded with gifts and caressed in public. Brought up as a Protestant, he was educated to the brink of pedantry. In 1590 he had married Anne, daughter of the King of Denmark. He had three children: Henry, Prince of Wales, who was thirteen when he was brought to England (he died in 1612), Charles who succeeded his father as King, and Elizabeth who, by marrying the German Elector Palatine, became the ancestress of King George I.

The Scottish King lost no time in coming to take over his new kingdom. He arrived in London three weeks after Elizabeth's death, and a few days later, on 3 May 1603, paid his first visit to the Tower, where earlier Scottish kings had been brought as captives. He travelled to the Tower by royal barge from the river-gate of Whitehall Palace. The Councillors waiting to receive him at the Wharf saw the oarsmen shoot past, and His Majesty had to land at the eastern end, by St Katherine's Hospital. A great many guns were fired in greeting—20, the records tell us, from the top of the White Tower, 100 from the Wharf, and 130 more from the ramparts, making 250 guns in all. Never before had so many been fired for any monarch. At each boom King James blinked his eyes and made the most hideous faces, while trying desperately to maintain a grave and dignified posture.

Plague was raging in London at the time. No less than 875 persons died of it in a week. James nevertheless stayed in the Tower for a few days and spent his time inspecting the guns, the Armoury, the ordnance factories, the Mint, the White Tower and many of the lesser towers. What aroused his greatest delight was the zoo.

He came back to the Tower for his coronation, but wanted all the arrangements simplified on account of the plague. Triumphal arches were already being erected along the route, but James ordered that all work on them must be stopped and that they should be left uncompleted. The procession was small: the King, riding on a white horse with a rich canopy above his head carried by six Privy Councillors, was accompanied by the Queen, by his heir Prince Henry, and by an escort of nobles.

The Tower became a favourite resort of his. He often came to stay and brought friends to share his delight in the zoo. What excited and amused him was to put some mastiffs into the lions' cage and watch the lions and dogs fight over the meat thrown to them. This cruel sport was practised again and again. But better diversions were provided at other times. On one occasion William Shakespeare was invited to the Tower with eight other players from what became known afterwards as 'The King's Company', and after the performance they 'walked from the Tower to Westminster in the procession which accompanied the King'. Each actor was given four and a half yards of cloth to wear as a cloak. Shakespeare's name appears at the top of the list. Ben Jonson also organized and presented many masques in the Great Hall of the Palace in the Tower or, if the weather was fine, in the gardens outside.

Very early in the reign an attempt was made to overthrow this 'alien' ruler and have his first cousin Lady Arabella Stuart crowned as Queen. She was the granddaughter of the Countess of Lennox and a niece of Darnley, who had married Mary Queen of Scots. A very beautiful but empty-headed young girl in her twenties, Arabella had an English upbringing, but by descent was at the time of her birth the next successor after James to the thrones of both England and Scotland. Intrigues had been going on for years to ensure that she and not James should succeed Elizabeth. She was in consequence regarded with the utmost suspicion by Elizabeth and at the Queen's orders had been kept under a strong guard at the home of her English grandmother Bess of Hardwick, the Dowager Countess of Shrewsbury.

Arabella was herself so eager to attain the crown that she wrote secretly to the Earl of Hertford, who had married Lady Jane Grey's sister Katherine, to suggest a marriage between herself and his grandson Edward Seymour, and thus strengthen her claim to the throne; both were descendants of Henry VII—she from Henry's elder daughter Margaret, he from Henry's younger daughter Mary. But the nervous old man immediately informed the Council, and the Queen took further measures to prevent the girl's escape. All this took place only a week or so before Elizabeth's death, and is said to have hastened it.

When James succeeded, Arabella's situation changed entirely. He received his cousin at his court and treated her with the courtesy due to a close relative. But, because of her continued intrigues and her resolve to marry Hertford's grandson, a hope she never gave up, she was later expelled from the court. In December 1609, on hearing rumours of her plot to marry a foreign prince, the King arrested her and sent her to the Tower, but the rumour proved groundless and she was released. Six months later she secretly married Hertford's younger grandson William. As soon as this became known they were both arrested; Arabella was held prisoner at Lambeth while her husband was sent to the Tower.

She escaped a year later, dressed up as a man, with long yellow riding-boots and a wig. It had been arranged that her husband should escape too and meet her just outside London. But she arrived first and, not seeing him, rowed out to a French vessel lying in the Thames. Her husband had by now managed to get out of the Tower. He had been confined in St Thomas's Tower and had seen a cart come in daily to sell hay and faggots. Putting on a carter's hat and smock, a black wig and beard, he climbed on to the cart and drove out through the Bulwark Gate. The French ship had already sailed, but Seymour boarded another boat leaving for Calais. At once a hue and cry was raised; all ships were searched, and warships were despatched to intercept vessels already at sea. Halfway across the Channel, Arabella's ship was stopped and she was brought back and imprisoned in the Tower: she was lodged in the Lieutenant's House to begin with and was later moved to the nearby Bell Tower. Seymour's ship was blown off course and he landed at Ostend.

Many begged the King to release Arabella, but he was deaf to their entreaties. In 1613 there was a plot to help her escape. It failed, and she died two years later in the Tower after a long illness, insane, according to some accounts. She was buried in the tomb of Mary Queen of Scots in Henry VII's chapel in Westminster Abbey. Her husband returned to England in 1616 and married the daughter of Queen Elizabeth's Earl of Essex.

One of the men accused of being implicated in the plot to depose James and make Arabella

Sir Walter Raleigh: miniature by Nicholas Hilliard (National Portrait Gallery, London)

Queen was Sir Walter Raleigh. He was arrested in 1603 before Arabella herself was implicated, and was taken to the Tower with a number of others, chief of whom was Lord Cobham, a descendant of Sir John Oldcastle (Falstaff). It was Cobham who had incriminated Raleigh.

It was not Raleigh's first imprisonment in the Tower. He had been arrested twelve years earlier by Queen Elizabeth for seducing and then marrying (without her consent) one of her ladies-in-waiting, Elizabeth Throgmorton, whose relative Nicholas Throgmorton had been imprisoned for taking part in the rebellion at the time of Mary Tudor's marriage with Philip of Spain. On that occasion Raleigh was confined in St Thomas's Tower, but he was released after a time and restored to favour.

He was over fifty at the time of his second arrest and had lived a varied and adventurous life. After serving as a soldier, he went with his half-brother Sir Humphrey Gilbert on an expedition to colonize 'any remote barbarous and heathen lands not possessed by any Christian prince or people'; and later he set sail in search of Eldorado in Guiana, in South America. He had served as Captain of the Queen's Guard and led the attack on Cadiz with Essex. Master of one of the most famous privateers, he was rightly regarded as the last of the great Elizabethans.

King James, who had looked upon Essex as a supporter of his, had never been well disposed towards Raleigh because of his part in Essex's trial. He began by dismissing Raleigh from the captaincy of the Guard, then turned him out of Durham House on the river where, with Elizabeth's consent, he had lived for twenty years. He was now confined in the Bloody Tower but was allowed to walk across to the Lieutenant's House and dine with him. A friendship soon developed between the two, and the Lieutenant, Sir John Peyton, was promptly dismissed. Aware that James was resolved on ruining him and possibly even executing him, Raleigh is said to have attempted suicide by plunging a knife into his breast. But he hotly denied this, saying, 'Why, man, if I wished to die, could I not dash my head against that wall?'

Together with the others accused of plotting to dethrone James in favour of Arabella Stuart, Raleigh was taken to Winchester for his trial because plague was again raging in London. He travelled in a carriage with the secretary of his brother-in-law Robert Cecil, suffering from a rheumatic ague caused by the cold damp of his cell. As they drove through the streets of London the mobs yelled abuse at him, threw mud and threatened to drag him out and lynch him. The secretary reported to Cecil, 'It was hob or nob if he would escape alive through such multitudes of unruly people.' Raleigh remained unmoved. He told the secretary, 'Dogs do always bark at those they know not.' Among the things hurled at him by the unruly crowds were tobacco pipes, for he had introduced pipe-smoking into the country and was growing tobacco on his own vast estates in England and Ireland—'so vile and stinking a custom,' Lord Henry Howard, a cousin of the Duke of Norfolk, called it, 'loathsome to the eye, hateful to the nose, harmful to the brain, dangerous to the lungs', an opinion shared by the King, who wrote a treatise denouncing smoking.

The prosecuting counsel was Sir Edward Coke, described by G. M. Trevelyan as 'one of the most disagreeable figures in our history'. He was himself to be imprisoned in the Tower some years later. Charged with having conspired with Cobham against the King in order to advance Lady Arabella to the throne and to procure foreign, that is to say Spanish, 'enemies to invade England', Raleigh pleaded not guilty. 'I will prove all,' shouted the dapper, bearded Coke. 'Thou art a monster! Thou hast an English face but a Spanish heart.' If this was meant to provoke the man who had spent his life fighting Spain, it failed. 'Thou art the most vile and execrable traitor that ever lived,' shouted Coke; to which the prisoner answered, simply and quite calmly, 'You speak indiscreetly, barbarously and uncivilly.'

Cobham had written earlier to the new Lieutenant of the Tower, Sir George Harvey, confessing his remorse at having falsely accused Raleigh. This letter was not referred to at the trial and only became known when the Lieutenant's son revealed his father's perfidy. The son was arrested and jailed. Raleigh now asked that Cobham be brought into court to face him. 'He is in this very house,' he added. But the judges refused, although it was only on Cobham's evidence that Raleigh was being charged.

Raleigh was found guilty and was sentenced to be beheaded. Cobham, on the other hand, was to be imprisoned 'during His Majesty's pleasure' and was confined in the Lieutenant's House. Raleigh was taken back to the Bloody Tower to await execution. But the sentence was not carried out. On the day fixed for his execution he was told that a reprieve had been granted, but he was kept in the Tower for a further thirteen years. The reprieve was in fact due to Robert Cecil's intervention, prompted by a twinge of conscience after receiving a desperate appeal from his sister-in-law Lady Raleigh for 'compassion and justice'. He also called off those who, like vultures, were stripping Raleigh of all he possessed.

That first winter in the Tower was exceptionally severe. The prisoner ached and shivered in his cell, with the foul water from the river seeping in through the stone walls. His wife and young son Wat, aged twelve, were allowed to stay with him. But the plague was still rampant, and Raleigh complained, 'My poor child has lain this fortnight next door to a woman with a running plague sore and but a paper wall between them, and her child is, this Thursday, dead of the plague.' He himself had become thin, his cheeks pale, his eyes sunken. But he applied himself to work and began writing his *History of the World*. Friends were allowed to visit him. Many came: court ladies, ambassadors with their wives, even the Queen, Anne of Denmark, and Henry, Prince of Wales, who was the same age as young Wat. The Prince, handsome, highly intelligent and an idealist, did not share the crude enthusiasms of his father, for whom he already had nothing but contempt. Of Raleigh's imprisonment he said, 'Only my father would keep such a bird in a cage.'

The King had by now reorganized the Tower zoo and had appointed the famous actor Edward Alleyn to be Master of the Bear Garden; Alleyn later founded the well-known public school for boys, Dulwich College. He organized bull-baiting exhibitions for the King and his friends, as well as James's favourite sport of watching a fight between three mastiffs and two lions. Prince Henry was taken by his father to see one of these spectacles; after two of the mastiffs had been

Raleigh's Walk, looking towards the upper chamber of the Bloody Tower. (Ministry of Public Building and Works)

killed and the third badly mauled, he cried out angrily that the show must be stopped. The King told him that such 'a bonny fight' must go on to the finish. The mauled mastiff had gamely leapt on one of the lions and was tearing at its belly. But the Prince, addressing Alleyn himself, told him to take the injured mastiff home and 'make much of him'.

Guests at the Tower, however, were less interested in the zoo than in the great man confined in the Bloody Tower, of whom they tried to catch a glimpse as he walked along the rampart from the top of the Bloody Tower to the roof of the Lieutenant's House, which was later known as Raleigh's Walk. They would wave and cheer, and the tall, distinguished but emaciated man with a small pointed beard would bow in acknowledgement. One of Raleigh's visitors was an Indian chief he had met in Guiana; they sat together in the cell and talked of old times. Many prominent scientists also came to see him, and he was given the use of a shed in the Tower grounds, which he called his 'garden house', in which he and his visitors used to experiment with chemicals and drugs. One of his notable successes was the turning of salt water into fresh water. Other friends came to discuss his *History of the World*, for which Ben Jonson, another famous visitor, wrote a brilliant preface. Raleigh made a model of a ship for Prince Henry and told him of his many adventures. The boy developed such an affection for this remarkable prisoner that, when he was a little older, he looked up the records of Raleigh's trial and together with his mother begged the King to release him. But James refused.

Yet another Lieutenant, Sir William Waad, took office; he had been one of the judges at Raleigh's trial, and was resolved to make his prison conditions much more trying. He refused to allow Lady Raleigh to stay in the Tower, and she was forced to rent some lodgings near the Church of All Hallows, Barking, so that she and her two sons (a second boy had been born in the Tower) could be near her husband.

It was the King's desperate need for money that led eventually to Raleigh's release. James had showered gifts on his handsome favourite Robert Carr, whom he created Earl of Somerset in 1613, and in 1609 had given him Raleigh's vast estate at Sherborne, in Dorset. When Somerset fell from grace in 1614, the estate was given to the new favourite George Villiers, later made Duke of Buckingham. Raleigh hardly protested at all, realizing it would be of no avail. Villiers, apprecia-

tive of his forbearance, pleaded with the King and even provided money to obtain Raleigh's pardon. But what finally induced the King to release him was the knowledge that Raleigh might bring back vast quantities of gold for him from Guiana. On the morning of 19 May 1616 Raleigh, who had been moved by now to the Brick Tower, was released.

At the same time Frances, Countess of Somerset, was imprisoned in the Bloody Tower. She was a niece of the Duke of Norfolk and some years before had married the young Earl of Essex, son of the man Elizabeth had executed. But she refused to let Essex consummate the marriage because even at that time she was secretly having an affair with Carr. In 1613, as we have seen, Carr became Earl of Somerset; flushed with power, having succeeded Robert Cecil as First Secretary in 1612, he decided that she should divorce Essex on grounds of impotence and marry him. The besotted King agreed to this and spent a vast sum of money on the wedding. Meanwhile Somerset, utterly incompetent in his role of Secretary, persuaded his friend and confidant Sir Thomas Overbury to do the work for him privately.

All went well for a time, for Overbury was a man of immense skill and learning. Moreover, when Somerset was only eleven, Overbury had become infatuated with him and they were inseparable. Overbury now suffered the King's infatuation for Carr because it helped his own advancement; he was also prepared to overlook the affair with Frances Howard, and even composed Somerset's love-letters to her. But the thought of the couple marrying was abhorrent to him. Servants in the Palace of Whitehall overheard Somerset and Overbury quarrelling in the gallery and repeated Overbury's angry description of her as 'a filthy base woman, nothing but a whore'. When this reached the lady's ears, she resolved that Overbury should no longer come between them. The King was persuaded to send him on a mission to Russia. Overbury refused to go and was sent to the Tower for 'disobedience'.

Shortly afterwards, Somerset married his mistress. She aroused a contemptuous titter when she appeared at the ceremony dressed in a low-cut bodice that only just covered the nipples of her breasts. Having attained her goal, she was nevertheless determined that Overbury should not emerge from the Tower to discredit her. She persuaded her husband to replace the Lieutenant of the Tower, Sir William Waad, by a man of her own choice, Sir Gervase Helwyss, who was 'well acquainted with the power of drugs'. With the further aid of a procuress she knew, a physician's widow named Mrs Turner, the desired end was achieved. Overbury fell ill and died. Poisoning was suspected and both Somerset and his wife were taken to the Tower. Later the Countess confessed her guilt. The King did not execute her, but kept her and her husband in the Tower for seven years.

Their accomplices were hanged. Mrs Turner was dressed in the height of fashion when she was brought to Tyburn; the judge, Sir Edward Coke, who had been Raleigh's prosecuting counsel, had ordered that she should wear the ruff and thus bring what to him was a 'detestable fashion' to an end, and by way of mockery the hangman also wore a ruff made of yellow paper—Mrs Turner was the inventor of a yellow starch used for stiffening ruffs. Helwyss was hanged on Tower Hill in 1515 for complicity in Overbury's murder and for cheating him out of his best clothes. In 1615 Prince Henry suddenly fell ill and died. Poisoning was suspected, and it was believed that Carr, whom the Prince disliked, was responsible. The succession thus passed to the twelve-year-old Duke of York, later to become King Charles I.

In 1617 Raleigh sailed for Guiana with his son Wat, his nephew George Raleigh, and his friend Lawrence Keymis, who had explored Guiana with him twenty-two years earlier. Raleigh was appointed Admiral of the expedition, commanding a fleet of seven warships and three pinnaces. On equipping it he spent what remained of his fortune. Terrible storms delayed his departure. The journey was long. Not until the end of the year did he reach Guiana. By now Raleigh had fallen ill and had to be left behind in Trinidad while his son, his nephew and Keymis went on up the Orinoco.

King James had been warned by the Spanish ambassador, to whom he paid sedulous attention in his anxiety to keep the peace with Spain, that there were Spanish settlements in that country. But Raleigh explained that the Spaniards were trying to get to the same gold mine, which was not in their territory at all, but had been taken over by him many years before in the name of the Queen of England.

On landing, the expedition found the Spaniards actually in Guiana. A battle ensued in which Raleigh's son was killed; he died fighting gallantly with a dozen lance wounds in his breast, crying 'Go on! Go on!' By a headlong charge his pikemen took the town of San Thomé, but were hemmed in on all sides by the Spaniards. In the Governor's house in San Thomé they found full details of Raleigh's plans, the strength of his expedition in ships and men as well as their armament. It was evident that the plans had been supplied by King James himself in a letter to the King of Spain. Night sorties were made in the hope of finding the mine through the tangled, steaming jungle, but it was impossible to go on with the quest with 250 men dead out of 400. So Keymis returned to Trinidad, broke the news to Raleigh of his son's heroic death, and then committed suicide.

When Raleigh returned to England, he was arrested. Everyone wondered why, knowing what his fate would be, he had not gone on to France. Sympathy for him was openly expressed everywhere. But he was taken back to the Tower and imprisoned in the Lieutenant's House. Later he was moved to the Wardrobe Tower because the Lieutenant, Sir Allan Apsley, was too friendly with him. Spain insisted that Raleigh should be handed over for execution. King James was told that England would rise against him if that was done. Raleigh's erstwhile friend, Francis Bacon, now Lord Chancellor, found an alternative solution: Raleigh had already been condemned to death, and all that was required now was to revoke the reprieve. He had been condemned, it will be recalled, for being a friend of Spain; he was to lose his life now for being Spain's enemy. The King signed the warrant for his execution.

On the evening of 28 October 1618 Raleigh was taken from the Tower to the Gatehouse in Westminster. Seeing an old friend as he crossed Palace Yard, he advised him to get up early if he wanted to see the execution. He told his valet not to trouble much about cutting his hair unless he had a plaster to stick the head on again. He dressed carefully in a tawny satin doublet, black taffeta breeches, ash-coloured silk stockings, a long gown of black velvet and a lace skullcap over his snow-white hair 'lest the chill of the early morning air bring on my ague and they think I shiver from fear'. He was executed in Palace Yard in front of the Houses of Parliament; it is thought that he was sixty-six, the exact date of his birth being uncertain.

CHAPTER THIRTY-NINE

Guy Fawkes

The Lieutenant of the Tower, the Constable's deputy, took over the running of the fortress in 1189, in the reign of Richard Coeur de Lion. Thereafter the Constable, although still the chief official, left the executive functions almost entirely in the control of his Lieutenant, who dwelt in a suite of rooms in one of the towers until his lodgings were built for him by Henry VIII in 1530. Here most of the State prisoners were brought on arrival at the Tower, registered and searched. Some prisoners were tried here in the large room on the second floor, often referred to as the Council Chamber; it overlooks the River Thames. On 6 November 1605 Guy Fawkes and some of his fellow-conspirators were examined here by the Lieutenant, Sir William Waad, on the morning after the discovery of the Gunpowder Plot to blow up the Houses of Parliament.

It was a Roman Catholic plot—the third since the accession of James I. The Catholics had expected much from the son of their champion Mary Queen of Scots despite the fact that he had been brought up as a Protestant; and his efforts to maintain peace with Spain, the most powerful Catholic kingdom, which was employing the cruel torture of the Inquisition against all heretics, had greatly raised their hopes. But peace with Spain had only opened the door wider for the flood of Catholic priests and Jesuit agents who fomented political intrigues.

The first of the three Catholic plots was easily squashed. Some Catholics who were calling on the King at Greenwich to present a petition planned to overpower the guards, put on their uniforms and carry the King off to the Tower. The plan was discovered. The next, hatched by Lord Cobham and his brother George Brooke, was to place Arabella Stuart on the throne. As we have seen, the failure of this plot led to the arrest of Sir Walter Raleigh.

The Gunpowder Plot was a much more dangerous affair. Behind it were a group of Catholic aristocrats; one of them, Thomas Percy, was a close relative of the Earl of Northumberland. The State Opening of Parliament was due to take place on 5 November 1605, and it was their purpose to blow up the entire place while the King was present. As early as May of the preceding year Thomas Percy rented a house in Westminster amid the huddle of buildings between the House of Lords and the river, and for eighteen months a number of Catholic gentlemen were continually coming and going. The explosion was to be on an extensive scale, affecting not only the House of Lords, but the magnificent, historic Westminster Hall and the House of Commons, which sat in St Stephen's Chapel between the Hall and the river. The peers sat in the upper floor of their building; underneath were vaults and the disused kitchens of the old Palace of Westminster, which had been largely destroyed by fire many years before. One of these kitchens had been let to Dame Elizabeth Skinner, a vendor of coal, who used it as her storehouse. She agreed to sublet it to the plotters because she was planning to get married and no longer had any use for it.

Explosives were stored there, and Guy Fawkes, a Catholic from Yorkshire who had gained some experience of mining operations during his fight for Spain against her Dutch rebels, was to ignite the gunpowder. With the extermination of the King, the Government and the entire legislature, the rebellion was to begin. Armed Catholics in all parts of the country would rise simultaneously, help would be sent by Spain and James's young daughter Elizabeth would be proclaimed Queen.

The plot was discovered because too many

people were involved in it. Some of them had qualms of conscience about blowing up the innocent with the guilty, since those Catholics who were peers would also die. Robert Catesby, at the head of the conspiracy, brushed aside these objections: the end justified the means, he argued. But one of the plotters, an extremely rich Catholic whose sister was married to Lord Monteagle, sent an anonymous letter to his brother-in-law urging him to keep away from the House of Lords on that day. 'They shall receive a terrible blow this Parliament, and yet they shall not see who hurts them,' the letter said. Monteagle took it to Robert Cecil, the chief minister.

The words 'terrible blow' and 'shall not see' suggested an explosion. The vaults were searched. An immense amount of wood and coal was found, and when this was removed, thirty-six barrels of gunpowder and great iron bars were discovered. Thomas Percy's servant, 'a very tall and desperate fellow', was in the cellar with a dark lantern and a slow match. This was Guy Fawkes, though he said his name was John Johnson. He was seized, bound with his own garters and taken to the Tower.

He was brought before members of the Privy Council in the Council Chamber in the Lieutenant's House, but refused to say anything. Then, on the King's orders, he was tortured. Part of his torture was to be confined in the 'Little Ease', four feet square and completely without light or air; no doubt the door was opened from time to time to let in some air and keep him alive. This, the thumbscrew and the rack so broke and unnerved him that bit by bit he disclosed who his accomplices were. He was in intense pain when he signed his confession with a trembling hand.

Many conspirators had fled, including Catesby, but after a fight in which four of them were slain, the rest were captured and brought to the Tower. Two Jesuits were also brought in—Fathers Oldcorn and Fisher. Father Gerard was another accomplice, and a rigorous search was made for him also. The Earl of Northumberland, an immensely wealthy scholar and scientist, and a friend of Raleigh's, was already a prisoner in the Martin Tower for being involved in an earlier Catholic plot; it was now found that he was implicated in this one too. (He was the son of the Earl found mysteriously dead of dagger wounds in the Bloody Tower at the time of the Armada.) Others arrested were Lord Mordaunt, Lord Stourton and Sir Everard Digby. They were tried by special commissioners at Westminster.

Digby and three lesser conspirators were drawn from the Tower on hurdles to St Paul's churchyard in London and there hanged. The next day Guy Fawkes and three others were similarly dragged on hurdles to Old Palace Yard in Westminster, by the scene of their crime, and hanged. Fawkes made a short speech of repentance and had to be helped up the ladder. They were brought down from the gallows before they were dead, then disembowelled and beheaded. Their heads were displayed on London Bridge. Two peers, Mordaunt and Stourton, were kept as prisoners in the Tower for many years. Northumberland, known as the Wizard Earl because of

Page from the House of Commons Journal for 5 November 1605, with marginal notes by the Clerk describing the search for explosives in the vaults. (House of Lords Record Office)

The Council Chamber in the Queen's House, with Sir William Waad's plaque commemorating the Gunpowder Plot.
(Ministry of Public Building and Works)

his scientific experiments, was tried later by the Star Chamber and sentenced to return to the Tower of London 'from whence he came, and there to remain prisoner as before, during his life'. He was taken back to the Martin Tower and kept there for sixteen years; he was finally released on paying a fine of £30,000.

The Gunpowder Plot provoked intense anti-Catholic feeling all over England. Persecution of Catholics became much more severe. There was a Thanksgiving service for the great deliverance, and this was held annually on 5 November for the next 250 years. Even now the day is marked by bonfires and fireworks, and in the streets is sung the rhyme 'Remember, remember, the Fifth of November'. A plaque put up by the then Lieutenant, Sir William Waad, in the Council Chamber of his house commemorates the plot and can still be seen there.

Father Gerard, one of the Jesuits implicated in the Gunpowder Plot who managed to elude capture, had been a prisoner in the Tower some years before when he was sent there by Queen Elizabeth in 1597 for plotting against her life. Confined at that time in the Salt Tower, at the southeastern corner of the Inner Wall, he was taken to the Lieutenant's House and examined by the Lords of the Council in the very chamber where Guy Fawkes was examined eight years later. He refused to give any information about other Jesuits involved and was warned that he would be tortured. Still obdurate, he was taken, he records in his autobiography, 'in a sort of solemn procession, the attendants preceding us with lighted candles because the place was underground and very dark'. It has long been believed that an underground passage linked the Lieutenant's House with the White Tower.

'The torture chamber,' Gerard states, 'was a place of immense extent, and in it were ranged divers sorts of racks and other instruments of torture. Some of these they displayed before me and told me that I should have to taste them. They led me to a great upright beam or pillar of wood, which was one of the supports of this vast crypt.' His hands were placed in iron gauntlets attached to the pillar and the stool on which he stood was then pulled away so that he hung by his wrists. A man of great weight, he was questioned while suspended, but he still refused to speak. He was left hanging there for some hours and fainted many times. Later he was taken back to the Salt Tower. The next day the Lieutenant, Sir William Waad, instructed the chief superintendent of the torture chamber 'to wrack him twice a day until such time as he chooses to speak'. Gerard was taken back to the gauntlets and suspended once more, the agony being far more acute this time because his wrists were swollen. He was tortured yet again on the next day but bore his pain and suffering without speaking.

Back in his cell, food was given to him, but it had to be cut up as he could no longer use his fingers; they remained swollen for three weeks. 'Every day I did exercises with my hands . . . The food was provided at the Queen's expense and it was plentiful—every day they gave me six rolls of very good bread. (The grades of diet in this prison vary according to the rank of the prisoner).'

Some months later, the resolve to escape began to take shape in his mind. Within sight of the Salt Tower was the Cradle Tower, built in the Outer Wall; between the two towers was the Privy Garden of the Palace. In the Cradle Tower was a Catholic prisoner named John Arden. The two men could just see each other through their windows. Fortunately the same warder was in charge of both prisoners and, by bribing the man, Gerard was able to send Arden letters written in orange juice. He outlined his plan of escape. Arden's tower was near the moat encircling the outer fortifications. Outside help was needed, and Gerard wrote to friends to arrange it. Then, with the warder's aid, he began going across to Arden's tower to say Mass with him.

On the appointed night, when Gerard went to the Cradle Tower, the door was bolted behind him by the warder as usual; but that did not affect his scheme. His friends arrived in a boat after it was dark, bringing a rope fastened to a stake. Gerard and Arden, who had gone up the stairs to the roof, threw down a ball with a cord attached to it so that the rope might be tied to the cord and they could then draw it up. When it reached them the rope was almost horizontal, stretching across the moat and the Wharf. Both men managed to get down.

Gerard remained in England and met Sir Everard Digby and others who were later involved in the Gunpowder Plot. Gerard was deeply implicated. 'As soon as news reached us,' he wrote, 'that the plot had been discovered and that some of our friends had been killed and others captured, we knew that we would have to suffer.' But friends hid him in a priest-hole where food was brought to him every night. Stealthily he moved from one house to another, from one town to the next. Many of his Jesuit accomplices paid the ultimate penalty of 'martyrdom' for the plot of 5 November, but Gerard survived.

CHAPTER FORTY

Strafford and Archbishop Laud

The execution of the Earl of Strafford on Tower Hill, 12 May 1641. (By permission of the Trustees of the British Museum)

James I died in 1625 in his sixtieth year, leaving his only surviving son to succeed him at the age of twenty-five. King Charles I added to his lack of stature (he was almost a dwarf) and a bad stutter another grave, indeed tragic, failing: until his death on the scaffold he adhered obstinately to his father's obsessive belief in the divine right of kings. There was trouble enough over this theory in the closing years of James I's reign. It was strenuously opposed by Chief Justice Coke, the attorney-general who prosecuted Raleigh, and his opposition to the King on this point eventually led to his being confined as a prisoner in the Tower. John Pym, who was to be a prominent opponent in Charles's reign, was also imprisoned by James for insisting that parliamentary liberty was the birthright of the English people. Both were later released.

Coke's son, Clement Coke, was sent to the Tower for opposing Charles's marriage to the Spanish King's daughter, the Infanta, although in the end it never took place. Bacon too had his spell in the Tower—it was almost James's final fling. Bacon was imprisoned in the Lieutenant's House 'for many acts of bribery and corruption'. He wrote instantly to the King's favourite George Villiers, Duke of Buckingham, imploring him to obtain his release, for 'to die in this disgraceful place is even the worst that could be'. Villiers's intercession brought immediate action. Bacon was released the next day.

King Charles very rarely visited the Tower. His coronation procession did not set out from there because plague was again raging in London. But in the very first year of his reign a clash with the House of Commons brought two prominent Members of Parliament to the Tower. They were Sir John Eliot and Sir Dudley Digges; their offence was that they had censured the conduct of the Duke of Buckingham. As the King's chief minister, he was called to account for the mismanagement of affairs. Nor were they prepared, they said, to accept the King's haughty attitude, defined in the words 'Remember, Parliaments are altogether in my power for their calling, sitting and dissolution; and therefore, as I find them good or evil, they are to continue or not to be.' They demanded Buckingham's impeachment. Digges said, 'The laws of England have taught us that kings cannot command unlawful things and, whatever ill events follow, the executioners of such designs must answer for them.' The Duke greeted this with contemptuous laughter, which was followed by a fierce denunciation from Sir John Eliot.

After a time both men were released, but Eliot was sent back to the Tower two years later, together with eight other Members of Parliament, for opposing the King's right to levy taxes as he thought fit; he was imprisoned in the Bloody Tower. Some of the prisoners were released after a time; Eliot was fined £2000 before getting his freedom, but he was back in the Tower shortly afterwards to be held 'during the King's pleasure'. Once again in the Bloody Tower, he seems to have been fairly comfortable, and complained only of the clanking of the chains and windlasses as the tower's two portcullises were raised and lowered. He was able to use the walk on the ramparts as Raleigh had done, and one of his windows overlooked the garden by the Lieutenant's House and Tower Green. Visitors were allowed, and one who came often was the great Parliamentarian John Hampden, who later rose to prominence and was a supporter of Oliver Cromwell. A change of Lieutenant brought the severest restrictions for Eliot: he was moved from the Bloody Tower to a cold damp cell, where he caught consumption and died in 1632. He was buried in St Peter ad Vincula on the King's orders, despite his son's plea that his father should be interred in the family churchyard in Cornwall.

Eliot's room in the Bloody Tower had been used earlier for the imprisonment of John Felton, an ex-soldier who had stabbed the widely hated Duke of Buckingham to death in the streets of Portsmouth with a knife bought on Tower Hill. News of the assassination was greeted with great joy by the people. Felton became a popular hero and was cheered as he was led through the streets to the Tower. 'God bless thee, little David,' they cried. Ben Jonson wrote a 'Hymn to Felton' which had an enormous sale. The King ordered torture to make Felton reveal the names of his accomplices, but when Archbishop William Laud and the Earl of Dorset threatened Felton with it, he reminded them that torture was not permissible by the laws of England. In view of the strong public feeling for Felton, the judges refused to sanction its use. A Royal Commission was set up to enquire into the law, and it was found, as the State trial papers record, that 'no such punishment is known or allowed by our law', despite the use of it by certain sovereigns during the preceding centuries. Thus Felton must be credited with the abolition of torture in England. He was taken to Tyburn in 1628 and hanged there, and his body was suspended in chains at the scene of his crime in Portsmouth.

The next important figure to be imprisoned in the Tower was Thomas Wentworth, Earl of Strafford, once a leader of the progressive party in the House of Commons, but later one of Charles's staunchest supporters. After more angry scenes in the Commons, the King dissolved Parliament in 1629 and ruled without it for eleven years, relying mainly on Strafford and on Archbishop Laud, the vital members of the Council.

The country was at peace and was enjoying great prosperity. Trade was expanding and harvests were good. London had been growing fast and now had a population of about a quarter of a million; the provincial towns were also growing bigger. But the King, relying on the revenue from the existing taxes and the increasing customs revenue that the expanding trade produced, was still short of money. In 1626 he pawned the Crown Jewels, but since this did not help much, he resorted to imposing a series of highly unpopular levies without parliamentary sanction. One of his measures was to recognize defective titles to the ownership of land if the claimant paid enough. Another was to grant company monopolies—this brought in enormous sums. Monopolies were established for the sale of bricks, salt, starch, soap and a number of other commodities; when it was discovered that the shareholders of some of these companies were friends of the Lord Treasurer, the public were scandalized.

Then came the extension of the tax known as 'ship money', which was strongly resisted. Hitherto it had been paid only by the coastal regions, but now it was levied from the entire country. No doubt in a time of national danger this extension might have been accepted, had parliamentary sanction been sought. But there was no Parliament, nor was the country in danger. John Hampden, who had been an MP until Parliament was dissolved, refused to pay it. He was taken to court and, though the King won the case by the judges' vote of seven to five, the country was wholeheartedly behind Hampden.

The crucial conflict with the King was sparked off in Scotland, where the people, largely Presbyterian, defied Archbishop Laud's attempt to run their kirk. They did not want bishops, but were being forced to accept them. An army was recruited, and in no time at all it numbered as many as 20,000 men. King Charles had no standing army. The royal arsenals in the Tower and elsewhere in the country were practically empty. Some excellent ships had been built for the Royal Navy with the 'ship money', but these alone could not decide the issue. Charles appealed to Spain for help, but it was refused. Strafford offered to bring troops over from Ireland, where he had recently established order by his firm rule, but they were a mere handful.

Unable to fight, Charles gave in, but only to gain time to raise an army. The necessary funds could only be raised through Parliament, so elections were at last held. Parliament met in May 1640, but its mood was so critical that it was dissolved after three weeks and thus became known as the Short Parliament. By now the Scottish army was on the border, and after a clash with such troops as Charles had there, an invasion of England began, for the English troops ran away. As a contemporary noted, 'Never so many ran from so few with less ado.'

The Scottish leaders, declaring that they were also fighting for the liberties of the English people, appealed to the Parliamentary party and the Puritans in England for help. Now that the country had been invaded, there was a clamour for the recall of Parliament; the King gave in, and elections were held again. The new Parliament, to be known afterwards as the Long Parliament, met on 3 November. All the old opponents of the King had been re-elected, and at their head were John Pym and John Hampden. The King had on his side less than one-third of the House.

The Commons demanded immediate redress of their grievances and the punishment of Strafford, regarded as a traitor to the cause he had once championed in the House and hated for his ruthlessness. Locking the doors of the chamber, the Members drew up the articles for Strafford's impeachment and delivered the document to the House of Lords. The peers, who had cheered Strafford when he entered that morning, now told him to withdraw. On his return after their debate, his sword was taken away from him and he was arrested by Black Rod, the chief Gentleman Usher of the Lord Chamberlain. A few days later he was taken to the Tower. In less than two months Archbishop Laud, equally despised by Parliament and the people, was also arrested, taken by boat to the Traitors' Gate and imprisoned in the Bloody Tower.

For a time Strafford was lodged in the Lieutenant's House. His trial in Westminster Hall in the following March lasted eighteen days, and on each of those days he had to make the journey from his cell by water, escorted by a powerful armed guard travelling in six barges. The King and the entire royal family attended each hearing. The scene has been vividly described by one who

was present. 'It was daily the most glorious assembly that the isle could afford; yet the gravity was not such as I expected,' records Dr Robert Baillie, a Scottish minister, in his diary. 'After ten, much public eating, not only of confections but of flesh and bread; bottles of beer and wine going thick from mouth to mouth without cups, and all this in the King's eye.' Strafford defended himself doggedly and with great skill. The charge was treason—not against the King, as it was once phrased, but against the nation. The King spoke in the House of Lords in his minister's defence: 'I cannot in my conscience condemn the earl of treason, but,' adding a placatory gesture, 'I shall never again employ him in any office, no, not so much as a constable.' The Lords did not like this; they regarded it as an attempt to influence their vote.

The people of both England and Scotland were deeply interested in the trial. It seemed to them that their future depended on the decision of the judges. Londoners shut their shops and collected outside Westminster Hall, calling loudly for justice and Strafford's head. In case the impeachment failed, Pym took the added precaution of bringing in a Bill of Attainder, a parliamentary measure which did not rely solely on points of law, but could find a man guilty by decree; and to make sure that Parliament should not be dissolved in the meantime, a Bill was rushed through the Commons prohibiting the dissolution of Parliament without its own consent.

Strafford now had no chance. The King's conscience had been greatly troubled, for he had promised Strafford that no harm would come to him; Charles wept when he was faced with having to give his assent to the Act of Attainder. 'My Lord of Strafford's condition,' he said, 'is happier than mine.' He signed it and sent his eleven-year-old son, later King Charles II, to appeal to the Lords for mercy, but the plea was rejected. The King never recovered from this blow. He felt it was a betrayal of his greatest and most loyal minister, and when his own time came to face death, he said more than once that all his sufferings were a just punishment for his sin in letting Strafford die. Laud noted in his diary when he learned that Charles had signed the death warrant, 'The King was not worth serving, he knew not how to be, or be made, great.'

The execution was fixed for 12 May 1641. Strafford had asked the Lieutenant, Sir Thomas Lunsford, if he could see Laud to say farewell, but the request was refused. On his way to

Tower Hill, as he was being led through the large gateway of the Bloody Tower, he saw the Archbishop's face in the window just above him. They did not speak, but Laud leant out of the window; raising his hand, he gave Strafford his blessing and fell back in a faint into the arms of an attendant, to whom he said later, 'I hope by God's assistance and through mine own innocency that when I come to my own execution, I shall show the world how much more sensible I am to my Lord Strafford's loss than I am to my own.'

Tall, dark, dressed in black and holding himself with immense dignity, Strafford went past the dense crowds to the scaffold, lit by the May morning sun. He mounted the steps and said, 'I thank God I am not afraid of death nor daunted with any discouragement rising from my fears, but do as cheerfully put off my doublet at this time as ever I did when I went to bed.' That night bonfires were lit all over the country and there was much wild rejoicing. For the first time the records reveal the name of the masked executioner—Richard Brandon—who was sent to prison a year or two later for bigamy. He is reputed to have executed Charles I as well, but the records do not corroborate this.

Laud remained in the Tower for a further three years. He was a man of little breeding but great learning and boundless energy: 'a little, low red-faced man', irritable, self-opinioned and tactless. His pride in the Church led to his encouragement of Inigo Jones, who designed and built many simple and lovely churches; admired today, they were sneered at then as Laudian-Gothic. He also revived interest in church plate, vestments and stained-glass, which the Puritans detested and regarded as a form of 'popery'. His insistence on religious uniformity in a style akin to High Church today was rejected by Scotland, where the congregations hurled stools at the ministers who dared to adopt it.

There was deep resentment of Charles's marriage in 1625 to Henrietta Maria, the daughter of King Henry IV of France, a Protestant from Navarre who became a Catholic in order to gain the French throne because, he said, 'Paris is worth a Mass'. She was only fifteen at the time, lightheaded and given to frivolity, which the King did not like at first; in time, however, he became her slave. Laud was himself disquieted by the Queen's strong support of Catholicism and of the Catholic friends she gathered around her with the King's devoted encouragement. There were Spaniards at the court, and even constant contact with Rome.

The anger of the people was directed against the Archbishop, who was hated not only because his religious intolerance had led to the arrest and imprisonment of a great many churchmen who opposed him, but also for his unwavering support of the King in his arbitrary and dictatorial decisions. In 1632 an attack by the Puritan pamphleteer William Prynne on masques and plays, which the Queen loved, led to savage action by Laud, no doubt on the King's instructions. Prynne was branded on the forehead, placed in the pillory, his nose slit and his ears cut off; he was further fined £5000 and sentenced to life imprisonment in the Tower.

Laud's downfall was heralded on May Day 1640, when some London apprentices joined angry seamen and dockers and marched on his palace at Lambeth. The Archbishop fled, but his servants prevented the crowd from breaking in. The ringleaders were arrested, but the rabble broke into the gaol and released all the prisoners. Just before Christmas, Laud was impeached, arrested and sent to the Tower. The old man, now nearly seventy, asked if he might go home and collect some papers and then be taken to the Tower when it was dark 'to avoid the gazing of the people'. Both his requests were granted. Nevertheless, as his barge went down the river 'hundreds of my poor neighbours,' he recorded in his diary, 'stood there and prayed for my safety and return to my house. For which I bless God and them.'

Ironically it was Prynne, released on the instructions of Parliament, who came to the Bloody Tower early one morning to search Laud's papers, leaving two musketeers at the door and bringing in three others, 'their muskets already cocked'. They found Laud in bed. Not enough evidence was available to support the charge of treason, but it was argued at his trial in 1644 that 'when all the Archbishop's transgressions of the law were put together they made many grand treasons'. To this Laud's counsel replied, 'I never understood before this that two hundred couple of rabbits made a black horse.' Laud was found guilty of 'attempting to subvert religion and the fundamental laws of the realm'.

He was condemned to death, and on the bitterly cold morning of 10 January 1645 he was taken out on to Tower Hill. His petition to be executed with an axe was granted, and as it was about to descend he raised his voice and cried, 'I am coming, O Lord, as fast as I can.'

CHAPTER FORTY-ONE

Oliver Cromwell's Prisoners

Speaker Lenthall asserting the privileges of the Commons on Charles I's attempt to arrest the five Members. Wall painting in the Lords Corridor. (By permission of the Serjeant-at-Arms, House of Lords. Photo: Ministry of Public Building and Works)

The execution of Strafford, the denial of the right to dissolve Parliament without its consent, the cancellation of all taxation not sanctioned by Parliament were so strongly resented by the King that he embarked on a series of actions that inevitably led to civil war. In June 1641, a very few weeks after Strafford's execution, he was engaged in a secret attempt to bring the army into London. In August he went north to persuade the Scottish army to fight against Parliament; in this he failed. He was also intriguing with the Roman Catholics in Ireland for military help.

On his return to London in November, he was met by a demand for further reforms and the appointment of ministers acceptable to Parliament. The King gave a non-committal answer and shortly afterwards, on 4 January 1642, he violated the liberties of the House of Commons, where no monarch had ever been allowed to enter, by striding into the chamber with an armed force, intending to seize Pym, Hampden and three other distinguished Members whom he regarded as the ringleaders of the resistance. Warned of the King's intentions, the five Members had taken refuge in the city of London, which refused to surrender them. At this the King left Whitehall to prepare for war. Both Houses of Parliament replied by setting up a Committee of Safety and enlisting a force of 10,000 men for active service. Civil war broke out on 22 August 1642, when King Charles set up his standard in Nottingham. Nor did it end in 1646, when the King surrendered to the Scots, who later handed him over to the Parliamentarians in return for £400,000. There was a lull for two years then a further outbreak of fighting.

Meanwhile a new figure had emerged as political and military leader of the Parliamentarians. Until 1641 Oliver Cromwell, though a Member of Parliament for thirteen years and a cousin of John Hampden, had rarely spoken in the House. A man of heavy build, with a swollen, reddish countenance, poorly dressed despite his comfortable means, he was an ardent Puritan, eager for the abolition of episcopacy, and was on the point of emigrating to America when the prospect of war provided him with a fresh field of activity. On the King's attempt to seize the five Members of Parliament, Cromwell moved in the House that the kingdom should be put in a state of defence, contributed more than £1000 out of his own purse for this purpose and enlisted for service in the cavalry. Shortly afterwards he raised his own regiment, formed strictly of 'men of religion' called by God to leave their homes, their farms and their work to fight in what Cromwell regarded as a religious war. No blasphemy, drinking or disorder was tolerated in their ranks. In the closing year of the Civil War his was the commanding voice in the affairs of the Parliamentarians.

Until the autumn of 1648 he was in favour of preserving the monarchy, and protracted negotiations with King Charles went on. But when it was found that concessions were only being made in order to gain time, the Council of the Parliamentary Army demanded that the King should be brought to trial. In December Colonel Thomas Pride, a former drayman, acting on the Army's orders, removed from Parliament all those who were likely to support the King (Pride's Purge), and on 1 January 1649 the remnant of Members in the House of Commons resolved that Charles was guilty of treason by 'levying war against the Parliament and Kingdom of England'.

A high court of justice was set up to try the King. On 20 January at Westminster Hall the trial began. The King, escorted by twelve halberdiers, was dressed in black with the glittering star of the Order of the Garter on his cloak, and a tall black hat above the long grey hair falling on to his shoulders. He refused to recognize the authority of the court on three successive days, and on the fourth was sentenced to death. Many of the commissioners seated in judgement refused to sign the death warrant. A few days later, on the afternoon of Sunday, 30 January 1649, he walked through the great Banqueting Hall of the Palace of Whitehall between two lines of soldiers and stepped out through one of the windows, enlarged for this purpose, on to the scaffold, the small platform of which was crowded with soldiers and shorthand writers with notebooks and ink-horns. The executioner and his assistant were not only masked but heavily disguised. In his last words he made an allusion to Strafford: 'An unjust sentence that I suffered to take effect is punished now by an unjust sentence on me.' The street was filled with people; mounted troops stood between them and the scaffold.

The King with the help of the Bishop of London pushed his hair under the cap he was given to wear and said he would pray briefly and then give the executioner the sign. His head was severed with one blow, and a groan went up from the watching crowds who had until now been silent. Charles was in his forty-ninth year. Oliver Cromwell was later proclaimed Protector of the Commonwealth.

Nearly two hundred years had passed since the outbreak of the Wars of the Roses had plunged England into thirty years of turbulent conflict, but the six years of the Civil War disrupted the country far more grievously. In the former wars only the rival claimants of the royal house and their immediate supporters had been involved. Now the entire country was affected: brother fought brother, father fought son, as they lined up with the Cavaliers (royalists) or the Roundheads (Parliamentarians). The Tower was not directly drawn into the war—there were no battles for its possession—but prisoners were confined there and the lieutenants came and went in bewildering succession.

The funeral of Charles I: a modern painting by E. Crofts. (Bristol City Art Gallery)

The first incident occurred in May 1641, more than a year before the outbreak of war. A body of one hundred royalist troops arrived at the Bulwark Gate and demanded admittance. London was strongly in sympathy with the Parliamentarians, and it was realized that this was an attempt by the King to strengthen the garrison of the Tower with forces he could rely on. The Lieutenant, Sir William Balfour, aware that their admission might provoke the Londoners to besiege the Tower, barred their entry. A battle seemed imminent, but Balfour knew that the King had no wish to fire the first shot, and asked the royalist force to withdraw. Afterwards Balfour was dismissed.

The new Lieutenant, Sir Thomas Lunsford, was a reliable royalist. The corporation of the city of London immediately petitioned Parliament for his removal, stating that a man of his questionable reputation was unsuitable for such an important position of trust—he was described as 'fit for any wicked design'. A deputation from the Commons went to see the King, and informed him that the merchants of London, conscious of the Lieutenant's unsavoury record, refused to supply any more bullion to the Mint in the Tower. This meant that the coining of fresh money would be brought to a complete standstill. The King thereupon dismissed Lunsford and appointed Sir John Byron, later the first Lord Byron and an ancestor of the poet, who arrived at the Tower in January 1642 with a brigade of gunners and weeded out all members of the garrison suspected of having Parliamentary sympathies. Just as the dismissed men were marching out, a large body of the city's train-bands arrived on Tower Hill, and Byron thought it prudent to recall the men who were leaving. Instead, the royalist gunners he had brought with him were sent away.

A week or two later, Byron records, while he was away from the Tower attending a meeting of Parliament where his removal was being discussed, 'Capt Skippon towards the evening marched to the backside of the Tower and stayed at the Iron Gate with his men, which were about five hundred. He sent one into the Tower to the Sergeant who commanded the [Tower] Hamleters that he should march out of the Tower that night and come to him. They desired to be excused.' Byron adds that all the arms in the Tower had already been sent out for use by the troops and none had been brought in to replace them. 'The powder likewise decreases apace ... and by the time the Navy is furnished there will be little or

none left.' In the following year, when the Parliamentary forces had gained the ascendancy against the King, a man whom the city could trust was appointed Lieutenant. This was Sir Isaac Pennington, a fishmonger and a former Lord Mayor of London.

After this, Cavaliers formed the greater part of the prisoners in the Tower. Among them was Sir John Hotham, who was brought in with his son. Both were tried in the Guildhall and condemned to death for trying to arrange for the surrender of the town of Hull to the King's men. As the father was on his way to the scaffold on Tower Hill, a messenger galloped through the crowd with a reprieve and he was taken back to the Tower. When it was discovered that the reprieve had been granted by the House of Lords, the Commons cancelled it (Cromwell abolished the House of Lords a little later when he became Protector). Two days later, Sir John Hotham was again taken to the scaffold, in a most pitiable state of distress, for his son had been executed on the preceding day.

Five royalist prisoners made daring attempts to escape. Daniel O'Neill, a great-nephew of the Earl of Tyrone, dressed himself up as a woman. The sentries thought he was the wife of one of the warders; he was allowed to walk out and escaped to Holland. Two others, also Irish royalists, Lord Maguire and Colonel Macmahon, managed somehow to get hold of a saw and cut their way out of their cell. Outside they found a rope, which they attached to the bar of a nearby window; they then lowered themselves down to the moat, swam across and made for the house of a friend where they hid. The Lieutenant was severely punished for his negligence, and a reward of £100 was offered for their recapture. All the houses around the Tower were searched and the two prisoners were brought back and executed, the peer on Tower Hill, the commoner at Tyburn.

Another escape was that of Lord Capel. He had been captured by the Roundheads when Colchester surrendered in August 1648. A friend sent him a long rope and some grappling irons. He chose a dark night and, tying the rope to his window-bars, let himself slowly down to the ground. Then he cautiously groped his way through the darkness to the moat. Since he could not swim, his friends had sent him a diagram indicating the shallowest part, but he found it hard to locate. He stepped in at what he thought was the right point and soon the water was well above his chin. He struggled on, stumbling and slipping, his feet sinking into the squelching mud, and finally reached the other side, where his friends were waiting. They took him off to a room in the Temple, where he hid for three days before being moved, heavily disguised, by boat to a house in Lambeth.

Unfortunately one of the men had addressed him as 'My lord', and the boatman, having heard that Lord Capel had escaped from the Tower, followed the party to the house and passed the information on to the authorities. He received £10 reward, and Capel was taken straight back to the Tower. He was executed on 9 March 1649, with the Duke of Hamilton; the Earl of Norwich, also in the Tower, had a last-minute reprieve. Two other prisoners, the royalist Generals Middleton and Massey, taken prisoner at the Battle of Worcester, fared better. They got out of the Tower without detection and crossed to France.

The most important prisoner in the Tower during these years was Colonel George Monk. Born in Devon, he had obtained considerable military experience in the Dutch wars and at first had fought for King Charles. He was captured at the Battle of Nantwich in 1644 and spent three years in the Tower. He was then offered his freedom if he would take command of one of the Parliamentary armies. Being a soldier of fortune interested more in warfare than in the cause, he agreed, and fought for Cromwell in Scotland. He won the confidence of the Scots and brought that country into complete subjection. Later, after Cromwell's death, he played a vital part in the restoration of Charles II in 1660, and was made Duke of Albemarle in the same year. His new authority gave him the right to appoint the Constable of the Tower in the name of the new King. The man he chose was a Major Nicholas.

Although he filled the Tower with prisoners, Cromwell himself never stayed there. Towards the close of the Civil War he appointed Thomas Fairfax, the Commander-in-Chief of his armies, Constable of the Tower. After the execution of Charles I, however, he took over that office himself. He pulled down the Jewel House by the White Tower in which the Crown Jewels were once kept and also the Wardrobe Tower near it which housed the King's State documents and more costly personal possessions. The Coldharbour Tower on the other side, the formidable gateway to the Royal Palace, was also dismantled. The Mint received the Protector's constant attention and he retained Thomas Simon, the master craftsman Charles I had appointed. In 1650 Simon travelled to Edinburgh to draw a likeness of Cromwell for the medal commemorating the victory at Dunbar. 'Indeed the man is ingenious and worthy of encouragement,' said Cromwell.

Not all Cromwell's prisoners in the Tower were captives from the battlefields. Many were arrested for plotting to assassinate the Protector. A large batch of them, numbering more than fifteen and headed by the Earl of Oxford, were brought to the Tower in 1654. They had been planning to kill Cromwell, seize the Tower and bring back Prince Charles, then in exile in France, as the new King. Two of the plotters were executed.

Another would-be assassin was Miles Sydercombe. He had prepared a 'deadly machine', consisting of seven blunderbusses bound cuningly together so that all seven could be discharged simultaneously; he took this to a house in Hammersmith which Cromwell was to pass on his way to Hampton Court, but it failed to work. So Sydercombe adopted another plan—to set fire to Whitehall Palace while Cromwell was in residence. This time one of his accomplices betrayed him, and he was arrested and taken to the Tower. While awaiting execution he tried to bribe his warders to let him escape, but they refused. He then persuaded his sister, who was allowed to visit him, to bring a deadly drug; telling his warders on the night before his execution that he would like to be alone while he said his prayers, he committed suicide. Nevertheless, his corpse was dragged on a litter by a horse to Tower Hill, where, in the words of the chronicler, 'a hole being dug, he was turned in, stark naked, and a stake spiked with iron was driven through him into the earth; that part of the stake which remains above ground being all plated with iron, which may stand as an example of terror to all traitors for the time to come.'

The assassination plots became so numerous that Cromwell always wore a shirt of mail under his doublet and refused to eat any food that had not already been tasted by others. He also slept in a different room each night. The other palaces he stayed in were left intact but the Palace in the Tower he pulled down. The debris remained there until Charles II had it removed. The Palace was never rebuilt because monarchs had ceased to reside in fortresses; large, comfortable residences like Hampton Court served well enough in an era when a castle's stout walls and moat were no longer impregnable.

CHAPTER FORTY-TWO

Theft of the Crown Jewels

In 1660 the diarist Samuel Pepys sailed with his cousin Admiral Montagu, later the Earl of Sandwich, and the English fleet to fetch King Charles II from Breda in Holland. Pepys's family had been divided during the Civil War, like many families in England—his father and mother were Parliamentarians, but he remained a staunch royalist.

The round-up of Cromwell's active supporters had begun before the actual Restoration. After the Protector's death there was a great deal of uncertainty and uneasiness. A number of his adherents, aware of the plans for a restoration of the monarchy, took every possible step to prevent it. Colonel John Lambert, for example, one of Cromwell's more brilliant strategists, was preparing to bring 2000 sailors into the Tower, which was still nominally under Parliamentary control, and to provide enough provisions to enable it to withstand a long siege. But he was forestalled by royalist sympathizers. They secretly took over the Tower and put Lambert into it as their first prisoner. Pepys describes how Lambert contrived to escape. Having obtained some rope from friends outside, he persuaded the woman who had come to make up the bed in his cell to put on his nightcap, get under the sheets and pretend to be asleep. Then he slid down the rope from the window and joined six friends who were waiting for him in a barge. He managed to get as far as Warwickshire, but was recaptured and brought back to the Tower, together with his accomplices. After the Restoration, Charles II banished him to the Channel Islands, where he remained a prisoner for more than twenty years.

Charles's coronation followed the tradition established by earlier kings. It was the first to set out from the Tower for more than sixty years. Since the Palace had been destroyed, Charles arranged to stay in the old royal apartments in the White Tower. All the towers were already full of prisoners when he arrived on Sunday, 22 April 1661 to prepare for the ceremony. Most of those who signed the warrant for his father's execution had already been disposed of. The first of them to die was General Harrison, who was executed on the spot where the statue of Charles I now stands. Pepys witnessed this execution and noted in his diary, 'Thus it was my chance to see the King beheaded at White Hall and to see the first blood shed in revenge.'

Charles II was the last of the English kings to spend a night in the Tower before his coronation. He also revived the ceremony of creating Knights of the Bath—in fact he created more than sixty-eight of them in the Painted Chamber at Westminster, and the diarist John Evelyn states, 'I might have received this honour but declined it.' Charles also created six earls and as many barons. 'I spent the rest of the evening,' Evelyn adds, 'seeing the several arch-triumphals built in the streets through which His Majesty was next day to pass.'

The next morning the customary procession set out through the Bulwark Gate for Westminster. Pepys, 'having put on my velvet coat', watched from a window in Cornhill. 'It is impossible to relate,' he writes, 'the glory of this day, expressed in the clothes of them that rid, and their horses and horse-clothes, among others my Lord Sandwich's embroidery and diamonds were ordinary among them. The Knights of the Bath was a brave sight of itself, and their Esquires. Remarkable were the two men that represent the two Dukes of Normandy and Aquitaine. The Bishops came next after the Barons, which is the higher place; which makes me think that the next Parliament they will be called to the House of

Lords. My Lord Monk rode bare after the King, and led in his hand a spare horse, as being the Master of the Horse. The King, in a most rich embroidered suit and cloak, looked most noble . . . Glorious was the show with gold and silver, that we were not able to look at it, our eyes at last being so much overcome with it. Both the King and the Duke of York took notice of us, as he saw us at the window.' The King was thirty-six years old and a bachelor; his brother the Duke of York, who later became King James II, was three years younger. A night was spent in Whitehall Palace and the coronation took place in the Abbey on the next day.

There were no Crown Jewels left in the Tower

The State Salt, presented to Charles II on his accession by the city of Exeter and now in the Tower collection. (By permission of the Controller of Her Majesty's Stationery Office. Crown Copyright reserved)

because Charles I had pawned most of them, and Cromwell, resolved that there would never be a king again, sold the lot. The massive gold Crown of State, weighing $7\frac{1}{2}$ pounds, the Queen's crown, also of gold, weighing nearly 4 pounds, a smaller crown, the royal globe, two coronation bracelets adorned with rubies and pearls, two sceptres, a long rod of silver—all were gone. But much more important was the famous Crown of Alfred the Great, which was nearly eight hundred years old. It was made of gold wire inset with precious stones. Cromwell had the gold melted down and sold it for £238 10s 6d. The Crown of Edward the Confessor, more than six hundred years old, and the Staff, which is said to have contained in its head a portion of the Cross on which Christ was crucified, were also disposed of. Both these crowns and the Staff were well known to the goldsmith Robert Vyner, who was asked by Charles to replace them when the new Crown Jewels were made for the coronation, at a cost of £31,978 9s 11d.

It is possible that a great many of the new jewels were in fact the original Crown Jewels which Cromwell had sold. There is a complete inventory in the British Museum of the items sold, the price paid for them and the names of the purchasers; and it has long been believed that the owners kept them with a view to restoring them to the Tower when the new King came to the throne. That they were not given back as a gift, or even identified as the originals, is thought to be due to the fear that Charles II, being in desperate need of money, could have classified them as royal property and might even have punished the purchasers for having them in their possession— we know, for example, that some of the jewels lost by King John were found later and those who possessed them were punished. So it is thought that the pieces rescued from Cromwell's sale were secretly handed over to Vyner and passed off as part of the new regalia.

Some items were undoubtedly new, for, as we have seen, Cromwell melted down the Crown of Alfred the Great. We can only be certain of three pieces—the Ampulla, the Anointing Spoon and 'Queen Elizabeth's Salt Cellar', which we know to have been hidden by the monks at Westminster Abbey. The Ampulla, which was used at the coronation of Henry IV in 1399 and is certainly much older, is in the shape of a Golden Eagle, the head of which unscrews. The anointing oil is poured out of the bird's beak into the bowl of the Anointing Spoon, which was perhaps made for

King John. Into this the Archbishop of Canterbury dips two fingers and makes the sign of the cross on the monarch's forehead, breast and the palms of both hands during the coronation ritual. 'Queen Elizabeth's Salt Cellar' was made in 1572 and is believed to have been used by the Queen. It is a fine example of Tudor craftsmanship with a figure on the lid of a knight in armour carrying a long sword and shield (see page 166).

Charles II took a sustained interest in the Mint. While in exile he had met in Antwerp a gold engraver named Roettier and occasionally borrowed money from him. Soon after his return to England he sent for the old engraver's three highly skilled sons and installed them in the Tower Mint. The man in charge there at the time was Thomas Simon, who went to Edinburgh to design a likeness of Cromwell for a commemorative medal. Charles retained his services and was amused to learn that the coins he had designed for the Commonwealth had personally cost him £1700—he had applied to Cromwell again and again for payment and in the end received only £700. 'I beg you to consider,' he wrote to Cromwell, 'that I and my servants have wrought five years without recompense and that the interest I have to pay for gold and silver eats up my profit.'

Charles asked the Roettier brothers and Simon to send in designs for his new coinage. His choice fell on an admirable design by young John Roettier. Simon, not to be outdone, produced a medal known as the Petition Crown, which he sent to the King with a note: 'Thomas Simon most humbly prays Your Majesty to compare this, his trial piece, with the Dutch [the Roettiers], and if more truly drawn and embossed, more gracefully ordered and more accurately engraven, to relieve [pay] him.' Two years later, in 1665, Simon died of the plague. About this time a new method of minting money was introduced. Steel rolling-mills worked by horse and water power were set up for striking coins, and the old casting presses were removed.

Pepys often visited the Tower. He sometimes went with the King to inspect the work being done at the Mint by the Roettiers. 'So we by coach to them, and there went up and down all the magazines with them; but methought it was but poor discourse and frothy that the King's companions, young Killigrew among the rest, had with him. We saw none of the money; but Mr Slingsby [Master of the Mint] did show the King, and I did see, the stamps of the new money to be made by Blondeau's fashion, which are very

Medal of Frances Stuart, Duchess of Richmond, by John Roettier. (National Portrait Gallery, London)

neat and like the King.' Blondeau was the designer brought over from Paris by Oliver Cromwell. Pepys adds, 'We compared these with those made for Oliver.' Later: 'We were shown the method of making this new money, from the beginning to the end, which is so pretty that I did take a note of every part of it.' And again: 'My Lord Brounker and I to the Tower, to see the famous Engraver, to get him to grave a seal for the office, and did see some of the finest pieces of work, in embossed work, that ever I did see in my life, for fineness and smallness of the images thereon. Here also did see bars of gold melting, which was a fine sight.'

Pepys was particularly captivated by the court beauty Frances Stuart, who was the model for Britannia in the Roettiers' medals and coins. The first of these medals was struck at the Mint to commemorate the Peace of Breda, after an action against the Dutch in 1667, and another commemorated naval victories. She also figured as Britannia on all the halfpennies, and after her death in 1702 was shown on pennies as well. In spite of her name, 'La Belle Stuart', as she was called, was not a member of the royal family but a daughter of Dr Walter Stuart and granddaughter of Lord Blantyre. The King was so infatuated with her that, on hearing she was about to marry the Duke of Richmond, he put the young man into the Tower and later sent him to Denmark as ambassador. Eventually she did marry Richmond and returned all the jewels the King had given her. John Roettier was also in love with her and a wax effigy of her may be seen today in the museum in Westminster Abbey. Two other mistresses of Charles II also sat for the Roettiers in the Tower: the Duchess of Cleveland (Lady Castlemaine) and the Duchess of Portsmouth (Louise de Kérouaille), but these medals, though designed, were never issued.

Pepys paid many visits to the Tower for another purpose. Cromwell had appointed a man called Sir John Barkstead, a former goldsmith, Governor (in effect Lieutenant) of the Tower; at the Restoration he had fled to the Continent. Sir George Downing, nephew of the first Governor of Massachusetts, and himself one of the first graduates of Harvard, had first served Cromwell as a spy and then swore allegiance to Charles II (the street in which the Prime Minister lives today is named after him). He now told the King that he could round up the regicides who had got away. He was sent to The Hague as ambassador, and induced a Dutch businessman to trick the fugitives to come to Holland, promising to pay £200 for each man he got. Barkstead and two other men named Okey and Corbet were lured to Delft on the promise that several factories were being built at great cost and there would be most lucrative profits for them. The moment they arrived, they were arrested by Downing and brought over to England, where they were put into the Tower and later hanged at Tyburn. Ten years later, Downing was himself imprisoned in the Tower for leaving his ambassadorial post in The Hague without the King's permission, but he was later released.

It was generally believed that Barkstead had hidden £7000 (according to some accounts, £50,000) in the Tower just before he fled the country, and Pepys attempted to find it. The King authorized the search and was to receive a large share of the money. After four long and exhausting sessions of digging in several small cellars by the light of candles, nothing was found. 'And now privately the woman, Barkstead's great confidant, is brought, who do positively say that this is the place where he did say the money was hid in, and where he and she put up the £50,000 in butter firkins.' But it was not there. Then Pepys persuaded the Lieutenant to put some men to work. They tried the garden, 'in the corner against the Main Guard', while he sat by the fire in the Governor's House. The money was never found.

When the Great Plague broke out in 1665 and the court and the Government moved out of London, General Monk took charge of the Tower, and the Lord Mayor carried out the ceremony of installation in a barber's shop near the Bulwark Gate. A guard of honour was drawn up, and the Lieutenant, the Steward of the Tower and the Comptroller of the Mint acted as the chief officials. Fifty-eight members of the Tower garrison, as well as a large number of others working or residing in the Tower, were suspected of having caught the plague; they were moved to a pest-house in Stepney where most of them recovered.

In the following year, as though to cleanse the city of the contagion, the Great Fire broke out. It started in Pudding Lane by London Bridge in the early morning of Sunday, 2 September 1666. Pepys, who was living near the Tower, was awakened by one of the maids and went up to her bedroom window to look at the blaze. It seemed so far away that he went back to bed and fell asleep again.

Fires were everyday occurrences in the city at that time. This one, however, was to change the face of London completely. The narrow streets, the timber-framed houses with their sharp gables were soon alight and, as Evelyn noted, the sky was like the top of a burning oven. A great number of churches were destroyed or seriously damaged. Old St Paul's, its massive walls and its high position giving some hope of escape, was burnt to the ground. The London Shakespeare knew vanished. Until his death fifty years earlier it had remained unaltered; only westward beyond the city walls had there been persistent expansion.

By Sunday evening Pepys discovered that the fire was spreading, went to the Tower, and from 'one of the high places'—probably the roof of the White Tower—saw 'the houses at that end of the bridge [London Bridge] all on fire and an infinite great fire on this and the other side of the bridge. My heart full of trouble, to the Lieutenant of the Tower, who tells me that it burned down St Magnus Church and most part of Fish Street already.' The fire was for a time at its fiercest by the river. All the lanes and alleys off Thames Street were choked with people hurrying to the nearest churches with their possessions on their backs; and as the flames came nearer, the goods were quickly taken out again and carried to safer places, only to be moved once again. Those who could afford to pay the exorbitant prices demanded by the wherrymen dumped their furniture and effects into boats and had them ferried across the river.

The King and the Duke of York came that afternoon by river from Whitehall. His Majesty

The Great Fire of London, seen from the east: panel painting by an unknown Dutch artist, possibly an eyewitness. (By permission of the Trustees of the London Museum)

ordered that houses in the line of the fire but well ahead of it should be pulled down to prevent it spreading. But the wind was so keen that the demolition had constantly to be taken still further ahead. Most of the lovely halls of the city guilds were in flames. From the Goldsmiths' Hall they managed to remove all the money and wares, valued at £1,200,000, which were conveyed to the Tower for safety. The Guildhall, Bow Church, all Cheapside, almost the whole of Fleet Street were burnt down. The fire licked the western walls of the Tower by Tower Hill, but luckily it was prevented from going any further, for the Tower was stacked with gunpowder; had this been ignited, the explosion, Evelyn records, 'would not only have beaten down and destroyed all the bridge [London Bridge was the only bridge at that time] but sunk and torn all the vessels in the river, and rendered the demolition beyond all expression for several miles about the country.' To prevent this, the gunpowder was hurriedly moved out of the Tower and deposited well beyond its eastern walls. Tower Hill was filled with homeless refugees who brought their possessions in bundles. Many people fainted and some died. On the fifth day the wind dropped and the appalling conflagration was brought to an end.

Five years later a most daring and carefully planned attempt was made to steal the Crown Jewels. The thief was an Irishman known as Colonel Blood. The son of a blacksmith, he had fought for Cromwell, but it is uncertain that he was ever a colonel. He was no longer young and very far from being attractive—'pudgy-faced, large-nosed, heavy-lipped'. For some months this

dark, stocky man was seen about Petty Wales, the squalid, unsavoury street running from the river past Lion Tower to Tower Hill. Here he hoped to find accomplices who were bold, fearless and likely to hold their tongues on the promise of a share in the very substantial loot.

Since the Jewel Tower had been pulled down, the Crown Jewels and regalia were now kept in the Martin Tower, which was built into the Inner Wall in the reign of Henry III. Charles had been in arrears with the salary of the Master of the Jewel House, Sir Gilbert Talbot, so he had arranged to pay him a small sum but to allow him to 'show the regalia to strangers' and keep anything they paid in admission fees. The Crown Jewels were displayed on the ground floor of the Martin Tower. In the two upper storeys lived a caretaker, eighty-year-old Talbot Edwards, with his wife and daughter, and it was Edwards who showed the visitors round and pocketed the fees.

Blood, disguising himself as a country parson who had come to London to see the sights, arrived at the Martin Tower one evening in April 1671 with a woman whom he passed off as his wife. Edwards showed them the Crown Jewels, but while they were viewing the exhibits, admiring and exclaiming, the woman began to sway, held on to the wall and said she felt faint. Edwards called to his wife, who came quickly down the stairs and helped the woman up to her living-room where she made her comfortable on the settee. The 'parson' thanked them both profusely and came back a few days later with a pair of gloves as a gift for Mrs Edwards. Invited to sit and talk for a while, he spoke among other things of a nephew who was well-to-do and extremely anxious to get married. He even went so far as to suggest that perhaps a marriage could be arranged between him and Edwards's daughter. Mr and Mrs Edwards were delighted. The old man revealed that he was often worried as to what would happen to his daughter after he died. He invited the Bloods to bring their nephew to dinner, and, when they sat down to the meal, Blood, still dressed as a parson, said grace at interminable length and finished with a prayer for the King, the Queen (Charles had by now married the Portuguese Princess Katherine of Braganza) and the royal family, meaning the Duke of York's family, since the King had no legitimate children.

The dinner was a great success. Blood asked if his nephew might have a look at the Crown Jewels, and Edwards took them downstairs. Blood admired a pair of pistols he was shown, and asked if he might buy them to give to a nobleman who was his neighbour. Edwards agreed to sell them, and thus left himself unarmed. Blood then asked if he might come early the next morning with three friends who were anxious to see the Crown Jewels before leaving London. Obligingly, Edwards agreed.

Blood and his friends arrived at seven o'clock on the morning of 9 May. All were armed with pistols hidden in their pockets, daggers concealed in their belts, and rapiers in their canes. One of the men waited at the entrance of the Martin Tower, while Blood and the other two went in. The man outside was told to say he was Blood's nephew if questioned.

Talbot Edwards was waiting to receive them in the jewel room. After they had entered, as Edwards stooped to lock the door, Blood threw his cloak over the old man's head, stuffed a wooden gag into his mouth and tied it in position with leather thongs; then an iron clip was put on his nose to prevent his snorting to attract attention. The old man struggled desperately; fearing this might attract attention, Blood and his men hit him on the head with a wooden mallet and brandished a dagger in front of him, whereupon he fainted. One of the men, Parrot, took the Orb and dropped it into his baggy breeches. Blood seized the Crown, which he found too large to conceal, so he flattened the top with his mallet

Daggers traditionally believed to have been used by Colonel Blood and his accomplices in their attempt to steal the Crown Jewels. (Ministry of Public Building and Works)

and hid it under his cloak. The third man, Hunt, took the Sceptre. As it was much too long to put into the bag he had brought, he began to file it into smaller sections.

199

At this moment footsteps were heard going past the door and up the stairs. It happened to be Edwards's son, who had come home unexpectedly from Flanders. In panic, Blood plunged his dagger into old Edwards and unlocked the door, and all three men dashed out. They made for the Iron Gate on the eastern side. As they raced across the Inner Ward Blood, still in parson's attire, kept shouting 'Stop thief!' and pointing ahead of him. Hunt had dropped the unwieldy Sceptre and the file before leaving, but Blood still had the Crown and Parrot had the Orb bumping about inside his trousers, which must have impeded his progress. There was great confusion. Everyone seemed to be chasing somebody without knowing who it was.

Meanwhile Talbot Edwards's son had hurried down with his sister, and finding his father on the floor, wounded, gagged and in a faint, went to his aid. When he removed the wooden gag, his father said, 'Treason! The Crown is stolen.' One of the men engaged in the chase was Captain Beckman, an officer of the Ordnance. He was soon joined by Edwards's son and took up the cry of 'Treason! The Crown is stolen!' Guards and warders rushed out of the various towers. The servants from the Lieutenant's House also joined in the pursuit. As they began to gain on him, Blood fired and one of his pursuers fell. He fired again, this time at Beckman, who was almost on his heels, but missed him. As Blood began to reload his pistol, Beckman grabbed him. They struggled for a while and the Crown fell out from under Blood's cloak and rolled into the gutter. Some of the precious stones came away from their setting, but they were later retrieved.

Meanwhile Parrot, who had reached the Wharf, was seized by two of the guards and the Orb was rescued. Its top had broken off and lost one of its rubies, which had to be searched for in his trousers. Hunt had managed to reach their horses, which had been left by the Iron Gate with yet another of their accomplices, and these two quickly mounted and rode away leaving Blood and Parrot prisoners. Still quite calm and arrogant, Blood said airily, 'It was a gallant deed, although it failed. It was to gain the Crown.' While Hunt was galloping through the narrow streets outside the Tower, he collided with a projecting barber's pole and was knocked off his saddle. A crowd gathered at once; he was recognized and taken back to the Tower.

Blood was confined in the vaults of the White Tower. He seemed to regard the whole episode with amused detachment, saying that he would confess only to the King personally and to no one else. His insolence astounded everyone. It was mentioned to the Lieutenant, and eventually someone told the King as a jest. His Majesty laughed and declared he would like to see the ruffian. Blood was taken to Whitehall Palace; after his talk with the King, he was not only released from the Tower and granted his complete freedom, but was given estates in Ireland. Some said that the estates were originally his, had been confiscated, and were now returned, but not everyone believed this. Blood was also given a pension of £500 a year for life.

His accomplices were also released, but it is not known if they were rewarded too. Certainly Blood was often seen at court laughing and jesting and even dining with the King's friends. Evelyn records in his diary on 10 May 1671: 'Dined at Mr Treasurer's where dined Monsieur de Gramont and several French noblemen, and one Blood, that impudent bold fellow who had not long before attempted to steal the Imperial Crown itself out of the Tower . . . How came he to be pardoned, and even received into favour, not only after this, but several other exploits almost as daring both in Ireland and here, I could never come to understand . . . The only treason of this sort that was ever pardoned. The man had not only a daring but a villanous unmerciful look, a false countenance, but very well spoken and dangerously insinuating.' Many believed that the King, being in need of money, had hired Blood to steal the Crown Jewels. Since he had paid £32,000 for them only a few years before, doubtless with difficulty, it would not look right if he took them out of the Tower and sold them himself.

Blood died nine years later at the age of sixty-two. The gossip got round that his 'death' was just a trick, for the King had been using him as a spy. An exhumation was ordered, however, and it was found that Blood was indeed dead. He is said to have become a Quaker a short time before. The caretaker, Talbot Edwards, was ill for some months. The dagger wound was not serious, but the mallet blow on his head and the wooden gag made him very infirm. A pension was applied for, but was refused. He lingered on for some years and was eventually given a small pension. Captain Beckman of the Ordnance, who so bravely tackled Blood and took him prisoner, became a Major and married Talbot Edwards's daughter Elizabeth, whom Blood had earmarked for his so-called nephew.

CHAPTER FORTY-THREE

The Duke of Monmouth and Judge Jeffreys

As Charles II had no legitimate heir, his brother James Duke of York, who was a Catholic, was his obvious successor, and a number of plots to influence the succession were hatched during the closing years of his reign.

The first of them came to light in 1678 when Charles was gravely ill. Titus Oates, an Anglican cleric with an unsavoury reputation, who had gone among the Jesuits posing as a Catholic, unfolded to a justice of the peace a startling conspiracy to hasten James's accession. Almost every Catholic peer and baronet was implicated; he even named James and the Queen, also a Catholic, as being involved in it. The accusations seemed so far-fetched that they were regarded as a Protestant attempt to discredit James and forestall the Catholics. But the murder of Sir Edmund Berry Godfrey, to whom Oates had made his statement, put a different complexion on the affair. Lord Arundel of Wardour, Lord Petre, Lord William Howard, Viscount Stafford, the Earl of Powis, the Earl of Danby and a great many others were sent to the Tower, but the only one executed was Viscount Stafford; Petre died a natural death in the Tower and most of the others were released many years later. It was afterwards established that the charge against Stafford was false and that Oates's evidence had sent an innocent man to his death. A few months later a second plot, this time a Protestant one, involved anti-Catholics. Lord Shaftesbury was put in the Tower, but was later pardoned and fled to France. Two others, Lord Russell, son of the Earl of Bedford, and Algernon Sidney, son of the Earl of Leicester, were executed. A third man taken to the Tower, the Earl of Essex, committed suicide by cutting his throat in his cell.

Pepys was dragged into the first of these plots, chiefly because, as Secretary to the Navy, he was closely associated with the King's brother, who was head of the Admiralty. Pepys was accused of betraying naval secrets to the French, apparently to obtain help for James's accession. He was imprisoned in the Tower for six weeks, from 22 May 1679 to 20 June. The cost of this to the State was '£3 a week, ancient allowance, and 13s & 4d per week, present demands, according to retrenchments.' The State always paid for the prisoner's keep and deducted this sum from his estate if he had one. Prisoners of exalted rank were usually allowed to supplement their rations; the others were dependent on the Lieutenant's whims or greed. At times half the money allocated was pocketed by the Lieutenant; at others, a kindly Lieutenant used to draw on his own purse to provide extra food for a prisoner. Evelyn dined with Pepys one afternoon in the Tower, sending some venison in advance, which they shared. James pleaded with the King for Pepys's release. He was let out on bail in the enormous sum of £30,000, of which he himself gave surety of £10,000, the rest being provided by generous friends. He was eventually able to establish that he was in no way connected with the papists. In February 1680 the charges against him were dropped.

Another prisoner in the Tower, a friend of Pepys from the age of twenty, was William Penn, the founder of the American state of Pennsylvania. He had been born on Tower Hill and was a Quaker; his father, Admiral Sir William Penn, had served Cromwell, but later went over to Charles II. Returning from a raiding 'assault on the Spaniards in the West Indies' without success, the Admiral was for a time imprisoned in the Tower. The younger Penn was arrested and sent to the Tower in 1668 for publishing a violent attack on accepted religious beliefs, including the doctrine of the Trinity, in a pamphlet entitled *The Sandy Foundation Shaken.*

There was some doubt as to whether the warrant of his committal, which was signed by the Secretary of State instead of the King, was acceptable. The Lieutenant of the Tower, Sir John Robinson, refused to admit him until the Secretary of State, Lord Arlington, came in person and offered to take full responsibility. Penn was confined in the west wing of the Lieutenant's Lodgings for nine months, during which time he wrote his pungent pamphlet *No Cross no Crown*—a defence of Quaker doctrines and practices and an attack on the unchristian lives of the clergy. To those who tried to make him change his views he said, 'The Tower is to me the worst possible argument in the world. My prison shall be my grave before I will budge a jot.' In March 1681 he bought the vast tract of land in America which bears his name.

Quite the most serious of the plots favoured the claims of Charles II's illegitimate son, the Duke of Monmouth. There has always been some doubt as to whether he really was the King's son.

James Scott, Duke of Monmouth and Buccleuch: painting after Lely. (National Portrait Gallery, London)

The 'brown, beautiful, bold' Lucy Waters was Charles's mistress while he was in exile on the Continent, but until then she had lived with Robert Sidney, son of the Earl of Leicester and brother of Algernon Sidney; and the resemblance between Monmouth and Robert Sidney was very striking. But Charles accepted him as his son and he was brought up by his grandmother Henrietta Maria, widow of King Charles I, as a Catholic although he later became a Protestant.

When the boy was thirteen, Charles sent for him and placed him in the care of his current mistress, Lady Castlemaine, thus exposing him to the worst influences of a corrupt court. He was treated by the King as a prince of the blood, and in 1665, when he was sixteen, he was married to Anne Scott, Countess of Buccleuch, the wealthiest heiress in Scotland. Thereafter he adopted his wife's name of Scott. At twenty, on the death of General Monk, he was made Captain-General of the King's forces. Pepys described him as a profligate, and there is no doubt that he played a part in the wanton murder of a street watchman. He became politically important as the Protestant alternative to James. The strongest pressure was put on the King, especially by the Earl of Shaftesbury, to legitimize Monmouth, but Charles refused.

When anti-Catholic revulsion swept the country at the time of the Titus Oates plot, the King told his brother to leave the country, and James suggested that Monmouth should leave too. But the young Duke, now thirty, secretly returned after staying two months at Utrecht and was received with tremendous enthusiasm by the people. The King was furious. He stripped him of all his offices and ordered him to leave the country at once. Monmouth flatly refused to go. Weakening, the King then advised him to keep away from the court. This Monmouth did, but he set out on a series of tours through the country to show himself to the people. His youth and his engaging manner won him immense popularity. He was feted in the city of London, and it was seen that he had removed the bar of illegitimacy from his coat of arms. The King, fearing civil war, abruptly put a stop to all this. Monmouth lost no time in betraying the friends who had supported him; Lord Russell, Algernon Sidney and the Earl of Essex were sent to the Tower and executed while Monmouth became reconciled with the King and even with his uncle James.

Less than eighteen months later, in 1685, the King died. Monmouth, who had been living on the Continent with his mistress Lady Wentworth, a wealthy peeress in her own right, sold her jewels to raise money and returned hurriedly to England. On 11 June he landed at Lyme Regis in Dorset (Protestant country) and was proclaimed King Monmouth at Taunton nine days later; he did not use his first name, which was the same as that of the new King, James II. In his proclamation Monmouth accused James of poisoning his brother Charles in order to gain the throne. There was a sharp, swift battle at Sedgemoor on 5 July, at which Monmouth's army of 7000 men was defeated. He himself was found shivering in a ditch with an apple in his pocket beside his crumpled Order of the Garter. He was arrested and taken to the Tower. His wife and their six children, four boys and two girls, were already prisoners there. The warrant for his arrest read: 'James, Duke of Monmouth, 13 July, for High Treason in levying war against the King and assuming a title to the Crown'.

He wrote a most abject letter to his uncle James, casting all the blame on others. The next day he was taken to see the King. He begged for mercy and even offered to become a Catholic. James sent priests to talk to him in the Tower to see if his conversion was genuine, but they reported that he cared only for his life, not for his soul.

At ten o'clock on the morning of 15 July 1685, after a visit from his wife, to whom he bade a cold, unfeeling farewell, he was led out to Tower Hill, where a vast excited crowd had gathered round the scaffold. The guards in attendance had been given orders to shoot him dead if there was any attempt at a rescue. Flanked on both sides by soldiers, with their officers carrying pistols, he caused a stir among the public, who were obviously moved by his youth and his handsome countenance.

The scaffold was draped in black. Monmouth made no speech but handed a written statement to one of the clergymen. In it he said the title of King had been forced on him by others 'very much contrary to my opinion' and begged that the King would not let his children suffer on his account. One of Monmouth's daughters died in the Tower; the other children were released after a few months.

Turning to the executioner, Jack Ketch, Monmouth said, 'Pray do your business well. Do not serve me as you did my Lord Russell. I have heard you struck him four or five times; if you strike me twice, I cannot promise you not to stir.' He fared worse than Russell. It was not until the sixth blow with the axe that his head was severed. The infuriated mob shouted abuse and almost tore the executioner to pieces.

The King had two medals struck to commemorate the execution.

James abandoned the traditional coronation ceremony at the Tower as well as the processional ride to the Abbey. He stayed at Whitehall, created the Knights of the Bath there, and went without any pageantry to the Abbey. This brought to an end a ceremony in which the Tower had played so prominent a part and which had been observed with impressive and ever-increasing grandeur by the kings and queens of England for more than five hundred years. Roettier was asked to make a coronation medal for James in the Tower Mint. The King's profile appears on one side; on the other is a trophy of armour, with ships in the background to indicate his connection with the Navy when he was Duke of York (it is from his title that New York took its name). The profile was regarded by contemporaries as an excellent likeness—the lines of obstinacy are quite clearly discernible.

Four years later, when mounting opposition drove James from the throne, Roettier was dismissed from the Mint by James's son-in-law, who came to the throne as King William III; the engraver had to vacate his lodgings in the Tower and was accused of being a papist. His close association with Charles II, who though he imprisoned Catholics had confessed on his deathbed that he himself belonged to that faith, and also with James II was now held against him. Rumour had begun to assert that James had returned from his exile in France and was hidden in Roettier's rooms in the Tower; he was also said to be using old dies and still stamping coins with James's head on them. None of this was true, but a committee was set up by the House of Commons to decide what should be done about Roettier. 'It is too great a trust,' the committee reported, 'and may be of dangerous consequence for the said Rotier to have the custody of the dies, he being a Roman Catholic and keeping an Irish papist in his house, and, having the custody of the said dies, it lies in his power to let them out when he pleases, or to coin false money in the Tower.' So all his dies and puncheons, which were his engraving tools, were taken away and he had to leave.

James's troubles began when he openly encouraged Catholics to return to England. At the

Restoration in 1660, only twenty-five years earlier, his brother had given a solemn assurance that the country would be Protestant; that no doubt is why, despite his personal faith and the Queen's, Charles was careful not to flaunt Catholicism. The Test Act, passed by Parliament in 1673, required everyone who was given civil or military employment to take the Oath of Supremacy imposed by Henry VIII and to accept the doctrines of the Church of England. James II set aside the Test Act. Roman Catholics were given both civil and military posts. Catholic peers were added to the King's Privy Council. Jesuit priests opened a school at the Savoy in London. The streets of the city and of other towns were full of monks dressed in the brown robes of the Carmelites and the white robes of the Franciscans.

Fearing trouble, James increased the size of his standing army and established a camp of 15,000 to 20,000 armed men at Hounslow to overawe the Londoners if they dared defy these new edicts. In the summer James used to go down to see the troops drill and stayed to dine with the officers, one of whom was General Churchill, later the Duke of Marlborough and an ancestor of Sir Winston Churchill. In the centre of the camp James had set up a wooden chapel so that Mass could be celebrated. A Catholic Admiral was in charge of the Channel Fleet, and the fort of Dover was commanded by a Catholic. The Pope's ambassador was given a public reception, although all papal officials had been banned by his brother.

There was no doubt what the outcome of all this would be. It came to a head in 1688, when James appointed a Catholic as President of Magdalen College, Oxford, and expelled all the Fellows of the college, twenty-five in number, who refused to accept him. This infuriated the clergy, and there were signs of revolt all over the country. To strengthen his hand, James tried to win over the Protestant Nonconformists, who had also been suffering from certain disabilities under the existing law. He swept away the disabilities and announced that in future there would be complete freedom of worship for all.

This was received with widespread suspicion and distrust. If the King was allowed to discard the laws of the country arbitrarily and at his whim, no one would be safe. His every action until now had indicated quite clearly that he intended to rule as a dictator. He had learned nothing from the fate of his father or the caution of his brother. His model was Louis XIV, who had just driven the Protestant Huguenots out of France by his cruel persecutions, an action of which James II wholeheartedly approved, as is manifest in his letters. The people of England and Scotland were no longer prepared to trust him. When he gave orders that his decree of religious tolerance must be read out in every church for two successive Sundays, it was felt that the way was really being cleared for a return to Catholicism and the hideous sequence of imprisonment and death by burning. The Archbishop of Canterbury, William Sancroft, and six other bishops humbly pointed out that the King's 'dispensing power hath often been declared illegal by Parliament, and particularly in the years 1662 and 1672, and the beginning of your Majesty's reign'.

The seven bishops were immediately summoned to appear before the Privy Council, presided over by the notorious Judge Jeffreys, recently made Lord Chancellor. Jeffreys had risen rapidly to power and was not yet forty. Callous and cruel, his sharp tongue prodded his unfortunate victims like a rapier. He was fond of hard drinking and boisterous company, but there is no evidence that he was licentious or immoral. His advancement was helped by his close friendship with the Duchess of Portsmouth, one of Charles II's mistresses. He was employed by the court, and became Chief Justice of England at the age of thirty-five. Notoriety came to him through the 'Bloody Assizes' which followed the defeat of the Duke of Monmouth in 1685. Jeffreys toured the west of England, inflicting the most savage punishments on those who had even the vaguest connection with the rebellion. The official figures show that 320 were executed. More than 800 others were sent to the West Indies and sold as slaves. An even greater number were whipped and imprisoned. Many women were among his victims. James wholeheartedly approved of this severity and it was as a reward for this mercilessness that Jeffreys was made Lord Chancellor.

Now he was to try the seven bishops. They were sent to the Tower on 8 June 1688. Fearing a popular demonstration in their favour, James ordered that they should not be taken through the streets of London. They were put in a barge under heavy guard, but all the way to the Traitors' Gate they were cheered by the enormous crowds who had gathered on the river banks, and even followed in boats of every sort and size. As the barge neared the Tower, large numbers of people waded into the water and knelt to receive the bishops' blessing. When they reached the dreaded gate even the warders knelt down before them.

The bells of St Peter ad Vincula were being rung for evening service, and the bishops walked across Tower Green to attend it. After the service they were taken to the Martin Tower, the scene of Blood's theft, and were confined together in one room. Three days later the Queen gave birth to a son and heir. This made the situation even worse, for it portended the perpetuation of the Catholic monarchy.

The Lieutenant, Sir Edward Hales, had the utmost difficulty in preserving order in the Tower. The soldiers of the garrison kept cheering the bishops whenever they caught sight of them. Every day Tower Hill was a seething mass of people. Brought to Westminster for their trial, the bishops received the same ecstatic evidence of popular sympathy and support. After a long session lasting until late evening, followed by an all-night deliberation by the jurors, the verdict was 'not guilty'. It was received with the wildest rejoicing everywhere. As the bishops emerged from the court room, the entire surging mass of people went down on their knees to implore their blessing. Many wept with joy. Bonfires were lit, bells were rung and the reverberant boom of cannon could be heard for miles outside London. James himself was in Hounslow with his army. Suddenly he heard a shout of cheering from his troops. 'What is that clamour?' he asked. 'It is nothing, Sire,' he was told; 'the soldiers are glad that the bishops are acquitted.' The King frowned. 'Do you call that nothing?' he said.

That same night a group of peers, headed by the Earl of Shrewsbury and the Earl of Devonshire, sent a message to William of Orange, the ruler of Holland, who was married to James's Protestant elder daughter Mary and was himself close to the succession as the son of James's sister Mary, urging him to come to England with his army. Four months later he set sail, and landed at Brixham near Torbay on 5 November 1688. James, having already sent his wife and son out of the country, fled on the night of 11 December. To plunge the kingdom into anarchy, he threw the Great Seal into the Thames while crossing from his palace at Whitehall. Mary and her husband became joint rulers of England and Scotland as William III and Mary II.

Jeffreys, realizing that retribution would now inevitably overtake him, went into hiding. Disguised as a sailor, he hid in a boat lying off

The seven bishops are brought to the Tower, 8 June 1688. (By permission of the Trustees of the British Museum)

Wapping laden with coal and bound for Hamburg. As the vessel was not to sail until the morning, Jeffreys's craving for a drink took him ashore, and he was recognized in a tavern by a clerk whom he had savagely trounced in court. When the others learned that the supposed sailor was actually the hated Lord Chancellor they were about to lynch him, but he was saved by the arrival of the city of London's train-bands. Jeffreys was taken before the Lord Mayor for committal. Seeing the dreaded Judge come in, the Mayor was so terrified that he had a seizure and died. Some peers were then assembled to sign the warrant for Jeffreys's committal to the Tower. He was put into a coach, which was pursued through the streets of London by an enraged crowd, brandishing cudgels, holding up halters and shouting for revenge. The prisoner was in a convulsion of terror, and kept pleading pitifully with his guard, 'Keep them off, gentlemen! For God's sake keep them off!'

He was taken to the Bloody Tower. A search of his boat revealed that he had concealed 35,000 guineas in it to take away with him. The Lieutenant of the Tower, Sir Bevil Skelton, possibly on instructions, was told to allow the former Lord Chancellor as much brandy as he could pay for. This is said to have brought on delirium tremens. Jeffreys died in the Tower four months later.

CHAPTER FORTY-FOUR

The Most Remarkable Escape

During the reign of William and Mary only one prisoner in the Tower was executed. This was Sir John Fenwick, who was implicated in a plot to assassinate the King in 1696, eight years after William came to the throne. Found guilty of high treason, he was executed on Tower Hill.

Another, and far more interesting, prisoner was brought to the Tower a few years earlier. He was John Churchill, Earl, and later Duke, of Marlborough. He was sent to the Tower by the King 'for abetting and adhering to their Majesties' enemies'. He was kept in close confinement; no one was allowed to see him except by written authority from the Secretary of State, Lord Nottingham. His wife Sarah Churchill, an intimate friend of Princess Anne, the Queen's sister, with whom she had been living in Syon House, moved into lodgings near the Tower to be near her husband. Many orders signed by Nottingham granting her permission to see Marlborough, are still in existence, each of them marked 'for this time only'. But later, after Anne's intercession with her sister, the Queen instructed the Constable of the Tower, Lord Lucas, to allow Marlborough's wife and other relatives and friends to visit him from time to time and even to dine with him. Anne had been shocked when she learned of his imprisonment. She wrote to his wife, 'I am certain they have nothing against him . . . yet I was struck when I was told of it, for methinks it is a dismal thing to have one's friends sent to that place.'

Marlborough was in the Tower for six weeks. He was brought before the court of King's Bench on 15 June 1692 on a writ of habeas corpus and was released on a bail of £6000 (equal to about £40,000 now) 'for his appearance when required'. In effect it was complete freedom.

The other prisoners sent to the Tower by William and Mary were, in the main, loyalist supporters of James. Many of them were peers: Lords Yarmouth, Newburgh, Morley, Dartmouth, Clancarty, Tyrone, Cahir, as well as the Earl of Clarendon, son of Charles II's famous Lord Chancellor, and some Catholic generals. They were all released after a time. Henry Grey, a Member of Parliament, and Lord Falkland were also sent to the Tower for taking bribes; they too were eventually freed.

The number of prisoners was so great towards the close of William's reign (Mary died in 1694) that the famous architect Sir Christopher Wren, who was Surveyor-General of His Majesty's Works, was called in to provide additional accommodation for them in the Tower. The official order, dated 15 April 1695, required him 'to view Beauchamp Tower and Bloody Tower and report what it will cost to repair and put them in condition to hold prisoners of State. Sir Christopher Wren is also to survey the ground behind the chapel in the Tower [St Peter ad Vincula] where it is proposed to erect some buildings for keeping prisoners, and to report in like manner what it will cost and how many prisoners it can be made to hold.'

Two days later Wren wrote to say that he had viewed the two towers named, which 'had already in the preceding summer been "whited, mended and made strong", but to make them fit for prisoners of State, if by that expression it be intended that they should be wainscotted and made fit for hangings and furniture, it may cost £200 or much more but with such walls, windows and winding stairs they never can be made proper with any cost without rebuilding.' With regard to the new building behind St Peter's, of which a draft sketch was supplied, Wren wrote, 'If it be well built in three storeys, cellars and garrets it will cost £600. As to the number of

The works of Sir Christopher Wren, shown in a group dominated by his masterpiece, St Paul's, which was completed in 1710. Drawing by Charles Robert Cockerell, exhibited as a tribute to Wren at the Royal Academy in 1838. (By permission of the Royal Institute of British Architects)

prisoners the place may hold, I can only report with number of rooms each place contains. Beauchamp Tower hath a large kitching, two large rooms and two small servants rooms. Bloody Tower hath a kitching, one room and one closet. The new building may contain nine single rooms, besides cellars and garrets and a kitching, all which is humbly submitted.'

Wren was by now sixty-three years old. He had served as Surveyor-General for a quarter of a century and was to hold that office for a quarter of a century more, working almost until the close of his life in 1723 at the great age of ninety-one, just before which he was dismissed as a result of a shameful intrigue by his younger rivals. His work on the Tower, spread out over those fifty years, was far from being his main preoccupation, as every visitor to London is aware. Many of the old churches of London destroyed by the Great Fire were rebuilt by him, the greatest of them being St Paul's Cathedral, his enduring monument. Indeed, he planned the rebuilding of the whole of London, but this was never carried out.

In the Tower itself, his constant attention was given to maintaining and repairing the numerous structures, including the White Tower; unfortunately, when he refaced this, he replaced the old narrow windows, possibly to let in more light. Only four of the old Norman windows used by archers were left untouched for some reason, and may be seen along the top floor facing the river. One of the four old windows is said to have been used by Flambard, Bishop of Durham, when he made his escape. Wren's new windows were large, wide and stonefaced and were given rounded tops in the Italian style then in vogue. They did not improve the appearance of the building; indeed, they are incongruous and even ugly in relation to the original style. Wren also modernized the Martin Tower, home of the Crown Jewels after Cromwell's destruction of the Jewel House, in a manner that has almost completely destroyed the building's original character.

Another change, which had been going on for some time, was in the Mint. As we have noted, small steel rolling-mills had been introduced to produce the new milled coinage which had replaced the old hammered coins. The cost of running these mills was £1400 a year, but it greatly reduced the old practice of clipping the coinage. The evil persisted, however, and William III was determined to stamp it out. The dishonest clippers were rounded up, and in one day seven men were hanged and all the old hammered unmilled coins were called in and melted down.

It was at this time, in 1695, that the scientist and inventor Sir Isaac Newton, who discovered the law of gravity when an apple fell on his head (according to Voltaire, who had the story from Newton's niece), was appointed Warden of the Tower Mint; he later became the Master. His residence was on the west side of the Bell Tower. He was given a salary of £600 a year and had a staff of forty principal officers with a great many workmen under them. Newton's chemical and mathematical knowledge proved of immense value in carrying out the re-coinage. He greatly increased the number of mills; and it is thought to have been on his advice that Queen Anne, on succeeding her brother-in-law William III in 1702, brought the engraver John Roettier back to the Mint. A few months later the celebrated artist Sir Godfrey Kneller arrived with the design for a medal to be struck for Queen Anne. Newton asked Roettier to undertake this but, now old and infirm, he was unable to do it. He died not long afterwards and was buried in St Peter's in the Tower. Among Newton's many visitors to the Mint were his friends Alexander Pope, the poet, Jonathan Swift, the satirist author of *Gulliver's Travels*, and Pepys.

Queen Anne had little to do with the Tower. But as most of her large family died in infancy, and the only child to survive—William Duke of Gloucester—also died in 1700, intrigues began towards the close of her reign over her possible successor. If the Protestant line was to be maintained, which an overwhelming number in the country desired, then the succession must pass to the Queen's cousin, the Elector George of Hanover, grandson of Charles I's sister, Elizabeth of Bohemia. Others, however, saw this as an admirable opportunity to bring back the Stuarts. James II was dead, but by his second marriage to Mary of Modena he had a son, also called James, who was to be known in time as the 'Old Pretender' to distinguish him from his son Charles, the 'Young Pretender', though more romantically referred to as 'Bonnie Prince Charlie'.

William Maxwell, fifth Earl of Nithsdale: painting attributed to Sir John Medina. (By permission of Mr P. Maxwell Stuart of Traquair. Photo: Scottish National Portrait Gallery)

Uprisings occurred, chiefly in Scotland, in support of both these descendants of James II. The first was in 1715, within a few months of George I's arrival in London. There were some disorders in the capital and elsewhere in England, but it was the Highlanders, resenting the Act of Union in 1707 which formally joined Scotland with England, who rallied to the Stuart cause. The support promised by Louis XIV of France never came because he died almost immediately afterwards. The risings in England were soon suppressed, and in Scotland the tremendous numerical superiority of the Pretender's followers availed them nothing. Part of their force crossed into Northumberland, but they were stopped at Preston and surrendered. The dilatory claimant to the throne did not arrive until later, and had to hurry back to the Continent. All the principal Scottish leaders were arrested and brought to the Tower.

One of these, the Earl of Nithsdale, with the aid of his wife, effected the most remarkable escape in the entire history of the Tower, eclipsing the many escapes of the past 650 years—from the successful getaway of Bishop Flambard in 1100. Together with the young Earl of Derwentwater, the only Englishman to play a prominent part in this rising, and six other noblemen, Nithsdale was taken prisoner at the Battle of Preston and brought to the Tower. They were lodged in the Lieutenant's House and were allowed to dine with him. Tried in Westminster Hall, they pleaded guilty and were condemned to death on 9 February 1716; the execution of Nithsdale, Derwentwater and Lord Kenmure was fixed for the twenty-fourth of that month. In those few days Nithsdale's beautiful twenty-four-year-old wife had to reach London from her home in Dumfriesshire in Scotland, work out a plan for his escape and accomplish it. He got away only a few hours before the time fixed for his execution.

Scotland was under a heavy fall of snow when she set out. All stage-coaches had been cancelled, so this determined daughter of the Earl of Powis made the long and difficult journey on horseback with her Welsh maid named Evans and a groom. On arriving in London she went to St James's Palace to see the new German King and begged for an interview. He was holding a reception in the drawing-room, and as he emerged she way-laid him. She pleaded, she wept, she knelt at his feet and clung to his long embroidered coat; she was dragged half across the room until the court officials ran up and rescued the King. She was

then lifted up and, seeing the King disappear through the door, she swooned. She herself later wrote an account of the scene.

Leaving the Palace, she resolved to find another way of saving her husband. She made straight for the Tower, but was told that she would have to obtain a warrant to see her husband. At the same time she was warned that if she did obtain the warrant, she would not be allowed to leave the Tower until after his execution. Nithsdale had a room to himself in the Lieutenant's House and, after bribing the warders lavishly, his wife was taken to see him. She told her husband that she was planning his escape, but he had the gravest reservations. They went to the window together. It overlooked Water Lane, and the drop was sixty feet.

Lady Nithsdale left to find some lodgings, and rented a room in Drury Lane. A new plan was soon evolved but it would need accomplices. She discussed it with her landlady, Mrs Mills, and her maid Evans. A third woman was necessary, and the landlady brought in a friend named Miss Hilton. They went over the plan in detail, and the next day Lady Nithsdale went back to the Tower, where the guards, having already been amply rewarded, made no difficulty about letting her in. She unfolded the plan to her husband; he still seemed reluctant to co-operate, but in the end she persuaded him.

There was by now no time to be lost. The execution had been fixed for the next morning, and she had a number of things to buy. Make-up was required. Miss Hilton had to wear two riding cloaks and Mrs Mills a second dress over her own. That evening the four women set out for the Tower. Not more than one woman at a time, Lady Nithsdale realized, would be allowed to go in with her, and she took Miss Hilton in first, telling the guards that as an old friend of Lord Nithsdale's she had come to say goodbye. Inside the prisoner's room, Miss Hilton took off her extra riding cloak. When she left, she was told to send in Mrs Mills.

'I went partly downstairs,' writes Lady Nithsdale, 'to meet Mrs Mills, who held her handkerchief to her face, as was natural for a person going to take a last leave of a friend before his execution; and I desired her to do this that my lord might go out in the same manner. Her eyebrows were inclined to be sandy, and as my lord's were dark and thick, I had prepared some paint to disguise him. I had also got an artificial head-dress of the same coloured hair as hers, and rouged his face and cheeks, to conceal his beard which he had not had time to shave. All this provision I had before left in the Tower. The poor guards, who my slight liberality the day before had endeared me to them, let me go out quietly with my company, and were not so strictly on the watch as they usually had been, and the more so as they were persuaded, from what I had told them the day before, that the prisoners would obtain their pardon.'

She lied boldly to save her husband's life. In Nithsdale's room Mrs Mills took off her extra dress and put on the spare riding cloak Miss Hilton had brought. Then, taking Mrs Mills by the hand, 'I led her out of my lord's chamber.' Passing through the outer room, she found it full of people, most of them the wives and daughters of the warders. 'I said "My dear Mrs Catherine, go in all haste, and send me my waiting maid; she certainly cannot reflect how late it is. I am to present my petition tonight, and if I let slip this opportunity, I am undone, for tomorrow it is too late. Hasten her as much as possible." ' 'Mrs Catherine' (Mrs Mills) hurried out; and the wives and daughters of the guard were so filled with compassion that the sentinel at the door held it open for her. 'I had taken care,' Lady Nithsdale adds, 'that Mrs Mills did not go out crying, as she came in, that my lord [since he would be wearing her dress] might better pass for the lady who came in crying and afflicted.

'When I had almost finished dressing my lord, I perceived it was growing dark and was afraid that the light of the candle might betray us, so I resolved to set off. I went out leading him by the hand whilst he held his handkerchief to his eyes. I spoke to him in the most piteous and afflicted tone, bewailing the negligence of my maid Evans who had ruined me by her delay. Then I said "My dear Mrs Betty, for the love of God run quickly and bring her with you; you know my lodging, and if ever you made dispatch in your life, do it at present." The guards opened the door and I went downstairs with him, still conjuring him to make all possible dispatch. As soon as he had cleared the door I made him walk before me for fear the sentinel should take notice of his walk . . . At the bottom of the stairs I met my dear Evans, into whose hands I confided him. I had before engaged Mr Mills to be in readiness before the Tower, to conduct him to some place of safety in case we succeeded . . . His astonishment when he saw us threw him into such a consternation that he was almost out of himself,

which Evans perceiving . . . conducted him to some of her own friends on whom she could rely and so secure him.'

Lady Nithsdale returned to her husband's room in a great state of anxiety about her maid being late and everybody sympathized at her distress. In her husband's room she talked as though he was still there and answered herself 'in my lord's voice as nearly as I could imitate it, and walked up and down as if we were conversing together till I thought they had time enough to clear themselves of the guards.' On leaving the room she turned and bade farewell through the half open door, then pulled the string of the latch so that the door, once shut, could only be opened from the inside.

It was an elaborate but successful plan and Lord Nithsdale got safely away. Disguising himself as a footman, he joined the personal staff of the Venetian ambassador, whose coach and six took him to Dover; from there he crossed to Calais and went on to Rome, where he was joined by his wife. They lived there happily together for nearly thirty years.

Derwentwater and Kenmure were executed the following morning. Their scaffold had already been erected and draped in black when Nithsdale slipped past it into the gathering darkness.

Another Jacobite plot in 1722 brought a number of further prisoners to the Tower, including still another Duke of Norfolk (the eighth Duke), the Earl of Orrery and Lord North, grandfather of the North who was Prime Minister under George III. One of these prisoners was Francis Atterbury, Bishop of Rochester; the poet Pope has written about him, telling us that his soul shone 'unconquered in the Tower'. He was a difficult prisoner. When the Lieutenant gave the order for him to be searched, Atterbury resisted and had to be held down by several warders while the Lieutenant rifled his pockets. On mention of this in the House of Commons, a Member of Parliament shouted, 'Fling him to the lions in the Tower!' After some months Atterbury was banished to France, where he died twelve years later. His body was brought back and buried in Westminster Abbey.

The next rising, in the name of 'Bonnie Prince Charlie' in 1745, yielded what was to be the final great influx of prisoners to the Tower. Many famous Scottish peers were taken after the terrible Battle of Culloden. The Prince escaped, but more than fifty of his followers were brought to London and hanged. Of the peers executed the most notable was Simon Fraser, Lord Lovat, who was the last prisoner in the Tower to be beheaded. At that time he was over eighty and had led a wild and wicked life. Notoriously immoral, he had raped the widow of the tenth Lord Lovat, his aunt by marriage, then forced her to marry him in order to obtain her estates. Surprisingly, this ugly man aroused her affection despite his continuous ill-treatment. Earlier his outrageous behaviour in Paris had led to his imprisonment in the Bastille and afterwards in a castle in Angoulême from which he escaped. He was involved in a number of acts of treachery, supporting first one side, then the other, always betraying his adherents in order to save himself. After Culloden he was found hiding in a hollow tree and said it was not he but his son who had supported the Young Pretender; indeed, he went so far as to say to the Lieutenant of the Tower, 'We can hang my eldest son and then my second son will be my heir and can marry your niece.' The suggestion was rejected with contempt.

Lovat was brought before the House of Lords to answer a charge of treason and was then put on trial in Westminster Hall. Horace Walpole, whose father Sir Robert Walpole had been a prisoner in the Tower before becoming Prime Minister (charged with 'breach of trust on two contracts for forage for the troops' when he was Secretary at War), attended Lovat's trial and wrote about it: 'When he was brought to the Tower he told them that if he were not so old and infirm they would find it difficult to keep him there. They told him they had kept much younger. "Yes," he said, "but they were inexperienced; they had not broke so many gaols as I have." ' On his way to Westminster a woman put her head into his coach and said, 'You ugly old dog, don't you think you will have that frightful head cut off?' To which he replied, 'You ugly old bitch, I believe I shall.' He used to say that every time he passed a gallows his neck began to ache.

He was lodged in the Lieutenant's House, and on 9 April 1747 was taken by coach the short distance to Tower Hill for his execution. There, as was customary, since the scaffold was in the city of London, he was handed over to the sheriffs of London, who gave a receipt for him, then put him into a second coach to take him to his place of execution. He had to be assisted up the scaffold steps. 'God save us!' he said to the guards. 'Why should there be such a bustle about taking off an old grey head, that needs cannot go up three steps without three bodies to support it?'

CHAPTER FORTY-FIVE

John Wilkes in the Tower

One man who regretted that Tower Hill and the axe were no longer used was Earl Ferrers. A brutal and wildly extravagant man whose wife had left him, he had invited to his house a man appointed by Parliament to manage his estates and shot him when he arrived. He was arrested in 1746 and imprisoned in the Middle Tower,

John Wilkes: pencil drawing by R. Earlom. (National Portrait Gallery, London)

now the main entrance to the fortress. Two warders were posted in the room alongside his and two sentries guarded the foot of the stairs. Tried by the House of Lords, he was sentenced to be hanged, and drove to the gallows in Tyburn in his own carriage drawn by six horses. From the platform he told the crowd that he would have preferred to have been beheaded on Tower Hill like his ancestor, Elizabeth's Earl of Essex; he was misinformed, for Essex was beheaded on Tower Green. Ferrars, being an earl, was hanged by a silken cord instead of the usual hempen rope.

There were many other prisoners in the years that followed, most prominent among them being John Wilkes, who was arrested in 1763 for his attack on King George III in his publication *The North Briton*. Forty-eight others associated with the publication were also arrested. Times had changed greatly. By now the King could only act through his Government. No specific warrant was issued because Wilkes was a Member of Parliament and had a large following in London. Wilkes suggested that the warrant should be served on his next-door neighbour the Lord Chancellor, Lord Bute. The officers, seeing that he would have to be taken by force, returned in greater numbers and took him off to the Tower. The Lord Chief Justice later decided that his offence was 'not sufficient to destroy the privilege of a Member of Parliament' and Wilkes was released. Expelled from Parliament shortly after his arrest, he was re-elected by Middlesex but not allowed to take his seat.

A few years later in 1771, two other Members of Parliament, Brass Crosby, who was also Lord Mayor of London, and Alderman Oliver of the city corporation were sent to the Tower for resisting an order made by the House of Commons ordering six printers to appear at the bar

of the House for printing and publishing reports of its debates. Some answered the summons and were admonished, but others refused and were arrested in the city of London. Wilkes, an alderman of the city, ruled with Oliver that the Speaker's writ did not run within the city. Summoned now to the bar of the House, he refused to attend unless he was recognized as an elected Member. The House thereupon proceeded to deal with the Lord Mayor and Oliver. As they were being brought from the Tower to answer the charge against them, the streets were blocked by angry mobs; when they saw the coach of the Prime Minister, Lord North (grandson of the man arrested in 1722, and himself responsible for the troubles in America which led to the War of Independence), they attacked it and reduced it to matchwood. They were about to lynch North when he was rescued. Crosby and Oliver were released from the Tower at the end of the parliamentary session, and it is to them and to Wilkes's unflagging fight for the liberty of the press that Britain owes the reporting of parliamentary debates and the frank criticism one can read of

what is said in both Houses of Parliament.

But other things were happening in the Tower during these years. In 1744, by an action at sea that Drake and Raleigh would have admired and envied, Commodore George Anson brought to the Tower an immense quantity of captured Spanish treasure, valued at the time at £500,000. In command of a squadron of six ships during a war between England and Spain, Anson lost five of his vessels, but his dogged perseverance captured the prize ship *Nuestra Señora de Covadonga*. The exciting news spread through London, and on his homecoming people rushed through the streets to the riverside to watch the unloading of the treasure on to a long line of wagons. Slowly the laden wagons lumbered up Tower Hill, escorted by armed guards. A share of the prize was given to the gallant commodore; in 1751 he was made a peer and was appointed First Lord of the Admiralty.

On the outbreak of the American War of Independence in 1775, a large number of cannon were taken from the Tower Armoury and put in ships for despatch across the Atlantic. Great quantities of firearms were also sent, and the foundries were kept busy turning out more cannon and muskets. The war was not yet over when arms were needed much nearer home. In 1780 the Gordon riots broke out in London. The easing of some of the restrictions against the long oppressed Catholics brought upon Prime Minister North the wrath of many Protestants, led by Lord George Gordon. There was disorder everywhere, Catholic churches were attacked and destroyed and many houses were set on fire. Twenty thousand troops were called out to deal with the rioters, three hundred of whom were killed, and Gordon was taken off to the Tower. He was tried, but acquitted because it could not be proved that he had incited the crowds to violence.

In 1789 the French Revolution was greeted with fervour by many radicals in England, including Tom Paine, John Horne Tooke and Charles James Fox, the formidable opponent of William Pitt the younger, then Prime Minister. When war broke out with France in 1793, Pitt imposed a series of stern measures to curb their activities. Tooke, Jeremiah Joyce and six others were promptly seized and put into the Tower, where they were held for five months before being transferred to Newgate prison. Next, three Irishmen passing through England to join the French rebels were sent to the Tower. One of these, Arthur O'Conner, was tried at Maidstone before his committal, and sturdily defended by the famous playwright Richard Brinsley Sheridan and by Lord Thanet. The latter was also sent to the Tower for striking a man in court who tried to prevent O'Conner's escape. Thanet was imprisoned for a year, then fined £1000, and had to find securities for £20,000 before he was released.

Another witness in the same trial, Sir Francis Burdett, a young baronet who happened to be in France when the Revolution broke out, was sent to the Tower some years later. He was an ardent reformer and a Member of Parliament. When a fellow-Member, speaking bluntly about the liberty of the individual, was sent to prison by the Speaker, Burdett attacked this decision and sent his speech to the *Weekly Register* for publication. Although many years had passed since the previous battle for the right to report parliamentary debates, Burdett's action was regarded as a breach of privilege and his arrest was ordered.

He barred the doors of his house in Piccadilly and defied the authorities. An escort of soldiers was sent to force their way in, and Burdett was cheered by an enormous crowd as he was taken off to the Tower. At the end of the parliamentary session he was released. His supporters waited on Tower Hill to cheer him, but he left from Tower Wharf and returned to Westminster by boat. Burdett married the daughter of Thomas Coutts, the banker, and their daughter, raised to the peerage as Baroness Burdett-Coutts for her philanthropy, was one of the outstanding figures of the nineteenth century and a close friend of Charles Dickens.

CHAPTER FORTY-SIX

The Duke of Wellington's
Changes in the Tower

A fire was responsible for many of the changes in the Tower that were carried out in the following century. The fire broke out in 1788 and completely gutted the Lanthorn Tower, built 650 years earlier on the south side of the Inner Wall by the Palace. Forming, as it did, a part of the Palace, this ancient tower had a bedroom which was often used by Henry VIII and was hung with tapestries worked by Katherine of Aragon, her daughter Queen Mary and Katherine Parr, Henry's last wife. A large shed was put up on the site of this tower and was used as a storehouse by the Ordnance. But when the great Duke of Wellington was Constable of the Tower—for more than a quarter of a century from 1826 to his death in 1852—he brought in the well-known architect Anthony Salvin, whose work on Balliol College, Oxford, may still be seen, to carry out repairs and reconstruction and to erect new buildings; among his considerable activities was the erection of a new Lanthorn Tower. It is slightly to the north of the old tower but retains the old name; it is used as offices by a detachment of the Royal Army Ordnance Corps.

Another of the old mural or wall towers to go at the end of the eighteenth century was the Flint Tower, built into the northern section of the Inner Wall next to the Devereux Tower where Elizabeth's favourite Essex was imprisoned two hundred years earlier, and where the Duke of Clarence, uncle of the Princes in the Tower, is said to have been drowned in a butt of malmsey wine. The Flint Tower, which was in a completely ruinous state and about to collapse, was pulled down in 1796. It had two damp, noisome cells, one of which was known as 'Little Hell' and was regarded as being the worst prison in the entire fortress. A new tower was built to replace it—a strikingly ugly building.

The Duke of Wellington's characteristic briskness and resolution found an ample outlet during his long term of office as Constable. There were tremendous changes. Buildings were pulled down, others were put up, but his aim always was to adapt the Tower of London so that it could be put to the most advantageous use in the changed conditions of the nineteenth century. He found the moat dirty, with an unsavoury smell—despite centuries of effort to keep it clean—and a constant danger to the health of the residents in the Tower and in the surrounding areas of London; so the moat had to go. When the water was drained out, a large number of human bones and Tudor bottles were found. The base was filled with oyster shells to a height of fifteen feet. The sunken stretches of land were grassed over; they were wide enough to serve as parade grounds— and parade grounds they became.

Many more troops could now be drilled, and the Duke decided to build new barracks to accommodate them. A fire in 1841 providentially provided him with a suitable site. The Tower had escaped the Great Fire of 1660, but had suffered a number of other, smaller fires in the course of the centuries. On that particular site there had once stood a picturesque row of small houses where the officers of the garrison lived. When these attractive houses were destroyed by a fire in the reign of William and Mary, a large building was put up for the use of the Armoury. It had four storeys and a handsome stone pediment with a lovely carving of battle trophies by Grinling Gibbons. The fresh fire in 1841 caused this building too to be replaced; the pediment survived and is now mounted upon a wall just by the Martin Tower. The Duke called in Salvin to design the new barracks, and laid the foundation stone himself in June 1845. The architect

*Grinling Gibbons pediment from the William and Mary
Armoury building, now mounted near the Martin Tower.
(Ministry of Public Building and Works)*

surmounted the structure with ramparts, to be in
harmony with the rest of the Tower; the building
is not attractive, but it has been of the greatest
use to the forces in the Tower. It is known as
Waterloo Barracks, after Wellington's great
victory over Napoleon. For a century it has been
occupied by various units from which the guards
for the Tower were drawn. The Brigade of Guards
used it for many years. In 1949 it became the
Regimental Depot of the Royal Fusiliers; the
regiment was raised in the Tower of London under
royal warrant on 11 June 1685 by George Legge,
first Lord Dartmouth, and has been associated
with it ever since. To the east of the Barracks,
Salvin built the Officers' Mess, in a style in
keeping with the adjacent structure.

The bulk of Salvin's restoration work was
carried out after the death of Wellington, much of
it under the supervision of Prince Albert, the
Consort of Queen Victoria. Albert insisted that

St John's Chapel in the White Tower, which had
been used for two hundred years to house
records, should be restored and used again—as a
chapel and not a military tailoring store, as was
planned in 1857.

Three years earlier, astonishing rumours spread
through the city that Prince Albert and Queen
Victoria had been arrested on a charge of treason
and were being taken to the Tower of London.
Large crowds gathered on Tower Hill to see the
Queen and her German husband led in by the
guards. The rumours had been inspired by scur-
rilous broadsheets, accusing the Prince of being
pro-Russian when the country was on the verge
of a war against Russia in the Crimea, and also of

plotting to force Palmerston out of the Government because he was anti-Russian. One of the broadsheets had this verse:

Last Monday night, all in a fright,
Al out of bed did tumble.
The German lad was raving mad
How he did groan and grumble.
He cried to Vic, I've got my stick:
To St Petersburg go right slap.
When Vic, 'tis said, jumped out of bed,
And whopped him with her night-cap.
You jolly Turk, now go to work
and show the Bear your power
It's rumoured over Britain's isle
That Albert's in the Tower.

Queen Victoria was convinced that these rumours were prompted by Palmerston, who was Home Secretary at the time and made no effort to contradict them. The war came, and a series of early reverses made Palmerston Prime Minister.

Prince Albert died in 1861, but Salvin's work in the Tower went on. Restoration was carried out on all the four turrets of the White Tower. More than half of St Thomas's Tower, the sixty-foot span above the Traitors' Gate, was rebuilt. The overhead passage which links this tower with the Wakefield Tower, where the Crown Jewels were kept, was also repaired. In addition, Salvin restored the Chapel of St Peter ad Vincula and the Beauchamp Tower. The old atmosphere still survives despite the large window he put in. Another tower to receive his attention was the Bloody Tower, which has witnessed more tragedies than any other in the fortress. Salvin continued his work until his death in 1881; he erected a hospital block and a number of buildings which were required for residences, administrative offices or store-rooms.

It was during these years of refurbishing, on the afternoon of Saturday, 24 January 1885 to be exact, that the visitors making a round of awe-filled admiration were startled by a terrifying explosion in the White Tower. It sounded 'like the firing of a large cannon' and caused great panic among the crowd of weekend sightseers in the Banqueting Hall on the second floor, where the explosion took place. In an early attempt to set up an Irish Republic, some Fenians, backed by Irish exiles in America, had embarked on a series of indiscriminate outrages in various parts of the country, and had hidden an elaborate mine amid the racks of rifles on display in the Hall.

The explosion occurred at two o'clock in the afternoon; at precisely the same time other mines went off in the Houses of Parliament. The women and children in the Banqueting Hall screamed; some fainted as the flames leapt as high as the ceiling and set fire to the Council Chamber above. All the gun racks, being of wood, were ablaze, hundreds of rifles kept clattering as they fell, the large room was filled with smoke, and there was the recurrent crackle and tinkle of falling glass as the windows and casements were blown out. The crowd rushed for the staircase through the fog of smoke, and many were injured.

Fortunately, since the fire in 1841, a fire brigade had been established in the Tower. They arrived quickly with fire extinguishers and two more fire brigades came from London, hitched their hoses to the hydrants and eventually brought the fire under control. Meanwhile the warders and police were aiding the injured and escorting the others to safety.

By a miracle no one was killed. The charge of dynamite was large enough to destroy the entire White Tower. But the damage was not serious. The floor and ceiling of the Banqueting Hall were badly burnt, nearly all the windows and casements were severely damaged, the flagstaff at the top of the tower was blown away and the face of the clock was damaged. The Fenian responsible was caught. He had placed similar bombs two years before in Charing Cross Underground Station, and was sentenced now to fourteen years' penal servitude with hard labour.

CHAPTER FORTY-SEVEN

The Two World Wars

Sir Roger Casement in the dock at Bow Street police court, May 1916. (Radio Times Hulton Picture Library)

Throughout World War I the Tower carried on as usual. The public were allowed to come in and see the exhibits in the Armouries of the White Tower; even the Crown Jewels remained on view. No anti-aircraft guns were placed in position, nor were any barrage balloons put up. The blackout was not strictly enforced. Only after the bombing of London in the latter years of the war was the Tower pressed into service. The sub-crypt of St John's Chapel, where hundreds of prisoners had been herded together through the centuries, was converted into an air-raid shelter for the Tower residents. Fortunately, the only bomb fell in the old moat at the northwest corner near Tower Hill. The explosion shook the walls and the casemates, where the Yeomen of the Guard have their quarters, but no damage was done. The only casualties were two pigeons. A fragment of this bomb is preserved in the Bell Tower.

The war, however, brought prisoners to the Tower, the most notable of them being Sir Roger Casement. He was an Irish Protestant who had served the British Government with distinction in the consular service, especially in the Congo and in Peru, where he exposed the appalling conditions of the poor Indians working on the rubber plantations. He retired in 1912 at the age of forty-eight to help Ireland's fight for independence. On the outbreak of war he was in America, but left for Germany to obtain arms for an Irish rebellion and visited the prisoner-of-war camps to urge Irishmen to form a brigade and fight for the Germans. In 1916 he left Germany by submarine to assist the planned Easter rising in Ireland; at the same time the Germans sent a large cargo ship filled with arms for the rebels. Casement, a tall, bearded man, landed late at night on the sandy coast of Tralee in a collapsible boat. Early the next morning, Good Friday, the boat was found, as well as three loaded revolvers and a box containing 900 rounds of ammunition. Betrayed by a companion who had come over with him, Casement was arrested and taken to the Tower. The vessel carrying German arms was also stopped by the British, but blew up after the sailors had taken to the boats.

Casement was confined in one of the rooms of St Thomas's Tower, charged with high treason. He was tried by the Lord Chief Justice and was found guilty. His knighthood was stripped from him, and he was hanged at Pentonville in August 1916.

Eleven other war prisoners, all of them spies, were brought to the Tower at various dates from Brixton prison and shot. The first of these, a German naval officer named Carl Lody, is said to have been responsible for the rumour that Russian troops had arrived with snow on their boots to join the Allies on the Western Front. He was shot in November 1914. All the spies were allowed legal aid at their trial. Brought to the

Tower on the evening before their execution, they were taken out early the next morning to a miniature rifle range in the Outer Ward by the Martin Tower, where they were blindfolded and strapped to chairs as they faced the eight rifles of the firing squad.

Between the two wars, in 1933, a young Lieutenant in the Seaforth Highlanders, Norman Baillie-Stewart, was brought to the Tower accused of betraying secrets to Germany. He was confined in the Officers' Mess built by Salvin near Waterloo Barracks and was required to pay for his own food. During his court-martial he said a German blonde named Marie-Louise, whom he had met in Berlin, had given him money for passing on the secrets. The prosecution described it as selling his country for £50. He was sentenced to five years' penal servitude. After his release, he went to Germany and worked with William Joyce, 'Lord Haw-Haw', who broadcast to Britain and the Allied forces during World War II. At the end of the war he was captured by the Americans in the Tyrol, handed over to the British, tried at the Old Bailey and sentenced again to five years' imprisonment.

In World War II the Tower was completely barred to the public, and the Crown Jewels and the more valuable armour were removed to safe custody elsewhere. A total blackout was imposed, by no means an easy thing to achieve because of the innumerable arrow-slits and small apertures in the White and other towers. The procedure adopted was to switch off the entire electric supply whenever an air-raid warning was sounded and to use only hurricane lanterns. A solitary barrage balloon was tethered at the Tower. It was flown from the west section of the old moat alongside the Byward Tower; it broke loose from its moorings no less than four times and had to be replaced. A detachment of the Women's Royal Air Force took charge of the balloon later; they lived in huts in the old moat.

A barbed-wire camp was set up for prisoners-of-war in the hospital block, east of the White Tower. A fortnight after the outbreak of war, on 18 September 1939, forty-two German sailors were interned there. Early the next year Herr Gerlach, the German consul in Iceland, was brought to the Tower; being a civilian, he was confined separately in a room in the Lieutenant's House. When the bombing became intense in 1940 the sailors and the consul were removed elsewhere.

Rudolf Hess, Hitler's Deputy Führer, who had flown to Scotland on what was said to be a peace mission, was brought to the Tower in May 1941 and confined in a first-floor room in the last of the row of half-timbered Tudor houses by the Lieutenant's House. After four days he was moved to another prison. Only one spy, Josef Jakobs, was dealt with in the Tower during World War II. He was brought from Brixton in August 1941 and shot in the miniature rifle range.

Quite a large number of bombs fell in or very near the Tower. Fifteen of these were high-explosive bombs, three were flying-bombs, and there were also a great many incendiaries. The Yeoman Warders' alertness as fire-watchers and their skill in fire-fighting, with the help of the garrison, saved almost all the historic buildings. The North Bastion, built in 1848, and Queen Victoria's Canteen, used as the main guard room, were completely wrecked. The canteen's hideous architecture almost entirely obstructed one view of the lovely White Tower. Nevertheless, the Yeomen fire-fighters fought valiantly to preserve it, but the unceasing attack by incendiaries on that awful December night in 1940 caused such a fall in the water pressure that the building could not be saved. A portion of the hospital block was demolished by a bomb shortly after the German prisoners were moved out of it, and some of the houses used as residences suffered too.

Two bombs fell within a few yards of the White Tower. Every building was affected by these explosions: there were broken windows, a widespread litter of shattered glass, damaged roofs and collapsed ceilings. Considering the havoc suffered by Wren's churches and other historic buildings in London the escape of the Tower is a matter for great gratification. One of the bombs exposed an underground tunnel said to have been built in the reign of Charles II. One Yeoman Warder, one Welsh Guardsman and three others were the only people killed in the Tower by enemy action; eighteen more, sailors and lightermen, lost their lives on the Thames by Tower Wharf.

The Tower was floodlit for three nights to celebrate the defeat of Germany and for two more on the surrender of Japan. Not long afterwards, an American carrier pigeon was honoured in the Tower for its services with the 56th London Division in the Italian campaign. It was awarded the Dickin Medal, which is known as the animals' VC.

CHAPTER FORTY-EIGHT

The Tower Today

Much has changed in the past nine hundred years, but the Tower still stands and looks very much as it has for most of those centuries. Its range and variety of uses are not so extensive. It is no longer the residence of the monarch, and jet fighters and rockets are harder to make in that restricted space than bows and arrows, firearms or even cannon. The Courts of Justice are elsewhere, and the Privy Council meets where the sovereign happens to be. The Mint was moved in 1810 to just beyond the Tower wall. The Observatory, located at the top of one of the turrets of the White Tower, where Charles II's first Astronomer Royal, Sir John Flamstead, had once presided, was moved out even earlier when the Royal Observatory was constructed in Greenwich in 1675. The records stored in the Chapel of St

John in the White Tower and in other towers for so many centuries are now in the Public Record Office in Chancery Lane. The zoo, the greatest attraction for kings and other exalted visitors since the thirteenth century, and later for the British public, was taken to Regent's Park in 1834. Dr Johnson always asked visitors to London if they had been to see the lions. There were 627 animals in cages in 1829 and the number was greatly increased by the time King George IV transferred them to Regent's Park. In the eighteenth century the charge to see the beasts was 6d; the Keeper got a personal payment of 1s 6d a day and was allowed 1s a day for feeding each lion, lioness and leopard. In a guide book published in 1730 the visitor was told that on entering the Tower he would see on the

The Mint in 1800, shortly before it was moved out of the Tower. (Ministry of Public Building and Works)

right the figure of a lion painted over the door, and for 3*d* (the charge was doubled a hundred years later) he could go in and see the lions, panthers, eagles, vultures and the other caged exhibits. To visit the Mint the visitors had to pay 3*d*, and a like sum was demanded for going into the Horse Armoury, the Small Armoury and the Grand Storehouse. The Jewel House cost much more—2*s* 6*d*.

The Crown Jewels are, of course, still there. They have been moved from one tower to another ever since this priceless collection was brought to the Tower of London from Westminster Abbey in 1302, after the robbery for which the Abbot and a number of Abbey monks were sent to the Tower. As we have seen, the jewels were at first placed in the Wardrobe Tower, which housed all the King's personal possessions. Then in the fourteenth century a two-storied Jewel House was specially built for them near the White Tower. After Cromwell pulled that down, the Crown Jewels were displayed in the Martin Tower,

from which Colonel Blood tried to steal them: they were still kept in the same tower thereafter, but protected by an iron grille. More recently, in 1870, they were transferred to the Wakefield Tower, but in 1967 they were moved to an enormous underground vault below the Parade Ground in front of Waterloo Barracks, where they are easier to view and much more secure; queues of eager visitors have the further advantage of being sheltered from the rain while they wait to go in.

Of the eight crowns, the one used for the coronation of the sovereign is St Edward's Crown, which weighs five pounds. After the actual crowning ceremony, the Imperial Crown of State, which is only half that weight, is substituted; it is larger and more magnificent, with the Black Prince's ruby as the centrepiece in front and about 3250 precious stones; notable among them are the second largest 'Star of Africa', cut from the Cullinan diamond, and the Stuart Sapphire on the band. Under the arches forming the upper section of the crown are four large pearls which were traditionally worn by Queen Elizabeth I as earrings or pendants. This crown was made for Queen Victoria's coronation in 1838, and is worn by the monarch on such State occasions as the opening of Parliament.

One of the most famous jewels in the regalia is the Koh-i-Noor diamond, set in the Crown of Queen Elizabeth the Queen Mother; this gem once belonged to the great Mogul Emperor Shah Jehan, who built the Taj Mahal in Agra. Its weight is 186 carats. The Cullinan diamond in the Imperial Crown of State is nearly twice as heavy.

Of particular interest is the tiniest of the eight crowns. It was made for Queen Victoria from her own design and is not much bigger than an orange. Finding the State Crown too heavy, she wore this perched on the top of her head on public occasions, as can be seen in her many portraits on coins and stamps.

Like the Crown Jewels, the Armoury has remained in the Tower, and is today one of the finest collections of armour and weapons in the world. Started in the early Middle Ages, it was added to by Henry VIII, whose own armour may be seen there, and further extended by Charles II, who concentrated the collection chiefly in the Tower. It has since been developed by gift and purchase, and has been exhibited to visitors for nearly three hundred years.

Also still in the Tower, not moved out or ever likely to be, are the Yeomen of the Guard, commonly called 'Beefeaters', from the Norman-French word 'Boufitier', because they were once the guardians of the King's buffet. The company of 'Yeomen of the Guard of our Lord the King', to use the official title, was formed by Henry VII in 1485 after his victory at Bosworth and was composed of members of his private guard who fought in that battle. They attended his coronation at Westminster Abbey as his personal bodyguard; it was their duty to be the King's personal attendants at home and abroad, and they were responsible for his safety within the palace. No one except the Yeomen of the Guard could make the King's bed; and they searched the vaults of every house the King was to visit. It was they who seized Guy Fawkes. They have an unbroken record of service going back five centuries, and retain to this day the ancient uniform they wore in 1485, together with the ruff added by Queen Elizabeth, which still forms part of their State dress. The uniform consists of the Tudor bonnet with a red, white and blue ribbon round the base of the crown; the ruff round the neck; the frock, scarlet in colour, which has the royal crown, the Tudor rose, the thistle, the shamrock, the leek, and the insignia of the monarch embroidered in gold both on the front and the back; a full skirt reaching to the knees, with double lines of gold braid on each side of strips of black velvet; scarlet knee-breeches with red, white and blue rosettes on the knees; scarlet stockings and black shoes with rosettes on the insteps.

Originally there were only fifty members. Henry VIII raised their number to six hundred, but in the succeeding centuries this was gradually reduced. There are now two distinct sections. Those Yeomen in the Tower are known as Yeomen Warders; those stationed at St James's Palace as Her Majesty's Bodyguard are called the Yeomen of the Guard: it is the latter who are on duty as the sovereign's guard at the Guildhall, the Mansion House or on a royal occasion at the opera or the theatre.

The Yeoman Warders at the Tower are thirty-eight in number. They wear the same uniform as the Yeomen of the Guard save for the red and gold crossbelt from the left shoulder to the right hip which once carried the arquebus. The Chief Warder has four gold stripes on his sleeve with crossed keys; on State occasions he wears a short sword and carries a mace surmounted by a model of the White Tower in silver, while the Yeoman Gaoler carries the historic and beautiful ceremonial axe (it is normally kept in the Lieutenant's House). The Yeoman Clerk, who acts as Secretary to the Governor, has four stripes and a crown on his sleeve. The rest of the Yeoman Warders carry eight-foot pikes, which are known by their Tudor name of partizans. They wear State dress for the visit of the royal family to the Tower and at church parades on Christmas Day, Easter Sunday and Whit Sunday, as well as for picturesque ceremonies such as the installation of the new Constable. Only two Yeomen Warders take part in the nightly Ceremony of the Keys, when the three main gates of the Tower are locked. The Yeomen are the official custodians of the Tower; they also act as guides and take visitors round, supplying details about the buildings and the exhibits of historic interest—for this they have to undergo a rigorous training.

Recruitment for the force is from retired warrant officers of the Army and the Royal Air Force. At one time the Yeoman Warder was required to pay £309 when he joined; he was able to sell his position on retiring, but if he died while in service, the money could not be recovered. Hence the toast that is still given when they drink to each other—'May you never die a Yeoman Warder.' The Duke of Wellington abolished the sale and purchase system of recruiting. The alternative blue uniform worn by the Yeomen on non-ceremonial occasions was sanctioned by Queen Victoria in 1858; it is less heavy, much less expensive and more suitable for everyday wear; trousers are worn instead of knee-breeches and stockings but the Tudor bonnet is retained and the frock conforms in style and length to the State uniform of Henry VII.

The Tower has many uses today. It is still a garrison fortress, though the garrison now is very small. It is still a prison for traitors and spies. It is the depository for the Crown Jewels and houses the Armoury, although it no longer manufactures weapons. And last of all, it is a tourist attraction—the most important in all England, for its total number of visitors in a year is more than two million.

To certain sections of the Tower the public are not admitted, because they are used as residences. One of these is St Thomas's Tower, where the Keeper of the Jewel House lives; another is the Queen's House, which is occupied by the resident Governor and Major of the Tower. Visitors can, however, see a great deal besides the Crown Jewels and the Armoury. They can view Tower Green, where three queens—Anne Boleyn, Katherine Howard and Lady Jane Grey—were executed, and can wander into the Bloody Tower and the Beauchamp Tower, where they may try to decipher the inscriptions on the walls made by some of the exalted prisoners. Three other towers can also be visited if you ask the Yeoman Warder on duty—the Martin, scene of Blood's attempted robbery, the Salt, where Father Gerard was imprisoned, and the Byward, where part of a fourteenth-century wall painting was recently uncovered in the principal room above the gate; it is one of the finest paintings of the period and shows the *Agnus Dei* and St Michael against a background decorated with the leopards of England and fleurs-de-lys of France. Also to be visited on application is St Peter ad Vincula, which is full of sad memories and the tombs of so many who perished after imprisonment in the Tower: it was restored as a chapel royal in 1966 and a new era of church music was ushered in. The Bell Tower's lower vaulted chamber (twelfth century) and the Cradle Tower's vaulted gateway (fourteenth century) are of particular architectural distinction. And you will, of course, see the ravens.

In the past thousand years empires have fallen, wars have swept away frontiers and destroyed dynasties all over the world. Human ingenuity and invention have devised breathtaking changes in the familiar patterns of life. The shape of great cities has altered beyond all recognition, but in London one massive landmark has survived it all—the Tower. It stands undaunted where it has stood for over nine hundred years, playing a continuous, vital part in the history of a small island that came in time to lead the greatest Empire and Commonwealth the world has ever known. Much indeed has changed of that Empire and its Commonwealth, but still the ancient grey towers and turrets of the Tower of London, steeped in the traditional ceremonial, can claim in the words of W. S. Gilbert:

O'er London town and its golden hoard
I keep my silent watch and ward.

The Chief Warder of the Tower, with his ceremonial mace bearing a model of the White Tower. (Pix Photos Ltd)

Glossary: Technical Terms used in Building

Abacus The uppermost section of a capital.

Arch: ogee A pointed arch of four or more arcs, the two uppermost or middle arcs being reversed, i.e. convex instead of concave to the base line.

Arch: segmental A single arch struck from a centre below the springing line.

Arch: segmental-pointed A pointed arch struck from two centres.

Arch: tierceron A subordinate arch springing from the point of intersection of two main arches of a vault.

Arris The sharp edge formed by the contact of two plane or curved surfaces.

Ashlar Rectangular building blocks of cut free-stone wrought to an even face with square edges.

Brattices Timber defences on top of a wall to command its base.

Cambered Cut so that the middle is higher than the ends.

Chamfer The small plane formed when the sharp end (or arris) of stone or wood is cut away, usually at an angle of forty-five degrees.

Corbel A projecting stone or piece of timber for the support of a super-incumbent weight.

Cusps The projecting points forming the foils in Gothic windows, arches, panels, etc.

Freestone Fine-grained sandstone or limestone that can easily be cut.

Jambs The sides of an archway, doorway, window or other opening.

Joggled Stepped stones toothed into each other for mutual support.

Lintel The horizontal beam or stone bridging an opening.

Newel The central post in a circular or winding staircase.

Quoin The dressed stones at the angle of a building.

Rebate A continuous rectangular notch cut on an edge.

Rubble Walling of rough, unsquared stones or flints.

Scalloped capital A development of the cushion capital in which the single cushion is elaborated into a series of truncated cones.

Soffit The underside of a staircase, lintel, cornice, arch, canopy, etc.

Spandrel Triangular-shaped space above the haunch of an arch.

Squinch An arch thrown across the angle between two walls to support a superstructure.

Stanchions The upright iron bars in a screen, window, etc.

String-course A projecting horizontal band in a wall, often of moulded stone.

Tie-beam The horizontal transverse beam in a roof, tying together the feet of the rafters to counteract the outward thrust.

Transom A horizontal bar of stone across the upper half of a window-opening or doorway.

Trefoil A three-lobed leaf with a pendent stalk.

Vaulting An arched ceiling or roof of stone or brick.

  Barrel vault A continuous vault unbroken in its length by cross-vaults.

  Groined vault Cross-vaulting by intersection of simple vaulting surfaces.

Voussoirs The stones forming an arch.

Further Reading

Baillie-Stewart, Norman. *The Officer in the Tower.* Frewin, 1967.

Baker, Timothy. *The Normans.* Cassell, 1966.

Bayley, John. *The History and Antiquities of the Tower of London, with Biographical Anecdotes of Royal and Distinguished Persons.* 2 vols. Cadell, 1821–5.

Bell, Walter G. *The Story of London's Great Fire.* Bodley Head, 1920.

Benger, Elizabeth. *Memoirs of the Life of Anne Boleyn, Queen of Henry VIII.* 3rd ed. Longman & Co., 1827.

Britton, John, and Brayley, E. W. *Memoirs of the Tower of London, comprising Historical and Descriptive Accounts of that National Fortress and Palace.* Hurst, Chance, 1830.

Brown, R. A. *English Medieval Castles.* Batsford, 1954.

Bryant, Arthur. *The Age of Chivalry.* Collins, 1963. *Makers of the Realm.* Collins, 1953.

Churchill, Winston S. *A History of the English-Speaking Peoples.* 4 vols. Cassell, 1956–8.

Collinson, Patrick. *The Elizabethan Puritan Movement.* Cape, 1967.

Colvin, H. *The History of the King's Works.* 2 vols. HMSO, 1963.

Evans, Joan, ed. *The Flowering of the Middle Ages.* Thames & Hudson, 1966.

The Diary of John Evelyn. Ed. William Bray. New ed. Frederick Warne, 1891.

Ffoulkes, Charles. *The Gunfounders of England.* Cambridge University Press, 1937.

Fitzneale, R. *The Course of the Exchequer.* Nelson, 1950.

Gilbert, W. S. *The Savoy Operas.* Macmillan, 1952.

Harvey, J. *Gothic England.* Batsford, 1947.

Hume, M. A. S. *Wives of Henry VIII.* Grayson, 1905.

Irwin, Margaret. *The Great Lucifer, a Portrait of Sir Walter Raleigh.* Chatto & Windus, 1960.

Jusserand, J. J. *English Wayfaring Life in the Middle Ages.* T. Fisher Unwin, 1905.

Lander, J. R. *The Wars of the Roses.* Secker & Warburg, 1965.

Mattingly, Garrett. *The Defeat of the Spanish Armada.* Cape, 1959.

Myers, A. R. *England in the Late Middle Ages.* Penguin, 1952.

Oxford History of England. 15 vols. Oxford University Press, 1936–65.

The Diary of Samuel Pepys. Ed. Henry B. Wheatley. 8 vols. New ed. Bell, 1928.

Pollard, A. F. *Henry VIII.* Longmans, 1905.

Powicke, F. M. *The Reformation in England.* Oxford University Press, 1941.

Royal Commission on Historical Monuments. Vol. V: *East London.* HMSO, 1930.

Salzman. L. F. *Building in England down to 1540, a Documentary History.* Oxford University Press, 1952.

Scarisbrick, J. J. *Henry VIII.* Eyre & Spottiswoode, 1968.

Sitwell, Edith. *The Queens and the Hive.* Macmillan, 1962.

Stenton, Doris Mary. *English Society in the Early Middle Ages.* Penguin, 1951.

Stow, John. *Survey of London.* Strype's ed., 1720.

Trevelyan, G. M. *English Social History, a Survey of Six Centuries—Chaucer to Queen Victoria.* 3rd ed. Longmans, 1946.

Warren, W. L. *King John.* Eyre & Spottiswoode, 1961.

Wedgwood, C. V. *The King's Peace 1637–1641.* Collins, 1955. *The Trial of Charles I.* Collins, 1964.

The Official Diary of Lieutenant General Adam Williamson, Deputy Lieutenant of the Tower of London. Ed. John Charles Fox. Camden Society, 3rd series, Vol. 22, 1912.

Ziegler, Philip. *The Black Death.* Collins, 1969.

Index